Under the Perfect Sun

Also by Mike Davis

Under the Perfect Sun

The San Diego Tourists Never See

MIKE DAVIS, KELLY MAYHEW
and JIM MILLER

THE NEW PRESS

NEW YORK
LONDON

Published in the United States by The New Press, New York, 2003
Distributed by W. W. Norton & Company, Inc., New York

LIBRARY·OF CONGRESS CATALOGING-IN-PUBLICATION DATA

Davis, Mike, 1946–
    Under the perfect sun : the San Diego tourists never see / Mike Davis, Jim Miller, and Kelly
Mayhew.
      p. cm.
    Includes bibliographical references.
    ISBN 1-56584-832-2 (hc.)
    1. San Diego (Calif.)—History—20th century. 2. San Diego (Calif.)—Social conditions—
20th century. 3. Social classes—California—San Diego—History—20th century.
4. Political culture—California—San Diego—History—20th century. 5. Right and left
(Political science)—History—20th century. 6. San Diego (Calif.)—Biography. 7. Political
activists—California—San Diego—Interviews. 9. Interviews—California—San Diego.
I. Miller, Jim, 1965– II. Mayhew, Kelly. III. Title.

F869.S22D36 2003
979.4'985'053--dc21

                                       2003051042

The New Press was established in 1990 as a not-for-profit alternative to the large, commercial
publishing houses currently dominating the book publishing industry. The New Press operates in
the public interest rather than for private gain, and is committed to publishing, in innovative ways,
works of educational, cultural, and community value that are often deemed insufficiently profitable.

The New Press
38 Greene Street, 4th Floor
New York, NY 10013
www.thenewpress.com

In the United Kingdom:
6 Salem Road
London W2 4BU

Designed and typeset by Steven Hiatt, San Francisco, California
Printed in the United States of America

10 9 8 7 6 5 4 3 2 1

To the future:
Abdullah, Andrea, Hassan, Iko, Jack, Mariana,
Miles, Ruiari, Roísín, and Sarah

Contents

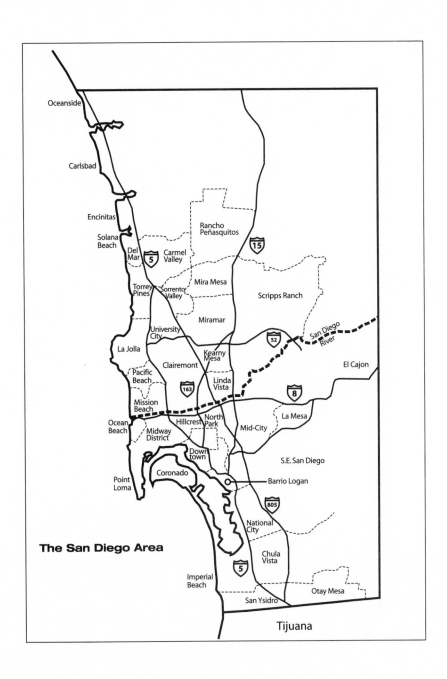

The San Diego Area

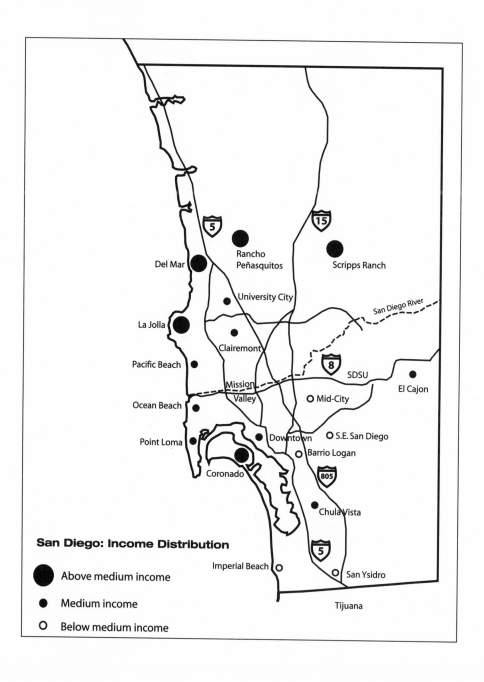

San Diego: Income Distribution

⬤ Above medium income

● Medium income

○ Below medium income

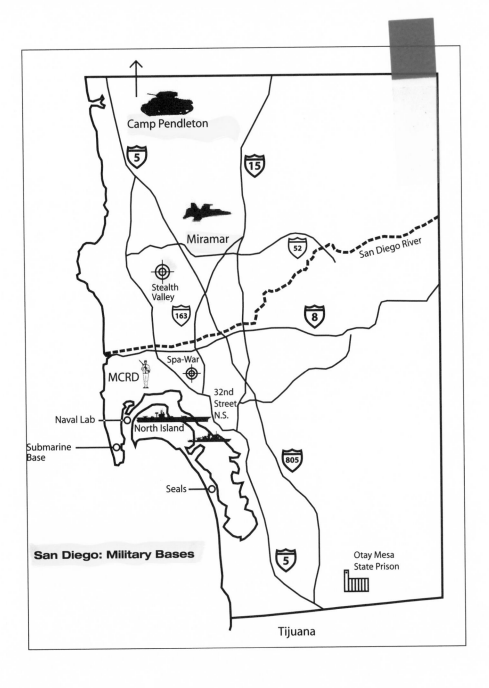

San Diego: Military Bases

Camp Pendleton

Miramar

Stealth Valley

San Diego River

Spa-War

MCRD

32nd Street N.S.

Naval Lab

North Island

Submarine Base

Seals

Otay Mesa State Prison

Tijuana

Introduction

It was one of those miraculous January days—as sunny as springtime in Virginia and as fresh as early autumn in Vermont—for which San Diego is world famous. The angry diesels of a big tug were straining to turn the bow of the USS *Tarawa* toward Ballast Point. A state-of-the-art amphibious and helicopter assault ship, the *Tarawa* was carrying battle-ready units of the First Marine Division to the Persian Gulf. The band had just finished playing "Anchors Aweigh" and rugged young crew-cut Marines were stowing their gear belowdecks. A television news helicopter hovered at a respectful distance. Back at the 32nd Street Naval Station, service families lingered at the dock—wiping away farewell tears, consoling their small children, and exchanging anxious gossip. War against Iraq seemed inevitable and it was likely that some of the 4,000 young sailors and Marines would never return.

Yet the rest of the city hardly seemed to notice the *Tarawa*'s ominous departure. Official San Diego is unctuously patriotic, but its attention was diverted by war's moral equivalent: Super Bowl XXXVII. Tourism is San Diego's other traditional cash crop, and sports play-offs are lucrative harvests. Municipal crews were already busy sprucing up downtown's gentrified tenderloin—the Gaslamp District—for affluent football fans. Once, this side of downtown belonged to the fleet, but the locker clubs, peep shows, clip joints, and chow mein palaces have been redeveloped into wine bars, nouvelle restaurants, and million-dollar condos. BMWs and Hummers cruise past the corner of Fifth and E, where radical orators once exhorted San Diego's toilers to throw off the shackles of John D. Spreckels's plutocratic rule. Ninety years earlier, Spreckels and other city fathers had used vigilante terror to repulse a famous "invasion" of Wobbly free-speech fighters led by Red Emma Goldman; now, in 2003, a new administration braced for an onslaught of rowdy Oakland Raiders fans from the tougher, less gentrified city to the north. This time the goal was not to tar and feather the barbarians but, if possible, to pick their pockets, pickle them in margaritas, and then send them on their way.

Two weeks later, while the *Tarawa* was steaming past Australia, San Diego's "NFL Experience" was reaching its pregame climax. Crowds of drunken revelers staggered past beer-company-sponsored stages featuring mediocre cover bands and little-known celebrities. Raiders fans screamed at Tampa Bay Buccaneers fans, and fights periodically erupted but were quickly quelled by San Diego police patrolling on mountain bikes. Inebriated packs of young women leered at equally blitzed hordes of muscular young men. At night, the Gaslamp became a kind of football hell, with constant war shrieks of "Rayyyyyderrrrrzzzzz!" People waited in lines for hours to get into suffocating dance clubs, while vomit and beer pooled in the gutters.

Hoping to interject some moral seriousness into this NFL orgy, War Veterans for Peace held a vigil outside of Horton Plaza mall on the edge of the Gaslamp. Wearing buttons bearing such slogans as "Peace is Patriotic" and "Veterans Against the War," the protesters passed out leaflets calling for sanctions rather than war against Iraq. Beer-swilling football fans, in response, gave them the finger and taunted them with insults: "You're not patriots!" and "Go back to Iraq!" One young male shook his fist in trembling anger: "Fuckin' traitors . . . fuckin' traitors." The vets finished the vigil fearing for their safety. The football fans returned to their street party, and the *Tarawa* continued on its voyage to war.

War, tourist spectacle, endangered dissent: these are the perennial axes of modern San Diego history. Here, where illusion is a civic virtue, reality has always nested inside spectacle like a set of Russian dolls. First, of course, is the happy tourist in shorts and a Sea World T-shirt proffering his credit card to the gods of commerce. Second is the heroic warrior, blue eyes fixed on the westward horizon of manifest destiny. Third is the smiling booster, handing out the brochures welcoming newcomers to "Heaven on Earth." Fourth is the low-paid service worker or enlisted person struggling to afford the cost of paradise. Fifth is the scorned dissenter, trade unionist, or civil rights activist. And sixth and innermost is the recent Latino immigrant, whose invisible labor sustains the luxury lifestyles of Coronado, La Jolla, and Rancho Santa Fe.

Unlike in Los Angeles, however, the existential discrepancies between tourist San Diego and working San Diego—as between militarism and fun in the sun—have never translated into an open clash of icons: of sunshine versus noir. Despite Philip Marlowe's final jaded vacation in La Jolla (in the last and most anti-Semitic of Raymond Chandler's novels), the cultural vigilantes have generally kept the noir sensibility north of the county line. San Diego's perfect sun, they would have us believe, doesn't cast a single dark shadow. The skeptical visitor or rebellious native will search in vain for a serious history of the city or a realistic portrait of its social extremes. Nor will she find much critical thinking in a local newspaper monopoly that has been characterized for generations by its vicious intolerance of liberal and radical opinion.

The present volume is a first step in redressing this deficiency of published social criticism of a city that so many conservatives extol as a utopia of patriotism and free enterprise. In truth, we argue, San Diego has too frequently been a town wide open to greed but closed to social justice. Like its Sunbelt siblings—Orange County, Phoenix, and Dallas—it has a long history of weak and venal city halls dominated by powerful groups of capitalist insiders. "Private government" has long overshadowed public politics. And, despite its sunny reputation, postwar San Diego has generally been the most corrupt city on the West Coast. But it also differs from other Sunbelt cities—indeed from almost any other metropolis of its size—by its exceptional degree of economic and cultural militarization (110,000 active-duty military personnel are currently based in San Diego County). Superpatriotism, in turn, has too often been used as a bludgeon against local movements for economic and racial justice.

But this is not an exposé for exposé's sake. Shooting holes in booster stereotypes can be an enjoyable pastime, but we are not engaged in mere target practice. The authors, rather, count themselves proud to be part of San Diego's large and growing progressive community. Building on a rich local tradition of underground journalism and muckraking investigation, we offer an alternative, people's history of San Diego (from the dual perspectives of its elites and their opponents) as well as autobiographical portraits of some of the "other" San Diego's everyday heroes. We hope, in the first place, that this will be a useful tool for activists and stimulate further explorations of San Diego's controversial past, especially the neglected histories of labor and communities of color. We also have faith that it will annoy some of the rabid radio talk-show hosts, sports franchise publicists, downtown renewal cheerleaders, and Pentagon lobbyists who too often pass themselves off as "San Diego public opinion." This is a partisan book, dedicated to the San Diego Left, past and present, and it is meant to sting.

Foreword

California (Southern C. at least, which, however, the real C., I believe
much repudiates), has completely bowled me over—such a delicious difference from the rest of the U.S. do I find in it. (I speak of course all of
nature and climate, fruits and flowers; for there is absolutely nothing else,
and the sense of the shining social and human inane is utter.)
Henry James, writing from the Hotel del Coronado, April 1905

A city is a body of fate, but unfortunately the world cannot be persuaded that San
Diego is anything other than a sunny congeries of tourist attractions. Here, crimes,
follies, and misfortunes that would stupefy and amaze if they were set in New York or
Los Angeles do not intrigue beyond the county line. Historically, it seems San Diego
cannot represent itself, and is barely represented by others. In history and literature,
though America's seventh largest city at the millennium, it scarcely registers. Beginning with Helen Hunt Jackson's novel *Ramona* (1884)—on which was founded the
lucrative romance of the missions—the most valuable literary properties, even if
nominally set in San Diego, are sooner or later annexed to L.A. It is typical that
Raymond Chandler, the master mythographer of Southern California in the twentieth century, who spent the last sad sodden decade of his life in La Jolla, writing
and drinking at 6005 Camino de la Costa, denied that he got the least inspiration

from his opulent surroundings, telling a friend: "I've lost any affinity for my back-ground. Los Angeles is no longer my city, and La Jolla is nothing but a climate and a lot of meaningless chi-chi." The historian Kevin Starr was asked by Neil Morgan, the *Union-Tribune* columnist, why San Diego got so little space in Starr's celebrated *Americans and the California Dream, 1850–1915.* Starr replied serenely, "From a historian's point of view, nothing much happened in San Diego before the Second World War."

It cannot be said that he is refuted by the dutiful "Chronology" filling four and a half closely printed pages in the 1937 Federal Writers' Project guide to San Diego, which shows the city just before the clouds of war began darkening over Europe and Asia, guaranteeing remote Southern California its prosperity—not uninterrupted—for the next several decades. Between the 1769 founding of the first mission atop Presidio Hill and 1850, the most dramatic episode in the region—leaving aside the mission's sacking by the ungrateful Diegueno Indians in 1775—was the bathetic Battle of San Diego in 1803: "The *Lelia Byrd,* an American ship under command of Capt. Wm. Shaler, attempts to leave port with 1,000 smuggled otter skins. The Spanish garrison at Ballast Point opens fire; the *Lelia Byrd* returns it and sails out. No casualties."

From 1850 ("With much excitement the first county election is held") to the opening of the Panama-California Exposition in Balboa Park in 1915, the tale is told as dry commercial chronicle, enlivened by occasional bizarre disasters (1882: "A snowstorm plays havoc with flocks of sheep within the city limits. Thousands die of exposure"). The growth of a "naval-industrial complex" (according to Mike Davis), commencing around 1915, unfolded in the period between the wars in a country where, as someone has nostalgically said, military affairs commanded little more public interest than the fine arts. (Those were the days.) According to Francis Fukayama, in his famous 1989 essay "The End of History?", the past in a place like San Diego before the war, off history's beaten path, is like the future of whatever obstinate parts of the world reject liberal democracy. Events do occur in such out-of-the-way precincts, of course, and they are of absorbing interest to those involved; but for the world (and history), they are too provincial to matter. Thus detached from the mainstream, provincial history becomes secret history—ignored by the great world; forgotten, suppressed, or bowdlerized by provincial rulers. It is not simply the adjacent Babylonish glare of Los Angeles that casts San Diego into obscurity. As Jim Miller writes, "Unlike Los Angeles, however, San Diego has largely managed to conceal [its] contradictions and market an image of itself that pushes the 'real' city to the margins and buries its history under a mountain of booster mythology."

Long delayed, the Angel of History, in its whirlwind, arrived in San Diego around 1940 as the huge airframe assembly plants in Southern California expanded to fulfill FDR's demand for 50,000 warplanes a year. A wartime visitor, the great reporter John Gunther, found that between the Navy base and the aircraft factories, this "shining plaque of a city," once the final destination for so many invalids and pensioners from the Midwest, was easily the most crowded ("congested" was the bureaucratic term of art) city in the country. As he writes in *Inside U.S.A.* (1947), "A transient body of 125,000 soldiers, sailors, and marines was jammed into the community on top of its violently expanding population," which desperately sought makeshift housing. Forty-eight thousand workers were employed in a single aircraft factory, Consolidated Vultee (later Convair), stretching a mile alongside the sparkling harbor and elaborately camouflaged at roof level to deceive Japanese bombers. Among those were my father and mother, Max C. Reid and Antonia Makis, who arrived from Oplin, Texas, and Salt Lake City, Utah, respectively, in time for Pearl Harbor. Luckier than most, they found decent quarters—my father in a boardinghouse, formerly somebody's stately home, on Golden Hill, and my mother in the grandiose U.S. Grant Hotel downtown, which had been converted to war housing. Working the swing shift together, they courted in movie palaces (the Fox, the Orpheum, the Spreckels) and nightclubs on Kettner Boulevard (in wartime, San Diego's entertainments, like the plant, ran twenty-four hours a day), and married in 1943. My father did a tour in the Navy, returned in February 1946, worked a shift, and joined the great Machinists' strike.

When, in 1996, the Republicans convened in San Diego to nominate Senator Robert Dole for president—a forlorn cause—the *New York Times* asked me to write a column about my hometown for their op-ed page. I obliged, observing how the

local Republican establishment had never admitted to itself how much of its prosperity was owed historically to decisions made by despised Democratic bureaucrats
in Washington, D.C., during the New Deal, World War II, and the Cold War. San
Diego, I noted, was recovering from the collapse of its old military-industrial order
and remained devoted to moneymaking and bronzed outdoor living. It retained the
feel of an "enormous village" (the phrase Louis Adamic used to describe Los Angeles
in the 1920s), and the arts suffered from an insufficiency of dedicated social climb-
ers to support them. (The symphony had just gone bankrupt.) I continued: "The
nouveaux riches seem content with their gated-community privacy, their electronic
games, and sports. They are socially moderate and fiscally conservative, meaning that
they disdain the creationists and pro-lifers who live in the less-affluent inland valleys
but disclaim responsibility for the poor and luckless who are the business of government." The column was datelined Berkeley, where I now live.

Punctually, a letter was published in the *Times* denouncing my remote place of
residence, my "beady eye," and my disrespectful remarks about the yacht harbor.
With heaviest irony, the writer, Alice Goldfarb Marquis of La Jolla,[1] urged readers to
accept my dismal characterization of San Diego and leave its many cultural amenities
for the lucky few who already enjoyed them: "Certainly, the region's writers don't
want more alien scribblers cluttering the local literary scene."

Certainly not, yet it occurs to me that until the last twenty or thirty years, almost
all of the significant writing about Southern California has been done by "alien
scribblers" rather than the natives, and as a cultural region San Diego would have
benefited from more rather than less of their attention.[2] Such alien scribbling as we
have, from Richard Henry Dana Jr.'s *Two Years Before the Mast* (1840) to Thomas
Pynchon's *Vineland* (1990), sheds a fitful but necessary light on the secret and public
histories that unfold in this book. To begin: *Two Years Before the Mast* was a decisive event in the imaginative appropriation of California by the imperial United
States that preceded the actual plundering. When Dana first glimpsed California's
"remote and almost unknown coast" in January 1835, he was nineteen years old, a
delicate Boston Brahmin who had dropped out of Harvard College because of eye
trouble and gone to sea as a common sailor to defy his own fears of futile gentility.

Now he had arrived at one of the ends of the earth—"the most outlandish place in the world," as eighteenth-century Jesuit geographers had called the future fortunate coast—and its huge emptiness haunted him. An aristocrat himself, he admired the hospitable *Californios* on their vast land-grant ranches for their ease and grace, and yet—"sometimes they appeared to me to be a people on whom a curse had fallen, and stripped them of everything but their pride, their manner, and their voices." Lacking sound Yankee or British busyness, the locals were too indolent to live up to the splendor of their natural environment.

At the same historical moment, let it be noted, less adventurous travelers from England and America were apt to find contemporary Greeks and Italians also unworthy of their ruins. As Theodore Roosevelt, the Adams brothers (Henry and Brooks), and Jack London would later assure, Anglo America was ascendant: old (Southern) Europe was over, and its decadent descendants from Athens to Mexico were back numbers, and dubious as immigrants too. As Jim Miller suggests, self-serving contrasts between "Latins" and "Saxons" would become a staple of Anglo California's social mythology: "A new bourgeois utopia had arisen out of the quaint ruins of the Spanish past."

For several months, Dana was a beachcomber and day-laborer in San Diego, carrying and curing hides; in his free time he enjoyed sexual adventures in the canyons around Mission Valley, a detail omitted from *Two Years Before the Mast.* "From that book," he wrote in his *Journals,* "I have studiously kept out most of my reflections & much of the wickedness I was placed in the midst of." His shipmate Benjamin G. Stimson teased him in a March 1841 letter about "*the beautiful Indian lasses,* who so often frequented your humble abode in the *hide house.*" Thus, as Starr observes, the annals of California literature begin on the one hand with self-concealment and on the other with Dana's tendency to project his youthful fears of failure, moral and otherwise, onto the natural and social landscape around him. The degraded Yankee drifters who had washed up in distant California fascinated and appalled him. "Here he went dead to leeward among the *pulperias,* gambling rooms, &c," he writes of a Philadelphia tailor who had come to ply his trade at the Pueblo de los Angeles. ". . . One of the same stamp was Russell, who was master of the hide-house in San Diego.

. . . He spent his own money and nearly all the store's among the half-bloods upon the beach, and, being turned away, went to the Presidio, where he lived the life of a desperate 'loafer.'"

Sunburnt and longhaired, Dana returned after almost two years to Cambridge and college, graduated at the top of his class, wrote his book, became famous, and took the bar. *Two Years Before the Mast* was the *Uncle Tom's Cabin* of abused sailors—"the first book ever written about the sea, not from the bridge or the cabin, but by one of the hands" (Van Wyck Brooks). By exposing himself to the brutality of life at sea, Dana had proved himself deserving—unlike the "cursed" *Californios*—of privilege.

Returning to California twenty-four years later, Dana found San Diego eerily untouched by the great events that had transformed the San Francisco Bay Area, formerly a vast solitude, into the setting for a famous metropolis of 100,000—"one of the capitals of the American Republic, and the sole emporium of a new world, the awakened Pacific." Even the drifters had drifted away from San Diego: "Where were they all?" Undoubtedly, the companions of his youth were mostly dead ("But how had they died and where?"), and he was a disappointed man, his political ambitions frustrated, his marriage to a proper Bostonian a bitter disappointment, his application to the law a dutiful grind. His hopes, his dreams! "The past was real. The present, all around me, was unreal, unnatural, repellent."

By the time Henry James settled luxuriantly into the Hotel del Coronado in April 1905, San Diego had witnessed the several cycles of real estate frenzy, peopling, and unpeopling described by Mike Davis and associated with the names of William Heath Davis and Alonzo Horton, the builder of New Town (also known as "Horton's Folly"). John D. Spreckels, scion of the sugar fortune, had descended like a corsair to dominate the fortunes of the city for a generation. The Hotel del Coronado was his gaudiest acquisition. None of this James knew, nor would it have interested him if he did. The famous and difficult novelist—the legendary "Master" of John Singer Sargent's portrait and Ezra Pound's description in Canto VII ("the great head *e occhi onesti e tardi*")— was sixty-one years old, overweight, and on a lecture tour. "The days have been mostly here of heavenly beauty, and the flowers, the wild flowers just now in particular, which fairly *rage*, with radiance, over the land, are worthy of some purer planet than this," he continued in the letter to his sister-in-law, Mrs. William James, that is quoted in the epigraph of this essay. "I live on oranges and olives, fresh from the tree, and I lie awake nights to listen, on purpose, to the languid lisp of the Pacific." A "purer planet" but an empty one also.

Coronado Beach was a magnificent resort, no doubt, but it was not Newport, Rhode Island, with its complex civilization. It was more like Oz (in fact, L. Frank Baum spent time in San Diego, and there are scholars who believe the end-of-the-world splendor of the del Coronado inspired him). Certainly, as far as Henry James was concerned, the locals might as well have been munchkins.

Coronado has been a lure for alien scribblers. Rudyard Kipling's novel *Captains Courageous* (1897), about the spoiled son of a railroad magnate who is washed over-board while on a luxury liner and is rescued by sturdy fishermen who teach him to be a man (the affecting 1937 movie starred Spencer Tracy and Freddie Bartholomew), improbably locates the boy-hero's father's headquarters in Coronado, where, from a seaside palace, he commands by telegraph a transcontinental railroad empire and shipping routes extending to Yokohama. When his supposedly lost son wires that he is alive and in Boston, the father, Harvey Cheyne, clears the railway lines of the nation so that his private car can lunge across the continent in a terrific eighty-seven hours and thirty-five minutes, derailing all other traffic, and, incidentally, terrifying his rivals who, imagining a coup, frantically announce their surrender. Kipling is a romantic—he conjures up a fleet of Chinese junks that Cheyne keeps at anchor in the harbor—but also a realist: the first command Cheyne gives is to have his private car brought down from Los Angeles.

Physically, as Davis notes (and the canny Kipling realized), San Diego—with its hem of forbidding eastern mountains—is a "cul-de-sac." Its "intractable geography" frustrated generations of promoters who longed for the direct railroad connection to the east that might have made it a great entrepôt. Rather than becoming the hub of a railroad empire, however, San Diego was doomed to be a sideshow for remote capitalist deities like E. H. Harriman, master of "The Octopus" and Kipling's model for Cheyne. Rapacious even by the standards of his fellow robber barons, Harriman, who controlled the Union Pacific and Southern Pacific railroads, was the first to envision and almost to accomplish a global transportation network. According to Davis, the development of North County in San Diego was "retarded" for a generation as a remote consequence of Harriman's duel with the overmastered Henry Huntington.

Twenty-six years after Henry James checked out, Edmund Wilson, America's most brilliant literary journalist, checked into the Hotel del Coronado. It was the bottom of the Depression. Again, the interval had been eventful for San Diego, and perhaps now some of the world noticed. In 1915 the Panama-California Exposition at Balboa Park had been overshadowed by the Panama-Pacific Exposition in imperial San Francisco, which had looted the federal money originally intended for San Diego, but—unlike in San Francisco—San Diego's romantic churrigueresque exhibition halls, intended to be temporary, were left standing, to become the architectural focus of a great 1,400-acre urban park. San Diego had also survived an invasion by the Wobblies and Emma Goldman and acquired a civic religion—not being Los Angeles.

In the Progressive Era, the political class divided into "geraniums" and "smokestacks," giving birth to a perennial quarrel that John Gunther summarized a generation later: "The smokestacks want to bring in more industry, and the geranium folk resist this at all costs. They say, 'Let San Diego live as it always did, on tourists, on retired Navy pensionnaires, on celery, asparagus, and climate.'" The geraniums, led by the merchant George Marston, had prevailed, more or less, but in 1931 the old industrial order everywhere seemed to be dying, and many of those who had retired to San Diego on small pensions faced ruin in their tidy bungalows and garden apartments. The suicide rate was the highest in the country. Edmund Wilson commented on it:

> You seem to see the last futile effervescence of the burst of the American adventure. Here our people, so long told to go "West" to escape from ill health and poverty, maladjustment and industrial oppression, are discovering that, having come West, their problems and diseases remain and that the ocean bars further flight. Among the sand-colored hotels and power plants, the naval outfitters and waterside cafés, the old

spread-roofed California houses . . . they come to the end of their resources in the empty California sun . . ."

In this amazing dispatch from the depths of the Depression, the city of San Diego is a sun-lit necropolis and the grand old hotel a symbol of imperialism. San Diego is a double "jumping-off place": the "placid bay" in which the defeated "folks" drown themselves is a point of departure for manifest destiny's next chapter in the Pacific and beyond—in Hawaii, China, and Japan, in the Pacific War and Vietnam.

In *Vineland,* Thomas Pynchon's panoptic historical eye lights on "the brief but legendary Trasero County coast, where the waves were so high you could lie on the beach and watch the sun through them." Although fictitious Trasero County is "bracketed by the two ultraconservative counties of Orange and San Diego," it is recognizably North San Diego County, where "the madrone of wind-shaped cypresses of the clifftop campus of College of the Surf" rises, with "the military blankness at its back." Here, as of 1990, is the landscape shaped by seventy-five years of the naval-industrial complex, including an academic annex. (It is generally forgotten that Dwight D. Eisenhower's farewell warning of a "military-industrial complex" included a pointed reference to complicitous and ambitious universities. As a former university president himself—at Columbia—Ike knew whereof he spoke.)

According to Mike Davis, the "militarization of the San Diego economy after 1915, the epochal event in its twentieth-century history," began with the wiles of Democratic congressman William Kettner, master "seducer of admirals and generals," whose greatest catch was the young and vain assistant secretary of the Navy in Woodrow Wilson's cabinet, Franklin D. Roosevelt. Unlike his chief, Josephus Daniels, a landlubber from North Carolina who had first to be persuaded to move the Navy into San Diego, FDR loved ships and the sea; he was enchanted by the city and delighted by a royal reception arranged by the Chamber of Commerce in 1915. As the New Deal president and commander in chief during World War II, FDR continued the patronage of San Diego that began when he was a junior warlord, disregarding the stupid anti–New Deal prejudices of the local oligarchs, including the transplanted Reuben E. Fleet. On his occasional visits to the city, FDR entertained in Balboa Park, like an absolute monarch visiting one of his remote hunting lodges.[3] The Navy presence permitted San Diego to industrialize without prejudice to its geraniums, but as a socially conservative force, "it reinforced San Diego's tendency to become an ideological cul-de-sac," paralleling its unhappy geographical status. San Diego would become one of the anchors of the "Sunbelt," whose creation was the great geopolitical project of the New Deal. (FDR's ghost was repaid with generations of thankless industrialists—none more thankless than San Diego's, save Houston's —not to mention the presidencies of the apostate New Dealer Ronald Reagan and two Texas-based Bushes, one actually elected.)

Dictionary authority reminds me that "cul-de-sac" also means, finally and most poignantly, "a situation in which further progress is impossible." As such, the term appears as the title of Garrett Scott's masterful documentary film, *Cul de Sac: A Suburban War Story* (2002), which Scott describes in the *Harvard Film Review* as his attempt to reveal a particular terminal suburban tract of San Diego (Clairemont–Linda Vista) "as a geopolitical event continuously unfolding."[4] The same, it seems to me, is an ambition of this book: San Diego might even be developing its own unillusioned historical sociology.

In his great novel *Nostromo,* Joseph Conrad imagines a Central American republic, Costaguana, whose affairs are manipulated as a hobby by a financier, the great Holroyd, in distant San Francisco. Being a busy man, Holroyd can spare little time to this diversion, which involves backing the local oligarch, the deluded idealist Charles Gould. So, too, have San Diego's destinies been shaped, for much of its history, by a little pantheon of remote, mostly absent gods—Harriman, FDR, and, in more recent years, Jimmy Hoffa and subsequent masters of that enormous body of money known as the Teamsters' Pension Fund (Central States), in association with mobsters resident in Chicago and Las Vegas, to name the greatest—acting through and sometimes frustrating their local agents. As in imaginary Costaguana, politicians, realtors, mobbed-up developers, visionaries, criminals, reactionary publishers, and technocrats—read Spreckels, Marston, Ed Fletcher, Irvin Kahn, Glen Ricks, Roger Revelle, Pete Wilson, and Roger Hedgecock, a mixed bag!—have accommodated themselves to the realities defined by such world historical forces as these, or have pursued increasingly irrelevant careers. The resulting *combinazione* show exactly the unfolding of San Diego, from Horton's New Town to the "Golden Triangle," as a geopolitical event. In *Vineland,* again, the College of the Surf was intended by Southern California's monied classes ("oil, construction, pictures") "to have been their own private polytechnic for training the sorts of people who would work for them." So, too, the actual University of California at San Diego was originally envisioned "as a captive graduate school" for the military and the aerospace industry, and just as in Pynchon's novel, the undergraduate division that was reluctantly added turned surly and rebellious in the sixties: "A sudden lust for information swept the campus, and soon research—somebody's, into something—was going on 24 hours a day. It came to light that College of the Surf was no institution of learning at all, but had been an elaborate land developers' deal from the beginning, only disguised as a gift to the people."

Jim Miller's extraordinary "episodic history" of rebellion and resistance is counterpoint to the circulation of elites, the real estate deals, and the buying and selling of politicians pursued by San Diego's "private governments." This history from below has amazed even a reader who imagined himself reasonably informed about events aboveground. The range and corresponding documentation is enormous, unburying tracts of history encrypted beneath the official version, from unromantic mission days to the rise of the Globalphobics, surveying along the way such episodes in dissidence and reaction as the vicious hounding of Emma Goldman and violent persecution of the IWW in the 1910s; the 1934 lettuce strike; the efforts of Communist organizers such as Lee Gregovich of the Cooks and Waitresses Union and Luisa Moreno in the canneries; the Red-baiting of Harry Steinmetz at San Diego State College that preceded by two decades the similar pursuit by irritable authority and local prejudice of Herbert Marcuse at UCSD in the '60s; the battle for "Lumumba-Zapata College" at UCSD; the growth of the underground press (the *Door* of fond memory); Black Power; and generations of organizing on the waterfront.

Is it generally known that Henry Miller, in 1913, on his way to a whorehouse in Tijuana, stopped to hear Emma Goldman lecture downtown as a riot impended, and was converted to radicalism and free love? This may be the only curious happening from the tumultuous 1910s that Jim Miller omits. Otherwise, no episode is less familiar or more vivid—or Pynchonesque—than the anarcho-syndicalist Magonista revolt ("Red Flag Over Tijuana") led by the Los Angeles–based Mexican revolutionary Ricardo Flores Magón and which coincided crucially with the Panama-California Exposition. The revolt encompassed the "battle" of Mexicali, the brief seizure of Tijuana, and the Magonistas' betrayal by the absurd booster "Daredevil Dick Ferris." Quite rightly, Miller calls this affair both "the most bizarre series of events in the history" of San Diego and the birth of the Liberal revolution in Mexico. Needless to say, no other episode has been more deeply occulted by the official version.

More than Los Angeles, San Diego was a kind of Anglo crusader kingdom; such at least was the conceit of the political class and most of the polity. In a great demographic movement that began with World War II, the "mixed multitudes" that Lord Bryce found so distinctive in San Francisco in the nineteenth century are at last emerging as the commanding reality of San Diego in the twenty-first. The extraordinary portfolio of interviews by Kelly Mayhew includes self-portraits of veteran activists (labor, environmental, academic) and of the region's most recent arrivals; it contains retrospectives and conclusions, first impressions, fresh appraisals, political resolves. Emphatically and eloquently, San Diego begins to represent itself.

David Reid

Portions of the above draw on my essay "Under Eastern Eyes," in *University Publishing* 12 (Winter 1984), in which I discuss *Americans and the California Dream, 1850–1915* (Oxford University Press, 1972) and *Imagining America* by Peter Conrad (Oxford University Press, 1980).

The Next Little Dollar:
The Private Governments of San Diego

Mike Davis

JENNY: For we must find the next little Dollar,
                For if we don't find the next little Dollar
6 GIRLS: I tell you we must die!
          Bertolt Brecht, The Rise and Fall of the
                City of Mahagonny *(1930)*

1. The Secret City

San Diego hoped more, or longer, than the others.
Earl Pomeroy[1]

A narrowly political history of San Diego would tell us surprisingly little about its evolution from a dusty hide-and-tallow port to the tenth largest metropolis in the United States. Indeed, with the exceptions of Congressman William Kettner in the 1910s and Mayor Pete Wilson in the 1970s, its politicians have been an eminently forgettable succession of lackluster talents and poorly equipped ambitions. Its business elites, on the other hand, have included some acidly memorable robber barons: John D. Spreckels, Reuben Fleet, James Copley, C. Arnholt Smith, Irvin Kahn, and, today, John Moores. Big fish in a small pond, they enjoyed remarkable success in deflecting political reform or reshaping it in their own image. Indeed, as we shall see, the two most important watersheds in the city's political history were probably Spreckels's derailing of the Progressive movement in the 1910s and the savings-and-loan industry's co-optation of "slow-growth" protest during the Governor Wilson years.

This imbalance between government initiative and private power has been a constitutive feature of the local scene. On a comparative spectrum of large American cities, San Diego would be furthest from the examples of New York or Chicago, where strong mayors have to resolve complex algebras of interests that include powerful nonbusiness actors. In San Diego, by contrast, there have never been vote-rich unions, civil rights groups, or ethnic political machines to countervail the influence of local capitalists and developers. For much of its history, San Diego government has been closer to a private utility than a commonweal.

Certainly San Diego elites have had to pay deference to the commanding role of the Pacific Fleet in the regional economy, stoking a repressive culture of superpatriotism and opening the inner sanctums of power to retired naval and marine brass. Likewise, since 1970 big developers and landowners have deftly navigated around the bump in the road represented by San Diego's various environmental movements. Much of the energy of these protests, as we shall see later, has been shrewdly recuperated as political fuel for downtown and neighborhood gentrification.

Most of the drama of local politics, therefore, is generated not by populist uprisings but by wars between elite factions. Periodically the equilibrium of money and power has been upset by powerful outside intruders (Spreckels in the 1890s, Fleet in the late 1930s, Moores in the 1990s) or homegrown nouveaux riches (the Mission Valley Browns in the 1950s, Peterson and Silberman in the late 1960s, the Hoover-Dominelli clique in the 1980s). All hell is usually paid as a consequence.

Staid notions of *a* "power structure" or "growth machine" poorly capture the disorderly nature of these power struggles or the volatile hierarchy of San Diego's wealth, especially since 1970. In contrast to the reactionary but well-trained city of the 1920–70 era, when one "Mr. San Diego" happily followed another into the sunset, the losers in today's competitions tend to become economically extinct (like local banking dynasties after the 1989–91 meltdown) or to go to jail (like so many of the dominant figures of the 1960s-80s). Like Brecht's opera *Mahagonny* (the "city of nets"), modern San Diego thrives off ruin and downfall. The carnage of reputations and fortunes has become almost as reliable as the sunshine.

So has corruption. San Diego has an undeservedly benign reputation. In fact, the get-rich-quick ethos—here raised, literally, to the status of religion—causes endless civic mayhem. Wall Street aside, San Diego is arguably the nation's capital of white collar crime, specializing in Ponzi schemes (Westgate, J. David, MB Financial, and Pinn Fund USA—to name only the most infamous). It is also the seat of chronic municipal corruption to rival that of Youngstown or Providence. Two of its modern mayors have been hauled off in handcuffs, while another escaped a grand jury indictment by the skin of her teeth. A score more of council members, police chiefs, planning directors, judges, and commissioners over the last thirty years have been charged with perjury, bribe taking, or the illegal use of funds—a record unequaled by any other large city on the West Coast.

Moreover, "black capital" (as the Italians would call it) has played a significant role in building modern San Diego. In the 1960s and 1970s San Diego real estate was a preferred destination for mob-controlled union pension funds as well as for the gambling "skim" from Tijuana and Las Vegas. The city's most powerful business figures—including John Alessio, C. Arnholt Smith, Irvin Kahn, and Richard Silberman—had lucrative associations with crime family personalities. More recently, the murderous border drug cartels have laundered their cash flow in La Jolla dot-coms and Coronado condos.

San Diego, in other words, is a tougher town than the usual images of koala bears and wet T-shirt contests connote. By the same token, it is also a splendid place to observe how untrammeled greed is translated into politics. Although other Sunbelt cities—Phoenix, for example—can make similar claims to being the paradise of free enterprise, San Diego deserves special distinction. It was, after all, Dick Nixon's "lucky city," and remains the one true bastion of Christian patriotism on an otherwise pagan Left Coast. With the strongest local economy in California at the beginning of the twenty-first century, it is also a paradigm for evangelists of the New Economy.

In what follows, the political history of San Diego is retold from the "inside out"—that is, from the vantage point of an economic history dominated by a relatively small number of major individual or dynastic *wealth strategies*. As game plans for future accumulation, rather than just inventories of existing assets, these strategies are the ultimate molecules, so to speak, of dynamic, even visionary, self-interest. Famous examples include John D. Spreckels's successful attempt to control all of San Diego's critical infrastructures, C. Arnholt Smith's monopolization of tourist-related services, or, most recently, John Moores's manipulation of his baseball franchise to secure a dominating position in downtown redevelopment.

Individual wealth strategies can be brought into coordination through informal alliances (Scripps and Fletcher versus Spreckels), secret partnerships (Spreckels and E. H. Harriman), criminal conspiracies (Hedgecock, Hoover, and Dominelli), interlocking directorships (the First National Bank serving as a trust for old downtown wealth), and speculative syndicates (San Diego Security Company selling land to the U.S. Navy). More broadly, they can be institutionalized as campaign organizations representing a single sector of interests, like San Diegans, Inc. (major downtown landowners), and SEED (large developers); or as local capital in general, like the exposition commissions, the Chamber of Commerce, and the San Diego–California Club (ancestor of today's Convention and Visitors Bureau). Darwinian competition with larger, more powerful West Coast cities has given unusual discipline and urgency to the self-organization of San Diego business.

Although often impotent to control struggles within their own ranks, these business groups have otherwise constituted an efficient *paragovernment* dedicated to steering large-scale future movements of capital (as with downtown redevelopment) and setting parameters for public action (as in plotting infrastructure and resource investment). Their capacities for long-term planning and permanent lobbying of elected officials, moreover, entirely overshadow those of public-interest organizations. The peak business organizations routinely preempt the shaping of city policy, typically through alliances with powerful and secretive city managers and planning directors. This mutually beneficial alignment of business groups and the city bureau-cracy explains the paradox of how a city with such a famously weak executive and feudalized city council can provide such consistently high levels of support to major private-sector initiatives, whether donations of pueblo land for research centers or public subsidies to sports franchises.

This is the secret city where the future of a metropolitan area with now more than three million residents is shaped—sometimes consensually, other times in violent conflict—by a few hundred very wealthy people and their political and media func-tionaries. When radical political scientists define city government as an "engine of economic development for business elites," it causes no surprise to most rank-and-file San Diegans.[2] Indeed, local talk radio, when not bashing immigrants, is largely an endless speculation about the goings-on within this secret city. But most of the innuendo goes nowhere; it simply makes the mythology of power even murkier. It sharpens suspicion and sows apathy without increasing understanding. What activist San Diegans need, at least as preface and context, is a realistic (rather than conspira-torial) history of how wealth strategies have shaped local politics: a history, in other words, of the "finest city's" successive private governments.

2. Futile Speculations

> San Diego is bankrupt. Horton is busted and property nearly worthless.
> *Visitor's letter (1874)*[3]

Generations of San Diegans have been indoctrinated with the myth that their cel-ebrated harbor represents a manifest destiny: once world history fully arrived on the shores of the Pacific, a great city would follow almost syllogistically from its incom-parable advantages. Indeed, for the modern tourist or new resident, bewitched by the postcard beauty of San Diego Bay, the idea of geographical determinism is easy to grasp. But it is also illusionary, since the modern harbor is a social artifact: a century-long, billion-dollar work of jetty building, dredging, and infilling.

The "natural" condition of the harbor, as seen by its nineteenth-century Yankee conquerers, was less obviously a mandate to greatness. When John Quincy Adams's protégé Lt. George Horatio Derby, of the U.S. Army Topographical Engineers, arrived in 1853 to survey the proposed construction of a levee at the mouth of the San Diego River, he discovered a few hundred demoralized residents clinging to their dusty Old Town perched above the floodplain. The river, heavily laden with granitic sands eroded from the Cuyamacas, was picturesque, particularly in its meandering through the broad valley surrounding the derelict mission, but it was also seasonally unpredictable and dangerously flood-prone. In the 1850s, its course pivoted ninety degrees at the ruins of the Spanish presidio to empty into San Diego Bay through the large marsh that would someday be drained to construct the Marine Corps Recruit Depot. Derby discovered other channels, still subject to saltwater surges at high tide, that had recently provided the river with alternative outlets into False Bay (which on his map was not yet clasped nearly shut by the Mission Beach sand spit).[4]

San Diego Bay, in the lee of Point Loma, offered superb shelter from the northwesterly winter storms that so often made San Pedro and Santa Monica bays unusable roadsteads. On the other hand, this beautiful lagoon (the joint embayment of the San Diego, Sweetwater, and Otay rivers) was mainly shallow, with a tide-scoured deepwater channel that shifted treacherously. The channel was narrowest at the harbor mouth, where a notorious hook-shaped shoal brought unwary ships to grief throughout the nineteenth century. The true potential of the harbor could only be developed through expensive public works, beginning with the diversion of the river to False Bay and the dredging of Middleground Shoal. But the huge capital layout of making the bay into a working port could not be amortized unless San Diego was linked to the commerce of the Southwest and beyond by a transcontinental railroad. A railroad was thus the widely accepted sine qua non for any serious program of harbor improvement.

But San Diego's physical geography defied its dreams of railroad construction. It is easy to forget today what a remote corner it occupied on the Victorian world map. Few Americans, until the late 1880s, had ever heard of it. All of Southern California, in fact, has been accurately described as "an island on the land," isolated from the rest of North America by the furnace-hot Mojave and Colorado deserts. But as the Topographical Engineers, in their early 1850s surveys of possible routes for a transcontinental railroad, quickly recognized, the San Diego and Los Angeles regions possessed different schedules of geographical assets and liabilities.

Thanks to the San Andreas Fault, which shifts entire mountain ranges, the Los Angeles basin has two great natural gateways to the east—the San Gorgonio and Cajon passes—that were used by Indian raiders in the 1830s and 1840s before they became the routes of the Southern Pacific (1879) and Santa Fe (1885) railroads. The natural deficiencies of San Pedro Bay were compensated by these generous portals to the east.

San Diego, by contrast, is easily accessible from the north via the Camino Royal, and early boosters, especially Texas and Arkansas slave owners, held great hopes that army surveyors would find a convenient pass through its mountains to the east. Indeed, a thirty-second-parallel railroad route had become a geopolitical obsession with future Confederate statesmen like Secretary of War Jefferson Davis. But the army expedition led by Derby's comrade Lt. Robert Williamson discovered a wild, virtually impenetrable backcountry. "The most distressing conclusion of the Williamson surveys," writes the Topographical Corps' principal historian, ". . . was that no feasible railroad pass existed between the Gila River and San Diego. Both Warner's Pass and Jacum [sic—Jacumba] Pass were pronounced impracticable."[5]

San Diego, in a word, is a natural "cul-de-sac." This is a term that its promoters have always despised, but it accurately describes the bay's isolation by its bordering maze of high mountains and deep canyons—what an early geologist characterized as "an angry ocean of knobby peaks."[6] None of the early, bone-crushing stagecoach routes offered any shortcuts to railroad surveyors, and when John D. Spreckels finally surmounted the Lagunas and Cuyamacas with his San Diego and Eastern Railroad in 1916, it was only by dipping the line into Mexico for forty-four miles and then reentering mountainous eastern San Diego County through a series of twenty-one tunnels. It was an engineering feat comparable to boring through the Sierras or the Rockies, but in the end succeeded only in linking San Diego's commerce back to the mainline Southern Pacific (and the domination of outside capital) at Yuma. (The never-profitable line was washed out by hurricane Kathleen in 1976, and today San Diegans are still lobbying, as they were in 1853, for a rail connection to the East.)

In the face of such intractable geography, realists might have trimmed their ambitions to fit economic logistics. Yet, for the town's fervid boosters and would-be profiteers, the dream of San Diego Bay as the terminus of a great transcontinental railroad would not die. Indeed, it became a messianic religion. For sixty years (until the advent of the real *deus ex machina*, the U.S. Navy), and through four wrenching cycles of railroad-inspired booms and busts, they built a cargo cult around the steel road and the instant dispensation of wealth that its arrival would bring.

The first to go mad with railroad fever was William Heath Davis in 1850–53. A New England veteran of the hide-and-tallow trade, he joined forces with local landowner Miguel Pedrorena to develop a new town on a site recommended by the Topographical Engineers: a salient of flat, dry ground several miles south of Old Town that reached the bay through its otherwise daunting penumbra of marshes and wetlands. There, Davis and Pedrorena awaited the coming of the grandiosely named San Diego and Gila, Southern Pacific and Atlantic Railroad, which was being promoted as Dixie's window on the Pacific. But the Southerners' lack of federal or overseas financing, soon followed by the Civil War, turned Davis's New Town and the South's Pacific port into a ghost town.

When Richard Henry Dana, on a nostalgic reprise of the 1830s voyages that he so famously chronicled in *Two Years Before the Mast,* revisited San Diego in 1859, he found a defeated community ("certainly not grown" since 1835) living in a radical isolation comparable to the Russian colonies in Alaska or the Danish trading stations in Greenland. The town's only direct land-based communication with the East was an infrequent, hugely expensive ($400 in 1857 dollars), and dangerous (each passenger had to arm himself with a Sharps rifle and Bowie knife) stagecoach to El Paso. Dana was thoroughly depressed by the town's fallen prospects and atmosphere of defeat.[7] But the worst was soon to come.

The Civil War years brought literally biblical disaster to California south of the Tehachapis. The worst drought of the nineteenth century scorched the grasslands of Los Angeles and San Diego counties into ochre deserts and destroyed the livestock wealth of the region's mixed Anglo-*Californio* pioneers. In San Francisco, by contrast, the fabulous fortunes of the city's Nevada silver colony, the Comstock, as well as the profits from the construction of the Central Pacific Railroad, had created a boom of Medician splendor. After the end of the Civil War, the excess capital of the north soon flowed south to take ownership of the ruined ranchos. There was an almost complete turnover of elites as silver barons (like Baldwin and Irvine) and Central Pacific Railroad speculators (like Lankershim and Van Nuys) acquired an empire of former Spanish land grants at rock-bottom prices.

Their counterpart in San Diego was Alonzo Horton, a wealthy San Franciscan furniture merchant who arrived in San Diego in 1867 flush with cash and armed with a fervent belief that the railroad millennium was nigh. He discovered a town so ruined by drought and neglect that he managed to buy Davis's failed New Town site as well as much of the rest of present-day downtown ("Horton's Addition") at public auction, where he was the only bidder for a mere twenty-six cents per acre—a better deal than the legendary Dutch purchase of Manhattan. Horton also built a sturdy commercial pier and opened a comfortable hotel, employing as clerk a young Wisconsin fortune seeker named George Marston.

Horton's speculative investments were buoyed by the scoundrel wheelings and dealings of General John C. Frémont (controversial impresario of the Bear Flag revolt in 1846) and his proposed Memphis, El Paso and Pacific Railroad. When that collapsed in scandal, New Town was saved by Colonel Tom Scott's Texas and Pacific franchise. Scott was starting a war of giants with Collis Huntington's Central Pacific Railroad, which monopolized California's commerce. Huntington's cunning was legendary, but Horton and the San Diegans, like most contemporary Americans, regarded Scott, the president of the vast Pennsylvania Railroad, as invincible. Among the Pennsylvania's many assets was the largest corps of lobbyists in Washington: the better to wine, dine, and corrupt the Grant administration.[8]

While the *Union* rhapsodized that "hard times come again no more in San Diego," Scott's engineers reexplored the notorious backcountry.[9] Like Williamson a generation before, they were appalled by the ruggedness of terrain and endorsed his alternative railroad route through San Gorgonio Pass, east of Los Angeles. There could be no direct approach to San Diego Bay. But before construction could begin, Wall Street sunk into the Panic of 1873 and the Paris-based Rothschilds withdrew

Scott's financing. The ensuing world depression found its epicenter in an overbuilt American railroad system and its grossly overvalued (or overwatered) stocks.[10] Instead of building a new empire on the Pacific, Scott ended up battling insurrectionary railroad workers on his bankrupt Pennsylvania system.

The bursting of the railroad bubble ruined Horton, who for a glorious few months had been selling his twenty-six-cents-an-acre lots for as much as $6,000 each. He was now forced to auction off his wharf and mortgage his hotel (the creditors finally foreclosed on it in 1881). Simultaneously, New Town's swollen population of speculators and land investors, who were waiting for the Texas and Pacific to make them instant millionaires, melted away to the far corners. San Diego altogether lost nearly 70 percent of its residents and for the remainder of the 1870s was forced to earn a modest living from beekeeping, whaling, and vineyards, with an occasional mining boomlet in the mountains. Once again, in Hubert Bancroft's acid phrase, the forlorn town "crawled along . . . like a starved dwarf, wandering among trees laden with fruit beyond his reach."[11]

Finally, after the return of national prosperity in 1878, a new team of promoters, the Kimball brothers, traveled through the East trying to sell their National City development just south of New Town as a potential Pacific railroad terminus. The Kimballs, like Horton, were San Franciscans who had bought San Diego rancho land (in their case, the Rancho de la Nación) cheap after the 1860s drought, and, also like him, had been bitten hard by the city-building bug. Although they were rebuffed by Commodore Vanderbilt and Jay Gould, Thomas Nickerson of the Boston-controlled Santa Fe system was interested. In July 1880, the Santa Fe directors agreed to make National City their coast headquarters in return for a handsome bribe of 17,000 acres of land (including 485 prime lots) and $25,000 cash from the Kimballs and the city of San Diego. They proposed to construct the "California Southern" from San Diego to Oceanside, then through rugged Temecula canyon to the San Bernardino area, where it would eventually hook up with a route being built westward from New Mexico.[12]

Before the first locomotive could use the route, however, the deluge of February 1884 washed out more than thirty miles of track in the Temecula area and plunged the overextended Santa Fe into financial crisis. The eventual resolution was the abandonment of the inland route and then, in 1889, the relocation of the repair yards and business offices north to San Bernardino. In effect, the Santa Fe management double-crossed the Kimballs and then kept their bribe, the choice National City properties. All San Diego retained was a Santa Fe coastal spur to Los Angeles. However, this was all that it immediately needed to participate in the real estate mania that was sweeping Southern California in the wake of the transcontinental rate war between the Southern Pacific and the Santa Fe that began in early 1887.

A trickle of curious visitors to San Diego soon became a torrent of treasure hunters. Although there were no industries and few farms to support the increase, San Diego (population 2,637 in 1880) had swelled to more than 40,000 residents by the winter of 1887. The city's boom economy seemingly consisted of speculators selling land to other speculators. Four hundred realtors were busy subdividing enough lots for the population of one million that some zealots were predicting for San Diego by 1900. Poorer fortune seekers (denounced in the papers as "poison ivy") squatted in long rows of shanties across from the Santa Fe tracks at the foot of Broadway, awaiting the millennium. Like the cloud city of Laputa in *Gulliver's Travels*, San Diego defied the laws of economic gravity. Horton's worthless acres were now changing hands for tens of thousands of dollars, and big men were laying even bigger plans for dams, aqueducts, electric street lights, gingerbread palaces, buildings with elevators, and other marvels.[13]

Then, in 1888, the boom abruptly collapsed, and San Diego's inflated land values came crashing back to earth. The Santa Fe's move from National City the next year was a final nail in the coffin. Within mere months, 24,000 of the newcomers had packed their valises and swarmed back, chastened but suntanned, to Sedalia, Peoria, and Lansing. (As one ruined speculator supposedly told a local paper: "I had a million dollars wiped out in the crash, and what's worse, $500 of it was in cash.")[14] Assessed valuation plummeted from $40 million in 1887 to only $25 million by 1890. Such local celebrities as William Carlson, the developer of Ocean Beach, and William Babcock, the builder of the Hotel del Coronado, were outright ruined. The national panic of 1893 brought even more carnage: the embittered Kimballs of

National City went bankrupt in 1896, and "Father" Horton, now truly a pauper, was forced to sell his last heirloom, Horton Plaza, to the city. San Diego was once again a city of broken dreams.

3. A One-Man Town

> You have often heard the remark that San Diego is a one-man town. . . .
> This afternoon you can't give our great leader enough glory.
> *Mayor Louis Wilde, saluting J. D. Spreckels (1919)*[15]

One sunny day in July 1887, John D. Spreckels's yacht *Lurline*, looking much like a marauding pirate ship, sailed passed Ballast Point. As Spreckels's hagiographer would later hyperbolize, "the day of the *Lurline*'s arrival must forever remain the most important one in the history of San Diego."[16] Spreckels—curious about the San Diego boom—was a wealthy thirty-four-year-old San Franciscan, the owner of a Pacific steamship company. And, far more than any of his three brothers, he was also a chip off the old block.

His father, German-born Claus Spreckels, the so-called "Sugar King," was the third richest man in California history and probably the most piratical of all of San Francisco's Gilded Age robber barons. The founder of the Western beet sugar industry, he also built the world's most modern and profitable sugarcane plantation on the Hawaiian island of Maui while becoming the power behind the throne and free-spending lifestyle of Hawaii's King Kalakaua. Claus relished plundering the Pacific main and fighting epic battles against both the Eastern Sugar Trust and Hawaii's wealthy *haole* elite. John D., who served an apprenticeship managing his father's Hawaiian empire, inherited this love of conquest as well as a business philosophy based more on the dictums of von Clausewitz than those of Adam Smith.

Indeed, in hindsight, his enemies would later recognize that John D. had conquered San Diego like a Prussian general, systematically overrunning one stronghold after another. His first step, not long after docking the *Lurline*, was to construct a modern coal wharf at the foot of Broadway. Controlling the city's supply of imported energy, he was in a superior position to leisurely cherry-pick the best properties.

Thus, when the real estate bubble burst in 1888, he acquired ownership of the boom's crown jewel: Elisha Babcock's now bankrupt Coronado Beach Company. Babcock, who had opened the magnificent Hotel del Coronado just in time for the crash, was retained by Spreckels as his erstwhile junior partner and local front man, a humiliating role he always resented and would eventually repudiate.

Even more of a bit player was John D.'s unhinged brother Adolph, formally a partner in the San Diego venture of Spreckels Brothers' Commercial Company but seldom seen away from Barbary Coast pleasure houses. In 1884 Adolph had attempted to assassinate San Francisco *Chronicle* publisher Michael de Young after the paper had accused Papa Claus of swindling his Hawaiian stockholders.[17]

Brother John preferred to murder his competitors in the pocketbook. As land values and business equities crumbled, he bought cheap, like Horton in the 1860s. His acquisition of the *Union* in 1890, and the *Tribune* a decade later, gave him the loudest voice in town—the better to publicize the reservoirs that his Southern California Mountain Water Company was building to rescue San Diego from the severe drought of the early 1890s. In 1891 he purchased the local horse-drawn trolley franchise and converted it to electricity (generated, of course, by Spreckels's coal). His San Diego Electric Railroad, under general manager William Clayton, would define the main axes of urban growth in the early twentieth century as it built a network of lines across San Diego Mesa (today's "Midcity").

Many of the resulting mesa-top subdivisions from Hillcrest to East San Diego would be financed by the Spreckels-controlled First Trust and Savings Bank. Likewise, John D., by buying up the entire south side of Broadway (formerly D Street) from Sixth Avenue to the waterfront, pivoted the axis of downtown commerce from Fifth Avenue to Broadway, whose beaux arts skyline would consist principally of Spreckels's properties: the ornate Spreckels Theater, the San Diego Hotel, the Union Building, and the commanding Spreckels Building.

By 1900, according to one of his principal adversaries, Colonel Ed Fletcher, "Spreckels owned nearly everything of value in San Diego," and paid fully 10 percent of the county's property tax assessment.[18] It was a degree of absentee control (John D. did not move his residence to San Diego until after the 1906 San Francisco earthquake) unequaled anywhere in California, and editors and publicists had begun to routinely refer to San Diego as a "one-man town" or "principality."

But even the Promethean energies of Spreckels in consolidating and rationalizing the city's key infrastructures were of little avail against the depression that gripped San Diego for nearly a generation after 1888. (Even in 1910, its population would still be smaller than it was in 1887.) In 1893 John D. had to provide coal on credit to the bankrupt Santa Fe Corporation to prevent it from discontinuing rail service to what Los Angeles papers gleefully referred to as the "ghost town to the south."[19] Indeed, the 1890s ruthlessly clarified the differential growth potentials of the two southland cities. Although Los Angeles was also knocked flat in 1888, it was back on its feet and growing vigorously by the mid-1890s, largely due to its exploitation of hitherto unsuspected mineral wealth.

The most important discovery was that the Los Angeles basin and its inland valleys literally floated on millions of acre-feet of underground water, which, thanks to newfangled electric pumps powered by dams in the foothills, could be used to irrigate thousands of orchards and farms. Los Angeles, as a consequence, quickly became the richest agricultural county in the nation. Its other bonanza was oil, first discovered on the flanks of downtown in the 1890s, then in fantastically rich fields near Long Beach after World War I. Los Angeles, which had always relied on expensive coal imported from Australia and British Columbia, became the Saudi Arabia of the 1920s, with prodigious reserves of cheap fuel for its cars, suburbs, and new branch plants.

San Diego, by contrast, had no oil and precious little groundwater. Nor did it have a large constituency of wealthy citrus growers aggressively pushing for the comprehensive development of the water and power resources of its local mountains. Indeed by the time that imperial Los Angeles made its famed grab for the water of the Owens Valley, thirsty little San Diego was still embroiled in petty water wars between the Spreckels's Otay interests and the competing holders of water rights on the San Diego River. Unlike Los Angeles, which could afford to build vast infrastructures in anticipation of future growth, San Diego habitually failed to keep up with current demand. (Indeed, as we shall see, this historical shortfall in water provision, as well as in sewage treatment, would assume crisis proportions in the 1940s.) Whereas turn-of-the-century Los Angeles seemed to enjoy a virtuous circle of cheaper resources, more abundant capital, and high growth, San Diego stagnated without the capital to develop the necessary resources, or the resources to attract the necessary capital.

There was, however, a surprising silver lining to the region's slow growth. As George Marston (Alonzo Horton's humble room clerk, now the city's major dry-goods merchant) was perhaps the first to realize, San Diego had preserved the potential—which rapidly industrializing Los Angeles was squandering—to someday shape itself into a City Beautiful. Marston, a tougher businessman than usually depicted, recognized that landscape capital was perhaps San Diego's chief comparative advantage. Although John Nolen, the famed Eastern landscape architect whom Marston brought west in 1906, found the existing town "neither interesting nor beautiful," he was full of praise for its "advantages of situation, climate and scenery."[20] Unlike Los Angeles, which had recklessly alienated its public lands, San Diego still possessed 40,000 acres of developable "pueblo land," 1,400 acres of which had been providentially set aside for a great municipal park.[21] With proper planning and good adveritising, San Diego might yet become a bigger version of Pasadena, the celebrated town in the Los Angeles foothills that was a winter home for dozens of Midwestern millionaires.

Although Spreckels was hardly an Arts and Crafts aficionado like Marston, he owned major tourist assets and appreciated the obvious business logic of moderate public investment in parks, beaches, and pageantry. At least while waiting for the satanic mills to arrive from the East, it made sense to package the climate for sale to a leisure class of wealthy retirees, consumptives, and cultists—all of whom might stay in Spreckels's hotels and tent cities or buy lots adjacent to Spreckels's streetcar lines. John D. indeed would become the principal individual sponsor of the city's first national advertising campaign, the Panama-California Exposition of 1915. But the road to the famous fair was paved with contradictory intentions and had to pass through some hostile territory, including a railroad confidence game that Spreckels played on city voters and the surprising eruption of an anarchist republic in San Diego's own backyard.

4. Consummate Deceptions

> In San Diego reform victories were transient and superficial; Republican
> dominance soon returned and with it the centrality of John Spreckels.
> *Historian Amy Bridges*[22]

When Oscar Cotton, the former child actor who became one of San Diego's leading
boosters in the 1920s, first arrived in "the city of blighted hopes" at the turn of the
century, he was stunned by the landscape of dereliction and failure: "If you took the
steam train through National City to Chula Vista, you would pass rows of empty old
store buildings. It was quite appalling." After sixteen long years of depression, real
estate sales finally began to stir again in 1903, the beginning of a moderate boom
that lasted until the Wall Street crash in spring 1913. After getting his feet wet in a
Pacific Beach subdivision, Cotton partnered himself with Marston's brother-in-law,
R. F. Burnham, and made a fortune selling homes in the east San Diego area by the
then novel system of monthly mortgage payments.[23]

The return of prosperity to Spreckelstown also brought rumblings of mutiny.
Among the handful of newcomers to San Diego in the bust years were Ed Fletcher,
a young fruit peddler who quickly became the region's leading citrus packer, and
E. W. Scripps, a consumptive Cleveland newspaper baron who built a regal hacienda
on Linda Vista Mesa and called it "Miramar" after Maximilian's famed palace near
Trieste. Scripps in particular was an odd fish: a hard-drinking robber baron who
sympathized with Bellamyite socialism and whose San Diego *Sun* championed all
the causes—the American Federation of Labor, Robert La Follette, free speech for
radicals, and so on—that Spreckels's *Union* despised.[24] In the new century, Fletcher
and Scripps, often in tandem, began to earnestly chip away at the monolith of a
"one-man town." Eventually the two, joined by scrupulous George Marston, would
wrap themselves in the righteous banner of the Progressive revolt against the Old
Corruption of John D. Spreckels and the other McKinleyite oligarchs who controlled
California's Republican Party. But, as is usual in American history, idealistic political
insurgency was propelled by less visible and more selfish economic alignments.

In the San Diego case, the local power struggles of the 1900s, not surprisingly, were subsidiaries of more far-reaching regional and national conflicts. At the turn of the century, for example, following the death of Collis Huntington, the great E. H. Harriman—yearning to gird the entire globe with rail and steamship lines— obtained control of the Southern Pacific Railroad, which, added to his existing ownership of the Union Pacific and a large minority shareholding in the Santa Fe, gave him a stranglehold on the commerce of Southern California and the Southwest. He also inherited the corrupt and seemingly all-powerful political machine—the "Octopus"—that the Southern Pacific's founders, the Big Four, had built in the late nineteenth century to defeat the Populist revolt.

John D. Spreckels—whose portfolio was still divided between San Diego and San Francisco—became an ally and secret business partner of Harriman. One of their joint ventures was ownership of the San Diego city council—a generally craven body dominated at the turn of the century by Charles Hardy, a local meatpacker who acted dually as the Southern Pacific's political boss in San Diego and as Spreckelses' and Babcock's "fix-it" man. Contemporaries couldn't help but note the hypocritical contrast between the Spreckelses' born-again rectitude in San Francisco's graft trials and John D.'s loose morals in San Diego. Thus, while brother Rudolph was using the family paper, the *Call,* to thunder against Southern Pacific corruption in San Francisco, John D. (the *Call*'s publisher) was conniving with Hardy and other San Diego Southern Pacific henchmen.[25]

Harriman and Spreckels were supremely attentive to any threats to their allied dominions. Eventually, two local rail schemes cut across the prow of Harriman's dreadnought.

First, the ambitious Ed Fletcher—now describing himself as a "wholesale developer of land and water"—became the agent of Henry Huntington of San Marino, the powerful Southern Pacific heir who was seeking to extend his Pacific Electric Railroad down the coast to San Diego in direct competition to Harriman's mainline empire. As general manager of Huntington's South Coast Land Company, Fletcher was San Diego County's first megadeveloper, acquiring large tracts of land for new towns along the proposed Pacific Electric route as well buying their future water supply in the watershed of the San Luis Rey River. The plan nicely complemented

E. W. Scripps's strategy for the development of his extensive landholdings in the Torrey Pines–Miramar area, which would be only minutes away from downtown San Diego on the right-of-way through Rose Canyon (the route of today's I-5) that Fletcher had purchased for Huntington.[26]

Meanwhile, the city's third future Progressive leader, George Marston, had been drafted by the Chamber of Commerce to renew the crusade to build a railroad to the Colorado River. Irrigation was creating an agricultural gold rush into the Imperial Valley (until 1907 part of San Diego County), but Los Angeles was stealing most of the trade. As the L.A. men fomented secessionism among the Valley's growers, Marston raced against the clock to acquire right-of-ways for the proposed San Diego and Eastern Railroad that would defend and extend the city's interests east of the mountains. Tucson capitalists, some of whom were bizarrely agitating to make southern Arizona and San Diego County a separate state, offered their support. The prospect of an independent rail line to Arizona, however, was discomforting to Harriman, the Michael Corleone of Wall Street.

His responses to the twin challenges of Huntington's Pacific Electric corridor to San Diego and Marston's municipal line to Yuma were masterpieces, respectively, of cold-blooded betrayal and ingenious deception. First, Harriman bribed two of Huntington's most trusted associates, banker I. W. Hellman and developer Moses Sherman, to double-cross their bosom friend and sell him 51 percent of Pacific Electric's stock. Harriman immediately took a knife to Pacific Electric's proposed San Diego extension, throwing Fletcher out of a job and retarding North County's development by several decades. Having shut San Diego's "front door" by spiking the Pacific Electric, he then closed the "back door" by providing Spreckels with the wherewithal to take over construction of the Yuma line.[27]

Even Marston was moved to tears by the Spreckelses' patriotic magnanimity in assuming the burden of financing the railroad in 1906. The gesture seemed even more heroic when John D. announced that he was moving to San Diego to personally oversee the costly construction. As the Chamber of Commerce turned over title to its right-of-ways in a grand ceremony, none of Spreckels's perennial critics, not even Scripps's ornery *Sun*, fathomed that he was acting in collusion with that "enemy of the Republic" Harriman (currently the target of Teddy Roosevelt's antitrust crusade), or that the city's glorious railroad was secretly intended to become just a small tentacle of the hated Octopus.[28]

Instead, the city condemned a huge swath of downtown land to provide a hundred-foot right-of-way, as well as a roundhouse and terminal, for the new railroad. And, in further appreciation, the city council transferred the muncipal water franchise from J. W. Sefton's San Diego Flume Company (supplying water from the Cuyamacas since 1886) to the Spreckels-owned Southern California Mountain Water Company. Spreckels's transit monopoly in San Diego was now duplicated by his possession of the water franchise. Sefton, of course, was wiped out, and his aging flume system was sold off by its British bondholders at fire-sale prices to Ed Fletcher, who was shrewdly buying up water rights along the San Diego River and positioning himself to become the big power in east county.[29]

Thanks to his clandestine alliance with Harriman, John D.'s control of San Diego on the eve of California's so-called Progressive Revolution of 1910 seemed as unassailable as Porfirio Díaz's ongoing domination of Mexico. Ensconced in a gaudy granite pile in Coronado within eyesight of most of his choice possessions, Spreckels had less need of Babcock's services and so brutally shunted him aside. Although his control over local politics had been temporarily rattled by a revolt against boss rule in 1905, he took pleasure in watching his enemies fall out among themselves after it was revealed that Scripps, a chief supporter of the reformers' quest to obtain water rights for the city in nearby El Cajon Valley, was, in fact, secretly buying up land there.[30]

The formation in August 1907 of a statewide Lincoln-Roosevelt League, with Ed Fletcher, George Marston, and Edgar Luce as the chief delegates of the San Diego Progressives, seemed only distant thunder, since in November a Spreckels ally, title company owner John Forward, successfully reclaimed the mayoralty. Indeed, over the next few years, several of Marston's leading protégés—John Sehon and Grant Conard, for example—quietly (and profitably) made their peace with Spreckels, while voters scrapped the commission system of local government introduced to combat the Spreckels–Hardy machine. Perhaps to remind San Diego that he was still the king of pirates, John D. had his new yacht, the *Venetia,* painted buccaneer black.

In 1909, following one of the most famous antitrust investigations in American history, Harriman unexpectedly died, and, not unrelatedly, there was a brief panic on Wall Street. European credit temporarily dried up and Spreckels, who was also borrowing money to develop his lower Broadway properties, was forced to suspend construction on the Yuma railroad. Smaller businessmen filed for bankruptcy. With San Diego's future suddenly clouded, G. Aubrey Davidson, the former Santa Fe executive who was struggling to finish construction of the giant U. S. Grant Hotel on Broadway, proposed an international exposition to coincide with the opening of the Panama Canal in 1915. Although no city so small and off the beaten path had ever sponsored a World's Fair, Davidson and his Chamber of Commerce friends were convinced that an exposition, advertising San Diego's charms to the world, would be the best immunization against a new depression. Spreckels embraced the scheme and promised substantial financial support.

Contemporary San Diegans tended to imagine Spreckels as Midas, with unlimited financial reserves. Although the temporary shutdown of railroad construction shocked some, its resumption erased any anxiety about his resources. What almost no one knew at the time, however, was that the death of Harriman had plunged Spreckels Brothers into deep crisis. John D., recognizing that he was overborrowing to finance both skyscrapers and railroads, had tried to unload the Arizona project on the new board of the Southern Pacific in accord with what he claimed was his clandestine understanding with Harriman. But Robert Lovett, the Southern Pacific's hard-boiled CEO, turned the tables on him, insisting that he was, in fact, legally obligated to reimburse Harriman's investment and assume total financial responsibility for completion of the railroad. With Lovett threatening to air the dispute in court, it was only a matter of time before Spreckels's duplicity became a public scandal in San Diego.[31]

To make matters worse, his sister and two of his brothers were also preparing to sue him. For years E. W. Scripps had been gleefully irritating John D. by having his *Sun* lavish editorial praise on the "other Spreckels"—brother Rudolph, the patron of

San Francisco Progressives. But more than political ideology divided the Spreckels family: Rudolph and his two siblings accused their deceased father of having illegally willed their mother's community property (some $9 million) to John D. and Adolph. This bitter internecine dispute, which threatened John D.'s most prized assets, was ominously headed to court at about the same speed as the Southern Pacific litigation. Unless other more lurid distractions arose, the two lawsuits against John D. would probably dominate the headlines of the *Sun* and other Progressive papers for most of 1912.

5. Vigilantes and Geraniums

> Spreckels, of course, was the major force behind not only the suppression
> of free speech in San Diego, but also the open-shop drive. . . .
> *Philip S. Foner*[32]

In the event, there were indeed distractions, more dramatic than anyone might have imagined. Beginning in 1910, a violent labor war broke out in Los Angeles, a revolution overthrew Díaz in Mexico, and the Progressives captured Sacramento in an epochal election victory. These three events eventually had dramatic repercussions in San Diego in the form of an anarchist invasion of Baja California and a subsequent "free speech fight" and vigilante backlash in the streets of downtown San Diego. Since Jim Miller's chapter in this book chronicles this history and its oppressive legacies in splendid detail, it is appropriate here only to sketch how industrial violence, the Progressive breakthrough, and the Baja revolution were related to the recomposition of urban economic power in California and, in San Diego in particular, to a new round of conflict between the Spreckels and anti-Spreckels factions.

Both the Progressive movement and the simultaneous labor war of 1909–1911 were symptoms of "imperial" San Francisco's declining hegemony over the other cities of the Pacific Slope. The Progressives are usually depicted as an insurgency of the new professional middle classes: dentists, schoolteachers, architects, citrus growers, and grocers fighting for "clean," nonpartisan, and scientifically managed government. But Progressivism in California had another dimension much neglected in standard histories: it was equally an uprising of the younger urban business elites against the economic and political domination of San Francisco and San Francisco–allied local oligarchs.[33]

San Diego Progressives, of course, had special grievances against San Francisco. No sooner had they announced their proposed exposition than the Golden Gate's boosters produced plans for an even more lavish celebration of the Panama Canal's opening. Then the San Franciscans used their political clout to grab the entire $5 million subsidy for foreign exhibitors voted by Congress, a blatant attempt to kill San Diego's Balboa Park exposition.[34]

But after the statewide Progressive revolt broke the stranglehold of the railroads over Sacramento politics in 1910, San Diego had an opportunity to take revenge. At issue was the desire of all the California coastal cities to "municipalize" their waterfronts by reclaiming state-owned tidelands (like the marshes that ringed San Diego Bay) for port development. In the 1911 legislative session, a coalition of Oakland, San Diego, and Los Angeles won the fight that allowed them to build powerful port authorities, while San Francisco—which had abdicated administration of its waterfront to a state commission during the so-called "bulkhead wars" of the 1850s—failed in its initial attempt to wrest port improvements from the state. As a result, haughty San Francisco for the first time was forced to bargain with cities previously regarded as its mere satellites.[35]

The labor war itself was also as much about the struggle between cities as between their social classes. Although it ultimately embroiled the whole coast, the epicenter of industrial violence was Los Angeles, where General Harrison Grey Otis of the *Times* and his son-in-law Harry Chandler had been fighting unionism for almost a generation. To Otis and Chandler, the "open shop," as enforced by their militaristic Merchants and Manufacturers Association, was not only an expression of capitalist fundamentalism but also (as the *Times* constantly pointed out) a comparative advantage in L.A.'s competition with San Francisco, the most unionized city in the world. San Francisco's merchant princes and bankers, like Claus Spreckels and his sons, had reluctantly accommodated unionism in the 1890s only because the superprofits generated by the Golden Gate's dominance over the Pacific Slope and its extractive industries mitigated zero-sum class conflict at home. By the advent of the 1909 recession, however, San Francisco's spatial-economic monopoly was rapidly eroding in the face of the competition of lower-wage cities, especially Los Angeles, but also Oakland, Portland, and Seattle.

San Francisco's capitalists literally ordered the San Francisco Labor Council and California Labor Federation to equalize wage levels and working conditions by organizing Los Angeles or face an all-out open-shop offensive in the Bay Area. "The ultimatum," Grace Stimson notes, "was a powerful incentive for a supreme effort to organize Los Angeles." Otis and Chandler, in turn, countered the campaign by the northern unions with the harshest antipicketing ordinance in the country. Hundreds of trade unionists were jailed and the *Times* was bombed in retaliation. Los Angeles's embattled unionists called for solidarity from San Diego and elsewhere, while Otis issued bloodcurdling demands for California's capitalists to crush labor "terrorism."[36]

Initially, San Diego seemed immune to the warfare in Los Angeles. Partially because of its industrial backwardness, it had little history of violent class polarization. There were few large employers, and neither the open shop nor the union shop clearly prevailed. If Spreckels's San Diego Electric system was notoriously nonunion, both of his newspapers, by contrast, had been successfully organized by the Pressmen in 1908.[37] The Chamber of Commerce had not yet been put on a class-war footing nor was there a local counterpart to L.A.'s bellicose Merchants and Manufacturers Association.

This idyll ended when the Red flag was raised above the Tijuana customs house in 1911. Although the *Magonista* republic (discussed in the next essay) lasted only a few months, it directly threatened the considerable interests of California gamblers in border bars and bordellos (mostly gringo-owned) as well as the immense landholdings of Otis and Chandler in the Mexicali Valley.[38] Moreover, the Red Menace of 1911, followed by the entrenchment of the Wobblies in San Diego's tenderloin district—the so-called "Stingaree"—provided hugely convenient pretexts, respectively, for Otis to bring San Diego into alignment with his antiunion crusade, and for Spreckels to distract public opinion from the duplicity of his railroad machinations.

To the disgust of local Progressives, who despised the Los Angeles *Times*'s incessant disparagement of San Diego (the city was often deleted in *Times* maps of
Southern California),[39] General Otis was given a hero's welcome at a banquet at
the U.S. Grant Hotel in October 1911. He urged the hundred or so businessmen
in attendance to smite subversion and "labor terrorism" by adopting the model Los
Angeles ordinance outlawing street meetings and picket lines.[40] Spreckels's *Union*
soon intimidated the city council into passing the ordinance and San Diego's famous
Free Speech fight punctually followed. The little city, previously characterized by
the mild temperature of its labor relations, experienced nearly a year of fascistic rule
by self-appointed vigilantes under the impassive gaze of its supposedly Progressive
police superintendent.

There was broad speculation at the time that Spreckels was the secret leader of
the vigilantes. It would not have been a new role. As a young plutocrat in 1870s
San Francisco, John D. had armed his employees and led them into the sandlots
to oppose Dennis Kearney and the Workingman's Party.[41] Moreover, in "Spreckelstown" it was unlikely that anything so extreme as vigilante rule could arise without
John D.'s instigation or at least tolerance. Some of the identified ringleaders indeed
were clearly Spreckels's men, including a *Union* reporter.[42] The *Union* and *Tribune*
likewise surpassed even Otis's virulent *Times* in their hysterical calls for violence, even
murder ("hanging is too good"), against the Industrial Workers of the World (IWW)
and its supporters.[43]

Spreckels, moreover, had a compelling motive for staging a civic coup d'état: it
was a splendid diversion from damaging news coverage of the Southern Pacific suit
against him. According to Richard Pourade, "The suit confirmed what financiers
knew and most of the public had suspected. The San Diego and Arizona was a crea-
ture of the Southern Pacific and there had been no intention on its part, regardless of
the hopes of Spreckels, of extending its line beyond El Centro to the Colorado River
and thus competing with its own main line into Los Angeles."[44]

Unlike the Los Angeles Progressives, most of whom eventually rallied to Otis's
antiunion banner, the major reform leaders in San Diego denounced the reign of
terror. But no great anti-Spreckels movement emerged in response to vigilantism

or the exposure of the Harriman deal. In effect, local Progressives' hands were tied by the need to keep Spreckels onboard the California-Panama committee. The success of the exposition had become a supreme cause, more important than the civil liberties of labor, and, since San Francisco had stolen federal subsidies, Spreckels's financial support was more urgent than ever. With real estate once again booming and possibly millions of visitors on the horizon, there was an overriding interest in returning the city to "normalcy."

Spreckels made shrewd use of this situation. Although his railroad project was almost as mired in skyrocketing costs and engineering problems as de Lesseps's ill-fated Panama Canal Company a decade before, he was able to raise desperately needed cash by the profitable sale of his water system to the city. Moreover, his chief antagonist, Lovett, was replaced at the helm of the Southern Pacific and, although the railroad was unwilling to advance further capital, the new regime left Harriman's original investment in place. Simultaneously, by dangling his proposed $100,000 subsidy to the exposition in front of local voters, John D. exploited one of the Progressives' key antiboss reforms, the intiative and referendum, to win a twenty-five-year extension of his lucrative street rail franchise. He also used his financial clout to blackmail the exposition committee into changing its site from the Sixth Avenue west end of Balboa Park to the undeveloped central mesa.

The logic behind this move was revealing. Spreckels and others wanted to ensure a maximum serendipity between civic goals and their own profits. Even before the brush was cleared for the first exposition building, it was clear that the event had even more ambitious aims than simply advertising the city to the world and winning support for its major improvement projects (a transcontinental highway and a major naval installation). In addition, the fair was intended to directly sell real estate to the benefit of Spreckels, Oscar Cotton (of the Pacific Building Company), and other key backers.

The public explanation [Robert Showley emphasizes] was that the new site would offer more space for exhibitors; the private reason was Spreckels's desire to extend his street car system through the park and toward North Park and University Heights. He and other fair directors had real estate interests that stood to benefit from this move. Research indicates that Spreckels withheld his $100,000 pledge to the exposition until he got his way.[45]

In contrast to Spreckels's impressive recuperation of his power, the Progressives suffered surprising setbacks. In 1913 Marston ran for mayor with support of the Progressives and some of the Socialists. In a city of artful dodgers and self-promoters, where even Scripps and Fletcher seldom supported a reform without some eventual personal dividend, Marston had a unique record of almost selfless civic patriotism, including his leadership in the beautification of Balboa Park, his sponsorship of the 1909 "city beautiful" plan of John Nolen, his tireless work on behalf of the Arizona railroad, and, currently, his frenetic efforts to make San Diego the terminus of a cross-country motor highway. In the eyes of the San Diego labor movement, however, Marston's halo was worn crookedly. Despite his oft-expressed sympathies with the working classes and his generally decent record as an employer, he had used nonunion labor to cut construction costs on the new department store he opened in 1911. Moreover, the Labor Council was deeply worried about his advocacy of the "city beautiful."

As previously noted, Marston was no mere aesthete: rather, he had a coherent vision of developing landscape capital to attract wealthy retirees, tourists, academics, and lighter, nonpolluting industries. He "stood most emphatically for the kind of man and business that fits in with our natural conditions," said Oscar Cotton. Civic beautification was a priority "because it pays in dollars and cents."[46] Most of the old-guard leadership—bankers and developers with their assets in real estate and tourism, like Babcock, Fletcher, and Luce—generally supported Marston's ideas, as did Scripps, who was already pushing hard for the navy as the city's ideal partner.

But labor, quite rightly, failed to see where horny-handed sons of toil fit into Marston's garden city. In the 1913 city primary, the working-class vote split. A large minority supported the Socialists, whose objective was not the mayoralty but unseating an antiunion councilman who had been the police superintendent during the Free Speech fight. More of the labor vote, however, went to realtor Charles O'Neall and the less genteel camp of local capitalists who advertised themselves as the party of growth and jobs. Said O'Neall, "We don't want San Diego to be the 'amen corner' of the United States." Although much of the Socialist vote returned to Marston in the final election, O'Neall kept enough of the blue-collar constituency to win by a small margin.[47]

Four years later, Louis Wilde, a banker and former O'Neall backer, beat Marston—despite Marston's unprecedented endorsement by both the *Union* and *Sun*—by a far more commanding margin and effectively ended Marston's political career. The 1917 election, on the eve of the United States entry into the World War, was dominated by both the local slump in real estate sales and Wilde's gift for comically portraying Marston as the leader of no-growth "geraniums" and himself as the champion of "smokestacks" and full employment.

The two elections, in 1913 and 1917, were molds for the city's future in a double sense: First, despite his electoral defeats, Marston's vision of amenity-based "clean growth," with preference to retirees, tourists, and sailors rather than heavy industries and industrial unions, would provide an enduring template to which the city's dominant business elites would repeatedly return—until, in the 1980s, it simply became holy scripture. Second, the labor movement, except for a brief left-wing interval in the New Deal years, would perennially put "growth" ahead of any other issue of principle. In effect, this would propel the San Diego Labor Council into serial marriages of desperation with the demagogic politicians and reactionary local capitalists.

6. Seducing the Navy

> He [William Kettner] has hypnotized not only the committee but Congress.
>
> *Illinois congressman (1920)*[48]

The militarization of the San Diego economy after 1915, the epochal event in its twentieth-century history, owed something—mostly in the form of unintended consequences—to the rise of the Progressives. First, by stoking anti-Japanese hysteria in California to a fever pitch and producing the first "war scares" with Japan in 1906 and 1913, the Progressives contributed to the geopolitical tensions in the Pacific that would eventually realign U.S. naval deployments. Indeed, the creation of a Pacific Fleet to protect California from the "yellow peril" was a principal Progressive demand. Second, by splitting the Republican Party, the Progressives helped elect a San Diego Democrat, William Kettner, to Congress in 1912. He would eventually surpass his notorious contemporary, Mata Hari, as the era's most skillful seducer of admirals and generals.

Kettner, whose sales skills had been honed in the insurance business, had won acclaim as the Chamber of Commerce's chief lobbyist to the Navy. It was a difficult sales pitch. Despite San Diego Bay's much advertised charms, naval planners had shown surprisingly little interest in its strategic potential. Admiral George Dewey, the key architect of U.S. naval policy in the Pacific, spurned the daunting expense of dredging a deep harbor in San Diego in favor of existing facilities in San Francisco Bay and forward deployments at Subic Bay and Pearl Harbor. San Diego was excluded from the first iterations of War Plan Orange, the secret U.S. strategy for war with Japan. The only concession to the city was a tiny coaling station opened in 1904. When Teddy Roosevelt in 1907–08 sent the Great White Fleet around the world to impress potential allies and future enemies, San Diego wasn't included on the itinerary.

Kettner showed his chutzpah by borrowing Spreckels's yacht to intercept Admiral Bob Evans's armada at Magdalena Bay in Baja California. In return for Evans visiting San Diego, Kettner promised an Arabian Nights reception: rapturous flag-waving crowds, vast banquets, and a bumper crop of pretty girls. Spreckels agreed to underwrite the festivities and to regale the officers at his sumptuous Coronado hotel. The inducements were irresistible, although the great battleline of dreadnoughts was unable to safely enter the bay and had to anchor instead off Coronado. During the brief visit, Kettner lost no opportunity to ply flag officers with juicy details of the exceptional opportunities for fortune hunting and leisure in San Diego. Although the fleet's visit produced no immediate windfall, it left scores of young officers, the future naval leaders of World War II, with exceedingly favorable impressions of the city.[49]

Indeed, the ingenuity of the Chamber's campaign, as orchestrated by Kettner, was to combine direct lobbying in Washington with a sales campaign targeting visiting officers and, especially, their wives. Although every port city on the coast was aggressively competing for new naval investment, San Diego was unique in the degree to which it welcomed U.S. Navy and Marine Corps brass into its elite inner sanctums. Stationed on barren North Island in 1914 during a brief flare-up of border hysteria, Marine Colonel Joseph Pendleton had expected to amuse himself shooting jackrabbits but was instead swept up into the glamorous social life of Spreckels's Coronado set. "It took Pendleton no time at all to establish himself as a leading citizen and socialite, even while he was camping on North Island."[50] His successors would have similar experiences. Flag officers, especially, were treated as local celebrities and welcomed to the most exclusive golf links and male retreats, while their wives were the guests of honor at the women's clubs and charity balls. On retirement, captains, admirals, and Marine generals were invited to join bank and newspaper boards, appointed to city commissions, and encouraged to run for local office—like Pendleton, who became mayor of Coronado after his retirement.

Perhaps even more important, they were also cut into lucrative real estate syndicates, including those that sold waterfront land to the Navy and Marine Corps. An early example was Rear Admiral Henry Manney, who became head of the Chamber's harbor committee, was elected to the city council in 1913, and later served as superintendent of police and public morals. Along with several of Kettner's other closest associates, Manney was a director of San Diego Securities, which owned the tidelands at Dutch Flats and Loma Portal that were sold for the Navy and Marine training bases. Manney was the pioneer figure in the rise of the naval-industrial power structure that would become so distinctive of modern San Diego.[51]

Meanwhile, in Washington, "Bruder Bill," as Kettner liked to be called, laid siege to Admiral Dewey, the intransigent opponent of naval investment in San Diego. Although the hero of Manila Bay refused to reconsider his commitments to the primacy of San Francisco and Pearl Harbor, he grudgingly gave the insistent Kettner an endorsement for dredging San Diego Bay's treacherous middle channel. Kettner skillfully used Dewey's letter to pry open congressional appropriations and, above all, to whet the interests of Secretary of the Navy Josephus Daniels and his young assistant secretary, Franklin Roosevelt, in the naval potential of San Diego. In 1913, Daniels, the old Progressive, was wined and dined by the old reactionary, John D. Spreckels, at Coronado. The next year Franklin and Eleanor Roosevelt came as a Washington advance guard to observe the final preparations for the exposition. Cruising the harbor with Spreckels on his *Venetia,* the Roosevelts reputedly fell in love with the city.[52] Indeed, FDR was the Chamber of Commerce's prime catch: the most powerful and ardent convert to the strategic importance of San Diego in a dawning age of U.S.-Japan rivalry in the Pacific. Later, as president, he would continue his favoritism toward a city that otherwise was the most incorrigibly Republican bastion in California.[53]

San Diego taxpayers, on their side, welcomed the Navy with huge donations of public land, including a precious corner of Balboa Park for a naval hospital. Their local elected representatives, however, were often peripheral in the crucial negotiations with the Navy. Rather, it was the Chamber of Commerce that became the "Navy's exclusive broker in San Diego." Working hand in hand with their alumnus Kettner, Chamber leaders were intimately involved in selecting sites for installations of ever-increasing size and economic value: advanced naval long-distance radio stations at Point Loma and Chollas Height; the Navy and Army airfields and training schools on North Island; the huge World War I Army training base on Kearney Mesa (later Miramar Airfield); the Marine base (later recruit depot) at Dutch Flats; and, finally, the West Coast naval training center at Loma Portal (transferred, thanks to FDR's instigation, from Goat Island in San Francisco Bay). Several of these transactions, not surprisingly, were highly profitable for leading members of the Chamber, including Spreckels's sale of North Island and San Diego Security Company's sale of the Loma Portal site.[54]

After the creation of a full-fledged Pacific battle fleet in 1919, San Diego soon won destroyers (based at 32nd Street in National City) and a submarine base (at Ballast Point), transferred from San Pedro. If the biggest plums, the new battleships and heavy cruisers, went to Pearl Harbor, San Francisco, and Bremerton, it was a blessing in disguise. San Diego's compensation was an unusual concentration of the Navy's infant, cutting-edge technologies: long-distance radio transmission, carrier aviation, and, later, undersea and amphibious warfare. This was San Diego's future high-tech economy in embryo. Moreover, as the bay was gradually deepened, San Diego was able to grab some cruisers and, far more important, the first generation of aircraft carriers, led by the Langley in 1922 and the Saratoga in 1932. (The sediment dredged for the carriers was used, in turn, to create Lindbergh Field in 1929.) In part, this was San Diego's just reward for its political support of Admiral William Moffett and other leading advocates of naval aviation.[55]

With Kettner as Mephistopheles, San Diego had signed a Faustian pact with the Devil and Josephus Daniels. The coming of the Navy, as Kevin Starr has emphasized, allowed the city to achieve a synthesis of its Marstonian ideals and economic growth.[56] Indeed, the Navy was an ideal industry: to most eyes, its handsome warships and soaring carrier planes beautified rather than disfigured the environment. Each cruiser or carrier, moreover, added to the economy the purchasing power of a small- or medium-sized factory. But these were factories without troublesome industrial unions, irksome strikes, or politically potent workforces. At the same time, the stability of naval expenditure mitigated San Diego's traditional tendency to extreme boom/bust cycles: during the Depression, the Roosevelt administration increased naval appropriations every year. Finally, the constant stream of retiring naval and Marine officers bolstered real estate sales and reinforced the city's influence within the Department of the Navy.

But there was also the Devil's side of the bargain. The Navy was (and is) a jealous guardian of its harbor and airspace prerogatives. In selling or donating prime waterfront, as well as choice interior land parcels, to the Navy, the city gave away opportunities to achieve crucial parts of the Nolen plan, such as creation of a waterfront esplanade, as well as to promote the commercial-industrial development of the harbor. The atrophy of the civilian harbor was almost total: in 1940 San Diego (the sixth largest West Coast city) was next to the smallest of twenty-four Pacific ports in volume of trade. It wasn't even officially designated a "terminal port of call" by the Pacific West Bound Steamship Conference.[57] (In Los Angeles the opposite process occurred, with the big oil companies on Terminal Island successfully opposing naval expansion.)

Moreover, the Navy was a profoundly conservatizing force and it reinforced San Diego's tendency to become an ideological backwater. The old Yankee navy of the nineteenth century had become in the twentieth century the armed service most dominated by Southerners and their white-supremacist attitudes. A patrician, often ultrareactionary naval culture thus overprinted the stolid Hooverism of the Midwestern immigration. The city's business leadership, especially the *Union*, reciprocated by zealously promoting San Diego as the "most patriotic city" in the nation—too often a euphemism for union-busting and intolerance of dissent.

And despite all the boasting about it being a "Navy town," San Diego's infatuation was strictly with officers and gentlemen. It had a more ambivalent attitude toward its surrogate proletariat of enlisted men. Ordinary seamen, in turn, had a love-hate relationship with the city. When Josephus Daniels introduced the unusual reform of allowing crewmen to vote on which local port they preferred for liberty, San Francisco—which had been catering to sailors' needs for generations—always beat San Diego hands down. This was one reason why Navy boosters favored turning a blind eye to the drunken-sailor-oriented fleshpots on lower Broadway and along Fifth Avenue. Later Tijuana allowed San Diego to eat its cake and have it as well. But no solution would be found to the perennial problem of housing Navy families. Sailors are a low-wage workforce, and they had no more luck finding affordable housing for their families in the 1920s than they do today.[58] The bluejackets and leathernecks who built the fortunes of San Diego also became its permanent pariahs.

7. The Sales Pitch

> Now was the time to reach these people, while they were newly rich, and
> bring them to San Diego.
> *Oscar Cotton (1919)*[59]

Spreckels finally drove the golden spike to complete his San Diego and Eastern Railroad at Carrizo Gorge on November 15, 1919. Congressman Kettner, accompanied by two generals and two admirals, "said he was proud to live in such a 'one-man town' as San Diego," while John D. for the first time acknowledged that the true paternity for the railroad belonged to Harriman, now ten years dead. Later, San Diego, forgiving his epic double cross, celebrated "John D. Spreckels Day" with a huge parade. In the evening, three "superdreadnoughts" of the new Pacific Fleet—the *New Mexico*, the *Idaho,* and the *Mississippi*—thrilled Spreckels's subjects by illuminating the city's mesas with their powerful searchlights.[60]

It was perhaps the most anticlimactic moment in the city's history. Although Spreckels's *Union* boasted tastelessly of the "commercial tribute" that Arizona and the Imperial Valley would henceforth pay to San Diego, Los Angeles and the Southern Pacific retained their monopoly, just as Harriman had intended, on the trade of the Southwest.[61] Despite all the years of hyperbole and scandal, the railroad would make only a minor contribution to the city's future growth. But its completion was an authenic punctuation mark, signaling the end of one era and the beginning of another.

The city's old elite, class of 1890, was running out of steam. Spreckels would continue to reign over San Diego until his death in 1926, but he had no more vast projects to unfurl or worlds to conquer. Broken in health by prodigious drinking, Scripps meanwhile had set to sea in his yacht with an attractive nurse, partially to avoid the bitter conflict between his sons over the management of his newspaper empire. While anchored off Monrovia, he died within a few months of his old nemesis, Spreckels. Babcock, always plagued by bad luck, had been ruined for a second time in 1916, when the famous "Rainmaker" floods of that year washed away his latest venture, a rail line to La Jolla. Kettner, meanwhile, retired from Congress in 1920 to bask in the glory of the naval infrastructure he had procured for San Diego.[62] (His successor was a rabidly antilabor Imperial Valley judge, Phil Swing, who continued to press for more naval investment in San Diego while also co-fathering Boulder Dam.)

Marston remained San Diego's geranium emeritus. He continued as a fount of civic wisdom and humane values for nearly two more decades but was marginalized by the rapid extinction of the Progressive ethos after the defeat of its hero, Senator Robert La Follete, in 1924. Marston spurned the conservative backlash and grasping business culture of the roaring twenties, often upbraiding associates who assumed that as a successful capitalist he too must be a knee-jerk Coolidge-Hoover man. He preferred the idealism of his radical daughter, the founder of the Women's International Strike for Peace, to these philistines. And in 1932 he became one of the few millionaires in the country to endorse Norman Thomas, the Socialist candidate for president.

Ed Fletcher was the only member of the old guard to keep a full ante in the game for another generation. After building and selling a water empire (the Cuyamacas Water Company) in the east county, he took charge of the campaign to make San Diego a terminus of one of the proposed national highways. It was another epic competition, like the railroad wars, with Los Angeles, but this time little San Diego—with the help of its "Navy mayor," Admiral J. S. McKean—beat the Goliath to the north, and for almost a decade Highway 80 from Savannah to San Diego was the only fully paved route to Southern California. This triumph boosted Fletcher into the state senate, where he ended his career as a close ally of Governor Earl Warren.[63] As always, "Colonel Ed" managed to feather his own nest while pursuing the public good.[64]

The successor cohort of San Diego business leaders was more simply interested in feathering their nests. As the homeric generation of city builders passed from the scene, it was now the turn of the Babbits, the closing-tent artists and get-rich-quick boys. Their outstanding representative was Oscar Cotton, the young actor-turned-developer who had become a fat cat selling bungalows in newly subdivided Pacific Beach and East San Diego before the war. Cotton was the type specimen of the business species (so well described by Sinclair Lewis) that would dominate post-Progressive San Diego: political and social reactionaries, with little connection to the real world of production, who worshiped the power of salesmanship as a supernatural force.

If engineers and genius tinkerers had been the heroes of the previous generation, salesmen of all kinds, including political demagogues and religious hucksters, were the 1920s' new men of power. Modern "scientific advertising" (whose chief guru and systematizer was Freud's son-in-law Edward Louis Bernays) was essentially a brand-new industry in 1919, an outgrowth of titanic wartime propaganda battles. Cotton's idea, elaborated to the local business leadership in 1919, was to use advertising's newly proven powers over the masses to market a mirage—a hyper-romanticized image of San Diego—which, in turn, would sell local real estate (which had been in a distressing slump since 1917). Although the railroads, the West's largest land-owners, had engaged in place promotion for decades, their geographical loyalties were contingent, and often promiscuous. Cotton—a rabid antisocialist—wanted to "municipalize" the sales pitch. With the 1915 exposition as a model of elite coop-eration, he proposed the creation of a "San Diego–California Club" that would tax leading businessmen to mount a scientifically designed campaign to advertise the city to targeted groups of potential immigrants.[65]

"To whom are we going to sell?" Cotton asked Chamber of Commerce lead-ers. "Shall we invite laborers?" Cotton's answer was no. Before further blue-collar immigration was encouraged, the city had to build a base of wealth in accord with the ideas long advocated by George Marston. But where would rich geranium-lovers come from? From the Midwest, where wheat was selling at an all-time high of $2.20 per bushel in 1918 and where farms, worth only $40 per acre before the war, were now changing hands for $300 per acre. The war boom had fattened a large layer of Midwestern farmers and small business people whom Cotton proposed to induce to retire along the shores of San Diego Bay. "The great outstanding opportunity San Diego has today is the opportunity to get these people *now*, while they have the money in the bank and before they locate elsewhere."[66]

To accomplish this, Cotton emphasized, "*we must make San Diego symbolize California* in the minds of the people of this Midwest district." The chief aphrodisiac would be Balboa Park, whose temporary exposition buildings would now be left standing, romantic follies to seduce wealthy hicks. The City Beautiful—or, rather, its simulacrum in Balboa Park—would be the heart of the proposed sales pitch. And, indeed, many of the eventual ads were headlined: "Built Around a Park—San Diego."[67]

The ad blitz, concentrated in key Midwestern papers, began in November 1919; by December, the club was receiving 900 inquiries per day. Under Cotton's instruc-tion, the inquiries were divided into "classes" according to the presumed wealth of the sender. Stenographers then addressed personal responses to each of the "Class

1" enquirees, who were enrolled as honorary members of the San Diego–California Club and sent "a large, maroon-colored book entitled 'Where Life Means Most.'" Cotton later wrote, "It contained many large pictures of our beautiful Balboa Park, the waterfront and the beach scenes."[68]

Just as San Francisco had copied San Diego's exposition, so now Los Angeles cribbed a lesson from the San Diego–California Club. Its version, unveiled in 1921, was called the All-Year Club of Southern California, and it was backed by a predictably huge advertising budget, seven times the size of San Diego's. Houston, Phoenix, and other rising cities of the future Sunbelt quickly created their own counterparts, most of which, like the San Diego template, evolved into today's tax-supported "convention and visitors" bureaus. Cotton was genuinely the Henry Ford of civic boosterism.

And in spite of Los Angeles's competing entreaties, the "Class 1" people—the flush Iowa farmers and wealthy Indiana dentists—came to San Diego in a quiet flood, along with many of their less well-to-do neighbors. Although San Diego's industrial employment in 1929 (3,836) was virtually the same as in 1919 (3,427), Midwestern savings and annuities fattened the construction and services sectors.[69] Cotton's Pacific Development Company alone sold forty subdivisions during the decade, ranging from a few hundred to several thousand lots in size. On the giant chessboard of San Diego Mesa, the boom filled in the vacant squares between the original streetcar subdivisions developed prior to 1917.

The success of San Diego's Midwest sales pitch, of course, was also a posthumous moral victory for Marston's maligned "geranium" platform of 1917, and in 1921 Mayor Bacon, a Marston man, invited John Nolen back to San Diego to update his 1908 proposals. Nolen's new plan urged the preservation of Old Town and envisioned the building of a city center and airport along the harbor front as well as a scenic parkway through still rustic Mission Valley. Its official adoption by the city council in 1926 was proof that beauty had proven its market value, although with no guarantee that it would generally prevail.

In any event, the boundaries between San Diego's elected government and its para-government of business organizations—the Chamber of Commerce, the Realty

Board, and the San Diego–California Club—had permanently blurred. Glenn Rick, the pioneer planning director hired in 1927 to implement the Nolen Plan, complained that he often was unsure who exactly he was working for, since the Chamber and the Realty Board usually vetted planning proposals, such as the city's Major Street Plan, before they were ever presented to the Council.[70] The council majority obediently obeyed business agendas and ambitious mayors were so frustrated by their weak authority that one of them, John Forward Jr. (of the Union Title dynasty), resigned in frustration soon after taking office in 1933. (His less fortunate and oft-lampooned successor, Rutherford B. Irones, took to drink and ended up in jail after a drunk-driving hit and run.)

While San Diego was growing fat on its new diet of naval dollars and Midwestern retirees, the chief beneficiaries of the boom decided to properly "aristocratize" themselves by creating an exclusive retreat in the backcountry, a local counterpart to the Bay Area's Bohemian Grove or Pasadena's Valley Hunt Club. Located near Pine Valley, it was called Corte Madera Ranch: 3,400 wooded acres with a lake and polo field. The dozen families who built cabins at the Ranch during the 1920s were, for the most part, the second- and third-generation offspring of the 1870s and 1880s speculators. They included the Belchers (now married to Spreckels), Goodwins, Whitneys, and Garretsons, as well as the more parvenu Cottons (who eventually married Fletchers). Their overlapping power base was the First National Bank, then headed by Frank Belcher, and several had a stake in the San Diego Securities syndicate that profitably sold land to the Navy and Marines. For the next fifty years, the "Corte Madera set" would be a synonym for San Diego's cloistered and incestuous old money.

But there was also new money on the scene in the 1920s. The death of John D. Spreckels in 1926 and the subsequent sell-off of his San Diego assets brought the Midwestern newspaperman Colonel Ira Copley into the inner circle of local power. Copley, who became a "colonel" leading the Illinois militia against the Pullman strikers, was an ex-Republican congressman with a fortune divided between downstate Illinois newspapers and power utilities. After losing a bruising battle with Midwestern utility czar Samuel Insull, Copley cashed in his utilities in 1928 and went on a newspaper buying spree. His two biggest acquisitions were Spreckels's *Union* and *Tribune,* with the former becoming the new flagship of the empire. A close friend and supporter of Herbert Hoover (who, in turn, was the first California-resident, if not native-born, president), Copley established the first in a series of significant liaisons between San Diego elites and Republican White Houses.[71]

Baron Long, who acquired downtown's U.S. Grant Hotel in 1919 as well as a stake in the famed Caliente racetrack in Tijuana, brought with him links of a different kind: to both the Hollywood movie colony and a border underworld of corrupt politicians, high-stakes gamblers, and vice operators. Although Long introduced himself to San Diegans as Los Angeles's most celebrated impresario, the owner of well-known cafes and nightclubs, and the chief investor in the famed Biltmore Hotel, this was only the tip of an otherwise very dirty iceberg. Long, in fact, was one of the original "Czars of the Bars," along with Carl Withington and James Coffroth. According to a recent history of U.S. investment in Mexico, "the three owned nightclubs, gambling establishments, and brothels along the border from the Pacific Ocean to Matamoros in the Gulf of Mexico."[72]

Tijuana's transformation in the 1920s from a dusty hamlet into the "Monte Carlo of North America" (or Las Vegas *avante le lettre,* if you prefer) was a considerable boon to the San Diego economy. The cornerstone was the racetrack, which Withington's ABW Corporation opened in 1916, after the Progressives had closed down racing in California, to exploit the tourist influx for the San Diego Exposition. Opening day's principal handicap was named "the Adolph Spreckels" and there was widespread speculation that the Spreckels brothers were secret partners of Withington's San Joaquin Valley–based gang of oilfield gamblers, bootleggers, and pimps. In any event, the success of the track buoyed the fortunes of Spreckels's Hotel del Coronado and other local hotels after the end of the fair. The track was managed by the famed San Francisco boxing promoter and saloon owner "Sunny Jim" Coffroth, an old drinking and whoring buddy of "Dolph" Spreckels. Baron Long, who already owned a bar in Tijuana, formally took charge of catering, but his real role was to entice his Hollywood friends, like Fatty Arbuckle, Jack Dempsey, and Charlie Chaplin, south of the border.[73]

Prohibition, of course, gold-plated this Tijuana gambling and vice franchise, with a considerable faction of Hollywood celebrity at all times ensconced in the elegant new Agua Caliente casino and resort, opened in 1926 by Long, in partnership with Baja governor (and soon, president) Abelardo Rodriguez. It was a preview of the world of Las Vegas in the 1950s, movie stars playing with gangsters, and it was famed for its gorgeous women, including the young Rita Hayworth in a dancing act with her father. But Rodriguez's reign was short. In 1935, President Lázaro Cárdenas decided both to reclaim control of the national border and to topple the corrupt empire of his predecessor. In a defiant gesture of "Mexicanization" (which some in San Diego claimed was really "Bolshevization"), the casino was closed down and replaced by five new schools. The net effect was to drive the big gamblers to Hollywood's new desert oasis of Las Vegas, while the smaller gringo and local vice interests adapted their product to the mass market of the wartime U.S. Navy. But regardless of these vicissitudes, the "sin industry" of Tijuana would continue to be an integral part of both the San Diego economy and—with names like Alessio and Hank Gonzalez—its business power structure.

8. The Other Fleet Arrives

Consolidated's forced growth was the greatest of any private enterprise in any line of endeavor in the history of the world.
Reuben Fleet (1944)[74]

What happened to the purchasers of Cotton's San Diego dream? As the tide of migration from the Midwest receded in the early Depression years, Edmund Wilson stopped in San Diego to observe the quality of life left on the beach. In his famous essay "The Jumping Off Place," he discovered that many pilgrims-to-paradise became, in fact, suicidal lemmings.

They stuff up the cracks of their doors and quietly turn on the gas; they go into their back sheds or back kitchens and eat ant-paste or swallow Lysol; they drive their cars into dark alleys, get into the back seat and shoot themselves; they hang themselves in hotel bedrooms, take overdoses of sulphonal or barbital; they slip off to the municipal golf-links and there stab themselves with carving-knives; or they throw themselves into the bay, blue and placid. . . .[75]

Although Wilson's essay has always infuriated San Diego boosters, he was only pointing out some civic statistics that were not included in the San Diego–California Club brochures: the highest suicide rate in the nation and the largest percentage of invalids and sick people (nearly a quarter of the population). Wilson suggested that self-murder was not a surprising response when sickness and depression, having escaped to the sunshine and blue waters, find neither cure or solace. (Wilson's essay would be dusted off and reread in 1997 after thirty-nine Heaven's Gate cultists decided to make San Diego's wealthy suburb of Rancho Santa Fe their "jumping off place.")

In other respects, the Depression was less devastating in San Diego than elsewhere, thanks both to the absence of heavy industry and to the large share of regional income contributed by the Eleventh Naval District. San Diego had received more than $136 million in naval investment—nearly as much as the San Francisco area—since FDR's visit to the 1915 fair.[76] Nonetheless, times were hard, especially for the real estate industry, whose heartbeat almost stopped dead during the summer of 1932. The collapse of the 1920s boom left investors with the huge carrying cost of 50,000 subdivided but unbuilt lots.[77] Although the newly formed "Heaven on Earth Club" attempted to restart the profitable migration from the Midwest, many of the newcomers arrived in battered Model-Ts with gaunt faces, hungry, and desperate for work. To attract a more affluent stream of visitors and to remind the world of the city's charms, the business leadership returned in 1934 to the panacea of an exposition in Balboa Park.

The extravaganza, which opened in 1935 and ran until the end of 1936, had little of the edifying purpose or cultural pretension of 1915's version. Schoolchildren were dutifully trooped through the secondhand Century of Progress exhibits and the old exposition buildings were nicely renovated with new Moorish gardens in their backyards. But the real spirit of the fair was pre-Depression Coney Island. Indeed, there were many cheap and surprisingly uninhibited thrills to divert morbid San Diegans from thoughts of suicide. The most popular spectacles included "Midget City," with "one hundred Lilliputians"; "a fourlegged pickanniny girl exhibited in the Believe-it-or-not show"; an authentic nudist colony (surrounded by a high fence); Mary Pickford's curls; a Parisian musical review; Dillinger's car; and, for the most credulous, a big display about the "Lost Continent of Mu," which scientists, using the new wonder of sonar, had supposedly just discovered off the San Diego coast.[78]

All the scantily clad burlesque dancers pretending to be Parisian *artistes* were a big hit with the Fleet. San Diego seemed to have shed much of its old puritanism. Some of the old Progressives complained that, in fact, the vice and gambling interests, "dominated by Baron Long, King of Tijuana Gamblers," were brazenly taking over the city.[79] *Time* magazine delighted in reporting a remarkable meeting in June 1935 between Mayor Percy Benbough and the so-called Liberal Businessmen's Association. Benbough, an undertaker and former police chief, assured the assembled bookmakers, saloon keepers, and peep show operators that they were making an important contribution to the public's happiness, even if some of their activities "were not strictly legal." He then urged them not to succumb to bribe demands from public officials.[80]

Although *Time* didn't publish any names, San Diegans knew Benbough was referring to Police Chief Sears's alleged side income. Most reformers believed that graft in San Diego, via Caliente and Baron Long, was a part of a larger pattern of gambler-controlled corruption that included the notorious Shaw regime in Los Angeles. From this perspective, Benbough's firing of Sears and City Manager Flack in spring 1939 after his supporters gained a majority on the city council was the counterpart to the famous housecleaning in Los Angeles the year before. But whereas the recall of Mayor Shaw was the prelude to a dynamic new progressivism in L.A., based on an unusual alliance of middle-class reformers and the labor movement, there was little sequel in San Diego. Benbough was a wholly owned subsidiary of the Chamber of Commerce, or so, at least, charged the San Diego *Labor Leader*.[81] Wartime demand, moreover, immediately restocked the shelves with all the old vices and more, and the police (as investigations in the 1960s made evident) resumed their traditional grafting from bookmakers and pimps.

What did change dramatically in San Diego during the 1930s was the manufacturing economy. Before 1935, the civilian industrial base of the city consisted almost solely of some medium-sized tuna canneries plus Claude Ryan's little aircraft plant where the *Spirit of St. Louis* was built by hand in 1927. John D. Spreckels had briefly started up a tire factory in 1919 using cotton from the Imperial Valley, but it was quickly driven out of business by the L.A. branch plants of the big Akron tiremakers. The debacle significantly undermined investor confidence in San Diego as a viable industrial location.

Bankers, however, began taking a second look in the mid-1930s as aircraft manufacture, stimulated by military demand as well as by the rise of national airlines, became one of the first industries to recover from the Depression. The bigger companies, moreover, were exploring the adaptation of Detroit methods to the mass assembly of planes. They were also looking for larger plants to accommodate the 60- to 100-foot wingspans of the next generation of passenger planes and army bombers. Although engine production was tied in place to the tool-and-die culture of New England and New York, airframe assembly was ideally suited to semiskilled labor in climes with year-round flying weather for which San Diego was already world famous.[82]

In the case of Buffalo-based Consolidated Aircraft (Consair), crammed into a "twenty-year-old plant with a patchwork of additions sprawling from it," there were two additional criteria. One was a calm harbor for testing the big flying boats it had contracted to build for PanAm and the Navy. The other was an open-shop labor climate. Consair's founder, Reuben Fleet, was a fierce antiradical who as a militia officer in Aberdeen, Washington, in 1911 had led axehandle-wielding vigilantes against the IWW. As an Army officer, he had also served on the San Diego border and learned to fly at North Island under the instruction of Major T. C. Macauley, who, serendipitously, was now leading the San Diego Chamber of Commerce. The city and port district offered Consair a prime plant site next to the new municipal airport for a dollar per year, and Emil Klicka of the Bank of America promised financing. Fleet was shortly headed west with 400 loyal employees and 157 freight cars of machinery.[83] As he told the Chamber of Commerce officials who greeted him on his arrival:

"We left all the bad Radicals there in Buffalo."[84]

The first of the famed PBY Catalina Flying Boats rolled out of the doors of the 450,000-square-foot Plant 1 in September 1936. Three years later, after the outbreak of war in Europe ended a brief defense recession, Consair doubled its plant space to accommodate expanded seaplane production as well as work on a new bomber prototype, the XB-24.

It would soon become to San Diego what the Model-T had been to Detroit. The ungainly looking "flying boxcar," the future long-range bomber workhorse of the Army Air Corps in Europe and the Pacific, made its official test flight in March 1940. Two months later, just after the fall of France, FDR appealed to Congress for 50,000 warplanes a year. The official Army history of aircraft procurement later called the speech "*de facto* M day," the real economic declaration of war.[85] Total mobilization was ratcheted up another notch ten months later when Congress approved the Lend-Lease Act after one of the most bitter congressional debates since the Civil War.

"Monstrous," howled California's aging isolationist Senator Hiram Johnson, but Southern California industrialists were delirious. Fleet's Consair and its local sub-contractors, Ryan and Rohr, were already staggering under a large backlog of orders when Lend-Lease brought delegations of desperate British procurement officers begging for speed-up on the already overworked B-24 Liberator assembly lines.[86] By July Consair had an astonishing $645 million in contracted orders and its agents were pouring into the Southwest from Arizona to Louisiana trying to recruit more workers. With financing from the Defense Plant Corporation, Plant 2 was opened near the Marine training base in fall 1941. By December, Consair had a staggering 25,000 workers on its payroll, more than a third of San Diego's total male workforce, and planned to add 20,000 more by the next summer. Aircraft's contribution to the San Diego economy was now as large as the Navy's.[87]

9. The War Boom

> Be careful what you wish for.
> *Old adage*

By the time the first waves of Japanese dive-bombers came screaming down on Battleship Row at Pearl Harbor, the West Coast economy had already been at war for a year and a half. For San Diego, the war boom was both a bonanza and a cataclysm. Searching for a historical precedent, observers couldn't decide whether the now frenzied three-shift town, overwhelmed by hundreds of thousands of war workers and transient servicemen, more resembled Gold Rush San Francisco in 1852 or San Francisco in 1906, after the earthquake.

Under tremendous pressure from Washington, San Diego had reluctantly yielded more than a quarter of its incorporated land area and 70 percent of the undeveloped county to defense plants, training camps, airfields, and bombing ranges. "The city's landscape had been scraped, leveled and built to meet the demands of the Army, the Navy and the aircraft industry. Two thousand acres of new land had been added to airports and parade grounds by moving the waterfront a mile out."[88] North of the city limits, the vast Santa Margarita Ranch was commandeered by the Marine Corps for Camp Pendleton, while Gillespie Field in El Cajon was built to train Army paratroopers.

But if the city could supply raw land to the military, it was incapable of providing shelter to the (1940) weekly influx of 1,500 workers and military families. San Diego had long manicured its City Beautiful ambience with housing policies designed to discourage immigration by poor families. As historian Christine Killory concluded: "Powerful economic interests in San Diego were more preoccupied with protecting real estate values than housing the poor." The rental market was oriented toward retirees and single adults, with 85 percent of landlords refusing to rent to families with children. "Reluctant to tarnish an image of affluence," the city also declined to apply for federal funds, as provided by the 1937 housing act, to build subsidized or public housing. Meanwhile, the least expensive apartments or duplexes in 1939 cost $27–$30 per month, clearly beyond the means of Navy families living on pay of $34 to $84 per month. In the interlude between the beginning of the "blitz boom" in 1940 and the introduction of federal rent controls in early 1942, landlords were free to gouge whatever they could from the pocketbooks of war workers.[89]

But, whatever the price, there was simply not enough housing to meet the soaring levels of demand. In 1941 the population increased by a staggering 50 percent, a decade's projected growth in a single year. The result—as investigating congressional committees confirmed in 1941 and again in 1943—was the nation's worst defense housing crisis. "Aviation Okies," as they were called, were often forced to sleep in their autos, abandoned rail cars, all-night movie theaters, or share beds in shifts. Mission Valley, whose Nisei truck farmers were now interned in Arizona, was a vast trailer camp for Consair workers and Navy wives.[90]

Similarly, San Diego's historical failure to adequately plan infrastructure for future needs now caught up with it with a vengeance, as the future arrived in an instant. Despite the increasing problem of Navy human waste (three-quarters of a million gallons every day by the late 1930s), the city failed to fund completion of the sewage treatment system started under WPA auspices.[91] Everything was still dumped into the bay, which, since the diversion of the San Diego River in the 1870s, had no natural mechanism to flush itself clean.

An even bigger problem was the inadequacy of the city's water supply. The Metropolitan Water District, largely financed by Los Angeles, had years before invited San Diego to join its Colorado River consortium, but the city refused, claiming that it preferred at some later date to build its own hugely expensive tunnel through the Laguna Mountains to the All-American Canal in Imperial Valley. In the meantime, San Diego proposed to live off the enhanced water supply made available by its new San Vicente Dam between Ramona and Lakeside. San Vicente, dedicated in 1941 and scheduled to reach capacity by 1943, had been designed to store water for a predicted 1950 population of a quarter million. This, as we have seen, was exceeded within a year. Moreover, military consumption was increasing almost exponentially (41 percent of total water usage by 1945) and the county was experiencing a severe drought.[92]

In any event, the bewildered city administration of Mayor Benbough, who dropped dead of stress in 1942, was totally overwhelmed by the housing and infra-structural crises. With the city's business leadership almost paralyzed, Fleet took matters into his own hands. To gain Washington's immediate attention, he telegraphed Secretary of the Navy Frank Knox that a deadly epidemic was imminent because of the sewage in the harbor. Then he spoke directly to FDR, warning the president that further expansion of B-24 production was being jeopardized by the city's inability to overcome the various bottlenecks. "The situation is now impossible without federal aid," Fleet said.[93] The White House punctually ordered the Navy and other agencies to undertake a crash program of housing and public works. San Diego became the first of the so-called "congested districts," crucial to war production, whose urban development was temporarily taken in hand by the federal government.

The first priority was to get the Consair workforce out of their cars and tents. The Lanham Defense Housing Act provided the formal mandate for the nation's largest war housing project at Linda Vista, just north of Mission Valley. Construction on 3,000 residential units for an estimated 15,000 people began in March 1941 with an unprecedented 300-day deadline. It was both an extraordinary experiment in the mass production of housing and an unmitigated planning disaster. Ingenious prefab-rication methods enabled builders to complete as many as forty homes per day, but community infrastructure was entirely neglected. One water pipe supplied Linda Vista and one jammed road took its inhabitants to work and brought them home. There were no sidewalks, grocery stores, or schools.

Other war housing projects had similar problems. Most of the homes were designed as temporary structures and the projects were usually segregated from existing neighborhoods. This reflected the city leadership's animus against socioeconomic diversity, as well as federal builders' preference for greenfield sites suitable for large-scale industrial construction. But, as Christine Killory has eloquently argued, this was a shortsighted policy that ensured high social costs downstream. Temporary homes were almost as expensive to build as permanent homes, and there was, in fact, plenty of vacant, easily buildable land within the existing urban fabric served by utilities and public transport. Instead, the federal government built future slums and ghettos.[94]

Other federal initiatives, however, had happier results. Harbor Drive was speedily completed and traffic unsnarled, while Lindbergh Field was modernized and expanded. The Navy built San Diego's first sewage treatment facility in 1943 and two years later began construction on an aqueduct to connect San Vicente reservoir to the Metropolitan Water District at Lake Mathews in Riverside County. In the end, San Diego's improvidence was turned to its advantage. Ungrateful business leaders complained about "New Deal socialism," but, thanks to federal intervention, more than 70 percent of San Diego's prewar ten-year plan of public works had been built in half the time and at less than half the cost to the city.[95]

In the meantime, the city's major new employer had changed hands in a deal that many Progressives denounced as blatant war profiteering. Even before Pearl Harbor, rumors were flying that the Army was disenchanted with Fleet's despotic management style, which it believed was slowing down production. Fleet, on his side, was reputedly unhappy with the union contract he had been forced to sign with the International Association of Machinists. An aviation paper made the strange claim that Vultee Aircraft, a much smaller Los Angeles manufacturer, was attempting to buy giant Consair and its bulging order book. This caused considerable surprise in San Diego, where no one had ever heard of a minnow swallowing a shark.[96]

Behind Vultee, however, was Tom Girdler of Republic Steel, one of the wealthiest and certainly most hated industrialists in the country. After police had massacred ten strikers outside his South Chicago mill on Memorial Day 1937, Girdler had snarled, "There can be no pity." Consair's unionized machinists, who had fought Fleet to a standstill, were deeply apprehensive about an even more reactionary boss. Nevertheless, Fleet signed over the company to Girdler just in time to avoid the new capital gains tax that Congress had enacted precisely to prevent war capitalists from speculating on their government order books.[97] A consortium of banks, with the Bank of America contributing as much as the largest Eastern participant, provided $200 million in financial fuel for the continuing expansion of the bomber assembly lines.[98]

It was craven profiteering at a time when many Consair workers were sharing beds in shifts and their sons were dying in the Pacific, but poetic justice of a sort was rendered two years later when an aggrieved Mrs. Fleet won the largest alimony payment in American history from her philandering husband: $11.5 million, almost exactly what he received from Girdler.[99] Meanwhile, Rosie and the other Plant 1 riveters—choking on the ungainly amalgam of "Consolidated-Vultee"—were already calling their new company Convair.

10. The Convair Era

> Here's to a bigger and better Convair and more contracts from the Defense Department.
>
> *San Diego housewife (1961)*[100]

Just as the economic war began long before the shooting war, so also it ended earlier. By fall 1944, the American economy, doubled in size in a mere four years, had produced not just 50,000 planes as FDR had originally demanded, but nearly 300,000, a tenth of which were built by Consolidated-Vultee. The war pipelines were clogged with enough planes, tanks, and landing craft to finish off Germany and launch an invasion of Japan. Up and down the West Coast, the giant aircraft plants and shipyards began to shed their workforces. There was widespread apprehension that victory would spell depression, just as it had in 1919.

San Diego industrialists, apprehensive from the beginning of the blitz boom that they might be living a charmed but short life, were the first on the coast to begin thinking about reconversion. In the summer of 1942, Consair and Rohr, along with the Bank of America and San Diego Gas and Electric, began meeting with city planners and Chamber of Commerce directors to discuss the postwar situation. This latest exercise in private government, officially the Postwar Planning Committee, hired the Philadelphia engineering firm of Day & Zimmerman, Inc., to carry out an unprecedentedly expensive study of San Diego's existing and potential industrial niches.[101]

The Day & Zimmerman report was voluminous (1,300 pages) but unremarkable. It pointed out the obvious—San Diego's relative isolation, its dependence on the Navy, the lack of industrial diversity, and so on—while recommending what, in fact, were already items of elite consensus: the need for a unified port authority, the recreational development of Mission Bay as a tourist attraction, and the revitalization of the San Diego–California Club. Despite 125 meetings of the Postwar Planning Committee, there was little creative thought on how to address the reconversion of the aircraft industry.[102]

Indeed, it was an especially hard landing for Convair, whose order book was like a giant balloon suddenly deflated by a pinprick. From 1944 to 1946, its military sales collapsed from $644 million to a bare $14 million. As a result, San Diego deindustrialized almost as rapidly as it had industrialized in 1940–41. A month after V-J Day, aircraft employment, 65,000 at its height in 1943 (and 40 percent female), had shrunk to only 8,500 (overwhelmingly male).[103] Amid soaring unemployment, there was widespread panic that San Diego was again becoming a "ghost town." In fact, it was becoming more of a naval monoculture than ever: in 1947, active-duty military personnel plus the Navy's civilian employees accounted for fully 41 percent of local employment and $105 million in local wages.[104]

During these economic drought years, Convair relied for survival on the modest flow of orders for its dinosaur-like B-36 bomber. This monstrous six-engine plane, the first intercontinental bomber, was originally designed to allow the Army Air Corps to strike Japan from Hawaii. By the time of its maiden flight in August 1946, it had been reconceptualized as the first strategic deterrent of the emergent Cold War, a long-distance nuclear bomber to scare Stalin away from China and Western Europe. The newly independent Air Force made the funding of at least four B-36 bomber groups a top priority in 1947. At the same time, the Navy was also aggressively lobbying Congress to build a new generation of 75,000-ton "supercarriers."[105]

San Diego, of course, wanted it all: both superbombers and supercarriers. But the Truman administration's 1948 defense budget provided the resources for only one or the other. The result was an extraordinary public battle between the Air Force and Convair on one side, and the Navy on the other. When Secretary of Defense Louis Johnson sided with the Air Force in April 1949 and canceled the Navy supercarrier, whose keel had been laid only a week before, he provoked the famous "revolt of the admirals." Navy brass led by the Pacific Fleet's commander, Admiral Arthur Radford, denounced the San Diego–built B-36 bomber as "a billion-dollar blunder" and charged that the "Air Force was endangering national security by neglecting tactical aircraft."[106] San Diegans nervously made jokes about the Navy bombarding Convair across the bay.

In the end, an obscure Asian Stalinist, Kim Il-Sung, by prompting the Korean War, inadvertently rescued all the big-ticket projects: strategic bombers, supercarriers, and, most providentially for San Diego, a previously canceled Convair contract to develop an intercontinental rocket for the Air Force. Simultaneously, as the airlines looked for replacements for the aging DC-3, Convair found great success with its 240 series of passenger airliners. The bloom was back on the boom. Thousands of former wartime employees returned from all over the Southwest to reclaim what they were assured were now lifetime jobs in Plant 1 on Harbor Drive.

This new defense migration also put the federal government back into the housing business, this time through the financial subsidies of the Critical Allotment Program. Chief beneficiaries were La Jolla–based Lou Burgener and Carlos Tavares, who were developing a huge tract-home community on Moreno Mesa. Second in size only to Long Island's famous Levittown, Clairemont (named after Tavares's wife, Claire), with 6,000 housing units and an instant population of 20,000, was a decisive step in San Diego's post-1939 expansion into the scrub-covered mesas north of Mission Valley. In contrast to purely federal Linda Vista, it also reestablished segregation as the suburban norm by excluding black families. The same was true of San Diego's other mega-subdivision: Allied Gardens, developed in 1953–57 by William Bollenbacher and Louis Kelton out of the old Waring Ranch in the eastern foothills of Mission Valley.[107]

Korean War–related growth also pushed over the hills into the formerly agricultural El Cajon Valley, destined to become San Diego's largest blue-collar suburb. Ellsworth Statler, of the famous hotel chain, had invested heavily in the valley on the eve of World War II and was responsible via his Circle S Ranch company for much of its explosive growth in the early 1950s. ("If we had left it up to the little guy in El Cajon, I don't think there would be any town there.") In fiscal 1956–57 building permits in the valley were exceeded only by those in L.A., San Francisco, Anaheim, and San Diego itself.[108]

Although El Cajon retained its independence, San Diego City Manager Tom

Fletcher pushed an aggressive campaign of annexation that added nearly 100,000 acres to the city between 1956 and 1962. In case of the South Bay annexation of 1957, San Diego first had to annex a corridor running down the center of the bay to create the contiguity required for absorbing Nestor and San Ysidro. In other annexations—Miramar, Rancho Bernardo, Los Penasquitos, Tierrasanta, and so on—Fletcher's goal was to grab prospective suburbs and their future sales taxes before they were developed. It was a strategy that eventually backfired in the late 1960s and 1970s, producing a populist antigrowth revolt when the costs of public infrastructure and schools raced far ahead of the new suburbs' tax contributions.

Meanwhile, the final bitter peace in Korea brought no end to Cold War tensions or to San Diego's reborn prosperity. In 1954 Convair merged with John Jay Hopkins's Electric Boat Corp. and other interests to form a new defense giant, General Dynamics (GD). The next half decade was the golden age of the aerospace industry in San Diego. Hopkins began construction of a huge Kearney Mesa plant for Convair's Atlas missile program (now the Astronautics Division of GD), while downtown assembly lines were retooling to produce the famous F-102 and F-106 delta wing fighters, the B-58 Hustler bomber, and myriad civilian 240 successors, the 340s and 440s. The GD space program, moreover, stimulated the growth of local electronics manufacturing. Little firms with wonderful egghead names like Cubic, Non-Linear Systems, Digital Development, and so on seemed portents of a brilliant future.

At the time of the Convair/GD merger, San Diego's military payroll was larger than its manufacturing income, but by 1958, thanks especially to the post-Sputnik acceleration of the Atlas program and its outlier subcontracts, the manufacturing payroll was one and half times bigger.[109] The same year, 50,000 awestruck San Diegans (including this author and his father) toured the vast Kearny Mesa Atlas plant on its opening day while Navy jets from Miramar flew overhead. Although most of its high-value electronics were made elsewhere, the Atlas missile was now San Diego's talisman.

11. Big Tuna and Missile Man

> San Diego industry in the fifties believed it needed to go nuclear to regain
> financial stability. For this it needed physicists and engineers. For them
> it needed a university.
>
> *Nancy Scott Anderson*[110]

Who ruled San Diego during the Age of Atlas? City government itself—a succession
of short-lived city managers, impotent planners, and corruption-tainted mayors[111]—
was only a pallid reflection of San Diego's business world in an era when unlimited
growth whetted limitless ambition. Of course, the rise of outside corporate control in
San Diego, as well as the centrifugal logic of suburbanization, made the question of
power a slightly more complicated one than in 1910 when Spreckels was enthroned
in Coronado, leisurely skirmishing with Scripps and Fletcher. It is perhaps most
useful to posit two distinct though overlapping systems of private government in the
high Cold War era. The first was the Downtown-based elite, which controlled San
Diego's leading banks, its news media, and, above all, the ruling Republican Party.
The second network comprised General Dynamics and its military-industrial associates, including the heavily Navy-funded Scripps Institution of Oceanography. They
were less interested in local politics per se than in creating a world-class regional
educational and research infrastructure to nourish aerospace and high-technology
profits.

King of the mountain, especially in his own eyes, was still Reuben Fleet. His castle
in Point Loma, with its long picture window framing a panorama of the bay, was the
breakfast meeting place for the so-called United Republican Finance Committee,
which, because it controlled Republican campaign financing, effectively controlled
San Diego. Since its pooled resources were used to vet the Republican primary process as well as to finance general elections, the URFC was feared and often hated by
Republicans outside its power circle. Although it had an illustrious list of directors,
Fleet's servants usually set breakfast for just two guests: C. Arnholt Smith and Roscoe
"Pappy" Hazard.

Smith, who owned the U.S. National Bank and California-Westgate Tuna as well as a controlling interest in the San Diego Padres, would dominate San Diego in the 1960s before perishing in greed and scandal like Macbeth in the early 1970s. His father was an escaped federal felon from Washington state and his elder brother was a notorious Los Angeles oil promoter (associated with former San Diego "smokestack" mayor Louis Wilde) who was widely suspected of murdering his mistress. With his brother's help, Arnholt in 1934 had wrestled control of the grandiose-sounding U.S. National Bank. He in fact took over a tiny institution whose main business was financing San Diego's tuna fleet and whose chief asset was a faltering shipyard called National Steel.[112]

The war fattened the shipyard and filled the bank's vaults, providing Smith with resources to undertake a ruthless postwar rationalization of the tuna industry. In 1950 he acquired the Wade Ambrose family's Westgate cannery and moved it next to the shipyard. Building larger, more modern tuna boats at National Steel, he sent them to sea under the Peruvian flag with foreign nonunion crews. To maximize fishing time in southern waters, the catch was processed in South America then transshipped to San Diego via small refrigerated freighters. The whole operation, eventually under the single banner of the Westgate Corporation, was a textbook model of successful vertical integration. It was also ruinous for the local Portuguese family fishermen who had been U.S. National's original clients.[113]

"Pappy" Hazard, meanwhile, was a leading financier of the Republican right. A famous collector of cowboy memorabilia, he was one of San Diego's "Big Four" paving contractors—the others were Daley, Dennis, and Griffith—who controlled every square foot of concrete and blacktop laid during the aerospace boom. Since San Diego County had an infinite supply of sand and gravel in its dry riverbeds, the paving monopoly was a strictly political creation, the result of restricted competition zealously enforced by the only full-time lobbyist at City Hall, one Richard Stecks. Although Hazard—who would become even wealthier building San Diego's new interstate freeway bridges in the 1960s and early 1970s—was a pig at the public trough like Fleet and the others, he showed his smug contempt for any form of government regulation, which he considered "socialism," by illegally expanding his brickyard in Mission Valley in the 1950s without city permission.[114]

Although seldom invited to breakfast, Jim Copley also must be ranked in the first tier of local power. One of the two adopted sons of Ira Copley, who died in 1947, he fought a bitter battle with his brother Bill over the fate of their father's conservative newspaper empire. Bill, a close friend of artist Man Ray and other surrealists, was a liberal art collector who loathed his brother's enthusiasms for Senator McCarthy and H-bombs. In the end, Bill was pensioned off to Montparnasse and Jim retained control of the newspapers and affiliated television stations. After the Scripps heirs sold the *Sun* to the *Tribune* in 1938, the Copleys maintained an almost Kafkaesque stranglehold on San Diego public opinion. Jim, a former Navy officer whose only combat experience during the war was fighting off hostesses in Washington *haute* society, turned the *Union,* in particular, into an ersatz warship with retired Navy and Marine brass at every level of management. Already notorious for its reactionary politics, the militarized *Union* surpassed all other national dailies in the shrill, inquisitorial fervor of its anti-Communism during the 1950s and 1960s. The *Union* moreover automatically backed the Navy in any controversy, even against the Chamber of Commerce, and almost never saw a scandal, even when one was screaming at its doorstep.[115]

A second tier of downtown power was constituted by the third generation of the Corte Madera (or, if you prefer, the First National Bank) set: the Seftons, Starkeys, Whitneys, Goodwins, and Belchers. They were less flagrantly invested in state and national politics than Fleet's breakfast club, but still maintained impressive local portfolios. Ewart Goodwin, the head of the Percy H. Goodwin Company, was the recognized spokesman for all the old money embalmed in downtown real estate.[116]

The independent aerospace pioneers T. Claude Ryan and Fred Rohr were meanwhile a faction unto themselves. Ryan, almost as fond of hiring retired Navy brass as Copley, was a major contributor, like Hazard, to the right wing of the Republican Party. Rohr simply owned the San Diego suburb of Chula Vista where he had moved his big plant that manufactured "power pods" for Convair and Boeing. When Chula Vistans attempted to recall three of his henchmen from the city council, Rohr retaliated with a mass resignation of his employees from city boards and commissions. So that local merchants would understand his stranglehold on the city's economy, he paid his employees one week in silver dollars. The city ended up apologizing to King Fred.[117]

Despite some occasional factional differences (including, as we shall see in a moment, a split between Smith-Hazard-Copley and the First National Bank crowd over the commercialization of Mission Valley), the San Diego power structure of the 1950s was aligned in the common cause of reinforcing and expanding the military foundation of the regional economy. Their Washington henchman was Congressman Bob Wilson (1952–80), the most effective lobbyist since Kettner, whose growing seniority on the House Armed Services Committee would become one of the city's most valuable assets.

In the mid-1950s the holy grail sought by Wilson and other boosters was homeporting the Navy's new supercarriers. Without costly dredging of the harbor channel and the construction of new wharf facilities, however, San Diego could not accommodate the huge ships, the most deadly weapons platforms ever constructed. Long Beach, on the other hand, had ample port facilities and was eager to see San Diego demoted to a mere destroyer base. To make matters worse, the Navy, which considered all of Kearney Mesa's airspace as the exclusive preserve of its Miramar-based jets, was angry at a city plan to develop nearby Montgomery Field as a replacement for overcrowded and dangerously situated Lindbergh Field downtown. In the end it was left to the *Union* to panic voters with the apocalyptic headline, "Navy Says San Diego May Lose Carrier Fleet in Airport Dispute." Duly intimidated, the city council scrapped its airport scheme, and, with the help of Vice President Richard Nixon, Congress approved funding in 1958 for a new supercarrier wharf on North Island.[118] Two years later, San Diego repaid Nixon's favor by providing him with the margin of votes to narrowly carry California in the 1960 presidential election.

While the downtown elites were saving their traditional Navy town, General Dynamics' John Jay Hopkins was crusading to assure San Diego's high-tech future. Hopkins's short tenure in San Diego (he died in 1957) was as epoch-making as Spreckels's long reign or even Reuben Fleet's instant industrial revolution. He brought big science (Cold War variety) to San Diego via his Kearny Mesa Atlas plant and, especially, the General Atomic Division research center he built on 300 acres of city-donated land on Torrey Pines Mesa in 1956. General Atomic, although it never achieved the sci-fi promises of 1950s atomic culture, became the mother hen of San Diego technology, eventually spinning off some fifty different scientific companies. But Hopkins's most important contribution was undoubtedly the decisive support he gave to the Scripps Institution director Roger Revelle's dream of building a world-class science and engineering graduate school, a "public Caltech," he called it, in San Diego.

Revelle, the only other San Diegan besides George Marston who possibly deserves his posthumous beatification, had overseen oceanography's Cinderella transformation from an obscure branch of geophysics into one of the most strategic and affluent tributaries of Pentagon research. A decorated naval officer as well as a renowned scientist, Revelle maneuvered Scripps men into key roles in the Navy's postwar program of undersea-warfare research as well as the famous H-bomb tests in Micronesia. (More alarmingly, Scripps also had a hand in top-secret Operation Wigwam in 1955, which detonated a thirty-kiloton atomic bomb 450 miles offshore of San Diego itself.)[119] By the mid-1950s, when Hopkins and Revelle began to collaborate, Scripps was a major spoke in the University of California's vast empire of Cold War science. Moreover, Revelle, who had married a Scripps granddaughter, was wealthy enough himself to move at ease in the ranks of aerospace millionaires and plutocratic University of California (UC) regents.

Although San Diego had been halfheartedly pursuing a UC campus since the 1920s, it never before had advocates with as much economic influence as Hopkins or as much driving ambition as Revelle.[120] With Convair's Bob Biron and General Atomics's Frederic de Hoffman as the GD point men, and the San Diego Aircraft Industries Association and the Office of Naval Research as key allies, Hopkins and Revelle mounted an unprecedented lobby for a San Diego campus at a key regents' meeting in late 1955. Legislation to enable such a decision had just been passed in Sacramento under the sponsorship of San Diego assemblyman Sheridan Hegland.

The San Diego proposal was opposed by the powerful statewide Academic Senate, custodian of Berkeley's and UCLA's preeminence, as well as by San Diego's historic foes in Los Angeles, represented by the most powerful of the regents, oilman Edwin

Pauley. It was a protracted, five-year fight, complicated, at least in Revelle's view, by the insistence, on the part of San Diego public opinion as well as of UC technocrats like Clark Kerr, that the campus had to include a full undergraduate program as well as a science and engineering graduate school. Although Hopkins died midway in the fight, GD's Biron kept the procampus aerospace–Chamber of Commerce coalition hard at work overcoming the various obstacles that Pauley planted in their path, including the precondition that the proposed Torrey Pines site be assembled from donated city and Marine Corps–owned land.

In the end, however, Pauley and Los Angeles were defeated by the Sputnik scare and the political clout of San Diego's aerospace industry. In 1960, the same year that Jonas Salk accepted the city's offer of free land in Torrey Pines for his new research institute, the regents cleared the way for the first undergraduate class to move into the new campus in 1964. Biron predicted, accurately, that UCSD would soon have as big an economic impact on San Diego as had the arrival of Consair in 1935.[121] The new campus, moreover, was a ratification of George Marston's vision of a clean, recession-proof, culture-enhancing engine of regional prosperity. Like the coming of the Navy in 1917–21, the winning of UCSD, as well as the capture of both General Atomics and the Salk Institute, owed much to the city's fortunate retention of pueblo lands in a choice location. Finally, as in that earlier era, some of the chief boosters ensured that they were also beneficiaries of collateral land sales—notably Roger Revelle, who used his Scripps fortune to buy several large parcels on the new campus's periphery. As UCSD's official biographer tersely notes, "Revelle's complicated and considerable land deals bothered even his supporters."[122]

12. Battle of Mission Valley

> Thus died planning in San Diego.
> *Arthur Jessop (1958)*[123]

As it suburbanized in the 1950s, San Diego faced land-use decisions of truly epochal importance. Unlike its smog-shrouded big sister to the north, it still preserved, largely intact and within a few minutes of downtown, two magnificent natural ecologies: Mission Bay and Mission Valley. Although much of the Marston-Nolen planning legacy of the early twentieth century had already been squandered or compromised, especially along the harborfront, the bay and valley together constituted an exceptional open-space corridor, larger than Golden Gate Park and Central Park combined. It is true that in 1950 a neon motel strip already disfigured the western end of Mission Valley, but from Texas Street eastward, the valley was still the domain of the meandering San Diego River, the ruined Franciscan mission, and alfalfa fields. As San Diego spread northward across Kearny Mesa and eastward around the flanks of Cowles Mountain, the river, its valley and estuary lagoon, were the green commons around which might still cohere a metropolis of genuine beauty.

In the case of Mission Bay, public opinion and business strategy coincided on recreational wetland development. The public wanted an aquatic playground for picnicking, skiing, and motorboating, while the city's business elite wanted a new engine for the tourist industry. Only the Department of Interior and some sportsmen and bird lovers favored maintenance of a natural-looking lagoonal ecosystem. In 1946 the voters overwhelmingly approved a $2 million bond issue that was the first step in an ingenious strategy of leveraging maximum federal subsidies by combining flood control on the San Diego River and recreational development of Mission Bay into a single project. (By 1968, accordingly, the city's $22 million share had been augmented by more than $13 million in federal and state funding.)[124] The San Diego River was subsequently leveed and diverted into a concrete outflow to the ocean, while Mission Bay was dredged and landscaped to create miles of new beaches as well as artificial islands and baylets for lease to private hotel and resort developers. The capstone, of course, was the coming of Sea World in 1964. A blatant imitation of Palos Verdes's famous (and now long defunct) Marineland of the Pacific, Sea World would expand, under the control of a succession of corporate owners, into an anchor tourist attraction rivaling the San Diego Zoo.

If the development of Mission Bay was a pole of civic unity, Mission Valley was terrain for some of the most bitter civic divisions in a generation. That it was a battleground at all, of course, was due to the recently completed upstream dams—El Capitan and San Vicente—which mitigated the flood danger that had always restricted the economic use of the valley to dairying and sand-and-gravel mining. Then, in the early 1950s, against the vehement protests of El Cajon Boulevard businesses, Highway 80 was rerouted through Mission Valley, enormously enhancing its commercial potential.[125] Simultaneously, C.J. Brown bought some grazing land at the west end of the valley and adroitly convinced the city council over the objections of the planning department to let him open a "private club." It was called the Town and Country Hotel and Resort, and it was soon followed by the Mission Valley Inn and other golf resorts of today's "Hotel Circle," most of them controlled by the Brown family.[126]

Brown had broken the zoning dike preserving the open space of the valley, and further breaches were opened by Roscoe Hazard when he ignored zoning to expand his brickyard, and by C. Arnholt Smith when he persuaded the city council in 1957 to let him move the Padres from harborfront Lane Field to a stadium across from his friend Hazard's brickyard. (Later Smith would join forces with Ernest Hahn to redevelop the stadium into trendy Fashion Valley Mall.) The May Company, the giant L.A.-based department store chain and shopping center developer, cited the Padres precedent when it announced its intention in October 1957 to build a major regional mall near the intersection of the new Mission Freeway and Texas Street.

Downtown retailers, led by old-time jeweler Arthur Jessop, and neo-Marstonites, including the new city planning director, Harry Haelsig, vigorously opposed any further rezoning of the valley. In response to their objections, the May Company's CEO Walter Burnmark curtly warned the city council: "If we are not given the privilege and the right to come to your city and locate in Mission Valley, we will not come here. This a final statement." The ultimatum sent a tremor through the council, whose members expressed fears that the May Company would locate in La Mesa, and San Diego would lose the huge stream of future sales tax revenue.[127]

But *San Diego Magazine,* in those days unafraid of controversy and editorially dedicated to the City Beautiful, charged that sheer "corruption" was involved, not tax revenues.[128] It also targeted blame at Mayor Charles Dail, the most zealous "smokestacker" in a generation, for conspiring to convert San Diego's "exquisite valley into a commercial alley."[129] The valley debate of 1957–58 coincided with growing statewide concern over California's increasingly blighted urban landscapes and lost open spaces. Photographers and essayists documented the rape of the Golden State's beauty by sprawling postwar development. In the same spirit, *San Diego Magazine*'s architecture writer James Britton sought to convince readers that the struggle to save Mission Valley was nothing less than a battle for the very soul of the city. He warned—presciently—that if the city council was traduced by the May Company, "the gorgeous open valley will become with miscellaneous profit-seeking operations, the whoppingest roadside clutter in America."[130]

At the council hearings in June 1958, the case against rezoning was presented by the alliance of downtown retailers, Linda Vista business interests, and traditional geraniums. Hamilton Marston, the son, together with eminent Corte Maderans like Guilford Whitney and Ewart Goodwin, joined with architects, planners, and environmentalists to press the case for keeping the valley "open and parklike, a rec-reational continuity of Mission Bay." Jessop told the council that the proposed shop-ping center would initially have a sales turnover equivalent to half of downtown's trade, and that "no planner would purposely create two major downtowns four minutes apart." Architect William Rosser, launching the battle cry of "not yet L.A.," warned that San Diego would quickly become a copy of its free-enterprise-gone-wild big sister, its tourist industries extinguished by asphalt and smog. *San Diego Maga-zine* sensibly suggested that the May Company locate in the Midway area, a hub location with plenty of redevelopable land.[131]

On the other side, the May Company hired a San Diego State College professor to produce a survey of "housewife opinion" heavily favoring a valley shopping center. Likewise, Philip Anewhal, a leading commercial developer, organized a pro–May Company petition drive that garnered unsurprising support from the R. E. Hazard Company, Bishop Buddy (the Catholic Church being one of the largest landowners in and adjacent to the valley), and forty-one other landowners eager to mine fortunes from commercialization. Although the antirezoning camp could count on the second tier of downtown power, the first tier—Hazard and Smith, as we have already seen—was firmly on the side of development. This included Jim Copley, whose papers were eagerly looking forward to the May Company as their largest advertiser.[132]

The council's unanimous vote for rezoning punctually brought about all the nightmares envisioned by opponents, and more. Concrete commercial sprawl and huge interstate freeway exchanges engulfed the greenest parts of the valley while the oldest developed portion, the motel and resort strip west of Texas Street, slowly lapsed into a tawdry decrepitude. In the 1970s, "progressive" planning added intensive residential development as well, but with no schools, libraries, or (until relatively late) supermarkets, so that only childless people need apply. In 1980, *San Diego Magazine* writer Susan Vreeland took wry stock of this "prefabricated singles lifestyle," with its incessant disco nights and dismal bar chatter. She discovered that as nuclear family life in the new subdivisions increasingly came to grief, the "broken parts"—including perhaps some of the young housewives polled in 1958—ended up in the huge stucco complexes of single apartments and condos. The paved-over valley, oddly enough, had become Southern California's biggest lonely hearts club.[133]

13. "Bust Town"

> We have all the facilities, all of the personnel and all of the money needed to retrain these workers. There is only one real problem: What do we train them to do?
> *State official, talking about former Convair workers (1962)*[134]

In the early summer of 1961, San Diego was swarming with rumors about the imminent bankruptcy or sale of General Dynamics's Convair Division, the city's leading employer. For weeks, GD executives had been cloistered inside the "Rock," as everyone called the sinister-looking corporate headquarters without windows on Pacific Highway across from Plant 1. Periodically, the *Union* would publish curt notes about the firing or resignation of another vice president or senior official. At the beginning of August, there was a real obituary for a young engineering executive who collapsed during one of these bitter confrontations, as blame was doled out like hemlock after the single biggest product loss in American business history.

Five years earlier, TWA's Howard Hughes had persuaded Convair executives to enlarge the capacity of the supersonic passenger jet they were developing—the world's first—to capture new markets in the early 1960s when prop planes were due to be replaced by jets. The eventual Convair 880, which one San Diegan called the "sweet bird of our economy," was much faster than previous passenger jets (or, for that matter, any contemporary airliner except the Concorde) but too large and expensive to capture the medium-haul niche and too small and fuel-inefficient to successfully compete with the new Douglas DC8s and already in-service Boeing 707s in the transcontinental market. Simultaneously the Air Force was ending procurement of Convair's breadwinning F-102s and F-106s. Although the full extent of the debacle was not yet public, management inside the Rock was tearing itself to pieces over a staggering $450 million in red ink. *Fortune* described Convair in December 1961 as a "great corporation . . . out of control."[135]

A year later, after the 880 and F-106 assembly lines were shut down forever and thousands of Convair workers were laid off, top management announced the corporation's retirement from the civilian airliner business. Henceforth, Convair would be a hewer of wood and carrier of water for their former competitors, seeking airframe subcontract work from Douglas and Boeing. Although the liquid-fuel Atlas was still in production, it too would soon be replaced by the solid-fuel Minuteman, made in Seattle by Boeing. The future seemed to melt away in mere months. Between 1960 and 1961, the gross income of San Diego's aerospace industry fell from $1.1 billion to $215 million, a staggering decline.[136]

The direct loss of 26,000 jobs, moreover, had a multiplier effect that wreaked further havoc through the ranks of the service economy. Many lost their homes. As one savings-and-loan officer recalled: "I would come to work in the morning and get keys and deeds to houses in the mail. It was a tough time." The fastest-growing city in the nation for most of the 1950s, San Diego now ground to a halt. Indeed, while the rest of the nation was enjoying a new boom, there was a net out-migration from San Diego in 1961–62 as former Convair workers—"tinbenders" in their own jargon—moved to the greener pastures in Seattle and Los Angeles. A *Time* magazine story cruelly contrasted San Diego as "bust town" to Atlanta's "boom town."[137]

The Convair disaster, moreover, coincided with parallel fears that downtown San Diego was dying. Since the 1940s, suburban shoppers driving into downtown had complained about the acute parking shortage.[138] After Sears Roebuck moved out in 1952, downtown retailers proposed municipal parking garages, but the plan was defeated after Oscar Cotton and other leading conservatives denounced it as a species of "socialism."[139] Yet, even as its proportion of metropolitan retail sales declined, downtown's primacy endured through the 1950s in the absence of competition from the kind of car-oriented shopping centers that were being built in most other cities. Then came the big bang of the early sixties, as one new mall after another opened in competition with downtown: College Grove in 1960, Mission Valley and Grossmont in 1961, and Chula Vista in 1962.[140] Marston's and a few of the larger downtown stores quickly opened in the malls, but many smaller retailers were wiped out and downtown property values slumped. The threat to land values quickly concentrated the minds of the Corte Madera set. To the enormous aggravation of the Labor Council and others, the renewal of downtown became a higher priority to business organizations and the city council than a campaign for new industries to reemploy ex-Convair workers.

Although retail interests had long been represented by the San Diego Downtown Association, a real engine for downtown renewal didn't exist until 1959 when San Diegans, Inc. (SDI), formed under the presidency of Ewart Goodwin. Composed of a much smaller group of elite downtown landowners—basically, old money plus the Copleys—SDI was concerned about property values, not retail profits per se. Its goal was to defend the old guard's sunk capital by using public policy and tax dollars to generate new headquarters, office, and tourist development downtown. City manager George Bean was "in perfect tune" with SDI's Goodwin and their collaboration epitomized public administration's role as handmaiden to the agenda of private government.[141]

SDI wanted to jump-start new development north of Broadway with a grandiose "Civic Concourse," incorporating a new city hall plus convention and performing arts centers. It was too important a project, at least from the SDI point of view, to be entrusted to public debate and vote by the city council. Instead, Bean and Goodwin, supported by C. Arnholt Smith, secretly assembled land for the concourse without formally notifying the council until after the deed was done. As Harold Keen, the

dean of San Diego political journalists, later described their "slick real estate dealings":

> Acting as Bean's front man, Goodwin quietly obtained options to the downtown prop-
> erty where the Community Concourse sits today. Without knowledge of the Council
> (and unknown to the private property owners that their land was being acquired for
> the city), Bean committed city money without direct authorization to seal the options
> into a package large enough for the project.[142]

When a bond issue to finance the concourse was defeated in 1962, Bean and SDI
simply raided the city employees' pension fund and let the construction contract to
Morley Golden—coincidentally one of the ten founders of SDI. The concourse, as
expected, triggered a "high-rise renaissance" north of Broadway over the next decade,
led off by C. Arnholt Smith's expensive U.S. National Bank Building in 1963. By
Goodwin's death in 1967, land values had dramatically increased and the fortunes
of the Corte Madera set had been recapitalized for another generation. New city
managers—Tom Fletcher, then Walter Hahn—plotted the next phases of downtown
renewal around Horton Plaza and south of Broadway. San Diego, meanwhile, won
the "All-American City" award for its "exemplary partnership" between city government and business.

14. Rumblings in Smithtown

> Let's just say there was good liaison between city government and business.
> *Ex-mayor Frank Curran on the 1960s*[143]

Frank Curran—elected mayor in 1963—was fastidiously attentive to the interests of
Smith and the SDI crowd, while seemingly going out of his way to reinforce populist
paranoia that there was a downtown conspiracy to discourage new industry. When
questioned by Harold Keen about his industrial goals, Curran, the born-again geranium, responded with a hymn to geriatric dollars that sounded as if the Convair era
had never happened: "San Diego has a backbone of annuity dollars that provides a

constant income, in bad as well as good times. These are the modest, but widespread sources of family revenue through social security, retirement pensions from business and industry, and military retirement pay."[144]

This was not what San Diego labor wanted to hear. Instead, it relished the vision of Port Director John Bate, who advocated the breakneck industrialization of the harbor with an oil refinery in the south bay and a second deepwater entrance cut through the Tijuana River estuary. Based on a 1962 study commissioned by the Harbor Commission, Bate's plan evoked the precedent of booming Houston and its famous Ship Canal.[145] Satanic mills and fire-belching refineries, not surprisingly, were of course less favored by Smith, the SDI crowd, and the tourist industry. The Houston Ship Canal, after all, was not a favorite honeymoon spot. As Walter Hahn (the next city manager after Fletcher) would later explain:

> The deliberate policy of the Council, which gave direction to the Economic Development Corporation, was to keep smokestack industries out and bring clean industries in—computers, electronics, research and education. During my five years as City Manager, we actually turned away two or three large plants, and I think we benefited by attaining real balance between defense-oriented and non-defense-oriented industry.[146]

Although C. Arnholt Smith's roots were in the smokestack sector of the economy (shipyards and tuna canning), his new interests were primarily in tourism and recreation. His Westgate-California Corporation was a "conglomerate" empire—including a local airline, the cab franchise, hotels, luxury real estate, choice farmland, advertising, and the Padres—long before that term was popularized by the business press in the late 1960s. Smith's seeming ambition was to collect a significant share of every visitor dollar brought to San Diego. The ideal tourist would fly in on a Smith airline (Golden West or Air California), take a Smith-owned cab to Smith's opulent Westgate Hotel, where he would eat a Smith dinner before catching a Padre night game at Westgate Stadium. Perhaps the next day, after cashing some travelers' checks at Smith's bank, the same tourist might visit Shelter Island, developed by Smith, or cross the border to bet on the ponies at Caliente Racetrack, owned by Smith protégé and business partner John Alessio. If the visitor were truly upper crust, he might even wrangle an invitation to Smith's elite Cuyamacas Club, the new inner sanctum of downtown power.

When the cash flow from tuna couldn't keep pace with his acquisitions and deal making, Smith simply lent money to himself from his U.S. National Bank. To conceal his transactions he created almost a hundred corporate shells registered in various states. When, on occasion, federal or state regulators came close to uncovering his machinations, Smith was ready with a gift or job offer. Thus in the late 1950s, as the *Wall Street Journal* later reported, "three Internal Revenue Service agents were assigned to examine the books of a Smith company . . . he wound up hiring two of them before the examination was completed."[147] Smith had a closer call in 1962 when a bank examiner discovered that fully 21 percent of USNB's portfolio were loans to Smith's other companies. Self-financing on this scale, of course, was illegal, and the examiner recommended a Justice Department investigation. Instead, Comptroller of the Currency James Saxon transferred the examiner to San Francisco and hushed up his allegations. Smith, according to *Forbes* magazine, avoided further embarrassment over the next decade by ensuring that bank examiners were "entertained lavishly and offered jobs." Indeed, one became a vice president of the bank.[148]

Smith, who one day would be denounced as one of the greatest corporate criminals in U.S. history, was able to rule for years as genial "Mr. San Diego" largely because of his shrewd investments in a covering flank of powerful politicians, including several police chiefs, longtime district attorney James Don Keller, Mayor Curran, and Congressman Bob Wilson. He also had important political stakeholdings in Orange County, where he belonged to the elite Lincoln Club, and in the Central Valley, where he was allied with some of the most reactionary enemies of the Farm Workers Union. His most important life insurance policy, however, was Dick Nixon. Smith was a venerated member of the old guard of Nixon backers dating from Nixon's congressional campaign in 1948. Time and again, San Diego—thanks to Smith's fund-raising and Copley's media blitzes—had delivered landslides for Nixon, regardless of the statewide or national trends. It was, Nixon said, his "lucky city," just as Nixon—as we shall see later—was Smith's ultimate rabbit's foot.

Smith's power waxed as the local economy recovered during the Vietnam War boom. Young military families flooded into the city and housing supply again lagged behind demand. Canny speculators, using low-interest FHA loans, knocked down attractive 1920s bungalows by the hundreds north and south of El Cajon Boulevard to build "dingbat" apartments—the future slum dwellings of the 1990s. More affluent electronics engineers and medical researchers were meanwhile moving into new tracts on the fringes of La Jolla and Del Mar. Indeed, the area around the new UCSD campus was being promoted as the "future super-center of the San Diego metro area," and smart money was "riding waves like surfers" in north county.

Although the geranium policies of Smith and Curran had turned back heavy-polluting industry at the city line, the apartment boom and the new suburbs were spreading their own stucco blight. Plans had been approved to add vast tracts of housing in Carmel Valley and "North City" in the UCSD periphery. Curran allowed developers to rush through subdivision maps for 500,000 new city residents before the city council woke up and recognized that it was beyond the city's or school districts' financial ability to pay for the required infrastructure and new schools. The planning department was a frequent but ineffectual critic of this growth explosion. Neighborhood groups were outraged and charged that the council, under the financial influence of developers, was deliberately sabotaging community planning.[149]

Even the lush retreats of the rich were under siege. When Scripps heir William Kellog, the operator of the La Jolla Beach and Tennis Club, proposed plans to "Miami-ize" La Jolla Shores with high-rise construction, he was opposed by a coalition of residents that included the unlikely "environmentalist" J. Edgar Hoover. The FBI chief had spent every August in La Jolla since 1938 and he urged Mayor Curran to support a height limitation on new development.[150] Similar movements to stop overscaled development through "downzoning" soon emerged in Pacific Beach, Ocean Beach, Mission Hills, and Kensington. Neighborhood preservation became the common slogan of La Jolla millionaires, UCSD professors, Ocean Beach surfers, and Kensington boutique owners. Indeed, by the end of the 1960s, San Diego was facing a major middle-class uprising against an eroding quality of life and the soaring fiscal burden of unrestrained growth.

15. The Mob and the Promised Land

*They take the skim money off the top from Vegas to the East and then
bring it back here [northern San Diego County] for investment.*
Deputy Attorney General Charles O'Brien (1973)[151]

Successful land developers, even more than great generals, must always be thinking
not just one battle, but one war, ahead of everyone else. Thus in the late 1950s, a
small elite group of developers, bankers, and large landowners were defining where
Californians would be living in the 1980s. In the Bay Area, for instance, plans were
already being made to subdivide the pasturelands of Contra Costa County and to
export Alameda County's future growth over the Oakland Hills to the lush Liver-
more Valley. The first model homes in Buena Park and Anaheim had barely been
open before schemes were hatched for the suburbanization of the vast Irvine and
O'Neill ranches in southern Orange County. Other developers were eyeing the
equally baronial Newhall Ranch north of Los Angeles, while Henry Kaiser himself
was poking around the vast Vail Ranch near Temecula in western Riverside County.

Their common strategy was to buy the surviving ranchos of the Mexican era—
the largest parcels of land remaining in semicoastal California—and systematically
develop them into suburban cities over the course of decades. Each phase of development, in a planned evolution from extensive single-family home tracts to intensive
apartment and office park parcels, was designed to maximally leverage the value of
land in the succeeding phase. Land was treated like wine in casks, with the most
mature vintages commanding the highest price. The building of entire cities over a
generational span of time by a single developer or coalition of developers had hardly
ever been attempted before World War II, and it required unprecedented financial
reserves, especially in the initial stages. But the new "community builders" had vital
collateral: first, a universal belief in California's continued breakneck growth; and,
second, good intelligence on the location of future freeways and interstate highways.
Like the diversion of water into a desert, freeway construction could accomplish
overnight miracles, turning a relatively marginal parcel of hinterland into a new
suburban retail hub or a dormitory for commuters.

In San Diego County, 1950s tract home growth was primarily on the mesas immediately north of Mission Valley and eastward toward the El Cajon Valley. It was well understood, however, that developers of future growth would prefer, first, the mesas of the famed "flower belt" immediately inland from the La Jolla-to-Oceanside coastline and, second, the attractive ranch and citrus corridor running from Miramar to north of Escondido along California 395 (the future I-15). "City North" and "North County" together comprised what 1960s boosters would call San Diego County's "Promised Land."[152] The foundation for the coherent development of the inland north coast had been laid by Ed Fletcher, acting as an agent of Henry Huntington, in the early twentieth century. Much of the adjacent watershed had been duly dammed and channeled, while the Metropolitan Water District aqueduct, finally completed in 1948, made Colorado River water—the true elixir of Southern California's postwar suburbanization—available as well.

Glen Rick, San Diego's longtime planning director, was one of the first key figures to fully visualize that both the San Diego city line as well as its suburban fringe were going to move north in dramatic fashion. In 1955, he left City Hall to work full time with his sons on the subdivision of Bill Black's oceanfront property above Scripps Pier. Black, a rich oilman whose name is now associated with California's most celebrated nudist beach, had purchased the land from the Scripps estate in 1948 and could smell money in the air as the UC regents (including his close friend Ed Pauley) debated a new San Diego campus. In the end, there was a memorable ruckus when the regents paid above-market value for the property in a deal that also enabled Black to avoid any tax liability.[153]

In any event, Rick had made a prescient move and continued to be integrally involved in the development of the area. As he had envisioned, the coming of General Atomics, the Salk Institute, UCSD, and the Veterans Hospital made Torrey Pines Mesa and nearby Sorrento Valley into a second urban core: an eventual Golden Triangle defined by its three intersecting freeways. It was a classic formula already well rehearsed in Palo Alto and Boston: big public science promiscuously births private-sector spin-offs; engineers, medical researchers, and administrators, in turn, need upscale housing, golf courses, and adjacent shopping. At the same time, federal plans for Interstate 15 (which would eventually provide a high-speed connection between San Diego and the "Inland Empire" of Riverside and San Bernardino counties, as well as Las Vegas) promised to open a corridor of suburbanization through the north county citrus towns of Vista and Escondido, as well as to rustic little Poway.

Accordingly, other pilgrims quickly followed Rick's Moses into the Promised Land in 1959–62. Clark Higgins, the major landholder in the Sorrento area, put up a concrete box purely on spec in 1963 in the hope it would attract a spin-off of General Atomic—it did, and others soon followed. Norman Smith and Carlos Tavares, meanwhile, conceived big plans for "University City" across from the brand-new UCSD campus. They were joined there by Irvin Kahn, a former lawyer who had been a junior partner of Tavares's in Clairemont during the 1950s. Kahn on his own account managed to buy 14,000-acre Rancho de los Peñasquitos just northeast of UCSD in 1962.[154] He confidently predicted that half a million people would eventually move into the area. Harry Summers, who had just purchased Rancho Bernardo between Peñasquitos and Escondido, was equally sanguine. Other developers were optimistically positioning themselves in choice locations from Del Mar to the future San Marcos.

Like their counterparts elsewhere along California's suburban frontier, the north county pioneers were basically staking a claim, raising a flag, and hoping that insurance companies, pension funds, and corporations with surplus capital would promptly irrigate their dusty mesas and former cattle ranges with torrents of money. However, San Diego was still stuck in the starting blocks while other areas in the state were sprinting ahead. The "Convair recession" of the early sixties had slowed population movement northward and made it difficult for Kahn and the other highly exposed developers to finance the carrying costs of their huge properties. Even when the San Diego economy recovered during the Vietnam War boom, higher interest rates continued to plague their operations. There was chronic talk, especially in 1963–65, about a full-fledged bust, and wags speculated whether coyotes or commuters would be living in their promised futuristic cities. Big capital was desperately needed.

Depending on your interpretation of congressional hearings, FBI investigations, and speculative journalism, the eventual financial messiah was: (a) Jimmy Hoffa's International Brotherhood of Teamsters, in intimate association with mob-related figures, or (b) the Chicago-dominated Midwest mob itself, in full control of Teamster pension funds. In any event, the development of the "Promised Land" became part of a complex triangle trade in pension capital involving the Midwest, Las Vegas, and San Diego County. Some of the leading characters have, of course, been long encased in concrete, but the major transactions are easily reconstructed from the huge literature on the mob and the Teamsters.

According to the most recent and reputedly comprehensive history of "the Outfit," as the organization built by Capone called itself, its chief strategist Murray ("the Hump") Humphreys played a key role in elevating Hoffa to the Teamster presidency. In return, Hoffa appointed Allen Dorfman, the son of an old Capone associate, to administer the Teamsters' Central Conference Pension on behalf of Humphreys and Tony ("Joe Batters") Accardo, the other Chicago mob supremo. Indeed, within the Outfit, the $400 million Teamster pension trust was jokingly known as "The First National Bank of Accardo." From 1959, Teamster money fueled the mob's expansion in Las Vegas. Chicago's chief ally in Las Vegas was Moe Dalitz, a legendary gangster from Detroit and Cleveland who had been sent west in 1948 to represent Meyer Lansky's interests in Vegas. Dalitz, now "Godfather of Vegas" from his base in the Desert Inn, helped Chicago's Johnny Rosselli open the Stardust, the most lucrative casino on the Strip, and built, with Teamster money, the huge Sunrise Hospital mediplex in partnership with Beverly Hills producer Mervyn Adelson. Aside from being hugely profitable in its own right, the hospital also provided perfect camouflage for transferring the casino skim to Chicago via visiting mob "patients."[155]

Dalitz and Adelson, together with Adelson's associates Irwin Molasky and Allard Roen, then recycled some of their Vegas money together with a $27 million loan from the Teamsters into Rancho La Costa, a world-class golf club, spa, and planned community that became the crown jewel of San Diego's developing north coast.[156] Later, after Hoffa was imprisoned for pension-fund kickbacks and the new Teamster president Frank Fitzsimmons, a wholly owned Chicago subsidiary, increased the mob's credit line, more pension money expanded La Costa. C. Arnholt Smith, a longtime business associate of Dalitz and other mobsters, also helped finance La Costa. In return, the Teamsters deposited $20 million in his U.S. National Bank—a deal that was arranged by a Smith underling, Lew Lipton, aka Felix Aguirre, "a former restauranteur with underworld ties."[157]

Federal officials openly referred to La Costa as a "playground for the mob," which only made it more popular with the wealthy San Diegans, like charter members Jim Copley and John Alessio, who packed its clubhouse to enjoy the frisson of rubbing shoulders with Dalitz and his Chicago and Las Vegas friends. However, when two Leftish journalists writing in *Penthouse* in 1975 repeated FBI claims that La Costa was mob-dominated, Dalitz and Adelson counterattacked with the largest libel suit in history ($630 million). After seven years, a jury found in favor of *Penthouse*, but La Costa's owners managed to have the verdict overturned. Eventually, after spending an estimated $25 million in legal fees, both sides simply gave up in exhaustion, issuing a joint statement that they were "not obligated to litigate forever."[158]

La Costa's notoriety contrasted with the happy public face of a far larger Teamster pension-fund-backed operation: Irvin Kahn's Rancho de los Peñasquitos. Kahn's hugely ambitious but faltering project was rescued in 1966 with an initial $50 million in Teamster funding, which later increased to probably $200 million. The deals were arranged by Kahn's new partner, Missouri-based Morris Shenker, a Hoffa lawyer whom former FBI agent Bill Roemer characterized as "the front man for the St. Louis Mob."[159] Indeed, Ronald Lawrence, who reported on Shenker for the St. Louis *Post-Dispatch*, described him as "a financial genius of the caliber of Lansky." Lawrence added, "It was Shenker who tapped the Teamster Union's Central States Pension Fund to finance much of the mob's penetration of Las Vegas casinos and other ventures. Shenker's influence extended far beyond the underworld and he was able to get two of his own federal indictments killed."[160]

Whether Kahn was sleeping with the mob or simply part of a ménage à trois is unclear. Jimmy "The Weasel" Fratianno, the L.A. mob's chief enforcer who later became an FBI informer, claimed that he was told by Johnny Rosselli—Chicago's famous man-about-town in Hollywood and Vegas—that it was a side deal: "Well, you know, Jimmy, it was Shenker who got Kahn about two hundred million dollars from the Teamsters. Shenker went right to Hoffa for the money without going through any of the families. At that time he was was one of Hoffa's top lawyers and on the finder's fees alone he must have made millions with Kahn."[161] Writing later in *Ramparts*, two investigative journalists suggested that Kahn shared mob connections with C. Arnholt Smith through their mutual courtiers John Donnelly and Lew Lipton (Felix Aguirre). They described Lipton in particular as Kahn's and Smith's "plenipotentiary in Syndicate relations."[162]

The Kahn-Shenker-Teamster relationship, although generally treated with kid gloves by local law enforcement, did attract scrutiny from state and federal investigators. In September 1970, for example, the mob's most famous inquisitor, Senator John McClellan, criticized the San Diego office of the Federal Housing Administration for approving questionable transactions involving Kahn and the Teamsters. The senator told the press he was concerned about "the possibility of a conspiracy to defraud the government." Intriguingly, the FHA administrator involved, one E. Tagwerker, retired to become president of Kahn's Great Western Mortgage Company.[163]

One of Kahn's last ventures was his partnership with Shenker in the mob-founded Dunes Casino-Hotel in Las Vegas, where FBI wiretaps once overheard godfather Joey Lombardo (a future suspect in the murder of the Teamsters' Allen Dorfman) reminding Shenker "where he belongs" (to the mob) and warning him that he wouldn't live another year if he forgot that.[164] Kahn himself died young at fifty-seven in 1973. Considered by doctors and his family to be "in excellent health," he suffered a fatal heart attack while watching the Ali-Norton fight on closed-circuit TV at San Diego's Community Concourse.[165] Most of his empire soon reverted to Shenker and the Teamsters.[166] Death spared Kahn a possible subpoena in the investigation launched the same year by the California attorney general's office. At a dramatic San Francisco press conference, the chief deputy attorney general warned that the "Mafia was investing big money in San Diego."[167]

But San Diegans—or rather, rich La Jollans, to be precise—also seemed to be investing big money in the Mafia, or at least their Las Vegas operations. The most celebrated Cinderella story, of course, was thirty-one-year-old Allen Glick, "the clean-shaven, mild-mannered San Diego real estate developer" who stunned Las Vegas when he took over its hottest property, the Stardust, in 1974.[168] Of course, as fans of the novel and film *Casino* know, Glick was simply a front man for the Chicago mob, who had appointed Lefty Rosenthal (played by Robert De Niro in the film) as casino boss, with loose-cannon Nicky Santoro (played by Joe Pesci) as his unwanted enforcer.

In 1975 one of Glick's La Jolla business associates, Tamara Rand, began to claim that she was also a partner in the Stardust and made veiled hints about revealing more. She was punctually murdered in her beautiful Bandini Street home: three shots under the chin, one through the left ear, and one in the back. Glick was immediately a suspect, but the FBI concluded he was too much of a figurehead to be able to order a hit. Roemer, then the FBI's top expert on the Chicago mob, believed that Spilotro did it and therefore that was the version depicted in *Casino*.

More than a quarter century later, the Rand case is still under investigation by San Diego police, who in April 2002 developed evidence pointing to other mob hitmen than Spilotro.[169] Glick, after providing invaluable evidence to the Feds, escaped both prosecution and a contracted mob hit, returning to La Jolla where he lives today in modest wealth while under the 24-hour guard of ex-FBI agents.[170] The legendary Dalitz died of natural causes in the late 1980s, while his La Costa partners went on to create Lorimar Productions, of *Waltons* and *Dallas* fame. Irvin Kahn's legacy, meanwhile, can be seen from the port side of any shuttle flight from San Diego to L.A.: thousands of pastel tiled roofs where the coastal sage scrub of Rancho de los Peñasquitos used to be.

16. Plotting a Revolution

> State power is a much-coveted prize in capitalist circles.
> Door *(1972)*[171]

The year 1968 was the pinnacle of C. Arnholt Smith's power. Copley's *Union* had crowned him "Mr. San Diego of the Century," and his Padres baseball franchise had been accepted into the National League expansion. Even more impressively, Dick

Nixon had invited him to his Waldorf Towers suite to watch the returns on election eve. It was confirmation of his membership in the most intimate circle of the soon-to-be Nixon presidency. Smith had originated the nation's first "Nixon for President" committee two years earlier and had personally contributed or raised over $1 million for the campaign. After two decades of investing in Nixon, Inc., Smith now owned equity in the White House itself.[172]

He also owned a new expensive wife. Helen Alvarez Smith, a former television station investor from Tulsa, was addicted to opulence: Louis XIV furniture, silk tapestries, and oriental jade. Under her influence, C. Arnholt, previously the most low-key member of San Diego's establishment, began to step incautiously, even grandiosely, into the limelight. His imprimatur was the color beige. "His suits are beige, he drives a beige car, even his wife's hair is beige." He was the beige king, and his wife, in the unkind phrase of a federal magistrate, was "San Diego's Marie Antoinette."[173]

But Danton and Robespierre—or, in this case, Bob (Peterson) and Dick (Silberman)—were already plotting his overthrow. Peterson and Silberman were the immensely successful principals of the fast-food giant Foodmaker, Inc. Peterson had pioneered San Diego's famous Oscar's drive-ins in the 1940s before inventing the hugely lucrative Jack-in-the-Box franchises. Silberman was a former Convair executive who had made a fortune in electronics. In 1967, they had shocked San Diego by taking over the citadel of Old Guard power, San Diego First National Bank, ousting Andy Borthwick and his cronies. Their allies in the coup included third-generation Corte Maderan Malin Burnham (a bank director) and as well as other young executives disenchanted with the Smith and Curran regime's mismanagement of San Diego's growing racial, environmental, and economic problems. Dubbed by *San Diego Magazine* as the "Young Turks," they brazenly advertised their intention of building a new power structure and making San Diego "more progressive."[174] They turned the bank's executive dining room into an exclusive members-only restaurant, Tampo d'Oro, which mocked Smith's Cuyamaca Club just across the street.

Although Peterson was a registered Republican, both Bob and Dick generally supported Democrats or maverick Republicans like supervisor Jack Walsh, a born-again environmentalist. Silberman was Walsh's campaign manager. With Walsh, they organized the Century 3 Institute, which brought together elite critics of unrestrained and fiscally irresponsible growth, including influentials from Salk and Scripps as well as superior court judge Hugo Fisher.[175] The Foodmaker duo also had reached out to insurgent black politico Ted Patrick during the long, hot summer of 1967, when southeast San Diego was wracked by violent clashes between local youth and the police. They were widely perceived as the potential allies and financiers of all of the city's disinherited elites: minority leaders, wealthy environmentalists, good-government types, alienated UCSD liberals, and pure and simple enemies of Smith. Their strategy for civic revolution was straightforward: to exploit the breaches opened in Smith's fortifications, first by exposés in 1969 of his use of U.S. National Bank to finance his network of real and sham companies, then in the following year by the indictment and conviction of his closest associate, John Alessio.

San Diego's scrappy underground press, led by the *Street Journal* and followed by the *Door,* were the first to hold Smith's feet to the fire, publicizing what *Union* and *Tribune* reporters had known for years but had never been allowed to publish: that Smith, in essence, ran San Diego through a vast spiderweb of swindled funds, bribed politicians, and underworld connections. The *Street Journal*'s allegations, in turn, were contested by terror rather than by lawsuits. On top of persistent police harassment of their vendors and distributors, the paper's staff suffered through several years of death threats, firebombings, and a sniper attack. A *Ramparts* writer noted that "curiously, this terror campaign intensified as the paper exposed more and more illegal activities of San Diego kingpin C. Arnholt Smith."[176]

However, it was hardly possible to terrorize the prestigious and conservative *Wall Street Journal.* In April 1969, the paper stunned San Diego, and delighted the anti-Smith camp, with a detailed exposé by reporter Byron Calame of how Smith was using the public capital of Westgate and U.S. National Bank to enrich himself at the expense of other shareholders. The *Journal* was likely prodded into action by one of the fiercest Smith-haters in San Diego: J. Floyd Andrews, the chairman of Pacific Southwest Airlines (PSA). Convinced that Smith still secretly owned Golden West Airlines, which he had officially divested in an antitrust action initiated by PSA, Andrews in 1969 was in a permanent rant about Smith's shell games and hidden interests, especially after a California Public Utilities Commission inquiry was quashed by Smith's friends in Sacramento.[177]

Although the *Journal* piece didn't directly focus on Smith's airline machinations, it did illuminate some spectacular examples of his "self-dealing." Calame, for example, described how Smith made a $650,000 profit selling and reselling an Arizona life insurance company (so small or fictitious that it had no salesmen or salaried managers) from one of his corporate entities to another. He detailed arch-Republican Smith's zealous support for the career of Bert Betts, the Democratic California state treasurer from 1958–66. Under Betts, state deposits in Smith's bank soared until it was second only to the behemoth Bank of America as an official repository. The *Journal* also referred to the charmed relationship between Smith and fellow Westgate-California director John Alessio.[178]

According to the legend, Alessio was Smith's former shoe-shine boy. In 1929, impressed with his savvy and ambition, Smith parachuted Alessio into a bank job in Tijuana. Twenty years later, Alessio and his brothers were running Caliente and a hugely successful bookmaking operation in a sleeping partnership with Mexican president Miguel Alemán Valdés. They would also eventually own the Hotel del Coronado and other San Diego landmarks.[179] From the beginning there was a murky boundary between their holdings and Smith's sprawling empire. Alessio capital appeared in Westgate ventures and, reciprocally, U.S. National Bank loans buoyed Alessio projects. Finally, after years of complex interpenetration, the Alessio Corporation merged in 1964 with Westgate-California. In partnership with Smith, the Alessios also attempted to grab the racing franchise at Del Mar in 1966 "under questionable circumstances" with the apparent aim of eventually transferring races to Smith-owned San Luis Rey Downs. When state commissioners subsequently investigated the lease arrangement, John Alessio—according to *Life*—bribed San Diego's police intelligence chief for confidential information about the inquiry.[180]

It had been rumored in San Diego for decades that the Alessios had intimate connections with the mob through their bookmaking operations. Two journalists even characterized John as the "reputed boss of San Diego's underworld" and accused the Alessios of using the Caliente "skim" to speculate in property north of the border:

For a long time the take was simply trucked past deferential guards across the line into the U.S.; hot lunches would often descend on the border officials, compliments of the Alesio brothers. But as the Alessio Corporation grew, the brothers managed to funnel the Mexican money through the fifteen corporations owned by Alessio in Mexico; an Alessio trucking firm in San Diego, for instance, would sell equipment of an Alessio company in Mexico—at inflated prices. Once in San Diego, the "skim" from Caliente often appeared transfigured into properties of prestige. . . .[181]

Customs officials were not the only recipients of Alessio largesse. State and federal investigations, initiated in 1966–67, revealed evidence that the San Diego police department's intelligence unit as well as its vice and pawnship detail were little more than subsidiaries of the Alessio gambling network and their alleged mob allies. Russell Alessio, the brother who oversaw the book, was, according to Harold Keen, a "sacred cow to local law enforcement" as well as to District Attorney Keller. When the corruption of the vice squad was revealed in 1962, it was quickly covered up and the paperwork destroyed. Indeed, the San Diego police department's reputation was so notorious that other agencies refused to share sensitive information with it and eventually ousted it from the national Law Enforcement Intelligence Unit.[182]

Ultimately DA Keller was compelled to investigate the allegations about police corruption, interviewing scores of suspect and uncooperative officers, but he refused initially to disclose the findings of the investigation or to press any indictments. His excuse was the "prosecutable wrongdoing uncovered occurred entirely beyond the statute of limitations"—from which he drew the extraordinary conclusion that "for this reason, no criminal actions have resulted."[183]

Federal investigators showed more persistence in their investigation of the Alessios' untaxed Tijuana "skim." Finally, in March 1970, after scrupulous review by the IRS hierarchy and Justice Department tax lawyers, the case against the Alessios was given to the U.S. attorney for the San Diego area, Harry Steward, who in turn was expected to present it before a federal grand jury. "At this point in the life of a proposed tax fraud prosecution," explained *Life* magazine later, "it is presumed to be a solid, comprehensive piece of work. The next step is indictment."[184]

But Steward, appointed by Nixon at the behest of Smith, balked, and the beige king made a pilgrimage to the White House to ensure the president's intervention on the Alessios' behalf. "Within days of Smith's alleged call on the President," said *Life*, "the proceedings against Alessio came to an official halt. Though some subpoenas had already gone out . . . and others were being drafted, Johnnie Walters, then an assistant U.S. attorney general and now [1972] commissioner of the IRS, ordered the grand jury presentation held up pending 'further consideration.'" In fact, Walters, on orders from the White House, was stalling until the statute of limitations ran out. The Feds had less than a month to make the deadline.[185]

At this point, the anti-Smith forces in San Diego gained an unexpected ally: J. Edgar Hoover. Hoover, whom we saw earlier as an opponent of high-rise construction in La Jolla, was intimately familiar with the San Diego ruling class. According to *Life*, he was also a loyal Del Mar fan who was furious at what his local agents affirmed was the recent "fraudulent conspiracy" of Smith and Alessio "to defraud the state of California" over the Del Mar lease. It is likely that the California racing industry, which was losing millions to the Alessios' Tijuana book, made a strong presentation to Hoover. In any event, he gave the White House an ultimatum to allow the Alessio prosecution to move forward. Eight days before the deadline that would have made them immune to prosecution, John Alessio, three of his brothers, and his son were indicted. It was one of the largest tax fraud cases in American history.[186]

While—thanks to Hoover—the earth was opening up beneath the Alessios, Smith was also losing the protection of DA Keller, who was retiring amid accusations that he had covered for the police while they, in turn, covered for Smith and the Alessios. When the Feds, for instance, gave one key witness immunity to testify against the Alessios, he was immediately picked up by the SDPD. Councilman Floyd Morrow told Harold Keen: "I can unequivocally state as a former prosecutor in the City Attorney's office that there is police harassment in San Diego of anything regarded as anti-Establishment or anti-Copley or anti-Smith." But the real hammer of Keller and his anointed successor, Robert Thomas, was San Diego's former federal attorney from the LBJ era, Edwin Miller. Miller knew from intimate and bitter personal experience that "the vice squad and Keller were doing all they could to frustrate the federal investigation that was embarrassing to the Alessio interests."[187]

Peterson and Silberman shrewdly decided to throw their full weight behind electing Miller the new DA. While Keller was launching the campaign of his protégé Thomas at Smith's lavish new Westgate Executive Hotel, Bob and Dick were assembling a formidable coalition behind Miller. Miller was talked into running by prominent attorney Thomas Hamilton, who had been an arch-foe of Smith and the Alessios in the battle over the Del Mar racetrack. Harold Keen, who chronicled the decline and fall of the Smith regime in his *San Diego Magazine* articles, described the DA race as nothing less than a life-and-death "struggle between two formidable wings of the Establishment—with Thomas supported by the old-line C. Arnholt Smith/Alessio interest seeking to maintain their longheld commanding position in the power structure, and with Miller backed by the Young Turks." If Thomas won, there was a good chance that the damage to Smith would be confined to the conviction of the Alessios. On the other hand, Miller was a pit bull who wouldn't let go of Smith until he was wearing beige prison stripes.[188]

The Miller candidacy had the immediate impact of forcing Keller to press forward with an investigation of City Hall that had originated during Miller's reign as U.S. attorney. Miller had formed a joint task force with agents from the state attorney general's office to explore not only official venality but also possible Mafia influence in local government. Although his successor Steward denounced the L.A.-based task force as "carpetbaggers insistent on needlessly tarnishing San Diego's reputation for clean government," neither he nor Keller could prevent the probe.[189]

Investigators initially had been intrigued by the brand-new Impala that Charlie Pratt, the head of San Diego Yellow Cab (a Smith subsidiary until 1967), had given to retiring police chief Sharp in January 1968.[190] This led them to look closely at the 1967 decision by the city council to grant Yellow Cab a 22 percent fare increase despite the warning of an outside consultant that "if the rate increase were put into effect, the Yellow Cab Co. would have the outrageous opportunity to pull in $1,036,000 more in revenues and improve its rate of return by 178 percent."[191] In September 1970, while Thomas was still battling Miller, Pratt told a federal grand jury that he had bribed Mayor Curran and the city council to obtain the increase.

In October, Curran and all but one member of the 1967 council were indicted for conspiracy and bribery. A month later, Miller was elected DA and took over the prosecution of the Yellow Cab case.[192]

This was the fundamental shift in the balance of power that Smith and his associates had long dreaded. But there was no simple storming of the Bastille. Smith, although now directly imperiled, still retained the friendship of Nixon, who was determined to defend his friends in San Diego. Thus when Miller attempted to put David Stutz—the special agent who had built the case against Alessio—on the stand against Mayor Curran, IRS Commissioner Randolph Thrower prevented Stutz (who would soon leave the IRS in anger) from testifying. According to a later investigation by *Life* magazine, Stutz's testimony, based on his long investigation of Pratt, would have directly impeached Curran's veracity and probably led to his conviction. Curran was acquitted.[193]

Desperate to save the remaining bribery cases, Miller tried to persuade Herb Klein, the former *Union* editor now working as Nixon's communications director, to intervene with the president. Klein never returned Miller's calls. Next, Miller hand-delivered a request to the Western White House in San Clemente imploring Nixon to authorize Stutz's testimony. John Dean, the president's counsel, invoked "executive privilege" and refused the request. Stutz, the prosecution's key witness, was silenced. All but one of the defendants walked. Nixon sent his warmest congratulations to his friend Frank Curran, a nominal Democrat.[194]

Nixon also decided to make a dramatic, even cavalier gesture in support of San Diego's embattled establishment. Overriding considerable opposition, Nixon insisted that San Diego—his "lucky city"—host the 1972 Republican convention. In nominating Smithtown, the president inadvertently tied yet another knot linking the scandals of his administration to the meltdown of the ancien régime in San Diego.[195]

17. The Beige King Overthown

> [C. Arnholt Smith] . . . perhaps the swindler of the century.
> Forbes *(1975)*[196]

In early 1971 Peterson, Silberman, and the other Miller supporters began to plot the next phase of the anti-Smith revolution in cahoots with the financial backers of Pete Wilson, a young Republican assemblyman with mayoral aspirations and an unblemished record. Wilson, whose first act on taking office as mayor in late December 1971 was to purge Smith henchmen from city boards and commissions, became the first, and so far the only, strong mayor in San Diego history. His eight years in power are the subject of the next section of this essay. Here it remains to continue the saga of Nixon and Smith in the period that overlaps the restructuring of San Diego's power structure under Wilson.

Wilson himself, although formally a loyal Nixonian, was not an enthusiast of the proposed Republican convention. The deal had been arranged before his election by the White House, acting through San Diego congressman Bob Wilson and C. Arnholt Smith. At his conglomerate's 1971 stockholders' meeting in Smith's extravagant Westgate Hotel, ITT's CEO Harold Geneen had promised Bob Wilson that he would contribute up to $400,000 to finance the convention if San Diego business would raise an equivalent sum. Congressman Wilson promptly advertised this promise as inducement to bring the Republicans to San Diego but disguised the contributor as "local sources." On July 31, 1971, eight days after the Republicans announced San Diego as their convention site, the Justice Department dropped an antitrust suit against ITT. The following February, columnist Jack Anderson published a memo from ITT lobbyist Dita Beard in which she bragged that "our noble commitment has gone a long way toward our negotiations on the mergers eventually coming out as Hal [Geneen] wants them."[197]

Beard punctually had a heart attack that put her in a hospital room off-limits to the press, while ITT denounced the memo as "mad and disturbed." Nonetheless, the ensuing firestorm forced the Republicans to reject the subsidy. Most of the national press coverage of the "payoff," however, overlooked a crucial local element.

ITT's stake in San Diego included a National City manufacturing facility as well as a recently acquired subsidiary, Sheraton Hotels, which controlled almost half the hotel space on Shelter and Harbor islands. All were located on tidelands leased from the Port Commission, which (according to the *Door*) had been aggressively lobbied on ITT's behalf by Congressman Wilson, Mayor Curran, and C. Arnholt Smith. At the same time that Geneen was making his convention offer to Bob Wilson, the Port Commission approved a $450,000 lease concession to ITT in light of "unexpected construction costs" on Harbor Island and in National City. The proposed "payoff," in other words, would actually come from San Diego taxpayers. It was a deal right out of the C. Arnholt Smith gamebook.[198]

While City Hall was scrambling unsuccessfully to save the convention amid apocalyptic rumors of monster demonstrations, riots, and even terrorism, *Life* magazine dropped another bombshell, this time set to detonate over both the White House and the Cuyamaca Club. Beginning with the grave sentence, "The Nixon administration has seriously tampered with justice in the city of San Diego," the *Life* article, written by Denny Walsh and Tom Flaherty, described five instances of White House interference in local criminal justice investigations involving Smith, Alessio, or their political allies. In addition to trying to halt the indictments of the Alessios (and then attempting to obtain confidential details of the prosecution's case) and blocking IRS agent Stutz from testifying in the Curran prosecution, the administration was also accused of twice intervening to protect Smith himself from arrest.[199]

Life detailed how U.S. Attorney Steward prevented federal officers from serving a subpoena on Frank Thornton, Smith's key political operative and chair of the 1968 Nixon campaign in San Diego. Thornton, as vice president of the Smith-owned Barnes-Champ ad agency, wrote checks to pay phony bills he made up from Yellow Cab and other businesses. The money was then diverted into the Nixon coffers or to local races such as Frank Curran's mayoral campaigns.[200] According to *Life*, Steward had shocked his staff by telling them that "Thornton was his long-time personal friend, had helped get him his present appointment, and would probably help him become a federal judge." In addition to preventing Thornton from being subpoenaed, Steward also blocked Stutz from obtaining crucial documents from Barnes-

Champ that would prove the money-laundering scam.[201]

The FBI began an investigation of Steward for obstruction of justice after Yellow Cab's Pratt confirmed that an invoice from Barnes-Champ indeed led to an illegal payment to the Nixon campaign. But the FBI was ordered away from the case in early 1971 by Richard Kleindienst, then U.S. Attorney General John Mitchell's chief assistant at the Justice Department and soon his successor. "I have evaluated the matter and determined there has been no wrongdoing," he decreed in the face of overwhelming evidence to the contrary. When pressed by CBS's Mike Wallace on his motives for protecting Steward, and thus Thornton and Smith, Kleindienst exploded: "I'm no penny-ante two-bit little crook. I testified under oath on ITT and I'll do the same on this matter. I came to Washington with my honor and a little money."[202]

While the *New York Times* was corroborating *Life's* charges in interviews with former federal investigators,[203] the IRS was stumbling forward with its own investigation of Smith. In January 1971 the IRS, vulnerable because of the derailing of Stutz's investigation by his chiefs, assigned a ten-person team to undertake an audit of Westgate-California. It was a strange operation. The agent in charge, for example, reportedly had the "basic outline for the investigation" stolen from his car and then was suspended for two weeks for lying to the agency about the location of his automobile at the time of the theft.[204] Nevertheless, the IRS, soon joined by the Securities and Exchange Commission, picked up the paper trail where Stutz had left it and soon found massive evidence of Smith's swindling of Westgate and U.S. National Bank stockholders.

In March 1972 the victimized stockholders filed a $300 million suit against Smith and his associates, including the imprisoned John Alessio. It was the first in an avalanche of lawsuits and charges over the next several years, as IRS and SEC investigators were followed by bank examiners and then the Justice Department. They discovered a business labyrinth that perhaps most closely resembled the famous Winchester Mystery House in San Jose: a scarcely imaginable proliferation of business entities, some of them designed only to shelter ghosts. By the beginning of 1973, however, investigators had mapped most of the myriad self-dealing interconnections, although some monies—fruits of Smith's long association with the Alessios—probably remained salted away in Mexico.

Federal investigators were stunned by the scale of Smith's greed: an incredible 575 percent of U.S. National Bank's capital (or $345 million) had been illegally lent to Smith entities. Since his marriage to Helen Alvarez and his conversion to conspicuous consumption, Mr. Beige seemingly had lost any self-restraint. His baroquely expensive monument to bad taste, the Westgate Hotel, which cost $100,000 per room to build, was a notorious sinkhole. Some bank examiners called the Westgate empire a classical "Ponzi scheme" but with a difference: "Ponzi did not control his victims; Smith did, since the bank itself and Westgate's public stockholders were the ones who were bilked and Smith was their representative."[205] (On the other hand, Smith may have simply been born too soon: his self-dealing methods uncannily anticipated the Enron capitalism of the late 1990s.)

In the final days, as Smith was losing control over Westgate, he brought in lawyer John Donnelly as the head of the audit board. It was a nomination that only whetted the appetite of investigative reporters who knew that Donnelly was the Southern California legal representative of Moe Dalitz as well as the alleged conduit for Yellow Cab bribes. Stories appeared in both the underground press and the *New York Times* about U.S. National's history as a "mob bank" and its ties, via the coin-operated amusement business, to such colorfully murdered San Diego mobsters as Tony Mirabile and Frank Bompensiero. The old money downtown began to measure its distance from Smith, calculating how much collateral damage might result from his now inevitable downfall.[206]

Watergate had seemingly put Smith outside the pale of Washington assistance. Indeed the underground press believed that C. Arnholt was deliberately being served up as a sacrificial dish to draw attention away from the White House. In succession, the IRS filed a $22.8 million tax lien—the largest in U.S. history—against him and the SEC charged him with fraudulent use of Westgate and U.S. National Bank funds. Smith complained to the *Union* that this was a "little Watergate" and he was being persecuted because of his friendship with Nixon. "I can't help but feel that I am on some bureaucrat's list of enemies and must be the No. 1–plus, or something."[207]

Forbes magazine in 1975 begged to differ. By that time, U.S. National was in the morgue, with no one to call for the body. Its collapse in October 1973 had wiped out 4,600 stockholders as well as the pensions (paid in USNB stock) of the bank's employees. It also cost the Federal Deposit Insurance Corporation "more than the failure of all other U.S. banks combined since 1933." Yet thanks to Judge Robert Schnacke, a Nixon appointee, Smith's penalty for what bankruptcy trustees called "one of the largest systematic lootings of a public company ever recorded in the history of this country" was a mere $30,000 to be paid at the rate of $100 per month over 25 years with no interest. It was not exactly the same fate as Pretty Boy Floyd's: Smith probably spent $100 every month on shoe shines. *Forbes,* uncharacteristically, paraphrased Woody Guthrie on the difference between "robbing a bank with a gun versus robbing it with a pen." Added the editors, "Little wonder that the young and the radical say there are two kinds of justice: one for ordinary men and another, more lenient kind for the rich and powerful."[208]

18. Welcome, Mr. Clean

> Pete Wilson: unquestionably, the most influential
> politician in the history of the city.
> San Diego Magazine *(2000)*[209]

The downfall of Smith in 1973, together with the deaths of Jim Copley and Irvin Kahn the same year, created a power vacuum that was filled by Pete Wilson, the first mayor in decades who was neither a political weakling nor a paid henchman. The son of an Illinois advertising executive and a graduate of Yale and Berkeley Law School, Wilson campaigned for Nixon in 1962 and, in fact, stood by his side during the famous "You won't have Dick Nixon to kick around any more" speech. Herb Klein recruited him to San Diego, where he was installed in a genteel law partnership with the influential Davies family of Chula Vista (son John would become his closest friend). Rear Admiral Leslie Gehres, the chair of the county Republicans, became almost a stepfather. Wilson also quickly hooked up with the third-generation Fletchers: land developer Michael and Home Federal Savings and Loan president Kim.

Through Michael Fletcher, Wilson additionally became allied with Frank ("Kip") Nicol, another leading young developer. These patrician friendships were crucial venture capital in launching his political career.[210]

His election to the assembly in 1962—he outspent his Democratic opponent seven to one—was heavily financed by C. Arnholt Smith and the Alessios, although Wilson wasn't encumbered by any personal loyalty to either. In Sacramento, where he represented Clairemont and north San Diego, he became the first freshman ever elected as GOP caucus whip and quickly fell under the influence of Bob Fitch, the "moderate" voice in the future Reagan regime. Wilson married one of Fitch's aides and distinguished himself by his ability to retain support from progrowth Teamsters and developers while sponsoring coastline protection legislation that won favor with conservation voters and nominal Democrats. (His secret: the coastal bill was chockfull of developer exemptions.)

Wilson, who as governor in the 1990s would polarize California with his shrill, nativist denunciations of immigrants, was in the late 1960s and early 1970s celebrated as a rare "centrist," even a "liberal Republican" in a state where the Republican Party had been captured lock, stock, and barrel by former Goldwaterites. He relished campaign support from environmental groups and thrilled independents by scolding his national party leadership for "dumping" San Diego during the convention fiasco in 1972. He continued to cling, lucratively, to the center until his support for Gerald Ford in 1976 brought down the wrath of Reaganites who subsequently deserted him during his first, disastrous attempt at the governorship in 1978. From that point on, Wilson began to tack heavily to his right, abandoning centrism for a marriage, first of convenience, then seemingly of conviction to the conservatives who funded his post–San Diego rise to the U.S. Senate and then the governor's mansion.

Back in 1971, however, Wilson was still the generous centrist, "Mr. Clean-Cut," who simultaneously offered a life raft to old-time Nixonites like Herb Klein and San Diego Federal's Gordon Luce, who were desperate to get off C. Arnholt Smith's sinking ship, as well as a helping hand to young progressives like Jim Bates and Maureen O'Connor, who were eager to reform City Hall. He enjoyed ardent support as well from the descendants of Teddy Roosevelt's Bull Moose—the anti-Spreckels Old

Money represented by the Fletchers, Goodwins, Jessops, Marstons, and Scrippses. They looked to Wilson to defend San Diego the Beautiful and to keep downtown's engines running.

But the real coup of the Wilson mayoral campaign, beyond his eventual defeat of Jack Walsh in the primary, was to win the endorsement of the anti-Smith "Young Turks," Bob and Dick, and bring on board their ally, hotelier M. Larry Lawrence, the powerful chair of the local Democrats. Only a fusion candidacy, it was argued, could sweep clean the Augean stables of Westgate. Certainly the endorsements of leading Democrats made it easier for Wilson to reap the university and beach vote.

Against this unparalleled coalition, Smith tested the primary waters by having some friends offer money to Wilson. The contributions were rejected and Wilson announced that he would only accept "clean money." He even appointed a committee of lawyers to scrutinize his contributions. Checks from big developers were promptly returned.[211] As a result, Smith, in alliance with Irvin Kahn, hung on grimly to the tainted but loyal Frank Curran.

In a primary overpopulated with candidates (seventeen in all), Wilson harvested enough downtown money and north city votes to crush both Curran (who came in fourth) and rebel supervisor Walsh, the real pioneer in advocacy of controlled growth. With Walsh's supporters now on his side, Wilson faced former city attorney Ed Butler in the runoff. Butler, a labor-supported Democrat, was outspokenly anti-Smith, but his appeal was undercut by unsavory ties to Harry Sugarman, implicated with the Smith-Alessio gang in the Del Mar racetrack controversy, and to Irvin Kahn's patron, Harry Farb.

Wilson ads, deftly managed by the Lane and Huff agency (located in the Fletchers' Home Tower Building), wasted little time on Butler personally, but instead hammered away at the Curran legacy of uncontrolled growth and spiraling taxes. Exhibit one was Mira Mesa, a sprawling development that dumped the cost of services and new schools on angry homeowners in the rest of the city. "It was Linda Vista, 1941–42, all over again. Schools were in trailers and unoccupied homes. Dirt lots doubled as playgrounds. Access to and from the outside was limited."[212] Wilson demanded that developers either pay for schools or face a moratorium on new construction.

He also supported regional planning, which Butler, now in an odd marriage with the far-Right antistatists, opposed. Wilson's positions were more popular and he overwhelmed Butler.

Left snarling on the sidelines were the traditional opponents of growth management: Bruce Hazard (Pappy's son) and the paving contractors, Irvin Kahn, the Teamsters Union's John Lyons, and former city manager Walter Hahn, now the executive director of SEED, the progrowth coalition. SEED regrouped to contest control of the board of supervisors in the next year's general election. Controlling the board, and thus the frontier of developable land outside the city limits, would put SEED in a powerful position to frustrate any attempt by Wilson and his allies to regionalize growth control through the new "comprehensive planning organization" that Washington had mandated to better coordinate federal transport funds with land-use planning.

The 1972 election produced even more surprising results than the previous year's city election. As Harold Keen described it, "Rarely have well-heeled vested interests in San Diego County taken a battering as extensive as that suffered by a combine of land developers and allied construction groups in the 1972 elections—a debacle in which every one of its preferred candidates for the Board of Supervisors, though buoyed by a golden tide of campaign funds, were engulfed at the polls."[213] The defeat was made even more telling by the passage the same year of the California coastal protection initiative.

Thus, by the beginning of his second year in office, Wilson was the beneficiary of a sweeping political realignment and generational change on both the city council, where he enjoyed a comfortable bipartisan majority, and on the board of supervisors, where the construction industry was, however temporarily, out of the loop. Despite these changes, SEED's propaganda exaggerated the radicalness of the changeover. It created an impression that the Sierra Club (which had endorsed Wilson) was now in power in San Diego, ready to drive a silver stake through the heart of the economic boom.

In fact, developers and bankers held the reins of power as firmly as ever, but the new factions in power—in contrast to the Hazards and Kahns—looked toward conservative environmentalism as a useful tool to rationalize residential development and sustain growth on a long-term trajectory. Wilson's campaign, after all, had been carefully crafted by leading savings-and-loan lenders, backed by high-end developers and downtown renewers, and even endorsed by Ronald Reagan. Moreover, he was the "responsible alternative" to the "loose-cannon" threat of Supervisor Jack Walsh with his hippie beard, populist rhetoric, and uncertain commitment to the downtown agenda.

"Controlled growth," as had been amply demonstrated by Bay Area precedents during the 1960s, restructured the real estate market to the benefit of large landowners and financially robust developers.[214] It was also the strategy preferred by San Diego's more sophisticated lenders. In a revealing interview with Harold Keen, Kim Fletcher expressed full support for Wilson's growth management strategy:

> After seeing what has happened in Los Angeles and Orange counties, we appreciate the brakes on the uncontrolled growth we had here for a good many years after World War II. People think a financial institution such as ours depends on tremendous growth and building at any cost. That's not true. There should be qualitative, not quantitative growth, and that's why I'm a strong supporter of Pete Wilson.[215]

Likewise, Gordon Luce—both a key Wilson backer and Ronald Reagan's chief local supporter—emphasized that "our association [San Diego Federal] was the first in the country to rate loans environmentally, encouraging those with high marks for open space, sound-proofing, landscaping, the position of parking, and so on."[216]

Fletcher and Luce, of course, had another self-interested stake in growth control. Together with Malin Burnham, they were the second-generation leadership of San Diegans, Inc. (SDI), which in the early 1970s was grappling with new threats to downtown as grave as those that first prompted the elite group's founding in 1959. C. Arnholt Smith and developer Ernest Hahn were buttressing Mission Valley as the city's retail hub with their conversion of the Padres's Westgate Park into the upscale Fashion Valley shopping center. Meanwhile, the famous urban designer Victor Gruen was warning civic leaders that their sputtering "downtown renaissance" was about to die at the hands of Hahn's other mega-project (this time with Irvin Kahn): the huge University City complex with offices, shopping, and residences.[217] Thus SDI believed it was essential to slow down growth at the periphery long enough for tax-driven redevelopment projects—a proposed Horton Plaza mall, a convention center, a marina village, a "gaslight district" along Fifth Avenue, and so on—to resuscitate downtown property values.

Wilson accordingly endorsed the priority of downtown renewal over centrifugal growth and he immediately set in motion the Horton Plaza project, recruiting Ernest Hahn—archenemy of traditional business centers—as the city's surprising partner. The idea was to replace the cheap thrills of San Diego's "sailor town" centered around the plaza with an upscale, suburban-type mall for tourists and gentrifiers. Wilson also supported SDI's campaign to leverage redevelopment exclusively with "tax increments" (sequestered taxes on new development) rather than with special business districts that placed part of the burden on existing property owners. At the same time, the new mayor consolidated his popularity by generally supporting the efforts of older, primarily professional-managerial neighborhoods to "downzone" themselves, while encouraging well-designed, "inner-ring" residential development that would pay as it went for infrastructure and schools, and would not heedlessly destroy open space or raise taxes for existing residents.

He favored (as had Curran, for that matter) clean high-tech industries that attracted multitudes of engineers, scientists, and administrators who bought expensive homes on thoughtfully landscaped cul-de-sacs. Opposing the unions, he supported tourism rather than heavy industry as a strategy for reemploying blue-collar workers stranded by the decline of aerospace. Wilson also encouraged the first experiments in substituting trolleys for freeway gridlock—a program heartily endorsed by Burt Raynes, Fred Rohr's successor, whose Chula Vista plant was now manufacturing mass-transit cars.[218] These were classical geranium positions, of course, although Wilson represented a new high-powered hybrid rather than a traditional sapling.

On other fronts, Wilson wooed minorities and women, without making more substantial reforms, by appointing them to seats on boards and commissions that he had purged of Smith appointees.[219] The mayor also developed a profitable relationship with African American councilman Leon Williams, who supported Wilson's downtown priorities in return for the "juice" that allowed him to eventually ascend to the board of supervisors while promoting the careers of his protégés William Jones and Wes Pratt. This "Williams machine" was the moderate ballast in Southeast San Diego that kept the peace while downtown tax dollars were sluiced away from schools and social services to service the debt of mall and hotel development.

Wilson had more difficulty reforming a police department headed by the feisty and ultra-conservative Ray Hoobler, but the chief was forced to resign in 1975 after being caught in a bald-faced lie to the city council. Wilson replaced him with Bill Kolender, in many respects the mayor's alter ego: college-educated, mediagenic, and shrewdly ambitious. Kolender's appointment immediately, although only temporarily, improved the fraught state of police-community relations. A pioneer of "community policing" in Southeast San Diego, Kolender had long enjoyed personable relations with the Chollas Democrats and church leaders like the influential Grandison Phelps. As a Jew, he also offered reassurance to traumatized liberals and alienated academics that the police—for so long, mere bagmen and goons for Smith-Alessio—were now civilized guardians. Indeed, Kolender embarked on an ambitious program of professionalization and decentralization: "By 1984," boasted one admirer, "everyone on his staff held a college degree."[220]

The structural reform, however, that most concerned Wilson was redressing the imbalance of power between the mayor and the city manager. San Diego's weak mayor–strong council/city manager system did not fit with either Wilson's personality or his ambitions. The city charter devoted two full pages to the city manager's powers but a mere paragraph to the mayor's. Wilson frequently contrasted the enfeebled status of the mayor with the line authority exercised by county supervisors or, even more tellingly, the sweeping powers of Port Director Don Nay, who was the landlord of Lindbergh Field and all of San Diego's tideland industries.

When a frontal assault—an unsuccessful 1973 charter reform initiative—failed to provide Wilson with enhanced power, he resorted to stealth. He succeeded in forcing the council to accept a new committee system whose proceedings were controlled by a rules committee of which the mayor was chair. No agenda item, as a result, could come before the council without Wilson's approval. Likewise, he began to systematically undermine the power of City Manager Kimball Moore, creating, in Roger Hedgecock's words, "a parallel bureaucracy to the city manager's bureaucracy that would answer to him." Finally, he created a fund-raising network that allowed him to dominate San Diego's system (established in 1931) of citywide council runoffs. Council candidates were pared to two finalists by district primaries, but success in the runoff depended upon one's resources to mount citywide television ad campaigns. Wilson controlled the crucial purse strings.[221]

His key ally in this "silent revolution" was the ambidextrous Dick Silberman, who served as Wilson's troubleshooter for both the proposed trolley system and center city redevelopment. Indeed, Silberman seemed to be everyone's best friend in the middle 1970s. When not advising Wilson, he was huddling with his other compadre, Democratic senator Alan Cranston, or escorting his new date, Helen Copley, to a museum opening. (He reportedly turned away from the "hard-drinking eccentric" Copley when she "demand[ed] that he marry her.")[222] He would soon steer Jerry Brown's surprisingly strong presidential bid and end up in his Sacramento cabinet. (His old partner Bob Peterson, meanwhile, confined his political ambitions to supporting the career of his young wife, council member Maureen O'Connor, whom he married in 1977.)

Harold Keen, in one of his periodic reflections on "Who rules San Diego?" made Silberman and Copley co-equal with Wilson in the post-Smith hierarchy of power. But it was a hierarchy, in Keen's opinion, with no clear-cut lower levels. "Beyond the Wilson-Copley-Silberman triple alliance," Keen explained, "most political analysts see a power vacuum." He attributed this to the erosion of local economic power by the absorption of local businesses into national chains, the decentralization of commerce to new suburban centers, and the "venality or ineptitude of big-time local entrepreneurs whose plunge into indictments or bankruptcy destroyed the credibility of once mighty economic forces."[223] But San Diego, like nature, abhors vacuums. Ruthless Darwinian competitions were already selecting San Diego's new elites, while Pete Wilson—under the spell of a future presidential candidacy—was changing skins for higher office.

19. Wilson Devolves

> His image is no longer one of being concerned with the welfare of San
> Diego, but of one who is concerned with the welfare of Pete Wilson.
> *Councilman Mike Gotch (1982)*[224]

In his second and third terms, Pete Wilson, the soft furry mammal, began his famous transformation into a fierce scaled reptile. It was a devolution dictated, of course, by his environment. If post-Smith San Diego was temporarily Middle Earth, the world outside remained Jurassic Park. California Republican politics in the late 1970s were dominated by huge flesh-eating dinosaurs like Ed Meese, Evelle Younger, and George Deukmejian. Watergate may have tamed the GOP elsewhere, but not the party led by Ronald Reagan. To compete in this larger world, Pete Wilson had to change his diet from soufflé to trade unionists and welfare mothers.

First, however, he had to consolidate his hold on City Hall. The 1975 election—in the shadow of Nixon's götterdämmerung—has been described as a repeat of the legendary 1915 contest between "smokestacks" and "geraniums." Wilson faced Lee Hubbard, a cement contractor with seemingly bottomless financing from SEED. He outspent Wilson two to one.[225] Likewise, progrowth money poured into the campaigns of candidates trying to unseat Wilson's crucial council allies, especially those nominal Democrats O'Connor and Williams, most susceptible to charges that they were anti–new jobs.

It was the last hurrah of Wilson as righteous geranium. "We don't want to be another sprawled-out Los Angeles monster," he militantly told voters.[226] One of his key planks was that there was "no case" for a huge proposed development on the North City land reserve that was supposedly off-limits to development until the build-out of the city core sometime in the mid-1990s. Tampering with the urban reserve was also opposed by the tiny neighboring city of Del Mar, whose rusticity would be imperiled by "North City West." Leading the Del Mar resistance were three names soon to be San Diego household words: council members Nancy Hoover and Tom Shepard and Del Mar's ambitious city attorney Roger Hedgecock, who typed himself "the young Pete Wilson" and was preparing to run for the county board of supervisors. In the election Wilson and his key allies easily survived the deluge of developer money. But at the very moment that their victory was consolidating "slow growth" as a political majority, the mayor was beginning to backpedal on his commitment to oppose further satanic suburbs. Hedgecock had claimed that "a yes vote on North City West is quite simply a sellout to L.A. developers."[227] But this is precisely what now made political sense to Wilson, who was ready to venture out into the bigger political world. After Nixon's resignation, it was common knowledge that Reagan would run for the Republican nomination in 1976. Wilson wanted to move into the vacant governor's mansion and he needed the financial backing of megadevelopers like the two firms proposing to build North City West: Pardee Construction (a subsidiary of Weyerhaeuser) and Irvine-based Baldwin Construction.

At the same time, both Wilson and SDI also needed the help of big corporate developers to save the faltering downtown redevelopment machine. Wilson had campaigned on the premise that the revitalization of downtown was the alternative to fiscally irresponsible and environmentally destructive growth on the periphery. In reality, political logic dictated a different relationship between center and edge. Even with the leverage of massive public subsidies, downtown renewal as envisioned by SDI demanded the resources and reputations of the very largest developers. These developers, in turn, were unwilling to commit to center-city projects unless they were unleashed in the more immediately profitable suburbs.

Thus a series of quid pro quos emerged: Ernest Hahn—a former associate of C. Arnholt Smith—agreed to develop Horton Plaza, while Wilson supported Hahn's huge University City project. Pardee got Wilson's turncoat endorsement for North City West, and Pardee, accordingly, became involved in the redevelopment of the Marina. Pardee also hired Wilson's chief planning adviser, Mike Madigan. Development rights in supposedly protected zones of the north city were traded under the table for commitments to save downtown. Funds originally earmarked for open-space preservation were diverted to finance the downtown convention center. At the same time, Wilson, who had eagerly used federal funding to develop middle-class condominiums downtown, promised his new allies that he would leave the problem of affordable housing to be solved by the private sector. The city's role was confined to leasing or selling land at below-market values to residential and commercial developers—a policy that generated many conflicts of interest.[228]

Wilson also pushed through an ordinance that provided for the unrestricted conversion of rental apartments to condominiums. Housing advocates interviewed by the *Los Angeles Times* were appalled by the Wilson regime's double standard: "He's for subsidies for downtown. But when you talk of subsidies for people who need them—people who are poor—that's a different ballgame."[229] Indeed, ignoring the poor became a hallmark of the meaner-leaner Wilson administration after 1976. Questioned by the *Los Angeles Times* in 1982 about his administration's neglect of Southeast San Diego, Wilson shrugged his shoulders and said, "That is not something that you can simply wave a wand and create."[230]

As a result, downtown was gradually gentrified while affluent subdivisions spread across coastal mesas. Environmental planning remained holy dogma in San Diego, but open space continued to be devoured by development and traffic congestion rapidly approached the threshold of L.A.-style gridlock. Kevin Lynch, the famed urban designer who studied San Diego in 1974, was particularly shocked by the city's neglect of traditional blue-collar neighborhoods like North Park. He enumerated the symptoms: "The dangerous traffic, the heavy parking, the lack of parks, the threat of uncontrolled apartment growth, the aircraft overhead, the poor walking conditions, the deteriorating commercial strips"—and, he might have added a little later, the cataclysmic bisection of North Park by the 805 Freeway.[231]

But if "growth control" under Wilson failed to either stop the suburban juggernaut or address the condition of an older neighborhood like North Park, it did achieve the goals advocated by Fletcher, Luce, and other Wilson supporters of raising land values and channeling most new construction into the upscale market. Blue-collar San Diego—including the thousands of noncommissioned military families—was priced out of the new-home market while shoddily designed apartment construction ransacked older single-home neighborhoods.

While stealthily opening the floodgates to these forces, Wilson was loudly trying to lock out the city's unions. Again, higher political logic dictated his moves. In 1976—after battling local firefighters—he spearheaded the most antiunion initiative since the ban on street speaking in 1911: Proposition J, which not only outlawed public-employee strikes in the city of San Diego but also prohibited the rehiring of striking workers. The next year he tried to make a statewide version of Proposition J the bandwagon for his gubernatorial campaign (and a precedent for his analogous deployment of anti-immigrant Proposition 187 twenty years later). The image he was trying to market to Republican primary voters was that of the tough public executive who would now defend them against greedy workers and power-hungry union bosses, just as he had previously protected taxpayers from the spiraling costs of uncontrolled growth.[232]

But Wilson's 1977 campaign was doomed from the beginning. In 1976, hoping that he might be nominated as President Ford's vice presidential running mate, he had campaigned for Ford against Governor Reagan in the New Hampshire primary.[233] Now the Reaganites were determined to crush him. It was not hard. With little name recognition outside San Diego, Wilson came in fourth with a miserable 9 percent of the statewide primary vote. The San Diego County vote was even more humiliating: he barely won third place.[234] Yet in 1979, he easily secured a third term as mayor with a victory over former California Democratic Council president Sy Casady.

The object lesson was clear: Wilson might be a deity in his own City Hall but he was strictly a nonentity to statewide and national Republican voters. The nonpartisan centrism that was so popular in city elections was a kiss of death in the highly ideological statewide primaries. Most of all, Reagan's "Kitchen Cabinet" remained the gatekeepers of Republican power in California, and if Wilson hoped for a career on a bigger stage, he needed to grovel at their feet and win their forgiveness. This he set about doing with his usual button-down fastidiousness.

Locally, he continued his transformation into Pistol Pete, promising to "win the war on crime whatever the cost."[235] (Years later in a public television interview, he would claim his crackdown on crime as his greatest single accomplishment in San Diego.) A few critics contested the coded racial politics of Wilson's unleashing of the police department, but it was a generally popular policy with middle-class voters. More important, it was an essential credential in running for higher office against such red-in-tooth-and-claw types like attorney general George Deukmejian.

The terms of his reprieve were eventually revealed by Reagan henchman Lyn Nofziger in an article widely reprinted in summer 1982. In essence, Wilson had been ordered to divert his ambitions from the gubernatorial primary—where he was again hapless competition for better-financed Republicans like Lieutenant Governor Mike Curb or Deukmejian—to the senate race against Jerry Brown. Nofziger warned Wilson in so many words that he was still largely regarded as a wimp and that his only hope of redemption was to chew Brown to pieces. This was his road to Canossa. President-elect Reagan, as a symbol of his pardon, had earlier appointed him head of a task force on urban strategies.[236]

Wilson, who barely survived the bitter primary battle with incumbent senator Hayakawa and liberal Republican Pete McCloskey, had a slightly easier time with Jerry Brown, still in hot water with voters for his mishandling of the Jarvis tax rebellion and Proposition 13. Wilson's positions—carefully calibrated to win the hearts of big developers and agribusiness—horrified many of his old-time San Diego supporters. He was now a passionate advocate of, for example, the proposed Peripheral Canal, which would divert more water for Southern California suburbs while inflicting incalculable damage on the ecosystems of the Sacramento–San Joaquin delta. Equally, he was a heavily subsidized mouthpiece for the enemies of the farm workers' movement. "California cannot afford," he thundered, "a U.S. senator who takes his farm policy from Cesar Chavez, his social policy from Tom Hayden and his foreign policy from Jane Fonda." [237]

So Wilson took his farm policy from the growers, his social policy from the prison guards, and his foreign policy from the White House. As official Reagan urban spokesman, Wilson advertised a bowdlerized version of his accomplishments in San Diego. Growth control and regional planning were not on the Reagan agenda, so Wilson emphasized their opposites: "The trick toward the saving of American cities is to encourage and stimulate private sector's reinvestment in them. And you don't do that by overtaxing the investor or overregulating him or making it difficult for him to employ people." He also proposed withholding federal funds from cities with rental control ordinances: "We're not going to spend money in a city that is inflicting upon itself a disease." The former white hope of the Sierra Club was now just another Southern California reactionary.[238]

20. The Ponzi Scheme

> I'm really here. I'm sitting at the mayor's private desk. I'm on the mayor's private phone. And it's great. I'm having a ball.
>
> *Roger Hedgecock, on the phone to Nancy Hoover (1983)*[239]

If the 1960s saw the uprisings of the "have-nots," the 1970s were the decade of the angry "haves." Across the country, postwar "growth coalitions" were under siege from suburbanites protesting rising taxes and declining quality of life. If the tax revolts and anti–school integration protests of the early 1970s were primarily captured by the New Right, the "slow growth" movements of the later 1970s—geographically concentrated in the explosively growing Sunbelt—were fertile ground for post-Watergate centrists of both parties. But San Diego was an exceptional case, even among its cohort of high-speed Western cities.

Indeed, the slow-growth revolt of the 1970s led to a far more sweeping restructuring of San Diego politics than had either the New Deal or the Progressive movement. Among the distinctive features of the new political era were: first, the dominance of land-use controversies over all other issues, including job creation and racial justice; second, the shift of the city's political center of gravity to the new professional-managerial classes of the burgeoning north city; third, the renewed marginality of blue-collar unions and their agendas; fourth, newfangled campaign mechanics dominated by political consultants (Pete Wilson's George Gorton and his California Group were the local pioneers) and financed by political action committees (PACS); fifth, accelerated generational turnover as thirty-somethings used environmental issues to prematurely push aside the World War II cohort; and, finally, an epidemic of political hermaphroditism as centrist Republicans and Democrats wooed the same constituencies and made promiscuous alliances with each other.

In a city whose political culture had been defined for so long by Republican fundamentalism, the rise of amorphous, new-age centrism was an especially surprising development, and it was often difficult—even for the veteran observers like Harold Keen—to decipher the partisan credentials or belief systems (if they existed) of the innumerable Pete Wilson clones who dominated San Diego politics for the last quarter of the twentieth century. "How do you explain," wrote Keen in fall 1976, "the fact that a leading Democrat, Larry Lawrence, not only supported a strong Republican, Pete Wilson, for reelection as mayor, but also committed the ultimate apostasy of openly and arduously backing for governor a Republican, Houston Flournoy, against the bright new commander of the Democrats in California, Jerry Brown, one of whose publicly proclaimed admirers was County Supervisor Jack Walsh, a Republican?" Keen himself drew two conclusions: First, that the slow-growth revolt had skewed and made obsolete old-line politics; and, second, "Pete Wilson symbolizes the era in which local government cast free from subservience to powerful business interests."[240]

Keen's first conclusion was conditionally true on a local level, but the second was clearly wrong, contradicted indeed by his own careful analyses of the uncanny alignment between Wilson's conservative version of growth management and the economic interests of Fletcher, Luce, Silberman, and company. Moreover, Wilson's successors, although defending gnatcatchers and mouthing slogans about participatory democracy, were as eager as Oscar Cotton's generation to bind themselves to the latest highrollers and fast-buck artists. If in the 1920s and 1950s greed had superpatriotically wrapped itself in the flag, the 1980s were the age of venality impersonating environmental politics. The case in point was the extraordinary rise and fall (and, then, rise again) of Roger Hedgecock, Pete Wilson's successor.

By all justice, Wilson's mantle should have passed smoothly to Maureen O'Connor, the young Mission Hills neighborhood activist who had been elected to the council in 1971 at age twenty-five. The very definition of hermaphroditic centrism, she had been Wilson's most loyal council ally while also garnering praise from unions and community groups for her leadership in the battle for affordable housing. Moreover, in 1977 she had married the famed wealth and political influence of Bob Peterson while simultaneously becoming best friend and confidante to reactionary curmudgeon Helen Copley. Wilson, Peterson, Copley: three aces on the table that should have beat any hand in the 1983 special election.

But thirty-eight-year-old Hedgecock was a wunderkind in his own right. He had put a down payment on his first house when he was a teenage Goldwaterite, then furloughed himself to Haight-Asbury for a few years of long hair, dope, and promoting rock bands. This was punctually followed by law school and entry into a top-flight San Diego partnership. He was a fiscally conservative Republican who, after a hard day fighting big government, went into a telephone booth, stripped off his Brooks Brothers uniform, and changed into his alter identity as the surf-loving regional chair of the Sierra Club. His eloquence and angular good looks during the battle for California's 1972 coastal protection initiative particularly impressed Nancy Hoover and Tom Shepard, two hungry Del Mar city council members looking to hitch a ride on a comet. In 1974, according to the *Los Angeles Times,* they "pressured the city attorney into resigning and quickly hired Hedgecock"[241]

A year later, they were backing Hedgecock's long-shot bid for the board of supervisors. He won in a big upset in 1976 and quickly—because of "his unrelenting aggressiveness"—became the dominant personality on the board. He delighted environmentalists with his rants against the incipient "Los Angelization" of San Diego, and charmed libertarians with tirades against the "new fascism" of big government. He professed to be a follower of Scripps's and Marston's idol, Bob La Follette, as well as his two contemporary heroes: Barry Goldwater and Pete Wilson.[242] His progressive supporters, which soon included the local leadership of Tom Hayden's Campaign for Economic Democracy, tended to see only the La Follette side of Hedgecock, overlooking his Goldwaterite attacks on welfare recipients, indigent legal rights, and public employees.[243]

In 1980, Hoover and Shepard began to help Hedgecock plot an audacious assault on the mayoralty. They had new resources to play with. A little earlier, Hoover had left her wealthy broker husband to become the mistress of one of his former employees, a previously luckless stock hustler named J. David Dominelli. By the opening of campaign season in 1982, Hoover and Dominelli had synergized charm and guile into San Diego's hottest investment scheme, J. David & Co., and were operating out of an opulent La Jolla headquarters that also housed Shepard's new political consultancy, almost totally devoted to Hedgecock's dark horse campaign against O'Connor.

Since both of the leading candidates were carefully walking in the footprints of Pete Wilson, it was initially unclear what issues would distinguish Hedgecock from O'Connor. In any event, O'Connor was sucker-punched by Hedgecock's allegations—not entirely untrue—that she was a fat cat living in a La Jolla mansion and riding to power on her husband's money (he invested $400,000 in the campaign) and her odd friendship with Helen Copley. Hedgecock portrayed himself, by contrast, as a feisty populist, living in a modest Pacific Beach bungalow, whose more than half-million dollars in campaign contributions had been raised from thousands of mom and dad contributions, none exceeding the city's $250 legal limit (candidates' own fortunes and their spouses' were exempt).

Although O'Connor retained strong support in Southeast San Deigo neighborhoods as well as the endorsement of most unions, Hedgecock's anti-Copley tirades won considerable support from old-line Democrats who, like Harold Keen, were confused by a new-age politics that put a union-endorsed candidate in bed with the *Union.* Likewise, Hedgecock was able to divide the increasingly powerful gay vote in Hillcrest and Normal Heights while decisively winning the environmental vote in the beaches and the UCSD area. *Newsline,* the "New Left" weekly edited by a former *Door* writer, was particularly effective in building progressive support for Hedgecock over "Downtown O'Connor." Few were aware that *Newsline,* like Hedgecock himself, was now being largely financed by Dominelli, a right-wing Republican.[244]

Hedgecock's narrow but incontestable victory put into office someone who was as strong-willed as his predecessor and determined to defend all the mayoral prerogatives that Wilson had wrested from the council. Although Hedgecock had little respite before campaigning resumed for the 1984 regular election, some battle lines were quickly drawn in the sand. First, deputy mayor William Cleator—the third-place candidate in the special election—squared off as the proponent of the status quo ante Wilson, vowing to strip Hedgecock of the power to control committee appointments and thus council agendas. Second, Hedgecock—the supposed foe of the downtown power-structure—surprised many of his supporters by energetically endorsing an initiative, generaled by political consultant Shepard, to build a huge new downtown convention center. The cognoscenti, of course, knew that a potential beneficiary of the initiative was a key Hedgecock supporter, Doug Manchester, who was developing two huge waterfront hotels.[245] They wondered if it was not the first symptom of the Wilson devolutionary syndrome.

What no one was aware of, apparently, was the extent of Hoover's and Dominelli's investment in Hedgecock, or—what amounted to the same thing—Shepard's actual terms of employment. But it was difficult to peer closely at such dazzling, almost blinding success. In 1983 the gods were certainly smiling on the quartet and their extraordinary coordination of ambitions. While Hedgecock was upsetting O'Connor and Shepard was becoming king of consultants, Hoover and Dominelli were redefining luxury lifestyles in La Jolla with the remarkable success of their investment scheme, largely based on foreign currency speculations, that reportedly was earning an incredible 40–50 percent per annum. Although blue-collar San Diego was on the ropes with 11 percent unemployment in 1983, life had seemingly never been sweeter for the investor class. Together with their hundreds of triumphant clients, Hoover and Dominelli were living proof of the contemporary belief, to quote La Jolla evangelist Terry Cole-Whittaker, that "prosperity was your divine right."[246]

Then, in early 1984, rumors began to fly that J. David was really just a Ponzi scheme, like C. Arnholt Smith's empire of corporate boxes-inside-boxes, but more poorly built and near collapse. There was panic in the tea shops of La Jolla. Democratic honcho M. Larry Lawrence, who had loaned Dominelli $1 million, sued him and others soon followed. J. David declared bankruptcy. Dominelli, after unsuccessfully trying to scrounge a $125 million loan from the Bonnano crime family in New York, fled to Montserrat, where he was quickly arrested and extradited back to San Diego.[247]

As federal investigators dug deeper into the gilded world of Hoover and Dominelli, they discovered a fantastic plot not simply to bilk investors, but to take over City Hall. "They're buying the mayor's job," one J. David employee told the FBI. "They're corrupting the place and they're doing it in the name of good government."[248] District Attorney Ed Miller—the old terror of Smith—began to find plentiful evidence of the conspiracy as his staff investigated Hedgecock's campaign financing. His myriad populist contributors, investigators discovered, turned out to be primarily Nancy Hoover and David Dominelli. Likewise, humble Roger himself now owned a mansion in south Mission Hills, which he had renovated with a $130,000 "loan" (or was it a gift?) from Hoover.[249]

Two weeks before the 1984 primary, Miller filed a civil suit—he didn't have time for a grand jury indictment—alleging that Hedgecock, with Shepard's help, had concealed more than $357,000 in campaign contributions from Hoover and Dominelli. A lesser soul might have run for the border, but Hedgecock boldly stood his ground, counterattacking that Democrat Miller—whose campaigns had been heavily financed by O'Connor's hubby, Bob Peterson—was in cahoots with Helen Copley and antienvironment developers. He claimed that Miller had deliberately misconstrued Hoover and Dominelli's investment in Shepard's consultancy as a campaign donation to him. At the most, Hedgecock protested, he was guilty of simple absentmindedness due to his heroic absorption in civil duties.

But in September—two months before the runoff between Hedgecock and La Jolla savings-and-loan executive Richard Carlson—the grand jury backed up Miller with criminal indictments of the mayor, Hoover, Dominelli, and Shepard for laundering the finances of the 1983 campaign. A month later the Fair Political Practices Commission, citing 450 violations of campaign financing law, slapped the quartet with a $1.2 million lawsuit, the largest of its kind in California history.[250]

Hedgecock again portrayed himself as the victim of an establishment vendetta. When the Chamber of Commerce haughtily demanded his resignation, it only seemed to confirm Hedgecock's claim to be the people's champion against San Diego's traditional private governments. He rallied the support of talkshow hosts and local television commentators, exasperatedly waving his arms on the air and demanding, "Where's the crime?" His trial began a few days before the election, with Richard Huffman, a close associate of former attorney general Ed Meese, as prosecutor. It looked to many people like the revenge of the Nixonites. Most voters sympathized with Hedgecock the underdog, and he whipped Carlson in November by a commanding margin.

Hedgecock's first trial ended in a deadlock, with eleven of twelve jurors voting for conviction. At his second trial in fall 1985, he surprised prosecutors by hiring Oscar Goodman, Las Vegas's famous "attorney for the mob," who had defended both Tony "the Ant" Spilotro (of *Casino* fame) and his San Diego henchman, Chris Petti. (Coincidentally, Spilotro's former associate at the Stardust, La Jolla's Allen Glick, had been one of the few investors who had walked away from the J. David scam with his profits intact.) Goodman used the same tactics that he traditionally employed in defending "goodfellows": refusing to let Hedgecock testify while assailing the backgrounds of the prosecution witnesses. Nonetheless, Hedgecock was convicted in October on thirteen felony counts. Private investigators working for Goodman promptly claimed to find evidence of jury tampering, but the California attorney general's staff discounted the story and Hedgecock was sentenced to a year in jail. Compelled by statute, he resigned from office. The following February, Dominelli, as part of his own confession, confirmed Hedgecock's guilt.[251]

But felonious ex-mayor Roger refused to bow his head like Hoover and Shepard, who plea-bargained charges of campaign money laundering. Instead, he continued to claim that the real conspiracy was the one against him. While he appealed his jail time, he acquired a new bully pulpit as a "rage radio" host in the manner of Rush Limbaugh. "No more Mr. Nice Guy," Hedgecock now crusaded on the "deep environmental" issues of overpopulation and illegal immigration. Among other wild allegations, he claimed that thousands of Mexican women were having babies on the U.S. side of the border so they could collect welfare payments from San Diego County and then live in luxury in Tijuana.[252] These Mexican-bashing tirades, which undoubtedly influenced Pete Wilson's later gubernatorial frenzies, sent his show ratings into the stratosphere, particularly after Hedgecock instigated "Light Up the Border," which came perilously close to vigilantism. Angry Anglos in their Dodge pickups and Mercedes sedans were encouraged to shine headlights on the border fence where the "invasion of North America" was supposedly taking place.[253]

To the horror of his enemies, especially his successor Maureen O'Connor (elected in 1986), Hedgecock-the-unscrupulous was more popular than ever, even if he had traded the support of genteel tree-huggers for the angry adulation of the east county *herrenvolk*. Moreover, unlike poor Dominelli, he managed to escape the hoosegow entirely. In 1990 the State Supreme Court overturned his twelve perjury convictions because of judicial error. Former jurors expressed their helpless incredulity at the justices' decision. ("There was evidence ten times over to convict that man," fumed one.)[254] To avoid a new trial, Hedgecock accepted his conspiracy conviction and paid a $30,000 fine to the FPPC. After completing three years of probation, his conspiracy charge was reduced on his record to a misdemeanor. Hedgecock triumphally (and untruthfully) claimed total vindication.

21. The Brat Pack

He was a heel who worshiped only one god—HIMSELF!
San Diego novel[255]

The 1980s were the yuppie gilded age. The protesters of the previous decade were now miniature potentates sitting on the thrones of the routed 1960s establishment. The sins of the fathers were soon surpassed by the avarice of a generation whose benchmark was fame and fortune by age thirty. The Hoover-Dominelli plot to take power through Hedgecock was simply the most infamous and interminable of many celebrity scandals. San Diego retained its crown as the nation's capital of white-collar crime.

In 1980, for instance, the Feds arrested Joe Bello, the head of MB Financial, in a classic pyramid scheme that ripped off 1,200 local investors. In 1981 popular newscaster Mac Heald was convicted of child molestation; the next year, Judge Lewis Wenzell was busted in a call-girl scandal. In 1984, swindler Clifford Graham, the founder of Fotomat and the promoter of a bogus process for extracting gold from sand, vanished without a trace after being indicted. A stalwart local Republican, Graham had used endorsements from GOP congressmen Bob Wilson and Jack Kemp to entice hundreds of gullible La Jolla investors to invest in his fraudulent scheme.

Even more shocking to many San Diegans, famed evangelist Terry Cole-Whittaker fled La Jolla in 1985, leaving "behind hundreds of thousands of dollars in debts, longtime employees who hadn't received their final paychecks, stacks of bills from local businesses, and a $2.5 million, seven-year lease." Once she had been the very incarnation of the Southern California "Me Generation": "I'm a graduate of EST; I've done Gestalt, transactional analysis, rolfing, actualization. I'm into parties, fun, total living." Now, fleeing her debts and broken promises, the author of *How to Have More in a Have-Not World* told reporters that she was searching for "high-energy spiritual places." An associate explained she was talking about a television show.[256]

The same year, up-and-coming young Republican Uvaldo Martinez, who also liked "total living" (especially on a city credit card), caused a scandal with his bar-hopping and lewd conduct with female staff. He was indicted by a grand jury in 1986 on twenty-four felony counts of misusing city funds and kicked off the council.[257] In an astute commentary on San Diego's sick electoral system, veteran journalist and former Democratic congressman Lionel van Deerlin pointed out that progrowth Martinez had been overwhelmingly rejected by his Eighth District constituents in the 1983 primary in favor of opponent Celia Ballesteros, but then won the citywide runoff thanks to support from developers and the Wilson machine. Van Deerlin blamed Martinez less than the private governors of San Diego politics who had parachuted him into the council in the first place—"people who have used him to help maintain their grip on public business."[258]

The nature of that grip was further elucidated in 1986 when councilman Mike Gotch pushed through a deal to turn city-owned Belmont Amusement Park into a shopping center—to be built by his chief fund-raiser's husband. Soon afterward, veteran politico Nick Johnson declared that "San Diego currently has the worst city council in the world." The 1987 elections, with four open council seats for the first time since 1931, resulted in the substitution of identically coiffed and centrist new faces for those slightly old. All the brat-pack candidates seemed to have been spawned from the same Peter Wilson identikit. [259]

Presiding over this sprawl of yuppie greed was Mayor Maureen O'Connor, struggling to establish a more generous grassroots persona by her highly publicized tours of duty as a trash collector and homeless lady. Unlike Wilson and Hedgecock, who were buoyed by the rising tide of affluent north city, O'Connor's real political base was the solidly Democratic midcity: the older, mixed neighborhoods of blue-collar workers and young professionals. Although a "woman under the influence"—of Helen Copley's lavish art openings and billionaire heiress Joan Kroc's Fairbanks Ranch soirees—she also had a genuine empathy with the outcast San Diego being created by downtown renewal's displacement of the poor and the housing market's squeezing out of blue-collar families. "I am not a cocktail mayor," she claimed. O'Connor's Catholic conscience was best displayed in her attention to affordable housing, after-school programs in poor neighborhoods, and her generally friendly attitude toward a labor movement badly abused by the devolving Pete Wilson.[260]

She also, at least in the beginning, displayed a refreshing lack of deference to the SDI types accustomed to privileged access to the mayor's office. Promising to "make government more honorable," she had refused campaign contributions from large developers.[261] One downtown real estate executive even complained that she had "disenfranchised" business leaders. Her poor relations with downtown also stemmed from her previous opposition, as port commissioner, to the deindustrialization of the city's waterfront in favor of tourism. Her financial backers (in addition to millionaire hubby Peterson) included assorted port-related businesses who wanted the district's funds reinvested in the working harbor rather than in a harborfront convention center. O'Connor attributed a crucial margin of Hedgecock's upset victory in 1983 to support from downtown business interests after he endorsed the convention center initiative. She had remained neutral.[262]

Although a Wilson protégé like Hedgecock, O'Connor in office was probably the most liberal mayor in San Diego history. But she found little reinforcement from her political environment. Reaganism was at its zenith and the local, post–Lionel van Deerlin Democratic Party was in internecine disarray. (She herself was frequently accused of failing to support fellow Democrats in close contests.) Likewise, the strong-mayor regime established by Wilson did not outlive the Hedgecock scandal, and O'Connor was hemmed in by a city council that regained control over committee appointments and agendas. The limits of her power were brutally demonstrated by her failure to win support for a new, internationalized airport on Otay Mesa.

It had long been obvious that the continued growth of San Diego's tourist economy was constrained by its undersized and dangerously situated downtown airport. Earlier attempts to build a new airport on Kearny Mesa were, as we have seen, vetoed by the Navy, then made infeasible by the encroachment of suburbs. Largely undeveloped Otay Mesa, shared by San Diego and Tijuana, was the obvious alternative, but only with the participation of Mexico. Leading Republicans, however, objected to shared sovereignty and the spectre of drugs and illegal immigrants sneaking through the proposed terminal. Moreover, the Port Commission, whose vast waterfront developments like the new convention center were supported by income from Lindbergh Field, planted a series of land mines in O'Connor's path. As San Diego's new radio pundit, Roger Hedgecock, pointed out, "moving the airport would upset the whole relationship of money and power in San Diego."[263]

At the same time, O'Connor was stumbling almost as badly in her leadership of the managed-growth coalition. San Diego was the fastest growing large city in the country during most of the 1980s, in part as a result of Reagan's remilitarization of the economy. Wilson-era growth controls proved ineffective in the face of soaring population and congestion, and there were extraordinary economic incentives to breach the city's urban reserve. As developers organized to push through a series of new mega-projects, the environmental movement sprang back into life, and O'Connor was forced to deal with some of the most bitter land-use battles in city history.

The new cycle of protest began in 1984, during Hedgecock's tempestuous incumbency, when hundreds of angry Rancho Bernardo residents had been unable to get into a critical hearing about a proposed adjacent development in the urban reserve. The La Jolla Valley site was owned by the Campus Crusade for Christ, which packed the meeting with aggressive supporters bused in from out of town. By 1985, San Diegans for Managed Growth, including the Sierra Club, the League of Women Voters, and Common Cause, had beaten off the Christians and passed Proposition A, which required voter approval (retroactive in the case of La Jolla Valley) for further developments in the urban reserve.[264] A year later, the council, advised by famed growth management consultant Robert Freilich, imposed an interim control ordinance, which capped new housing at 8,000 units per year, a measure that was supported by all eight finalists in the 1987 council runoff, although a strong growth control ordinance simultaneously lost.

Although O'Connor had been previously credited by the Sierra Club as "the council's most dependable environmental vote," she seemingly dawdled as the council's majority launched an initiative campaign for a permanent version of its annual growth cap. Also on the 1988 ballot was a more radical proposal from PLAN (Prevent Los Angelization Now!), a new coalition headed by UCSD economics professor Peter Navarro, as well as two comparable measures to control growth in unincorporated county areas. Although O'Connor ultimately endorsed both the council and PLAN initiatives, she angered environmentalists by her failure to effectively campaign for either.[265]

Developers and real estate interests, on the other hand, unleashed an unprecedented negative ad blitz, the largest in San Diego history. Mike Madigan, Wilson's former planning adviser and now a Pardee executive, generaled the campaign with the support of two of Wilson's early backers, Gordon Luce and Malin Burnham. The San Diego battle was widely seen as a national test of the slow-growth movement, which, from a developer's perspective, had to be stopped at any price. After a $3 million blitz of misleading television ads, it was. Although a majority of voters endorsed some form of tighter growth management, their votes were dissipated across the four initiatives.[266]

Mayor O'Connor, herself originally the product of a neighborhood insurgency, also alienated supporters with her opposition to district elections, which she argued would balkanize the city along ethnic and income lines. Opponents denounced her reasoning as mere rationalization for the continued dominance of special interests over the city council. In November 1988, they succeeded in passing pro–district elections Proposition E over her opposition. Minority neighborhoods provided the highest percentage of "yes" votes.

Instead of fighting to hold on to power, O'Connor in January 1990 proclaimed herself a lame duck two years in advance of the next mayoral election. While O'Connor watched helplessly, the council ruthlessly demolished much of her legacy, ending funding for her proposed triennial arts festival, reneging on her promise to bring sewage treatment into compliance with federal clean-water standards, and blocking her dream of a "storybook" civic library. The mayor, for her part, lobbied for a sweeping package of charter reforms, including term limits, public campaign financing, and a ban on council members' long custom of voting on projects from whose sponsors they had received campaign contributions. It was a quixotic crusade, opposed in part or whole by every vested interest, without a populist base of its own. Moreover, voters were not surprisingly distracted by the abrupt end of the boom in 1989–90 and the onset of the worst recession since the Convair downturn of the early 1960s.[267]

22. Early Retirement

> This is not a virgin here.
> *Dick Silberman to arresting FBI agents (1989)*[268]

On April 7, 1989, FBI agents broke into a Mission Bay hotel room and arrested Dick Silberman, the former "Young Turk" who had helped overthrow C. Arnholt Smith. They caught Silberman as he was consummating a deal to launder $1.1 million in Colombian cocaine money. His associate, and the original object of the two-and-a-half-year investigation, was Chris Petti, reputedly the Chicago mob's local representative and former henchman for the recently murdered Tony Spilotro. According to the FBI, Silberman, who bragged of his past record of money laundering, had asked Petti to put him in touch with Colombian *narcotrafficantes*—one of whom turned out to be an FBI undercover agent. When some of Silberman's associates in the transaction attempted to shortchange him, he invoked Petti's much-feared muscle to adjust the accounting.[269] After his arrest, he tried unsuccessfully to save his skin by offering incriminating evidence against Willie Brown, the flamboyant speaker of the California assembly.[270]

The FBI, which had never been able to nail down the suspected mob partnerships of other San Diego influentials, was delighted to find Silberman writhing in their trap. In the late 1960s he and Peterson, in command of the Southern California

First National Corporation, had been accused of Smith-like self-dealing. In 1978, Silberman again appeared on law-enforcement radar screens when he approached mob fronts—La Costa Land Company and the Stardust's Allen Glick—for contributions to the Democratic Party. The FBI was also interested in Silberman's role in procuring an alleged $60,000 in unreported contributions to the Brown campaigns in 1974 and 1978 from Baja millionaire Carlos Bustamante. Finally, Silberman had partnered with Bob Peterson, Allen Glick, and swindler J. David Dominelli to take over from Las Vegas interests a scamlike and money-losing gold-mining venture called Yuba Natural Resources. Federal investigators suspected Silberman used Yuba securities to launder drug monies.[271]

Silberman's arrest—followed by his eventual conviction and prison sentence—set off a small earthquake inside the San Diego ruling class.[272] As Pete Wilson's former right hand in transportation and downtown development issues, as well as a high-ranking veteran of the Brown regime in Sacramento, Silberman was everyone's unwanted relative. His most intimate association was with ambitious county supervisor Susan Golding, the daughter of a former president of San Diego State, whom Silberman had married in 1984 despite the fact that she was a rising young Republican and he was a leading middle-aged Democrat. Golding, a shrewd political survivor, immediately denied any knowledge of her husband's dealings with mobs and cartels or the possible use of tainted money in her campaigns. Following in the footsteps of Nancy Hoover, who a few years before had cast adrift her prison-bound lover Dominelli, Golding portrayed herself as a victimized woman and lucratively divorced Silberman.

But the destruction of Silberman was only the most lurid episode in a more general decimation between 1988 and 1992 of the economic and political elites that had risen to power in the late 1960s and early 1970s. Helen Copley, Silberman's old date and the second member of Keen's dominant "triple alliance," also faded from the scene, preferring to cloister herself in her leafy La Jolla mansion, while her son David practiced his skills at drunk driving and yachting on the French Riviera.[273] Democratic congressman Jim Bates, the hope of San Diego progressives when he was elected to the city council in the early 1970s, was disgraced in front of the

House Ethics Committee in 1989 as his female staffers testified about sexual harassment. Likewise, powerful Planning Director Robert Spaulding was forced to resign in spring 1991 after revelations that city funds (authorized by his former boss, City Manager John Lockwood) had been secretly used to pay off a former mistress. Horton Plaza developer Ernest Hahn, who had made his fortune destroying the downtown districts of San Diego suburbs like El Cajon and Escondido before becoming yet another "Mr. San Diego," died in 1993. Don Nay, often criticized for running the all-powerful port district like his private company, retired the next year.

At the same time, the locally controlled savings-and-loan industry—itself having become a kind of super-Ponzi scheme—collapsed in a chain reaction: Imperial Savings was seized by federal regulators in 1990; Great American Bank went belly-up in 1991 along with trust deed lender Pioneer Mortgage; and then mighty HomeFed Bank collapsed like a beached whale in 1992. Although progrowth forces immediately tried to blame the extinction of local S&Ls on growth control legislation and the environmental movement, their downfall had little to do with local housing markets, but reflected, rather, the speculative frenzy in out-of-state commercial real estate. The Reagan Tax Reform Act of 1981 had created perverse incentives to develop mindless redundancies of minimalls and shopping centers while leaving huge shortfalls of needed affordable housing. Cleaning up the Great American mess alone cost federal taxpayers $1 billion, while the heads of HomeFed's real estate development subsidiary were indicted for conspiracy and fraud.[274]

The key power brokers of the Wilson era—Great American's Gordon Luce and HomeFed's Kim Fletcher—were virtually wiped out. San Diego–based finance, the traditional locus of the Corte Madera set's power, was just a smoking crater. Henceforth, big up-and-coming developers like Scripps Ranch's Corky McMillin, who once depended upon his alliance with Kim Fletcher, would go routinely to Southeast Asia to obtain loans for their subdivisions.[275] The fall of Luce—the very incarnation of the power of old money—prompted the *Union* to publish what was, in effect, an obituary for San Diego's former ruling classes: "Gone, retired, inactive or interested only in their hobbies are the Marstons, Jessops, Wangenheims, Alessios, Smiths, Fletchers, Hopes, Seftons, Hazards, Burnhams, Jones and Klaubers."[276] As predicted by Harold Keen in the late 1970s, San Diego had become a "branch town," with the crucial financial levers located elsewhere.[277]

Close on the heels of the S&L meltdown was the even bigger trauma of the post–Cold War plant and base closures. As in 1961, a burst of hypergrowth was again stopped in its tracks by the vulnerability of San Diego's military-industrial complex. What once would have been San Diego's own version of the apocalypse—the total shutdown of local General Dynamics production—began in 1992 when General Motors's Hughes subsidiary bought the Tomahawk missile program and transferred it from Kearney Mesa to Tucson. San Diegans were furious at GD's steadfast refusal over the years to seriously consider job-saving reconversion or diversification. "It seems they owe us something more than ten thousand pink slips," fumed council member Bob Filner. Five years later, GD completed its pullout by closing down Convair and razing historic Plant 1. Local economists estimated that altogether the region lost 58,000 defense-related jobs by 1996.[278]

San Diego was also traumatized by the decommissioning of its Naval Training Center in 1997, and the Navy's transfer of its famed "Top Gun" school to Nevada (the Marines took back Miramar). But the "Base Realignment and Closure Act," along with the downsizing of the Navy by 200 ships, brought more boom than bust to the local economy. Although San Diego lost a few cruisers, it gained a supercarrier. And, as in the past, naval restructuring favored the concentration of high-tech activities in San Diego, now headquarters of the U.S. Third Fleet. The debit of the Training Center's closure was more than balanced by the credit of the Space and Naval Warfare Systems Command relocation from the D.C. area to the former Convair Plant 2 at Pacific Highway and Barnett Boulevard.

According to defense experts, San Diego's comparative advantage was no longer so much its vaunted bay as the secretive and little-known offshore island of San Clemente. The true "crown jewel of the San Diego Navy" in an age of stealth warships and electronic warfare, San Clemente (legally in Orange County) provided "convenient instrumented test ranges above, upon, and underneath the sea—a resource unmatched anywhere in the world." Infinitely bombed, strafed, and torpedoed, this offshore landscape of destruction had become as important to the San Diego economy as Sea World or the zoo.[279]

Meanwhile, the recession was recentering San Diego's manufacturing economy around the mighty engine of UCSD/Salk Institute research. University science, financed by state tax dollars and federal research contracts, was irrigated with venture capital to grow scores of robust high-tech firms. Congress in 1980 (the Bayh-Dole Act) had legalized the licensing of federally funded university-developed research to the private sector. From 1985, this marriage of university research and local capitalism was accelerated by UCSD's CONNECT program led by Bill Otterson, the former CEO of Cipher Data Products. CONNECT, whose goals were the privatization of public science and the training of researchers as entrepreneurs, was the triumph of an antipodal agenda to the New Left's earlier attempt to build an inner city–UCSD alliance. Instead, major Republican donor Otterson was praised by UC President Richard Atkinson for creating a program that "multiplied exponentially the connections between UCSD and the region's business and industry."[280]

Indeed, by 1997 the university would claim that 124 companies, with more than 15,000 employees, were direct spin-offs of faculty research and entrepreneurship.[281] Torrey Pines Road just north of campus was lined with biotech firms with roots in UCSD's bioscience departments and medical school, while nearby Sorrento Mesa and Sorrento Hills were home to telecommunications and software firms fathered by engineering school faculty or alumni. These firms, in turn, were the scientific and geographical core of a larger north San Diego technology economy that by 1995 comprised some 600 companies with almost 100,000 employees. *San Diego Magazine* in the same year would claim that "among U.S. metropolitan areas, San Diego boasts the most college graduates and Ph.D.'s per capita, the most home computers, [and] the most miles of laid fiber-optic cable."[282]

The fairy-tale hero of the new San Diego economy was UCSD engineering professor Irwin Jacobs, who founded a little telecommunications company called Linkabit in 1971. By the mid-1990s Linkabit had become Qualcomm, San Diego's largest industrial employer, with some 7,000 workers. Another mythologized figure was UCSD bioscience researcher Howard Birndof, who transformed new diagnostic techniques developed in a university laboratory into an incredibly profitable private business. His Hybritech, San Diego's pioneer biotech success story in 1978, was later sold to Eli Lilly & Company for $418 million. Birndof and his venture capital backers subsequently founded half a dozen other widely publicized biotech start-ups. By the late 1990s San Diego was (depending on the basis of comparison) either the second or the third largest biotech center in the nation.[283]

The biggest San Diego–based technology firm of the 1990s, however, preferred shadow to light. Science Applications International Corporation (SAIC)—by the end of the decade a $6 billion company with 41,000 worldwide employees—was founded by Robert Beyster, a General Atomics (GA) physicist who left in 1968 after Gulf Oil took over GA and massacred its research program. Originally SAIC primarily performed contract research for nuclear weapons programs, but Beyster, who cherry-picked the cream of San Diego's laid-off engineering talent during successive aerospace recessions, quickly expanded into the development of surveillance and data-interpretation technologies for the CIA and other intelligence agencies. His board soon became crowded with the cast of a Tom Clancy novel: former spy chief Admiral Bobby Inman, ex–Secretary of Defense Melvin Laird, and, more recently, ex–White House antiterrorism adviser General Wayne Downing. By the early 1990s, SAIC was the hub of La Jolla's "Spook Valley," a rapidly growing cluster of firms developing technologies for homeland defense, border control, industrial security, and military surveillance (including "three of the seven programs to build unmanned spy-planes for the Pentagon").[284]

Local plutocracy—including the survivors of the S&L and General Dynamics debacles—reorganized itself around these new totems of the technology economy. Old elites supplemented their north-county real estate fortunes with tech stocks, while new elites sprouted up overnight in the miracle humus of the dot-com boom. "Sorrento Associates" took over the role—once performed by the First National Bank and the Cuyamaca Club—of providing a visible peak for San Diego's hierarchy of wealth. Described by the *Union-Tribune* as "a private group of thirty or so wealthy San Diego business executives committed to investing in homegrown high-tech and biotech firms," its select membership included a few traditional Republicans like that last Corte Maderan Malin Burnham, but was otherwise skewed—like the high-tech sector itself—toward opportunist Clinton Democracy (Irwin Jacobs, Sheila Lawrence, Lyn Schenck, and so on).

23. Playing the City

> The Padres: the team that ate San Diego.
> *Steve Erie (2002)*[285]

Larry Remer, the former antiwar activist turned political consultant, once observed that San Diego was actually as blue collar a town as Buffalo or Pittsburgh. But the political salience of class was reduced by the fact that such a large part of the working class was in uniform. "If even a fraction of the more than 100,000 active-duty service personnel stationed in the county were instead workers in a GM plant or a Bethlehem Steel plant and thereby belonged to the United Autoworkers or the United Steelworkers, the politics of this region would be dramatically different."[286]

During the 1990s this discrepancy between majority social needs—above all, affordable housing and living wages—and elite-shaped political agendas became greater than ever. In 1999, the *San Diego Union-Tribune* reported with embarrassment that since 1980 poverty in "America's finest city" had increased from 11 percent to 19 percent of the population, with fully one-third of San Diego's children under the line. Defying the usual Republican stereotypes of indolent welfare moms, almost two-thirds of San Diego's poor had full-time jobs, many of them as Marines or sailors.[287] The larger universe of low-income families (under 80 percent of median household income) constituted two-fifths of the population, with about 110,000 families paying a third or more of their income for housing.[288]

But economic justice issues, eclipsed for decades by homeowner-versus-developer struggles, now took a backseat during the 1990s to something truly trivial: professional sports. At a time when tens of thousands of San Diego families were caught in the widening scissors between stagnating wages and the rising cost of housing, city politics, thanks to the avarice of its officeholders, became the private playing field for two very rich and spoiled franchise owners: Dean Spanos of the Chargers and John Moores of the Padres.

Spanos and Moores, at first sight, were opposites. Spanos was a Stockton-based construction contractor and Republican mega-contributor who "poured millions of dollars into some of the nastiest campaigns around the country."[289] Former Texan Moores, on the other hand, was the paradigmatic wealthy nerd whose $400 million software fortune allowed him to become a major financial power in the Clinton wing of the Democratic Party.[290] In the bitter 1994 California gubernatorial race, Spanos and Moores went at it *mano a mano*, although largely behind the scenes. The Chargers' owner was Pete Wilson's most generous individual backer, while the Padres' boss (in the midst of moving from Houston to Rancho Santa Fe) was Kathleen Brown's biggest contributor.[291]

But Spanos and Moores also had two things profoundly in common. First, they held their sports franchises like guns to the heads of San Diego voters; and, second, they shared the services of Mayor Susan Golding. "I see in her," veteran politico Ed Butler observed shortly after Golding's inauguration in 1992, "a reprise of John Dean's book *Blind Ambition*."[292] She, indeed, held a formidable franchise on ruthless yuppie ambition. Her initial political resource was being the girlfriend of Wilson's political consultant George Gorton, notorious for his role in organizing a "kiddie spy corps" to infiltrate anti-Nixon groups during the 1972 election.[293] Through his influence, Golding was appointed to a city council vacancy, where she served for a short time before taking a more lucrative position in the Deukmejian administration in Sacramento. Later, having traded in Gorton for the even more influential Silberman, she was elected to the board of supervisors. When Silberman's arrest and the loss of his financial resources foreclosed her long-planned campaign for a statewide office, Golding opted for a temporary detour through the San Diego mayoralty.

Her runoff opponent in 1992 was Pete Navarro, the leader of PLAN. Although Navarro had come in first in the primary, he was the target of developers who, as he put it, "saw me, even in my best moments, as the environmental Antichrist." Golding, on the other hand, promised a "business friendly" City Hall and support for the expansion of border industries. With triple his campaign contributions, she unleashed a flood of cleverly crafted television calumnies that accused Navarro, among other things, of being financed by the porn industry and plotting to inundate

San Diego with drug addicts. Navarro, who nonetheless ended up with 48 percent of the vote, might have overcome Golding's negative ad campaign if he had won the endorsement of fellow Democrat and slow-growther O'Connor. Navarro later speculated whether O'Connor had been talked out of supporting him by friend Helen Copley, "or whether it was a sober recommendation against the endorsement from confidant and developer-lobbyist Paul Peterson":[294]

It was a pity, too, that upon her election Susan Golding dismantled practically all of O'Connor's favorite programs—including Maureen's annual Christmas homeless-shelter project. This destruction of the O'Connor legacy came, by the way, just as I had told Maureen it would if Golding won, but Maureen wouldn't listen to me.[295]

Golding's inauguration coincided with an economic recovery whose local emblem was the new completed downtown Convention Center. The convention trade finally provided a motor for the faux French Quarter "Gaslamp District," which had been treading water since the second Wilson administration. It also unleashed a tidal wave of gentrification as the council quintupled the catchment area of tax increment–financed downtown redevelopment. Finally, the convention center gave the new mayor splendid opportunities for self-advertisement as she impatiently waited for a shot at a higher office.

Golding pursued a two-part strategy whose conflation of personal ambition and civic interest was barely disguised. First she became the Chargers' best friend, supporting Spanos's controversial demands for guaranteed season ticket income and a gentrified stadium. "The idea was," an "insider" later told the *San Diego Reader,* "that Golding was to get on Spanos's coattails and meet his monied friends who would give it to Susan later." Second, she proposed to erase an old blot from San Diego's past by sponsoring the 1996 Republican Convention. The convention, of course, would also provide her with national limelight.[296]

Golding's projects cut against the grain of San Diego's fiscal conservatism as well as grassroots suspicion after so many political scandals. Unlike O'Connor, however, she had the support of like-minded ambitions on the city council and, more important, of powerful City Manager Jack McGrory. McGrory shrewdly nourished Golding's megalomania—including the Republican extravaganza, the giveaways to the Chargers, and, later, the construction of a new ballpark for Moores—in return for noninterference in his tenure as the city's real ruler. While the powers of the mayor, as we have seen, were severely pruned during O'Connor's term, those of the city manager had been augmented by the transfer of the planning department to his control after the 1991 sex scandal.

The year 1995 was the climax of Charger mania after San Diego finally made it into Super Bowl XXIV. Flying back from Miami on the Chargers' private jet, Golding—according to the *San Diego Reader*—had a notable conversation with Spanos. According to an "insider" interviewed by columnist Matt Potter, Golding readily agreed to support Spanos's demands for a ticket sales guarantee and public financing for the rebuilding of Jack Murphy stadium. Golding, still unknown to most ordinary voters outside of San Diego, "hoped and expected that Spanos [in return] would pave the way for the big money to come in [to her campaigns]."[297]

San Diego, like other cities, already had a long history of being raped and pillaged by the holders of its professional sports franchises. Back at the beginning of the 1960s, taxpayers had financed the rebuilding of Balboa Stadium to attract Barron Hilton's Chargers from Los Angeles. When Charger coach Sid Gilman expressed his dislike for Balboa Stadium, the taxpayers built a new stadium in Mission Valley in 1965. Hilton promptly offloaded the Chargers onto Eugene Klein for a handsome profit, although, as *San Diego Magazine* emphasized at the time, "what he really sold was our stadium."[298] Subsequently, the owners of the Chargers and Padres whipsawed the council for new subsidies and bigger promotion budgets. But Spanos's demands for keeping the Chargers in San Diego were the most outrageous yet.

He threatened to move the team unless the city guaranteed 60,000 sold seats per home game, with taxpayers making up any shortfalls in ticket sales. This would allow the Chargers to sell cable rights to home game broadcasts without worrying about the impact on attendance. In addition, Spanos demanded a radical renovation of Jack Murphy stadium, including more corporate skyboxes, VIP lounge areas, and a $17 million off-site training facility. When the Stadium Authority opposed the stadium expansion, Golding and McGrory bypassed it and used another agency to issue $60 million in bonds to meet Spanos's demands.[299] When taxpayers, invoking both the city charter and the state constitution, went to court to demand a referendum on the expansion, McGrory denounced them as "urban terrorists" and the council hired the city's leading law firm, Luce, Forward, Hamilton and Scripps, to oppose them:

> Though the firm also worked for Spanos, representing a legal conflict of interest, the city council, meeting secretly, agreed to waive the conflict and ultimately agreed to pay the firm at least a million tax dollars for its work to keep the stadium and convention issues off the ballot.[300]

High-powered lawyers, as usual, triumphed over populist insurgency, and Superior Court Judge Anthony Josephs quashed the taxpayers' lawsuit in 1997.[301] The shortfall between the city's $60 million and the total $78 million expansion cost was then made up in the most tawdry manner—at least to the many admirers of legendary sports writer Jack Murphy (who died in 1980)—by selling the stadium's name to Irwin Jacobs's Qualcomm.[302]

While Spanos was collecting his windfalls, his fellow Republicans were nominating ill-fated Bob Dole in the new Convention Center. The 1996 GOP convention, as intended, allowed Golding to bask in reflected glory. Conservative writers gushed fountains of praise for the mayor's leadership and San Diego's "pro-business, small government political culture." To enthusiasts like Malibu pundit Joel Kotkin, Golding's town was the new model for urban America: a "millennial city" blessed, he emphasized, because it had "no vast municipal welfare state, no entrenched urban underclass, no powerful municipal unions to skew spending priorities, and no industrial union tradition to make its labor force rigid."[303]

San Diego's taxpayers, meanwhile, were struggling to find out how much the Republicans had actually cost them. The council, foolishly or collusively, had given McGrory control over the finances in return for a detailed accountancy later on. But he and Golding had no intention of ever providing such data. Moreover, the *Union-Tribune* management allegedly "squelched a wide-ranging investigation into the costs by the paper's reporters."[304] Two years later, after McGrory's abrupt and rather mysterious resignation, the *Union-Tribune*'s Pat Flynn was finally able to publish a story about the convention cover-up.

> For more than a year, McGrory and Golding contended the city was not keeping track of the $30 million–plus that it was shelling out for the four days of festivities. Even council members conceded that they had no idea how much public money was involved.
>
> McGrory continued to deny the existence of a written budget until a reporter obtained a copy. Thereafter, sources said, McGrory banned all convention documents from City Hall and insisted that meetings with the Republican National Committees be held off premises.[305]

Golding, as everyone expected, was reelected in 1996, thanks to a campaign treasury bulging with contributions from Wilson appointees, Spanos and Moores associates, and local recipients of city largesse.[306] One of her opponents, gay activist Patrick Coleman, accused her of manipulating stadium subsidies and sewer contracts to build a special-interest leviathan:

> She is using the issuance of city contracts and lease-revenue bonds similar to how the oldstyle politicians back East assign patronage jobs. Each of these projects benefits somebody who can help her or assist her in fundraising and put money into her coffers either directly or indirectly.[307]

The next year she launched her long-planned campaign for the U.S. Senate, again with the blessing of Spanos and Wilson. "Troubling questions," wrote the *Los Angeles Times,* "have surrounded her vaunted campaign team, acquired lock, stock and barrel from Gov. Pete Wilson's political operation."[308] "By the end of 1997," added the *Reader,* "Golding had raised almost a million dollars from a combination of the Spanos connections, the San Diego hotel business, and other special interests. . . . [But] Golding's attempt to conceal the Spanos influence by delaying its disclosure was regarded to have backfired." Scandals over the stadium—both the thwarting of a popular vote on expansion and the soaring costs of ticket sales' shortfalls—hoisted Golding on her own petard. She had to withdraw from the campaign.[309]

Golding fell back to earth only to be caught in the waiting (and Democratic) arms of John Moores. The Padres' owner, not surprisingly, had been carefully taking notes from Spanos's deft playing of the mayor and city council. He argued that if the Chargers were rewarded with new sky boxes and ticket guarantees, then the Padres—who shared Qualcomm stadium—deserved nothing less than a new city-built ballpark. Indeed Moores's hubris was breathtaking: in addition to a downtown stadium, he demanded priority development rights (twelve prime parcels) in a proposed ballpark district. The Padres, in other words, were the Trojan horse to open the gates of downtown to his new subsidiary: JMI Realty. It was a strategy, moreover, that corresponded to the old SDI dream of pushing redevelopment into the warehouse and ice-storage district below Market Street.[310] In elite financial circles the ballpark, in tandem with an expansion of the convention center, was correctly understood as an archimedean lever to generate an estimated $1 billion in new development in what was now being called—even in advance of gentrification—the "East Village." No wonder, then, that "Mr. Downtown" (and last Corte Maderan) Malin Burnham welcomed Moores's land grab as the "second coming of downtown redevelopment."[311]

To ensure the millennium, Mayor Golding appointed an "independent" Padres task force that most critics regarded as little more than a Moores dream team. Its members included Burnham, who owned a minority share of the Padres; Tom Hom, a ballpark district landowner; Herb Klein, Copley editor in chief; Robert Dynes, the ambitious UCSD chancellor, whose father-in-law was a business partner of Moores. When community groups protested the conflict of interests enshrined in the task force, the DA ruled that because it was only an advisory committee to the mayor and city council, it didn't have to disclose personal holdings or, for that matter, even open its deliberations to the public. In the event, the task force loyally endorsed a funding package ("Proposition C") that committed $275 million in public revenue to the ballpark.[312]

Meanwhile, Golding's chief of staff, Kris Mitchell, moved over in 1998 to become a Padres' lobbyist, while Tom Shepard (of Hoover/Dominelli notoreity) led the PR campaign for what the *Reader* denounced as Moores's "downtown pleasure palace, replete with luxury suites and an artificial beach." Although closer in conception to the Taj Mahal than San Diego's original Lane Field (the 1950s downtown ballpark torn down at C. Arnholt Smith's behest), Shepard's old pal Roger Hedgecock gave the proposal his neopopulist endorsement, as did most local radio celebrities. Indeed the boosters of the stadium bond issue surfed a wave of Moores's advertising money, as he outspent his opponents almost one thousand to one (the old "fairness doctrine" guaranteeing equal media time having long ago been scrapped by the Reagan administration).[313]

As a result, most voters thought they were being offered a local version of Camden Yards or Yankee Stadium. The People's East Village Association struggled in vain to explain that the new ballpark was, in fact, designed for "an elite audience . . . inconsistent with baseball being an affordable family pastime."[314] Nor did the broader public hear the voices of Barrio Logan residents complaining about their exclusion from a planning process that decisively impacted their community. As *La Prensa* explained at the time, the ballpark followed the "familiar scenario" of private interests, organized as a private government, making all the key decisions then "inviting an 'Hispanic Representative' to sit on some sort of board."[315]

The only real, if temporary, roadblock to the Proposition C juggernaut was the county grand jury. Shortly before the November 1998 vote, it issued a pair of scathing reports that criticized City Hall for withholding full information about the measure's impact and the astounding subsidies that Moores would reap. Following C's passage, polls indeed showed that voters who approved the measure "had a hazy understanding of the city's financial commitments."[316] In June 1999, the grand jury stopped just short of accusing Golding of bribing the San Diego Hotel-Motel Association to endorse Prop. C in return for an additional $4 million in its promotional budget. The grand jury's exact words were "wilful misconduct" and "collusion." The jurors also held the mayor responsible for disbanding the city's watchdog Public Utilities Advisory Commission at the exact moment when it should have been blowing whistles over the San Diego Gas and Electric Company's misuse of a $330 million surcharge that the city council, meeting in closed session, had authorized for the construction of underground powerlines.[317]

The final achievement of the Golding era was the adoption of a redevelopment plan in 1999 for the former Naval Training Center (NTC) at the foot of Point Loma. The Clinton administration's gift of the 435-acre former Navy bootcamp (closed in 1997) was a unique opportunity for San Diego to redress the city's shortage of affordable housing as well as to achieve some of the unfulfilled goals of the Nolen/ Marston vision of a harbor greenbelt. Golding and the council majority, however, again defied the recommendations of their own citizens' committee to turn over the renewal of NTC to Corky McMillin, the heir to Ernest Hahn as the region's most politically well-connected developer.[318] For a site whose estimated value ranged as high as $700 million, McMillin paid exactly $8 (one dollar per parcel) in return for splitting future profits—above a 12 percent threshold—with the city. And instead of a new civic commons, McMillin proposed "Liberty Station": 349 luxury homes, two hotels, offices, retail outlets, and a business park. The deal was sweetened with a few dozen acres of park space and some offsite affordable housing.[319] NTC's neighbors were appalled both at the giveaway of public land and the squandering of the site's potential:

> We were promised a waterfront Balboa Park, but instead we're getting dense residential development, a strip mall and a bunch of office towers. We're getting nothing, zero. Public land should be used for public purposes.[320]

Critics suspected that the $500 million McMillin project was a template for the future redevelopment of nearby Lindbergh Field and the Marine Corps Recruit Depot, should the city ever find a new airport and the Marines be persuaded to consolidate training at Camp Pendleton. The ultimate result would be a three-mile arc of highrise gentrification along San Diego Bay from Point Loma to the new baseball stadium: a utopian culmination of the SDI vision of reviving downtown. Surely in that case a future McMillin or Moores will find room to erect an appropriately handsome statue of Susan Golding, San Diego's sweetheart of the 1990s.

24. Once and Future Kings

> The basic creed of the gangster . . . is that whatever a man has is his only
> so long as he can keep it, and that the one who takes it away from him
> has not done anything wrong, but has merely demonstrated his smart-
> ness . . .
>
> The Gangs of New York *(1928)* [321]

The 2000 mayoral election was sheer atavism: an issueless, expensive battle between two aging clones of Pete Wilson. The front-runner, Supervisor Ron Roberts, had the support of big developers, city vendors, and prime contractors, as well as the endorsement of powerful Wilson *consigliere* John Davis. His opponent was Judge Dick Murphy, another Wilson protégé (from precinct worker to councilman), running on the silly chauvinist slogan of "San Diego for San Diegans" and backed by conservative senior statesman Clair Burgener.[322] In keeping with local tradition, Roberts was a moderate "smokestack" while underdog Murphy was seen as a somewhat wilted "geranium."[323]

Earlier in his career, Roberts had a narrow escape from a wide-ranging scandal involving illegal campaign contributions by Frank Gatlin, a wealthy Del Mar shopping-center developer. This time Murphy was able to successfully tar Roberts with a new scandal involving the always generous John Moores. Although Roberts, who had received free plane trips and other gratuities from the Padres' owner, escaped prosecution (in contrast to unfortunate city council member Valerie Stallings), his campaign was irreparably damaged.

Murphy took over the helm in a City Hall ruled by a handful of regal political consultants, where council seats had become virtually hereditary offices inherited by senior staffers. The ghost of weak mayors past, Murphy has been generally overshadowed by more heavily armored egos: especially the ambitious Alan Bersin, Janet Reno's former "border czar" who has made the superintendency of San Diego schools into a bully pulpit for his authoritarian views. Nor has Murphy shown much backbone in dealing with the onerous task of changing the diapers of San Diego's spoiled, tantrum-prone sports franchise-holders.

Moores, despite a simmering Enron-like scandal involving his profitable bail-out from the doomed Peregrine Systems Inc., has continued to impose his will on ballpark planning, adding lucrative new density and, in general, strip-mining "East Village" for its last ounce of gold. *Fortune* magazine honored his chutzpah by ranking him as the "fifth greediest corporate executive in the United States."[324] Spanos, undoubtedly to prove that he was even greedier, countered with another threat to move the Chargers unless the city gave him a baroque new stadium, or, alternately, ownership of the land (estimated value: $180 million). Murphy, wary of perceptions that he was in the pocket of Spanos, promised that the city would not negotiate with the Chargers until a citizens' committee had thoroughly explored all options. In fact—or so at least opponents charge—both sides were "caught red-handed" in secret negotiations at the law offices of Luce, Forward.[325]

After the bloodbath of the 1989–92 recession, which liquidated so much ancient economic clout in San Diego, a new ruling class has slowly emerged. Moores—whose public image has recently gone "from friendly philanthropist and dorky owner of the Padres to Evil Billionaire and weasely doubletalker"[326]—continues to pursue the ancient crown of Spreckels and Smith. More than any other elite figure he bridges the gaps: between La Jolla and Downtown, between Clinton Democrats and Wilson Republicans. Thus Moores (a UC regent thanks to massive contributions to Gray Davis) joined Pete Wilson and Roger Hedgecock to sponsor a lavish fund-raiser for fellow regent Ward Connerly's latest attack on affirmative action (the so-called "Racial Privacy Initiative"). Reciprocally, leading Republicans have allied with Moores and Jacobs in financing terrifying television blitzs against opponents of School Superintendent Bersin.[327]

Yet Moores is hardly indispensable to this era of bipartisan good feeling. Indeed, if he were dethroned by scandal tomorrow, the party crowds in Rancho Santa Fe would hardly stop to mourn. Bersin would step forward as San Diego's new savior, or, perhaps, another billionaire from Houston or San Francisco would fall from the sky. In any event, the old pros at Luce, Forward (San Diego Law) and at Stooza Communications (the prime political consultants) would work out a strategy for keeping the local growth machine—now increasingly fueled by the War on Terrorism and the remilitarization of the economy—purring along. The institutions of elite para-government—after more than a century of Darwinian selection—are now stronger than the sum of mere personalities.

Red flag over Tijuana (May 1911)

The notorious soapbox (1911 free speech fight)

Communist rally (New Town Park, 1933)

Chorus girls at the 1936 Exposition in Balboa Park

The military–industrial complex (General Hap Arnold, Reuben Fleet, and William Knudsen, 1940)

The Holy Trinity: Dick Nixon, Bob Wilson, and J. Edgar Hoover (1956)

Civil rights comes to San Diego (March 1960)

Irvin Kahn, Lord of Rancho los Peñasquitos (1962)

CORE versus the Realtors (January 1964)

United Farm Workers picket GOP convention headquarters (1972)

The birthday boy (Mayor Pete Wilson, 1973)

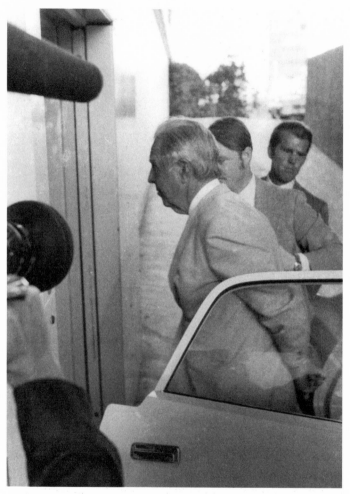

"Mr. San Diego" indicted (C. Arnholt Smith, 1975)

Just Another Day in Paradise?
An Episodic History of Rebellion and
Repression in America's Finest City

Jim Miller

Perhaps no other urban space embodies the logic of the theme park more than "America's Finest City." As the magical spell of Los Angeles has been broken by traffic, smog, earthquakes, and riots, San Diego has energetically sought to maintain its image as a quiet little beach town, free from the urban blight, pollution, and class and race conflicts that have forever soiled the reputation of its unruly neighbor to the north. On a sunny day in San Diego, a tourist might choose to wander through Balboa Park in search of the Spanish Colonial past that never was, shop by the harbor in a reconstruction of a New England fishing village in the vicinity of where the city's tuna and cannery industry once thrived, or have margaritas near the fictitious "Ramona's marriage place" in Old Town and stroll over to the conveniently relocated Victorian neighborhood in the Heritage District.[1] That same tourist might also eat at an expensive bistro in the Gaslamp Quarter where the red-light district was and the Wobblies were viciously beaten by police and vigilantes at the turn of the century, take a cruise on San Diego Bay past the Navy ships leaking invisible poisons into the water, or spend a day in the "natural beauty" of Mission Bay Park, which was constructed at the expense of 99 percent of the local wetlands and which frequently suffers from sewage spills.[2] Unlike Los Angeles, however, San Diego has largely managed to conceal these contradictions and market an image of itself that pushes the "real" city to the margins and buries its history under a mountain of booster mythology. If history is not dead in San Diego, it is certainly on life support.

In a 1983 essay, "Simulacra and Simulations," the French postmodern critic Jean Baudrillard argues that "Disneyland is presented as imaginary in order to make us believe that the rest is real, when in fact all of Los Angeles and the America surrounding it are no longer real, but of the order of the hyperreal and of simulation."[3] If this assessment of Southern California city-space seemed hyperbolic in the early eighties, the next two decades of urban development have proven it to be prophetic. Baudrillard's contention is that the fiction of the theme park no longer "masks and perverts a basic reality" or even "masks the absence of a basic reality" but rather "bears no relation to any reality whatever" and is "its own pure simulacrum."[4] Hence the sea of commodified simulations that comprise the contemporary city no longer tells the story of a city's past. There is no relation between the narrative of the street and the history of a given locality. Even nature, as Susan Davis points out in her book on Sea World, *Spectacular Nature*, has been transformed into spectacle. What we are left with is an ahistorical pastiche of styles and fantasies designed to aid commerce.[5]

Even those who do not share Baudrillard's utterly dystopian assessment of the American city have noted the trend toward the eradication of history in urban space in an effort to maximize consumption opportunities for the mostly white, middle and upper classes that San Diego exemplifies so well. In the seminal 1992 anthology *Variations on a Theme Park: The New American City and the End of Public Space*, Michael Sorkin argues that the line between theme park and city has been so eroded that urban spaces have been drained of memory and history.[6] As Mike Davis's entry about Los Angeles and Neil Smith's essay about New York illustrate, the theme-parking of the city is frequently accompanied by the erasure of older neighborhoods, the relocation of undesirable populations, and the banishment of unmarketable history and unpleasant contemporary realities to the urban dustbin, all in the service of a top-down class war.[7] Susan Davis notes the same process at work in San Diego, as it has relentlessly themed itself "while much of the city's real and recent history has remained unexplored."[8] The end result of this process has been the creation of attractions like Sea World that draw a population that is whiter and wealthier than San Diego as a whole.[9]

Outside the boundaries of the park, much of the rest of the city is comprised of themed zones like the Gaslamp, Sea Port Village, and Old Town that generally price out working-class visitors and provide nonunion low-wage service sector jobs for the local San Diegans who keep the tourist industry running.[10] Sea World's vigorous opposition to a project-labor agreement for its expansion plan is ample evidence of what happens when unions try to crash the party.[11] Thus the overall effect of the theme-park city is to replace this narrative of class division and labor squabbles with a space that is, as Susan Davis puts it, "as nonconflictual as possible."[12] Hence when the murals in Chicano Park or the house of African American city councilman George Stevens are defaced with racist graffiti, the local media portray such events as shocking aberrations, just as they do when local teenagers shoot and beat several elderly Mexican migrants or when a black Marine is the victim of a vicious racist beating in Poway. By doing so, they help perpetuate the mythology of San Diego as a mellow tourist paradise, free from the ugly conflicts that mar Los Angeles and other less blessed American cities.

The effort to create this illusion is as old as the city itself. What these "transgressions" really do, however, is expose the dark history of the city like the lightning bolt does the night sky. San Diego's boosters have always consciously sought first to avoid the importation of "undesirable elements" and, if that failed, to eliminate them by any means necessary. Nonetheless, despite San Diego's history of Social Darwinist city planning, Chamber of Commerce racism, reactionary vigilantism, and open class warfare, rebellions have cracked through the glossy veneer of the theme park if only to be brutally suppressed.

A Bourgeois Utopia

San Diego's 1915 Panama–California Exposition opened with groundbreaking festivities that featured an Anglo-Saxon interpretation of Spanish California. There was a "pontifical military mass" in Balboa Park, a grand fiesta that lasted half a week, and a "Pageant of the Missions." During one ceremony, a liberal interpretation of a

Spanish caravel sailed across the harbor from North Island to Broadway Pier. There, "King Cabrillo" was met by an eager crowd and carried up Broadway in a sedan chair by Anglos dressed as Indians. At the courthouse, his highness stopped for the coronation of "Queen Ramona" (based on the character from Helen Hunt Jackson's novel *Ramona*, the *Uncle Tom's Cabin* of California's mission Indians). Ramona awaited him dressed in an Edwardian interpretation of Spanish Renaissance clothing. After her crowning, the royal couple headed up Broadway to the carnival booths at the Isthmus.[13] As events such as these served to transform the city's history into an Anglo boosters' mythology, the *San Diego Union* explained what the Exposition meant with regard to the Social Darwinist struggle between the "Latin" and "Saxon" peoples:

> . . . the weaker was absorbed by the stronger; but with the passing of the weaker they left a legacy of their art and culture, which the survivor has gladly possessed to beautify and decorate his own. We have received this tradition gladly; we have made of this romance the background of our own history . . . in the fair port of San Diego and on this golden coast of California.[14]

Thus, according to the booster oligarchy, a new Anglo bourgeois utopia had arisen out of the quaint ruins of the Spanish past.[15] Such a mythology was easily fostered in San Diego at the turn of the twentieth century, whose population was 91.3 percent white and only 5 percent Mexican and Mexican American.[16] What this myth neglected, however, was the fact that the "romance" of the mission past had never existed. As Douglas Monroy points out in his essay "Brutal Appetites: The Social Relations of the California Mission," "The Spaniards had the best of intentions; they meant to bring reason and salvation to the Indians. Instead, they shredded their native culture and infested them with fleas and microbes. Then the padres buried the Indians."[17] California's "priest-civilizers," as the prospectus of the 1915 Exposition called them,[18] saw little of value in the culture of the *gente sin razón*. The native peoples' lack of a linear sense of time, their uninhibited sexuality, and their desire to work with rather than over nature struck the missionaries as barbaric. Indeed, Padre Junípero Serra noted their "pernicious disposition," and, as Monroy observes, "The priests unilaterally transferred their role of loving, kind, protective European father, and ruthless castigator of their errant, incontinent, and lesser charges, to the California Indians."[19] Hence the loving padres taught reason and conveyed their Christian charity with the musket and the lash. In response to such treatment, 10 percent of the Indians working in the missions fled. Some fought back by other means. In 1812, Padre Panto, the rigorous disciplinarian of Mission San Diego, was poisoned by his Indian cook.[20]

The secularization of the missions in 1834 did little to change the plight of the Indians. Debt peonage and vagrancy laws tied them to the ranchos of the *Californios,* where they occupied the lowest rung of the social order.[21] After the conquest of California, thousands of Indians continued to work in de facto slavery as laborers for whites in the fields and mines.[22] San Diego Indians rebelled against their Anglo masters just as they had against the Spanish. In 1851, Indians reacted to local officials who sought to tax them despite their lack of citizenship privileges by planning to drive these Americans off the land. The revolt failed quickly, however, after four Americans were killed and a leading San Diegan was expelled from his ranch. Antonio Garra, the leader of the rebellion, was betrayed and given over to the authorities for execution.[23]

From the 1840s to the 1870s, San Diegans were fearful of attack from wild bands of savages, according to most accounts.[24] In the 1880s, however, Helen Hunt Jackson's book *A Century of Dishonor,* along with her novel *Ramona,* briefly changed the image of San Diego's Indians from savage to victim. As the perceived threat faded, the "noble savage" of the past came into vogue in Anglo circles even as tales of the drunken "savage beast" of the present continued to fill the pages of local newspapers.[25] By the time of the Panama-California Exposition in 1915, Indians' best opportunities came through their ability to play themselves in an exhibit.[26]

After the American conquest, the *Californios* who had once oppressed the Indians also met a fate unfitting of a "romance." As Carey McWilliams notes in *Southern California: An Island on the Land,* "As the *gente de razón* lost their money and holdings, they began to be called Mexican and the old practice of referring to them as *Californios* or native Californians was abandoned.[27] Mexicans were frequently murdered by Anglos in Southern California and "[t]he practice of lynching Mexicans soon became an outdoor sport."[28] Although the level of mob violence against Mexicans that Los Angeles saw did not reach San Diego, individual acts of violence, slurs, and discriminatory legislation, such as "the greaser law," which made it easier to harass "vagrants," were daily facts of life for San Diego's Mexicans.[29] Rather than being "absorbed," as the *Union* proclaimed, Mexicans were driven off their lands and forced to become laborers or leave. This, combined with the huge influx of Anglo immigrants toward the end of the nineteenth century, seemed to the boosters to have permanently exorcised the Mexican influence. Thus San Diego's Anglo oligarchy could rewrite history and focus on limiting the influence of other "undesirable elements" and forging the city in their own image.

Even the San Diego labor movement, with the exception of its more radical elements, was more interested in limiting Mexican "immigration" than in organizing Mexican workers.[30] By the time San Diego reporter Harold Keen checked the "mood of the barrio" in the late 1960s, the legacy of this history was clear, as Mexican Americans had the highest unemployment rate of any minority group (25 percent) the highest school drop-out rate, the lowest level of educational achievement, and dilapidated, deteriorating housing and schools.[31]

Despite their small numbers in San Diego, African Americans were also unwelcome. A paragraph in an 1852 grand jury report bemoans the presence of "a den of sable animals" and demands that "these colored men be compelled to leave our town."[32] A little more than fifty years later, in 1907, the San Diego Chamber of Commerce received a letter from Los Angeles inquiring about the possibility of purchasing "a thousand acres of good farm or ranch land" to be sold as small tracts for "an industrious class of Negro farm families."[33] When the request was forwarded to the chamber's Transportation and Immigration Committee, it was not acted upon because, according to the chamber's own records, "negro colonization is not to be encouraged."[34] The African American population in San Diego did not increase much until World War II brought a large number of industrial jobs. Even then, displays of overt racism in employment were not uncommon. As the president of Vultee Aircraft told a group of African Americans, "It is not the policy of this company to employ people other than the Caucasian race."[35] Despite President Franklin

Roosevelt's executive order banning racial discrimination in the war industry and a concurrent labor shortage in San Diego, the U.S. Navy, the Chamber of Commerce, and San Diego city government all maintained a Jim Crow perspective. After the brief, modest gain in the black population, it fell again in 1946, and the city's de facto racial segregation continued for years.[36]

As Leroy Harris notes in *The Other Side of the Freeway: A Study of Settlement Patterns of Negroes and Mexican Americans in San Diego, California,* "Throughout its history as an American city, San Diego has contained a numerically and proportionally smaller number of Negroes and Mexican Americans than most other large American cities."[37] In addition to the overt social and economic discrimination faced by people of color in San Diego in employment and civil rights, the persistent efforts of realtors have also stood in their way. As Harris's study shows, "Restrictive covenants in real estate deeds" and the active "role of real estate agents in the formation of segregated housing patterns" were a very strong force in creating a segregated San Diego.[38] Indeed, as late as 1964, the San Diego Realty Board lobbied hard against the Rumford Act, California's fair housing law, and actively campaigned to have it annulled through a ballot proposition.[39] The Committee for Home Protection spearheaded the anti–Rumford Act drive. Their public relations consultant was William Shearer, an ultra-conservative former Oceanside newspaper publisher and then administrative assistant for Republican Assemblyman Richard Barnes of San Diego. Shearer, who also wrote for the segregationist journal *The Citizen* arguing that the GOP could win national elections if it could "kick free of the ball and chain of integration," helped frame the anti–Rumford Act fight as a defense of property rights and freedom of choice.[40] The California Real Estate Association may have been embarrassed by the support it received from the American Nazi Party members who marched outside the El Cortez Hotel, where they met in 1963, but when the realtors voted overwhelmingly to fight against the Rumford Act and all future legislation against housing discrimination, they were marching in lockstep with the fascists.[41] Proposition 14, which would have overturned the Rumford Fair Housing Act, passed with a large majority in the state and by more than two to one in San Diego County.[42] If not for the California Supreme Court, the far right would have won. Hence, when contemporary groups like the White Aryan Resistance, teenage skinheads in Lakeside, or nameless racist thugs and vandals make their way into the news, they are only saying out loud what the majority of San Diegans expressed in the not-too-distant past.

In 1965 the Fair Employment Practices Commission called San Diego one of the most segregated areas in the country and linked that segregation to employment discrimination.[43] The city's racism was also indicated by the fact that by the late 1960s there were only about one hundred blacks attending San Diego State College, and that it took until 1972 to break down racial barriers in the building trades.[44] As the city continues to grow and diversify, its largely unrecognized racial tensions are bound to re-emerge.

The Chinese were literally imported to San Diego as a cheap labor pool, exploited, and generally reviled by their fellow workers and the population at large. Very few Chinese people lived in San Diego until some local businessmen met Ah Quin in Northern California and asked him to come to San Diego as a labor contractor for the construction of the railroad. By 1884 there were hundreds of Chinese working on the line.[45] As that number grew to 800, San Diego developed its own anti-Chinese movement. In December 1885 the anti-Chinese Club was founded to call for the firing of Chinese workers "as long as a white man was out of work."[46] San Diego's first strike was also partly an effort to force companies "to pledge not to hire Chinese labor."[47] This was despite the fact that no Chinese worker held any of the highest-paid skilled jobs and suffered "the least pay and job security."[48] As a result, San Diego's Chinese population fell to 561 after the railroad was finished in the 1890s.[49] Those who stayed were segregated into the Stingaree, the city's red-light district, where they lived among prostitutes, pimps, criminals, gamblers, and drug addicts in quarters behind opium dens or illegal gambling houses.[50] Because of the federal Exclusion Acts, their numbers stayed low for most of the first half of the twentieth century, until some of the most repressive limitations on Chinese immigration ceased. Today, most of the traces of the original Chinese community have been erased, except for a tiny block on the edge of the Gaslamp Quarter and a few hard to discern historical markers.

The Japanese first came to San Diego in the 1880s as well. They made charcoal for the Hotel del Coronado and worked as waiters, gardeners, shopkeepers, handymen, farmers, fishermen, and cannery workers. They outfished the natives and brought innovations to agriculture.[51] Their competence, however, created a racist backlash and laws were passed that banned Japanese land ownership. When forced into wage labor, they were seen as an unattractive workforce because of their tendency to organize. As one writer put it, "They demand high wages and are exceedingly independent and untractable."[52] In 1914 James Phelan, a candidate for the U.S. Senate, argued that the Japanese government should be told that Japanese immigrants were "unassimilable" but "efficient human machines" who were "a menace to our prosperity and happiness."[53] A 1932 issue of the *San Diego Labor Leader* includes an article blaming "Japs" rather than the Depression for the woes of the fishing industry.[54] The bombing of Pearl Harbor provided the perfect excuse for exercising the already virulent hatred of the Japanese. In February 1942 Executive Order 9066 was issued, and all of San Diego County south of the San Dieguito River was designated a "military zone" and "all persons of Japanese ancestry, both alien and non-alien" were rounded up. The Japanese sold whatever they could and abandoned the rest, and then were forced to report to the Santa Fe Depot to be placed on guarded trains. Their first stop was a racetrack in Los Angeles. By August, most of the detainees had been shipped to a hot, barren Relocation Camp in Poston, Arizona, to choke on dust and ponder their fate as the desert wind swirled around them.[55] San Diego's Japanese community was gone. As if this were not enough, in 1943 the San Diego Chamber of Commerce passed a resolution protesting the "coddling of these Japanese in internment camps."[56]

The city of San Diego was not built on Anglo-Saxonism alone, however, as the boosters' aversion to major industrial development shows. From the beginning, San Diego's elite knew that if they were to build a garden city free of not just the ethnic conflicts but also the class strife that plagued other cities, they would have to devise a growth plan that avoided the importation of an unruly working class. Central to this strategy was their decades-long courtship of the Navy. As Abraham Shragge documents in his intensive study of San Diego's obsession with the Navy (*Boosters and*

Bluejackets: The Civic Culture of Militarism in San Diego, California, 1900–1945), the boosters saw the Navy as the answer to their dreams because, as the *Union* put it, "[Men] of that establishment [were] of a high class."[57] The Navy did not just bring in large amounts of federal money, Shragge adds: "The boosters believed that there were no radicals of the scurrilous IWW type in the Navy, nor petty crooks; as well, the pre–World War II Navy was almost exclusively white in its racial composition."[58] Thanks to the relentless efforts of San Diego's boosters, along with the political savvy of Congressman William Kettner, the plan eventually succeeded.

Even after World War II, the Chamber of Commerce was still working "to bring to San Diego the right type of people" by maintaining a "well-directed advertising campaign designed to reach a better class of resident and visitor."[59] The postwar city was still segregated, with a relatively tranquil labor movement. Even most of San Diego's "Rosie the Riveters" had been forced out of gainful employment by defense industry cutbacks and the wave of returning GI's.[60] While the civil rights movement and other 1960s upheavals challenged the city's status quo, the city's basic economic structure remains favorable to a conservative Anglo elite. The military remains a central economic engine, followed by federally subsidized aerospace industries, tourism, and higher education and academic research.[61] This has perpetuated a wide gap between affluent professionals and the growing low-wage service sector. Unionization has steadily declined and women and people of color are overrepresented in the lowest-paying service sector jobs. Part-time employment with no benefits is also on the rise as housing prices and rents soar beyond the reach of many workers. Overall, poverty in San Diego County has increased at a faster pace than elsewhere in California and in the United States as a whole.[62]

While the changing demographics of San Diego present a challenge to the new boosters, the city continues to reward corporations and sports teams with substantial benefits while largely failing to address the needs of the poor and racial minorities. Even in the midst of the nation's largest economic expansion in history, 61 percent of African American families, 51 percent of Latino families, 18 percent of Asian families, and 10 percent of white families were living in poverty in San Diego in 1997.[63] Seen in this light, the redevelopment of downtown into an entertainment complex for affluent consumers dotted with new condos "starting at only $700,000!" is just the latest installment in the same old story of booster class war fought from the top down. San Diego is no longer the lily-white Navy-tourist town it was for most of its history, and it remains unclear how long the city's elite can maintain the happy theme-park image of "America's Finest City." The weather is still nice, but the contradictions are growing, and they threaten to burst through the city's glossy veneer. As opposed to the boosters' version of San Diego's history, there have been rumblings and moments of rebellion in the theme park.

Red Flag over Tijuana: "Daredevil Dick" and the "Wretched Band of Outlaws"[64]

> Workers of the World Awaken!/Your comrades call from Mexico.
> *Laura Emerson, San Diego Wobbly poet*[65]

> You have got to haul down this red flag!
> *Dick Ferris, San Diego booster*[66]

> Man is worth nothing; the idea is everything.
> *Ricardo Flores Magón, anarchist*[67]

In 1911, San Diego, Tijuana, and the entire Southern California border region were swept up into a now obscure chapter of the Mexican Revolution, an anarchist uprising inspired by the brilliant but tactically incompetent Ricardo Flores Magón. Flores Magón, who had been imprisoned for his opposition to the Porfirio Díaz regime in Mexico in 1903, was released from jail after a year and fled to Los Angeles, where he reorganized his Liberal Party in exile and wrote searing attacks on the Mexican dictatorship in his party's main organ, *La Regeneración*. As opposed to Francisco I. Madero, whose forces eventually did overthrow Díaz, Flores Magón and his Liberal Party expressed not the wishes of the moderate, middle-class nationalists of Mexico but the unspoken desires of the majority working class.[68] The Magonistas were unique because, as Flores Magón put it in a letter from a Mexican jail, "No liberal party in the world has the anti-capitalist tendencies of we who are about to begin a revolution in Mexico."[69] In a manifesto written on September 23, 1911, he clearly differentiates the Liberal Party's aims from those of Madero: "All others are offering you political liberty when they have triumphed. We Liberals invite you to take immediate possession of the land, the machinery, the means of transportation and the buildings, without expecting anyone to give them to you and without waiting for any law to decree it."[70]

The son of an Indian mother and a Mestizo father, Flores Magón grew up idealizing the communal lives of Oaxaca's Indians as opposed to what he saw as the corrupt artificiality of Mexico City. As an adult, his reading of Kropotkin, Bakunin, and Marx, as well as his brutal treatment at the hands of the Díaz dictatorship, fused with the lessons of his youth to create a passionate utopianism rooted in a belief that only communal ownership of the land and the dissolution of organized government would create real human freedom.[71] Hence, when the Magonista army took Tijuana, they hoisted a red flag emblazoned with the slogan "*Tierra y Libertad*" and issued a proclamation calling on the people to "take the land."[72] Unfortunately, Flores Magón's powerful idealism was not accompanied by shrewd tactical thinking, and his dream of an anarchist utopia was hijacked by a shameless opportunist and San Diego booster, "Daredevil" Dick Ferris, in what is surely the most bizarre series of events in the history of the city.

Flores Magón brought his revolution-in-exile to a Los Angeles that was in the midst of its own labor war after the bombing of the *Los Angeles Times* building by AFL unionists in 1910 and the growing influence of the Industrial Workers of the World (IWW), which had inspired an open-shop drive and an antilabor propaganda campaign in Southern California.[73] In addition to this, *Times* owner Harrison Gray Otis, as well as *San Diego Union* owner John D. Spreckels, had extensive water, land, and railroad holdings in both the Imperial Valley and Baja California, Mexico.[74] Thus, as Lowell Blaisdell argues in *The Desert Revolution,* it should have been obvious to Flores Magón that the odds of mounting a successful revolutionary campaign in a sparsely populated area with little money and no military experience were slim.[75] Consequently, what little scholarship there is on the Magonista revolt has investigated the charge that the Magonistas were actually a front for a filibuster designed by American capitalists to capture Baja from Mexico.[76] Given the fact that no solid evidence of a real filibuster exists, what emerges is the farcical story of an anarchist revolution expropriated by boosters to sell the Panama-California Exposition that they hoped would help woo the military and promote real estate in San Diego. As the Panama-California Exposition solemnly celebrated the emergence of an imperial America backed by God as well as by massive naval firepower, and showcased San Diego's desirability as a strategic port,[77] the Ferris filibuster spectacle that preceded it grabbed headlines by crassly exploiting a life-and-death situation and making a joke of Mexican independence for the sake of publicity.

In the beginning, Flores Magón's cause was received well both in California and in national labor and Left circles. Partisans generated funds by selling *La Regeneración,* took in donations from individual workers and unions, and got fairly favorable press coverage. Italian anarchists and the IWW were their biggest supporters.[78] The IWW, with its anarcho-syndicalist philosophy of organizing all workers into "One Big Union" without racial, craft, or any other distinctions, and with its instinctive distrust of the bourgeois state and legal system, was the most likely, if not perfect, fit with Flores Magón's anarchism. Like the Liberal Party, the Wobblies were born of repression, believed in direct action, and had an open-door policy with regard to membership. As one IWW organizer put it, "One man is as good as another to me; I don't care if he's black, blue, green, or yellow, as long as he acts the man and acts true to his economic interests as a worker."[79] Flores Magón too had an internationalist perspective: "In the ranks of the Liberals are men who are not our nationality but are our ideological brothers. . . . They sacrifice themselves to destroy the chains of our slavery."[80] These attitudes help explain why the Wobblies supplied the largest number of soldiers for the Liberals. Still, the great irony of the Magonista army was that the majority of its members were gringos, not Mexicans fighting for independence. Richard Griswold del Castillo cites several reasons for the failure of the Magonistas to attract more Mexicans to fight with the American radicals, including the abstract nature of Flores Magón's rhetoric, the small population of northern Baja, the United States Army presence at the border, the junta's lack of connection with the region, and, most important, the perception of the Army as a filibustering expedition.[81] One might also add to this list the junta's careless recruitment of ideologically suspect mercenaries in the name of expediency, the fact that Ricardo Flores Magón never left the Liberal Party's headquarters in Los Angeles (making communication with the rebel army difficult, to say the least), Flores Magón's choice to distribute more copies of Kropotkin than bullets, the racial tension that existed between some of the troops despite the official rhetoric of the revolt, and the general chaos on the ground.[82] Nonetheless, in the face of these seemingly insurmountable odds, the revolt got off to a good start. After receiving the word from Los Angeles, the rebels began planning an attack on Mexicali at the IWW headquarters in Holtville, a small town near the border in the Imperial Valley. After a successful scouting operation, about thirty mostly Mexican Magonistas, led by José Maria Leyva, took Mexicali in a predawn raid on Sunday, January 29, 1911, killing only the town jailor.[83] The Liberal Revolution was born.

Less than a week after the fall of Mexicali, a meeting was held in support of the Magonistas at the Los Angeles Labor Temple. They raised $140, and Socialist novelist Jack London penned a manifesto in support of the rebels:

> We Socialists, anarchists, hobos, chicken thieves, outlaws, and undesirable citizens of the United States are with you heart and soul. You will notice that we are not respectable. Neither are you. No revolutionary can possibly be respectable in these days of the reign of property. All the names you are being called, we have been called. And when graft and greed get up and begin to call names, honest men, brave men, patriotic men and martyrs can expect nothing else than to be called chicken thieves and outlaws. So be it. But I for one wish there were more chicken thieves and outlaws of the sort that formed that gallant band that took Mexicali. I subscribe myself a chicken thief and revolutionist.[84]

In San Diego, the local Anti-Interference League sponsored a speech by Emma Goldman at Germania Hall that raised $113 on the eve of the battle of Tijuana. The league, whose members included prominent local Socialist Kasper Bauer and progressive lawyer E. E. Kirk, was formed to oppose United States intervention in Mexico. Bauer and Kirk were also the local contacts for the Magonistas.[85] Events such as these soon swelled the ranks of the rebels, which came to include around

150 men, comprised of Mexicans from the Mexicali area, Cocopah Indian scouts, IWW volunteers, and a number of soldiers of fortune.[86] Despite a lack of military funding from Los Angeles and constant chaos and squabbling in the field, the Mago- nistas managed to briefly take Tecate and hold off a lackluster attempt by Mexican federal forces to recapture Mexicali.[87] The leadership of the rebel army underwent several changes, with some of the Mexicans leaving to fight with Madero and the troops squabbling about tactics and leadership. By the time of their biggest victory, however, the Magonistas were under the command of Caryl Ap Rhys Pryce, a Welsh soldier of fortune who had fought in India and South Africa and, after reading John Kenneth Turner's condemnation of the Díaz regime entitled *Barbarous Mexico,* had developed a fledgling sense of social justice.[88] While his military experience proved a temporary asset, his lack of any deep commitment to the cause, along with his affin- ity for Dick Ferris, ultimately proved disastrous.

The new commander's greatest achievement was the result of either direct disobe- dience or a mistake. Flores Magón had sent orders directing the rebels to march east and attack the Mexican forces near Mexicali. Instead, the day after thirty Indians led by Juan Guerrero had taken the tiny port town of San Quintin, Pryce turned west and attacked Tijuana. At dawn on May 9, 220 Magonistas seized the small town after a fierce battle that killed 32 and wounded 24.[89] After the battle, while the rebels behaved with some restraint, a group of sightseers from San Diego crowded into the town and looted the shops.[90] This marked the beginning of the steady, farcical decline of the revolt, with the Los Angeles junta refusing to dismiss the untrust- worthy Pryce or to give him aid or more ammunition. As Flores Magón remained inactive, the rebels were forced to open Tijuana for tourism and gambling in order to raise money. Battle watching was a popular spectator sport along the border with the occasional spectator actually falling to a stray bullet.

Once the battle was over in Tijuana, the town received a large number of tourists who were just as interested in meeting members of the eccentric Magonista army as they were in watching the battle. San Diegans were fascinated by the wild mix of cowboys, Wobbly hobos, mercenaries, black army deserters, Mexicans, Indians, and opportunists. The army lacked any traditional class hierarchy and was characterized by the rough camaraderie that was common among the Wobblies and their fellow *lumpenproletariat*.[91] Magonista soldiers were happy to pose for pictures with visitors and also for postcard reenactments of the battle that were sold in A. Savin's Bazaar Mexicano, the town's most visited curio shop. The "*tarjetas postales*" sign is evident in still-existing photos of the post office where the rebels flew the red flag.[92] It is ironic that the Wobblies, who were so popular as a tourist attraction for slumming San Diegans in Tijuana, would be savagely driven out of San Diego in only a year's time. Apparently, revolution could be enjoyed as a commodity as long as it stayed across the border.

The spectacle of the Magonistas continued to draw visitors and was given a further boost when Dick Ferris reentered the scene. Ferris had been hired as the manager for the upcoming groundbreaking ceremony for the Panama-California Exposition in Balboa Park, and his job was essentially to drum up publicity for San Diego in order to draw attention to the upcoming event and the city itself. Less than a month after the Magonistas took Mexicali, Ferris launched his first scam, which involved giving the Mexican consul in San Francisco an "offer" to buy "lower California" or be faced with a well-funded filibuster. He then had an assistant place an ad in several newspapers calling for a thousand men to come fight for "General Dick Ferris." Ferris even sent a telegram to a Maderista general declaring that "The peninsula rightly belongs to our country, and must, in time, be part of it."[93]

Ferris's first stunt was successful enough to garner an angry response from the Díaz regime and plenty of press coverage about his plans for a "sporting republic" that would offer not just rights but "the pursuit of happiness, whether that happiness may take the form of horse racing, prize fighting, bull baiting, or betting where the little ball will fall."[94] A little more than a month later, Ferris had a Los Angeles horsewoman ride across the border and plant a silk blue flag with a rising sun and the scales of justice embroidered on it on the Mexican side of the border near Agua Caliente. The feminist filibusterer then told the *San Diego Union:* "Lower California, I claim you in the name of equal suffrage and model government."[95] Miss Flora S. Russell then fled across the border amid the Mexican consul's calls for her arrest.

With these two successful promotional scams under his belt, Ferris seized the opportunity that the fall of Tijuana presented. With the aid of a *San Diego Union* reporter he was introduced to Pryce. The *Union* followed this favor with extensive coverage of Ferris's publicity schemes that would seem to indicate the editorial approval of the paper itself, then owned by San Diego's own main booster and robber baron, John D. Spreckels. Whatever the case, Ferris proceeded to befriend the rebel commander and champion his cause, minus the troubling Mexican nationalism and anarchism. He brought Pryce to San Diego and introduced him to several prominent boosters and encouraged him to reconsider his position on "Lower California," which might do well as a "white man's" republic. When Pryce was arrested on his way back across the border, Ferris helped secure his release and tried to stage a hero's welcome for him back in Tijuana, for which Ferris was too late but which the *Union* helped him embellish nonetheless. While all of Ferris's efforts were, in fact, disingenuous maneuvers designed only for publicity, they did stir supporters of the Mexican government to action against the "filibusterers." In San Diego, an anti-Liberal group led by Dr. Horacio E. Lopez raised $1,000 and a good number of recruits to go help fight the mythic gringo filibuster.[96]

Throughout all of this comedic mess, Flores Magón continued to refuse to go to Mexico, aid the rebels, or dismiss Pryce, so Pryce came to the junta to convince them to fold their tents, join forces with Madero, or fight him. When no new directive was forthcoming, Pryce lost all interest in both social justice and filibustering and ended up in Hollywood acting in Westerns before disappearing from history for good. With Pryce out of the picture, Ferris bled the dying revolution of all the publicity it had before he bailed out. After the departure of Pryce, there was a power struggle between the adventurers, Wobblies, and Mexicans. The last gasp of Ferris and the adventurers came when Louis James, who was relentlessly unable to get the Ferris joke, strove to enlist Ferris as their leader and hit up John Spreckels for filibuster funds. When Spreckels refused, James stupidly threatened his Mexican interests, which may explain the *Union*'s eventual loss of sympathy with the filibuster story and Ferris's exploits. For his part, Ferris, with no intention of actually doing anything, went to Tijuana and gave an impromptu speech in which he chastised the rebels to "haul down this red flag" and "cut out your socialism, your anarchism, and every other ism you have gotten into, and form a new government" that would appeal to "the young blood of America."[97] According to James's version of events, Ferris was elected president after his departure, but when James returned with a new flag for a Ferris-led "Republic of Madero" that Daredevil Dick had flippantly sketched out and handed to his tailor, an angry group of Wobblies burned the flag and nearly executed James before deciding to expel him.[98]

None of this prevented Ferris from playing up his possible presidency of a filibuster republic in the press, even as his much-desired publicity gravely insulted Mexicans, destroyed what was left of the Liberal rebellion, and made a less violent end to the conflict impossible. Meanwhile, IWW man Jack Mosby was elected as the new rebel commander and proceeded to threaten to blow up Spreckels's railroad lines if he used them to transport Mexican troops.[99] Spreckels then pressured the United States government to intervene, and Mexican forces finally moved against the Magonistas. With the junta still unable to either offer aid or accept compromise, the Magonistas stayed and fought anyway. On June 22, in the second battle of Tijuana, Mosby led a contingent of 150 Wobblies and 75 Mexicans into a fight against 560 advancing Mexican Federal forces, including many recruited as a result of Ferris's antics. Badly outnumbered and seriously low on supplies, the rebels fought hard but were routed in only three hours. Thirty rebels were killed.[100] The "wretched band of outlaws," as the *Union* was now calling them, had been wiped out. Mosby was captured as he fled weeping across the border and was later shot trying to escape military custody.

Ferris fell from grace as the exposition's manager after his joke backfired. He was charged but not convicted of violating the neutrality law. His fortunes never did reach the same heights as they had while he was boosting for the exposition, although he did return to his original profession, acting, and played himself in a farce called *The Man from Mexico*, in which he continued to exploit the Mexican struggle for freedom as a bad joke for financial gain.[101] After they were released from Federal custody, most of the Wobblies drifted elsewhere, but some stayed in San Diego and sought work in the Wild West show proposed for the exposition.[102]

Ricardo Flores Magón, who had steadfastly refused to leave the junta's headquarters in Los Angeles, eventually lost the support of his fellow Mexicans, who saw him as a pawn for American filibusterers; of the American Federation of Labor (AFL); of the Socialists, who thought his anarchism was too extreme; and finally even of fellow anarchists and the IWW, who condemned him for failing to participate in his own revolution or help defend his comrades. As Lowell Blaisdell concludes in *Desert Revolution,* "As a leader of men, his incompetence was truly breathtaking."[103] Nevertheless, he held true to his faith in "the idea" of human liberation and was duly crucified for it. As opposed to Pryce and Ferris, who were not convicted of violating the neutrality laws, Flores Magón and the leaders of the junta were convicted of violating the neutrality laws and given the maximum sentence. Unrepentant after his release from prison in 1914, Flores Magón again took up the editorship of *La Regeneración.* Within two years of his release, he was again arrested for writing a vehement attack on the Mexican government, and while he was appealing the decision in that case, he was arrested yet another time for violating the Espionage Act by writing a manifesto with Librado Rivera that predicted the downfall of capitalist society, calling on intellectuals to prepare the masses. Although there was no specific reference to World War I in his piece, Flores Magón was convicted and sentenced to twenty years in prison, a clear victim of the Red Scare. When, in 1920, a later administration of the Mexican government offered Rivera and Flores Magón a pension to help ease their time in prison, Flores Magón thanked them graciously but turned the money down on anarchist principle, because, coming from the state, "It is money that would burn my hands and fill my heart with remorse."[104] For the same reason, he refused to even ask for a pardon, knowing that "This seals my fate. I shall go blind, putrify, and die within these horrendous walls. . . . I have lost everything . . . except my honor as a fighter."[105] He was found dead on the floor of his cell in Leavenworth on November 21, 1922.

Ironically, in death, Flores Magón became a hero honored by the Mexican poor. He came to be seen as a predecessor to Zapata, and was buried as a respected revolutionary figure. In *Rebellion in the Borderlands,* James A. Sandos argues that Flores Magón's legacy is important in the American context because his writings in *La Regeneración* expressed the anger of Mexicans and Mexican Americans and helped to inspire rebellions in the Texas border region that were not "an external conspiracy directed by enemies of the United States, but a domestic response to exploitation."[106] Perhaps, Sandos ponders, the old anarchist ideas went "underground" in the Mexican community and were preserved privately "within their families, thereby giving the Chicano community a later militancy."[107] If so, then maybe the San Diego activists who built Chicano Park, the janitors striking for higher wages, the maquiladora workers struggling for their basic rights, the Zapatista support groups, and the globalphobics challenging the excesses of neoliberalism are part of something started long ago. As a desperate Flores Magón wrote in the face of failure and death:

> The dreamer is the designer of tomorrow. Practical men . . . can laugh at him; they do not know that he is the true dynamic force that pushes the world forward. Suppress him, and the world will deteriorate toward barbarism. Despised, impoverished, he leads the way . . . sowing, sowing, sowing the seeds that will be harvested not by him, but by the practical men of tomorrow, who will at the same time laugh at another indefatigable dreamer busy seeding, seeding, seeding.[108]

Tijuana itself was saved from radicalism only to be turned into a playground for wealthy San Diegans, Hollywood stars, and other vice seekers that Ferris would have loved. Less than a decade after the failure of the Magonista revolt, Prohibition turned the Tijuana–San Diego region into a boomtown. One of the central players in all of this was "Sunny" Jim Coffroth, who built a racetrack with money from the Spreckels family.[109] The combination of liquor, gambling, and other illicit pleasures drew many visitors to San Diego and spurred an orgy of building. As Roberta Ridgely observes in her series of *San Diego Magazine* articles on "The Man Who Built Tijuana":

> While thirsting pilgrims funneled through Southern California on their way to the international line, hotels and apartments quickly became San Diego's hottest real-estate items. The tap-tap-tap of the hammers putting up Tijuana saloons and pleasure resorts was echoed by the noise of heavy equipment at work along San Diego streets as the epoch of the stucco-frosted bungalow court and neo-Mission apartment-hotel came into fully landscaped bloom. The future looked as rosy as a Tequila Sunrise.[110]

Largely because of this record building boom, San Diego was by 1924 "the only Pacific Slope city showing as a white spot (indicating good conditions) on the nation's business map."[111] In downtown, grand new structures such as the Balboa and Pantages theaters were built and suburban development exploded.[112] San Diegans' sense of ownership over their backyard was well exemplified when, in 1920, the American Legion successfully demanded the border be opened for their private convention in the midst of a standoff between the governor of Baja and the Mexican government.[113] Indeed, with the bars closed in San Diego, "racing fever was spreading to all walks of life."[114] Spreckels's *Union* was crowing about the amount of money spent by visitors at the track,[115] which exceeded Balboa Park and the beaches as a tourist attraction. Los Angeles was so worried by San Diego's unrivaled tourist attraction across the border that it sent in a "morals squad" to humiliate its southern neighbor. Many San Diegans hypocritically enjoyed the prosperity created by the border trade as they railed against the vices of Tijuana. As Ridgely points out:

> [T]hey liked to delude themselves that the only beginning-to-be-developed beaches, the tiny zoo, the Park, and a few fringe attractions . . . were entirely responsible for the accommodations shortage, for the rage of construction, and for the Pan Pacific luxury liners electing to make the town a port of call.[116]

Thus, pious reformers who had conveniently forgotten the city's history of brothels, gambling, and opium dens in its own Stingaree district engaged in an effort to preserve a mythological "Old San Diego innocence," and lobbied for the "nine o'clock law," which shut the border down early.[117] In response to their efforts, the twenties version of contemporary *coyotes* in reverse shuttled Anglo visitors back and forth through "the famous Hole in the Fence," which all the track employees knew about as well as Tijuana regulars and "the In crowd of San Diego and Hollywood."[118] The labor movement was also opposed to Tijuana's "illicit traffic in drugs, booze, and women." Apparently angered by a Tijuana promoter's effort "to break up the Labor Day celebration at Balboa Park," the *San Diego Labor Leader* threatened to expose the "prominent citizens" who owned the den of inequity.[119] The Labor Council's mouthpiece, which also frequently protested the importation of unskilled Mexican

workers to San Diego, was apparently unconcerned by the racist employment practices of the resort owners across the border. In 1923, the Tivoli was invaded by fifty
Mexicans who rioted, overturned gambling tables, and tried to make their way to
the Foreign Club, protesting the fact that only whites were employed in many of
the bars and casinos frequented by San Diego's wealthy Anglos.[120] This spontaneous uprising failed to disturb the fun seekers for long, but by 1926 a new group of
Mexican *insurrectos* along the border was enough to slow the party down.[121] While
San Diego's Anglo booster party animals were happy to chug down the czar's vodka
purchased from the Bolsheviks,[122] Mexican rebels with guns still made them nervous.
Flores Magón would have been happy.

Kissing the Flag: Terrorist Patriotism versus Free Speech and Public Space

> The little flags which the citizens of San Diego are wearing are outward evi-
> dence of the determination that treason shall never again be tolerated in San
> Diego, by word of foul mouths or by the flaunting red rag of anarchy.
> San Diego Union *(1912)*

> Your commissioner has visited Russia and while there has heard many
> horrible tales of high-handed proceedings and outrageous treatment of
> innocent people at the hands of despotic and tyrannical Russian authori-
> ties. Your commissioner is frank to confess that when he became satisfied
> of the truth of the stories, as related by these unfortunate men, it was hard
> for him to believe that he was not still sojourning in Russia, conducting
> his investigation there instead in this alleged "land of the free and home of
> the brave." Surely, these American men, who as the overwhelming evidence
> shows, in large numbers assaulted with weapons in a most cowardly and
> brutal manner their helpless and defenseless fellows were certainly far from
> "brave" and their victims were far from "free."
> *Colonel Harris Weinstock*[123]

> Out there in San Diego
> Where the western breakers beat,
> They're jailing men and women
> For speaking on the street.
> *IWW song*[124]

In an August 2000 issue of the *San Diego Metropolitan,* a local business journal, Jerry Butkiewicz, head of the San Diego–Imperial County Central Labor Council, is quoted as saying, "I really have no idea how San Diego's reputation [as an antilabor town] got started because it happened long before I was involved in the labor movement."[125] The feature, "Busting the Anti-Union Myth," briefly addresses the brutal history of the San Diego free speech fight but focuses mainly on giving a sunny picture of the local labor movement. While Butkiewicz deserves credit for working hard to create a strong and active labor movement, and it is certainly a good sign that the business press would spend time giving favorable coverage to local labor leaders, the notion that San Diego's bad reputation as an antiunion town is a "myth" is wishful thinking at best and disingenuous boosterism at worst. Even a casual review of what little labor history there is on San Diego reveals that if there is a "myth" about San Diego labor relations, it is that "America's Finest City" is an exception to the rule of class conflict that has frequently marred Los Angeles and San Francisco as well as other large American cities. The *only* full-length study of San Diego labor is the 1959 *A Short History of the San Diego Labor Movement,* a report by Frederick L. Ryan financed by the AFL-CIO and First National Trust and Savings Bank of San Diego. In it, Ryan makes the claim that a "reasonable attitude on the part of both business and labor leaders . . . made labor conditions different in San Diego. This tolerance is characteristic of a middle-class type of society in which the members on both sides are fairly prosperous and confident of their future."[126] This is the study's central thesis, the way it was reported in the local press,[127] and the way it has been noted by scholars who cite Ryan as the "Dean of San Diego Labor History." If one reads his work to the end, however, the narrative seems inconsistent, as Ryan concludes:

> The Gompers tradition has remained strong in San Diego, and for years the unions suffered one political defeat after another. They were continually "off-balance," fighting against proposed legislation that would introduce the open shop in one form or another or that would limit the unions' use of the strike and boycott. Nor were they able to rely on the common working man because the common laborer had little sympathy with the crafts.[128]

The successes Ryan attributes to the San Diego labor movement are the enforcement of "minimum standards" and the fact that the "existence of unions was protected."[129] These are hardly convincing arguments for a strong labor movement. Interestingly, Ryan also notes that with the elimination of the most radical elements of the movement, "Something . . . has been lost. . . . The long-term goal of a better society that appealed to the emotions and the ethical principles of the old-time unionists has almost disappeared."[130] Thus a critical reader of Ryan's own history might conclude that the story of labor in San Diego is something very different than a tale of "tolerance" and "reasonable" accommodation. In fact, the history of San Diego's labor movement shows the extreme limits of the Gompers tradition that has ignored unskilled workers and not served immigrants and people of color well, in addition to the extremely hostile and sometimes brutal reception received by all those who have chosen a more radical path. Ryan fails to make this harsher judgment because his study is top-down in nature, blind to issues of race, and apologist with regard to the faults of the conservatism of the Gompers tradition. Hence, while he is very critical of the vigilante response to the IWW, quoting a scholar who compares them to European fascists,[131] Ryan fails to see the full significance of the free speech fight for San Diego labor, no less the history of the city itself.

If Ryan's take on the free speech fight is lacking, other local historians have also failed to address it at all or have sought to diminish its importance. The predominance of booster history written to be sold to tourists explains much of this. A lot of local "history lite" treats the issue as a colorful but forgettable part of San Diego's otherwise pleasant past or as an amusing tale of when the eccentric radicals came to town. Most of the serious considerations of the free speech fights have come in sections of books on the IWW or California labor, not the city of San Diego.[132] To date, there is no book-length study on the San Diego free speech fight. One reason for this may have been hostility toward the Wobblies by local historians themselves. For instance, scholars researching the free speech fight at the San Diego Historical Society (SDHS) archives are likely to review the vertical file of periodical articles on the IWW. A careful observer of these materials will note a "Memorandum to the Files" dated April 24, 1954, by G. F. MacMullen, director of the SDHS from

1954–64, which states, "The foregoing is set forth as a starter for a file on this phase of San Diego's history—a phase which has been considerably garbled by present-day 'liberal' historians."[133] The rest of the memorandum gives an unsympathetic summary of several events surrounding the free speech fight during which, MacMullen tells us, he was fourteen. He then cites the *Union*, the mouthpiece for the vigilantes, as evidence for his point of view. The articles in the file are almost entirely collected from papers hostile to the IWW, with not one single document from the liberal or labor press. MacMullen's hostility toward "liberal" history is remarkable given the fact that, as Daniel Cornford tells us in the introduction to his 1995 anthology, *Working People of California,* the history of labor and people of color was slow to make inroads in the Golden State and "the new social history did not make a major impact on the writing of California history . . . until the late seventies and early eighties."[134] Attitudes like MacMullen's show why that history has been even more tardy in reaching San Diego.

Rosalie Shanks's award-winning [135] 1973 *Journal of San Diego History* article "The I.W.W. Free Speech Movement, San Diego, 1912," is probably more liberal than G. F. MacMullen would have preferred but it still mythologizes the past by portraying the free speech fight as a struggle between "two violent mobs,"[136] a move that inoculates San Diego against more severe criticism by admitting some wrongdoing. This kind of intellectual homeopathy is an ideological apologist's stock in trade, as Roland Barthes reminds us: "One inoculates the public with a contingent evil to prevent or cure an essential one."[137] The essential "evil" that Shanks's essay conceals is the fact that the vigilantes were not aberrations in San Diego's otherwise tolerant hegemony but rather an expression of the city's essential character. Shanks cites Ryan as her evidence of the city's otherwise liberal character when she argues that, "In direct contrast to the bitter opposition in the Los Angeles area, a distinctive attitude existed in San Diego that was reasonably tolerant toward organized labor."[138] She then goes even further by ludicrously suggesting that the *San Diego Union,* because it had supported child labor laws, was a bastion of "liberal if not radical" thinking on labor issues despite its overall conservatism. The fact that the *Union*'s owner, John D. Spreckels, was a major proponent of open shop, a member of the vigilante committee,[139] and owner of a business that had been organized by the IWW is not mentioned.

Shanks's own prose is also instructive as she puts quotation marks around "free speech"[140] when addressing the Wobblies' grievances, refers to the "hordes" of their membership,[141] and speaks sympathetically about San Diego's "anxiety" over the upcoming fair: "While in preparation for her debut as an important cultural and seaport city, San Diego could not afford to allow radicals to disrupt her labor force and flood her streets with inflammatory speakers of questionable 'moral' character."[142] She also notably refers to a *Tribune* editorial about lynching Wobblies as a call for "capital punishment,"[143] cites the virulently anti-IWW press for much of her evidence of IWW violence and wrongdoing, and inaccurately characterizes Special Commissioner Harris Weinstock's conclusions about the events in San Diego as "thoroughly confused" and equally condemning of both sides.[144] Thus, even though she ends the essay by defending free speech, it is clear that the Wobblies are to be "detested" along with the vigilantes.[145] While the handful of master's theses, dissertations, and periodical articles that exist on the subject do a better job than Shanks, the history of the IWW in San Diego has largely been ignored or underplayed by subsequent generations of San Diegans.

California's preeminent historian, Kevin Starr, has noted that despite the fact that labor and radicals were persecuted all over the United States during the early twentieth century, "No state pursued its radicals more remorselessly than did California."[146] Furthermore, he argues that "both the resistance and the suppression of the IWW revealed the paranoid underside to public life in the Golden State."[147] In no place was this more evident than San Diego. As Philip S. Foner argues in *The Industrial Workers of the World, 1905–1917,* the other free speech fights were "a tea party"[148] compared to the struggle the IWW and their sympathizers engaged in when they came up against "the worst enemies of organized labor in the United States"[149] and fell victim to "some of the worst brutality against prisoners in American history."[150] The paranoid hysteria, blind hatred, and eventual terrorism that the IWW inspired in the Anglo booster oligarchy and their petty bourgeois minions exposed the brutality that follows when the powerful come to perceive themselves as victims. In this case, the crime that had been committed against the aggrieved elites was not so much speech or any real threat to their power but simply the existence of an "other," which defined itself against their mythological version of the past and their Social Darwinist dreams of the future. The IWW and its constituency were, by their very existence, an affront to the booster's self-proclaimed identity. Because of this they could not be allowed to speak, occupy public space, or for that matter even exist in the presence of the boosters' version of the future.[151]

What the IWW threatened to do was upset the racial and class hierarchy that had been so carefully constructed and maintained in San Diego. Before the IWW came to the city, no one had even thought to organize unskilled laborers. The first IWW local, 245, which was then prophetically changed to the unlucky 13, was set up in 1904 at the urging of Frank Little to do just that.[152] The Wobblies sought to organize Mexican workers who had been neglected by the local AFL. Their efforts aroused criticism of the AFL and resulted in some unions leaving the Labor Council, which then denounced the IWW in the local papers.[153] As opposed to the AFL, which, as has been noted, was frequently hostile to immigrant and unskilled workers, the IWW was antiracist and internationalist in outlook, actually seeking out the most marginalized workers to organize. The Wobblies were the only American union to oppose exclusion laws and organize Asian workers as well as racially excluded blacks and Mexicans. Jews, Catholics, and recent immigrants were also welcome.[154] As a federal investigator into the Colorado mining wars put it, the Wobblies were "born out of the fires of that conflict."[155] They rejected contracts, believed in direct action, were suspicious of political organization, and mixed anarchism, syndicalism, Marxism, and an inverted form of Social Darwinism freely, as their rough and ready membership regarded such distinctions as useless nitpicking.[156] The IWW opened its doors to all comers with very low dues and gave its previously impotent and excluded membership a sense of community and a way to channel its deep grievances.[157]

In an obscure 1956 book, *Skid Row U.S.A.,* Sara Harris interviewed former Wobblies about what the union meant to them. One old Wobbly, "Rickety Stan," describes why he joined the IWW and what it meant to him:

Things was terrible. . . . Them bosses' hearts was made up from rusty iron. Say some workingmen had a argument with the bosses, the bosses was not worrying. By them in the head they had it figured out was always plenty men would work for nothing and never give the boss no arguments neither. They thought dumb workers was the cheapest things in the world. Till one time the dumb workers begun to get smart and says to each other, "Alone we ain't nothing but weakers." So what's to do, ha? Nothing? Nothing like hell! Is plenty to do. Is get together and organize a union. We won't be weakers no more if we got our own union. So the hobo workers organized and we got us the one big union. . . . Never did find a place to lay my head steady before my union came. No matter where I was working, things'd always get so bad I'd have to move on. After my union, I didn't have to move on unless I wanted to. If things got bad, I could stay right where I was and fight the bosses was making them bad. My union brothers would help me. I never felt like a brother to no man or woman till after I joined the one big union. Before I'd thought I was nothing but a bum. After I got in our union, I found out who the real bums was. Not me and my brothers but the bosses we was working for.[158]

Thus, when the IWW came to San Diego, they sought to turn "bums" into men by transforming the attitude of the town's small disposable labor force from individual shame and defeatism to solidarity and class anger. Their method was street-speaking. In *We Shall Be All,* Melvin Dubofsky explains that "[f]or the Wobblies free-speech fights involved nothing so abstract as defending the Constitution, preserving the Bill of Rights, or protecting the civil liberties of American citizens."[159] They were interested in "overcoming resistance to IWW organizing tactics" and demonstrating that "America's dispossessed could, through direct action, challenge established authority."[160] The aim was to show workers who were dubious about legal and political reform "the effectiveness of victories gained through a strategy of open yet nonviolent confrontations with public officials."[161] The IWW sought to win free speech fights in order to preserve and enhance their recruitment efforts as well as their ability to educate unskilled workers about how antiunion employers and the turnover of common laborers keep wages down.[162] Rickety Stan describes how he used to agitate:

I let them have it straight. I said, "How do you like living the way you live anyways?" The fellow's always say the same things I used to before my organization came. "What do you mean how I like it? All I know I got to *live*. Right?" So then I'd say, "Well my friend, there's living and there's living. Why should bosses live so good and you and me live so lousy? Who say the world's got to be like that?"[163]

While many of the press reports and unsympathetic historical accounts cite obscene language as one the primary offenses of the soapboxers, talk such as this was probably even more unwelcome to San Diego's oligarchy. Stan also describes the tenacity of the free speech fighters, recalling proudly that "they was sure scared of littler agitators like me. . . . A sheriff's man came with a whip and hit me over the face and punched me in the belly and threw me in jail. . . . I couldn't ever have quit. What did beatings or jail matter compared to the class struggle?"[164] This kind of commitment to endure numerous beatings and jailings in the name of the struggle partially explains the brutality with which the Wobblies were met. They were a tough bunch and hard to beat down, but San Diego, more than any other city, upped the ante of brutality in response to both its tenacious foes and the fellow citizens who chose to stand by them. As Dubofsky points out, San Diego was an odd choice for a free speech battle as it didn't have a huge migratory working class or large industry.[165] The reaction they inspired might also seem odd in that there was not a huge base for IWW recruitment. What the wave of intense terrorism unleashed on the free speech fighters shows, however, is how little tolerance there was for even the *idea* of an unruly working class in San Diego. By organizing Mexicans and other unskilled workers and making their presence felt on the streets, the IWW presented the antithesis of the boosters' vision.

The IWW claimed that the real reason for the street-speaking ordinances that banned public speeches was the business elites' fears of their efforts "to educate the floating and out-of work population to a true understanding of the interests of labor as a whole."[166] The Anglo booster oligarchy could be tolerant of a weak, craft-based AFL, and it was fond of using unskilled Mexican and other workers for cheap labor as long as they remained docile, but the thought of a unified, openly rebellious, class-conscious, multiracial working class sent chills down their spines. Hence, when the IWW organized Mexican workers in John D. Spreckels's streetcar franchise and struck, it was as if their worst nightmare had come true. There were only fifty members in Local 13, but the efforts to go after the poorest workers in the mill, lumber, laundry, and gas industries were a profound threat to the symbolic order, as was the location of the Wobblies' oratory, Heller's Corner, at the corner of 5th and E Streets, in the heart of the Stingaree. The Stingaree, which sprawled southward from E Street toward Market, was where the majority of working-class whites, white-ethnic immigrants, blacks, Chinese, and Mexicans lived.[167] Full of shops, saloons, cheap hotels, gambling houses, opium dens, and prostitutes, this district was at the center of the Anglo elite's sordid racist and classist imaginary. It represented the exotic and the debased, vice, violence, and the unruly others who did not fit the "mission" fantasy picture. As a *New York Call* article of that era recounts, one possible motivation for the ban on street speaking was that "it was unpleasant for 'ladies' to pass crowds of ill-clad and grimy-looking workingmen."[168] Rickety Stan describes what street life was like from his perspective: "Nobody knows how a man feels to get treated like a dog and to have nobody care if he lives or dies. I came into town and I seen the way everybody looked at me like I didn't amount to nothing. Just because I was shabby."[169] In the midst of crowds of such men, the Wobblies would stand on soapboxes, denounce the boosters, and try to educate and organize San Diego's working class.

The prospect of the Stingaree's combination of *lumpenproletariat* and unskilled laborers finding common interests across racial and ethnic lines against the boosters was a horror to be avoided at any cost. Hence, the war on free speech went hand in hand with a war on public space. As Foner points out, "San Diego had plenty of room for her traffic and no one believed that this little town in Southern California would suffer a transportation crisis if street meetings continued."[170] The fact that the "restricted district" encompassed forty-nine blocks in the city's working-class core was clearly an effort to eliminate the possibility of San Diego's "undesirable elements" coalescing into a unified group. Indeed, even indoor spaces like Germania Hall were made off-limits by local police.[171] This left the IWW and its sympathizers with two choices: resist or be utterly silenced and erased from the map of the city. The ban on public expression was so complete that it did not stop at radical politics but included the enunciation of more moderate ideas as well as religious ones, making San Diego's law the most restrictive in the country.[172] Hence, the free speech fight was not just a war on the IWW, but on the entire San Diego working class and anyone else who dared dissent from the fascist hegemony.

Even before the anti-street-speaking ordinance was passed, an incident occurred on January 6, 1912, when real estate man and off-duty constable Robert Walsh drove his car into a closed-off Soapbox Row with horn blaring in an effort to disrupt the speakers. His car was rocked and his tires slashed by onlookers even as a Wobbly speaker warned the crowd against giving the police an excuse to break up the meeting, which is exactly what followed.[173] The real action started when San Diego authorities, acting in response to pressure from Spreckels, passed an ordinance banning street speaking that went into effect on February 8, 1912, and was immediately met with civil disobedience by the California Free Speech League. The league, a coalition of AFL unionists, Socialists, Wobblies, religious leaders, and other people of conscience, elected local IWW man Wood Hubbard as secretary, Socialist Casper Bauer as treasurer, and E.E. Kirk of Magonista fame as attorney.[174] Local IWW member Laura Payne Emerson, two other women, and thirty-eight men were the first to be arrested for speaking in public. More arrests followed, and IWW headquarters announced it would flood the city with protesters. Because of this fact, many accounts fail to recognize that the free speech fight in San Diego was not just an IWW affair. It united them with their foes in the AFL, with Socialists, and with a large number of San Diegans who were outraged by the city's emerging fascist tendencies, as the league chastised the Weinstock report for forgetting.[175]

When Superintendent of Police John Sehon issued an order for a roundup of "vagrants," things heated up as the jails filled. City officials responded to the waves of incoming Wobblies by passing a "move-on ordinance" that further extended the powers of the police to break up public assemblies, which they did with increasing brutality, wading into crowds with batons flying and beating prisoners on the way to and in jail. A Labor Council committee sent from San Francisco found that accusations of police brutality were well grounded in fact and that, "Outside the jail *not a single act of violence or even wantonness* has been committed!"[176] Still, despite this and other chidings by state officials, the police's reign of terror continued. Sixty-five-year-old Wobbly Michael Hoey was arrested and savagely beaten by three policemen who kicked him in the groin repeatedly and left him to lie on the cement floor of the overcrowded, vermin-infested cell for weeks until he was finally transferred to the hospital, where he died as a result of his injuries. When 5,000 people showed up to protest the police brutality, they were greeted by a four-hour assault from fire hoses strong enough to knock many of them off their feet. One of the protesters who wrapped himself in the American flag to shield himself from the barrage of water was arrested, roughed up, and fined for "insulting the national emblem."[177] Agnes Smedley, a young girl at the time of the free speech fight, recounts her impression of the war on the streets of San Diego:

> The opponents of free speech were like the land speculators I had known . . . I heard my friends called unspeakable names, saw them imprisoned and beaten, and streams of water from fire hoses turned upon their meetings. I escaped arrest, but the fight released much of the energy dammed up within me. . . . It was in this struggle that I felt the touch of a policeman for the first time. Before me in a small group, two policemen walked deliberately pushing against a workingman who walked peacefully with his hands in his pockets. One of the policemen shoved him until he was hurled against the other policemen; the second policeman then grabbed him by the collar and, shouting that he was attacking an officer of the law, knocked him to the pavement. "That's a lie!" I screamed, horrified, thinking they would listen to me. "That policeman shoved him. . . . I saw him . . . the man had his hands in his pockets." The policemen were already upon the man. Blow after blow they beat into his upturned face, and I saw blood spurt from his eyes.[178]

In May of that year another IWW man, Joseph Mikolasek, was murdered by police who shot him in the leg as he stood outside of the IWW headquaters. After being shot, Mikolasek reached for an ax to defend himself and was then shot four more times. A roundup of Wobblies, not an investigation into the shooting, followed the murder.

The only response many of the prisoners could make was to sing. Rickety Stan recalls the IWW songs with fondness: "You should have heard us singing with all our voices together. Sometimes we used to put our arms around each other. We always sang about what us workers would do to the bosses and their tools. It was good."[179] The purpose of the songs was to express solidarity and defiance and, simultaneously, drive their jailors to their wits' end. Police Chief Wilson, for one, saw the singing as an expression of the depraved nature of the Wobblies, as he complained to the Labor Council committee sent to investigate from San Francisco:

> These people do not belong to any country, no flag, no laws, no Supreme Being. I do not know what to do. I cannot punish them. Listen to them singing. They are singing all the time, yelling and hollering, and telling the jailors to quit work and join the union. They are worse than animals.[180]

If the police chief thought the brutal treatment dished out by his charges was insufficient, he was not in need of help. Vigilantes, urged on by most of the local press, took up the terrorism where the official violence left off. IWW bard Joe Hill, for instance, was so severely beaten by a group of vigilantes that he could barely speak during an appearance at a solidarity rally in Los Angeles.[181]

The vigilantes were backed by many of San Diego's most prominent citizens, praised by the press, and left unmolested by the police, so that they were, in effect, an unofficial arm of the city's power structure. Prominent businessmen and exposition directors such as San Diego's own robber baron John D. Spreckels, banker Julius Wangenheim, and sporting goods manufacturer Frank C. Spalding, as well as lawyers and realtors John and George Burnham, and other booster elites John Forward Jr., Carl Ferris, Percy Goodwin, W. F. Luddington, and Colonel Fred Jewel, were the driving force behind the vigilantes.[182] Kevin Starr argues that the "oligarchs did not take to the streets," but the "threatened middle and lower-middle classes,"[183] as he characterizes the vigilante thugs, would not have been able to operate with such impunity if not for the encouragement and support of the elites in both the city government and the private sector.

However enlightened, the elites who opposed vigilante violence, such as George

Marston, Edward Scripps, Samuel Fox, Ed Fletcher,[184] and others, clearly lost the day and, if they spoke too loudly, paid a steep price for it. In an editorial entitled "Put This in Your Pipe and Smoke It, Mr. Anti-Labor Man," Scripps's paper, the *Sun,* argued in 1910 that "it appears that there are some people in San Diego who think they are able to run this town successfully in the way that General Otis of the *Los Angeles Times* has been trying to run the city of Los Angeles for the last twenty years" and then went on to attack Spreckels by name, suggesting that the city's number one booster believed he "ought not to be taxed for occupying the streets with his railways."[185] According to a contemporary article in the *New York Call,* the *Sun* "took the side against free-speech" and refused to print some accounts of police repression, leaving only the *Herald* and the *Labor Leader* as the voices of dissent. Vendors of these papers, the *Call* claims, were harassed and arrested, while sellers of the *Union,* the *Tribune,* and the *Sun* were unmolested.[186] A close examination of the *Sun,* however, reveals that Scripps's paper, while proclaiming that "San Diego wants none of" the "IWW invasion" or the "anarchist," was a firm supporter of the principle of free speech, the Weinstock investigation, and, at times, an end to police brutality.[187] Specifically, the *Sun* favored the moderate compromise of creating a site where public meetings could be held at all times.[188] This may not have pleased all involved in the free speech fight, but it was a far cry from the position of those who supported the vigilantes. It was probably a combination of Scripps's distaste for the far left and his prominence that saved him from the vigilantes.

Spreckels's *Union* praised the vigilantes and openly threatened anyone who might oppose them. Writing on the wave of terrorism that swept through the city, Spreckels's mouthpiece roared, "And this is what these agitators (all of them) may expect from now on." Flouting all criticism of torture and murder, the paper proclaimed, "If this action be lawlessness, make the most of it."[189] Utterly shameless in its support for some of the worst vigilante violence in the history of the United States, the paper went so far as to attack Colonel Harris Weinstock, the special commissioner who was sent to the city by the governor to investigate human rights abuses, for reading a threat he received from the vigilantes during an address at the Commonwealth Club. Claiming that the letter was probably "written by an I.W.W.," the editorial went on to chastise Weinstock for "the injustice he has so impetuously cast upon 'the ordinary good citizens of San Diego.'"[190]

When the editor of the *San Diego Herald* dared to take the other side in the free speech fight, he was kidnapped, bound, threatened with lynching and run out of town.[191] Defying the threats of the vigilantes, Abram Sauer returned to publish his paper and wrote an article exposing the fact that "The personnel of the vigilantes represents not only the bankers and merchants but has as its workers Church members and bartenders. Chamber of Commerce and Real Estate Board are well represented. The press and public utility corporations, as well as members of the Grand Jury, are known to belong." The vigilantes struck the paper again, breaking into its offices and destroying an upcoming edition, forcing the production of the *Herald* to move to Los Angeles, where it had to be smuggled back into San Diego as contraband.[192] As opposed to the muckraking of the *Herald,* the *Tribune* took a more politically correct line by openly endorsing the lynching of free speech fighters: "Hanging is none to good for them and they would be much better dead; for they are absolutely useless in the human economy; they are waste material of creation and should be drained off in the sewer of oblivion there to rot in cold obstruction like any other excrement."[193] Following Samuel Johnson's maxim that patriotism is the last refuge of a scoundrel, the supporters of extralegal violence proclaimed their love of country, exhorting the opponents of free speech to wear American flags on their labels, and associating their beloved terrorism with other great battles in American history. As the *Union* put it, "Let every loyal citizen of San Diego wear the little flag on his lapel. It is the flag of Yorktown and Gettysburg. No American citizen need be reluctant to wear it, and wearing it his neighbors and fellow citizens will know just where he stands on a question that just now is of vital importance to San Diego."[194]

On April 12, the *Union* ran an announcement by the vigilantes in which they proposed "the deportation of these undesirable citizens" after they had left their "mark on them."[195] The vigilantes taught "patriotism and reverence for the law," as one local journalist put it, by torturing and marking their victims.[196] In one of the most notorious incidents, a drunken, well-armed vigilante army of 400 men wearing white armbands stopped a southbound train from Los Angeles carrying 140 men, over half of whom were under twenty-one, kidnapped them, took them to a cattle corral in the vicinity of San Onofre, and tortured them for eighteen hours.[197] In the corral, the men were forced to run a gauntlet of over a hundred vigilantes, where they were punched, kicked, and struck with pickax handles, wagon spokes, and whips. As one victim, Charles Hanson, remembered it, "The first thing on order was to kiss the flag. 'You son of a Bitch, Come on Kiss it, God damn you.' As he said it I was hit with a wagon wheel spoke all over, when you had kissed the flag you were told to run the gauntlet."[198] As Albert Tucker, another victim, recalls, "Several men were carried out unconscious . . . afterwards there was a lot of our men unaccounted for and never have been heard from since."[199] "Codger" Bill Lewis, Wobbly and brother of one of the IWW men who went to San Diego, recounts, "They kilt two wobs and ya' don't know how many more bodies they mighta' dumped in the desert for the coyotes since a lot of us were what ya' might call foot-loose, without family ties and connections if we was to disappear."[200] One of the weapons reserved for special beatings of defiant Wobblies was an eighteen-inch hose filled with sand and tacks. Toward the end of the nightmare, those who could walk were made to sing the "Star-Spangled Banner" before being released and forced to walk up the tracks toward Los Angeles. This flag-kissing torture ritual was repeated a month later in Sorrento Valley, and other smaller attacks are too numerous to mention.[201]

By the time the famous anarchist Emma Goldman came to speak in San Diego with her partner Ben Reitman, vigilante terror was at its height. At Santa Fe station, she was met by an angry crowd of vigilantes, mostly the same upper-class women whose delicate sensibilities were supposedly offended by the vulgar soapboxers, screaming, "Give us that anarchist; we will strip her naked; we will tear out her guts." Goldman herself remembers that "Fashionably dressed women stood up in their cars screaming: 'We want that anarchist murderess!'"[202] Narrowly escaping this mob, Goldman and Reitman made their way to the U.S. Grant Hotel, where another mob gathered outside in Horton Plaza and the hotel manager warned her that "the vigilantes are in an ugly mood."[203] While Goldman met with Police Chief Wilson and Mayor Wadham to unsuccessfully demand they clear the mob or allow her to speak to the crowd, Reitman was kidnapped from the hotel. He later spoke of his ordeal after being threatened at gunpoint and captured by "several persons who looked like business men" with the help of the police:

> The twenty-mile ride was frightful. . . . As soon as we got out of town, they began kicking and beating me. . . . When we reached the county line, the auto stopped at a deserted spot. The men formed a ring and told me to undress. They tore my clothes off. They knocked me down, and when I lay naked on the ground, they kicked and beat me until I was almost insensible. With a lighted cigar they burned the letters I.W.W. in my buttocks; then they poured a can of tar over my head and, in the absence of feathers, rubbed sage-brush on my body. One of them attempted to push a cane into my rectum. Another twisted my testicles. They forced me to kiss the flag and sing "The Star-Spangled Banner."[204]

The *Union* celebrated the news of Reitman's sadistic, sexualized torture, cheering the departure of Goldman before she could give a scheduled talk, and crowing that "Dr. Ben Rietman is said to be somewhere on his way to Los Angeles, clad thinly in his underwear and a coat of tar and feathers acquired somewhere on the Peñasquitos Ranch twenty miles to the north of this city after being forced to kneel and kiss the Stars and Stripes and promise never to return to San Diego."[205] In *Living My Life,* Goldman recounts how Reitman was never the same after the assault: "His whole being was centered on San Diego, and it became almost a hallucination with him."[206] When, in 1913, the two returned after his recovery only to be driven out again by J. M. Porter and his vigilante fellows, Reitman was "consumed with terror"[207] and could not bring himself to return a third time, after the free speech fight was over, when Goldman finally spoke unharrassed by thugs in 1915.

Colonel Weinstock's report on the violence in San Diego illustrated that the Merchants and Manufacturers Association, the Chamber of Commerce, the San Diego press, and "much of the intelligence, the wealth, the conservatism, the enterprise, and also the good citizenship of the community" had organized and participated in criminal vigilante behavior and recommended the governor direct Attorney General Webb to intervene, but no substantial action was taken other than some public chiding.[208] As Melvyn Dubofsky puts it, "No agency of government was prepared in 1912 to defend the civil liberties of citizens who flouted the traditions and rules of America's dominant classes."[209] Indeed, the only serious consequence befalling the vigilantes was the citing of J. M. Porter for contempt of court, while the real powers behind the terror got off scot-free. In fact, Spreckels and others went over the heads of state officials and pressured the federal government to investigate the IWW. While this specific request never resulted in any arrests, the IWW was, in the years to come, to be the victim of the intense paranoia of the Red Scare, as laws were passed specifically to prosecute them.

Technically, as Carey McWilliams claims, the San Diego free speech fight was won,[210] and when Emma Goldman finally did speak in San Diego in 1915, an enthusiastic member of the Open Forum argued that "out of the fire [of the free speech fight] has come the intellectual salvation not only of the martyrs, but of all the inhabitants of the city."[211] Local IWW member Laura Payne Emerson was less optimistic: "The sacred spot where so many I.W.W.'s were clubbed and arrested last winter lies safe and secure from the unhallowed thread of the hated anarchist, and in fact, from all other human beings. . . . They have the courts, the jails and funds. What are we going to do about it?"[212] In the final analysis, while the heroism of the Wobblies and their supporters who endured brutal beatings and torture, on multiple occasions in some cases, for the right to free speech must be remembered, it is clear that the vigilantes won the more important battle. Their terrorism cleared the city of "undesirable citizens" and taught not just radicals but all working people, unionists, and other marginalized groups that the price for stepping outside the accepted parameters of political speech and activity in San Diego was very steep indeed. The boosters, via legal and extralegal violence, were able to maintain unquestioned control over the shape and future of the city. They would have their exposition, lure the Navy to town, and ensure the city's conservative course for decades to come.

The fight for free speech and access to public space reemerged in the 1930s as unions frequently struggled for the right to picket and/or leaflet businesses downtown. In the sixties, the Congress of Racial Equality (CORE) struggled for those same rights on the streets and Herbert Marcuse fought the American Legion for the right to teach unpopular ideas at UCSD. San Diego's countercultural newspapers, the *Door* and the *Street Journal*, were attacked by local authorities and right-wing vigilantes with regularity, and local activists were spied on by police. Hence, the notion that the free speech fight was a one-time struggle in San Diego is wishful thinking. Public art, which criticized racism and police brutality in "America's Finest City" in the 1980s and 1990s, lost its funding and caused a considerable angry backlash. Even recent petty battles over whether people without beachfront property can drink beer on the beach reflect the old struggle between those who think they own the city and those who believe in the democratic right for anyone to use public space. Perhaps the Wobblies' ghosts would be gratified to know that at the yearly Raiders-Chargers game, the Silver and Black's much-hated *lumpen* fan base invades the city and pummels genteel San Diegans with impunity in a farcical inversion of the city's vigilante past.

Today, in the gentrified Gaslamp, nothing marks the site of Heller's corner, and the tipsy crowds of tourists and locals strolling the Disneyfied streets have no idea that so much blood was spilled there in a battle for the right to criticize the government and the rich in public space. Even vice has been driven out of the quarter, and now expensive prices and high-end condos do a better job than the police at keeping the rabble from crowding the streets. Public spaces like Horton Plaza and celebratory events like Street Scene and its various holiday-inspired offshoots ensure that access to "public space" in the heart of downtown comes with a price tag hefty enough to filter out "undesirable citizens" like the homeless. "Noncommercial expressive activity," as the signs in the malls say, is not welcome and rarely present.

Fascist Valley, the "Communist Wrecking Crew," and the "Parasitic Menace"[213]

> California has become prosperous with the toil and sweat of Mexican immigration attending to its number one industry, agriculture. Now they have sustained a true and lasting patriotism to a democratic country that refuses to give them citizenship or even basic civil rights.[214]
>
> *Luisa Moreno, United Cannery, Agricultural, Packing, and Allied Workers of America (UCAPAWA)*

Sitting in the office we heard the commotion. I guess the thugs retreated. They later testified in court that they were trying to arrest myself and Dorothy Ray [Healey], who was a representative of the Young Communist League and participating in the strike organization. The first we knew of their presence was the sound of tear gas. This cordon of men we then discovered armed with pickaxe handles—pretty much a slaughter. As our people tried to escape the building, they were knocked back in, knocked down and Miss Ray and I escaped through a back window.[215]

Stanley Hancock, San Diego Communist Party

You red son of a bitch arguing constitutional law. We'll give you a taste of our constitutional law![216]

Chan Livingston, Imperial County official

In 1949, Carey McWilliams wrote of the Imperial Valley: "Today as yesterday, the valley is ruled by a set of power-drunk ruthless nabobs who exploit farm labor with the same savagery that they exploit the natural resources of the valley."[217] Writing a little over a decade earlier, John Steinbeck agreed, and while he wrongly predicted that the future of farm labor would be "white and American," he quite accurately portrayed the situation faced by the mostly Mexican migratory labor force working the fields of the Imperial Valley:

To the large grower Mexican labor offered more advantages than simply its cheapness. It could be treated as so much scrap when it was not needed. Any local care for the sick and crippled could be withheld; and in addition, if it offered any resistance to the low wage or the terrible living conditions, it could be deported to Mexico at Government expense. . . . Recently, led by the example of the workers in Mexico, the Mexicans in California have begun to organize. Their organization in Southern California has been met with vigilante terrorism and savagery unbelievable in a civilized state. . . . The right of free speech, the right of assembly and the right of jury trial are not extended to Mexicans in the Imperial Valley. . . . And if the terrorism and reduction of human rights, the floggings, murder by deputies, kidnappings and refusal of trial by jury are necessary to our economic security, it is further submitted that California democracy is rapidly dwindling away. Fascistic methods are more numerous, more powerfully applied and more openly practiced in California than in any other place in the United States.[218]

Kevin Starr's assessment, in 1996, is similar, as he says of the Imperial Valley in the 1930s, "Political power in the Imperial Valley had been organized into a vertical structure which even a moderate conservative might label fascist."[219] Specifically, as McWilliams tells us, in 1936, 43 percent of the land in the valley was controlled by less than 6 percent of the growers.[220] Their interests were promoted by the Imperial Valley Growers and Shippers Association and the Anti-Communist Association. These organizations were filled with officials from county government and were integrated into the highest levels of the county commissioners, the highway patrol, the police, and the courts. Some of the nastiest work was done by deputized vigilantes who were drawn from the American Legion, the Ku Klux Klan, and the Silver Shirts, a fascist group modeled after the German SS. Statewide strategic and financial help came from the Associated Farmers.[221] Thus, as with the free speech–era vigilantes, the terrorist army arrayed against farm workers was a de facto arm of local government and law enforcement.

Even the most extreme elements such as the Klan and the Silver Shirts had important connections to business and members in the local governments in the Imperial Valley and San Diego.[222] Richard A. Floyd, 1930s San Diego Klan leader, was active in the local Republican Party and, ironically, was a central figure in the American-Mexican Republican League, an organization designed to promote cross-border business.[223] The Silver Shirts were well known but, as Larralde and Griswold del Castillo inform us, "ignored by most city officials who did not consider their anti-Semitic and anti-Mexican propaganda a problem."[224] It is instructive to note that while San Diego elites had long feared and sought to repress radicals like the IWW, the Silver Shirts, with their desire to "cleanse society of undesirable characters,"[225] were tolerated until the federal government became concerned with the Nazis in the later thirties. One can only assume that Anglo-Saxon racists were less threatening to San Diego boosters than the groups they despised.[226] With their goal of keeping Mexicans and Mexican Americans out of the professional class and in the manual labor pool where they could be imported or deported when necessary, the far Right stood with many of California's industrial leaders.[227] Indeed, in May 1934, the San Diego Chamber of Commerce, the Associated Manufacturers of San Diego, and the

San Diego Merchants Association decried the "San Diego citizens" who were "promoting strife" in the Imperial Valley and pledged aid for their neighbors who were "ridding southern California of the insidious menace of Communism."[228]

Up against enemies like this, it should come as no surprise that, as an AFL official in the 1930s said, "Only fanatics are willing to live in shacks or tents and get their heads broken in the interests of migratory labor."[229] With the only other labor organization who aggressively sought to organize nonwhite migratory workers, the IWW, in ruins, the people who stepped up to the task in the 1930s were Communists and their fellow travelers. Whatever issues one might have with the brutality of Stalinism in the Soviet Union or the rigidity of the Communist Party of the United States, it must be acknowledged that, as Kevin Starr puts it, "While their ideology represented a dead end, the cause they served, justice and decency in the fields, almost exempts them from the negative aspects of their Communism. . . . There was no one else on hand to do a job crying out to be done, other than the young Communists, and they did this work with courage and high moral purpose."[230]

The danger and difficulty of organizing agricultural and cannery workers required so much focus on "bread and butter" issues and practical necessity that many Communist organizers became less ideologically rigid in the service of becoming excellent trade unionists. Vicki Ruiz claims that "[w]hatever the union's roots, [Communist organizers in the fields and factories] time and time again, proved to be dedicated, tenacious, and selfless organizers."[231] The result was a stunning wave of 180 agricultural strikes involving 89,276 workers between 1933 and 1939 in California. As McWilliams says of this flood of strikes, "No parallel of any kind can be found in the history of American labor."[232]

San Diego's Labor Council, while thinking of Imperial Valley unions as "branches of the San Diego unions,"[233] did not make much of an effort to organize Mexican agricultural workers in the valley. In fact, through the twenties, the Labor Council showed little interest in overcoming its own anti-immigrant, racially exclusive policies. While the Labor Council did seek to work with the Tijuana Federation of Labor and formed a Laborer's Union in 1927, the effort fell apart and the council resumed its old calls for controlling Mexican immigration. Racism undoubtedly played a role in this failure. Throughout the twenties and into the thirties, the conservative AFL old guard in the Labor Council maintained a preference for native skilled workers.

It was a local carpenter and Communist, Stanley Hancock, who first argued for the organization of the unskilled in 1924, saying, "You will never be secure in your wages until the laborers are well organized and their interests taken into account."[234] As early as 1921, Hancock pressed for the end of racial discrimination in the Labor Council and the admission of blacks into local unions. Unfortunately, even when nonunion blacks struck in solidarity with white union builders, the Labor Council still voted against admitting them into unions.[235] Thus it was not aggressive "dual unionism" that inspired the Communist-led Cannery and Agricultural Workers Industrial Union (CAWIU) to organize local Mexican, black, and Filipino farm workers in the thirties, it was the AFL's lack of interest combined with the Communists' antiracist, egalitarian idealism. Their first efforts came in 1930, when Communist organizers sought to help with a lettuce strike. In "The Story of the Imperial Valley," Frank Spector, a leading Communist Party organizer, tells of "numerous open air and mass meetings . . . in Brawley, El Centro, Westmoreland, Calexico, Calipatria and other points" that were attended by thousands.[236] These first efforts at organizing were violently crushed and Spector, along with eight other organizers, was imprisoned for "criminal syndicalism" after being tried in front of a judge who was a member of the American Legion, and convicted by a jury stacked with his fellow Legionnaires.[237]

It is also important to note that Communist organizers did not impose unionism on naïve partners. Starr notes that Mexican farm workers had already formed the *Confederación de Uniones Obreras Mexicanas* in the 1920s and won wage increases and improved working conditions. By 1933, however, their wage rates had dropped by more than 50 percent as a result of the Depression.[238] Nonetheless, the history of earlier struggles made many of the workers eager to be organized. As Communist organizer Dorothy Ray Healey remembers:

> Despite charges by the growers that the Communists were conspiring to destroy California's agricultural economy, we were rarely the instigators of these strikes. They

usually broke out spontaneously and then the workers would come and find us. Most of the workers we encountered in the early 1930s were Mexican, with some Filipinos, and only a scattering of Blacks and Anglos.[239]

Starr agrees and points out that, given the fact that farm labor was akin to slavery, the workers craved a way to fight back: "From this perspective, the farm workers of California—Mexicans and Filipinos initially and most intensely, but later whites and African-American as well—were more likely to be using Communist organizers than to be used by them."[240] This is what happened in 1933 when fifty Filipino and Mexican strawberry workers in Twin Oaks Valley near Escondido came to the Communists in San Diego for help in organizing and winning a strike by keeping the growers from pitting the two groups against each other.[241] That same year, the *Uniones Obreras Mexicanas* contacted the CAWIU about organizing farm workers in the Imperial Valley.

As Stanley Hancock puts it: "The San Diego Party was quite influential in Imperial Valley among the agricultural workers." In 1933, CAWIU workers were pouring into the valley from Salinas and the San Joaquin Valley, and Hancock remembers, "That came into my territory, and I spent quite a bit of time in Imperial Valley, setting up locals of this red union."[242] Healey's account is a little more revealing as she admits that "I had only given a couple of speeches. Stanley and I had a lot to learn when we set off for the Imperial Valley."[243] When they got there, Healey remembers:

The Imperial Valley was a self-enclosed feudally run barony, surrounded by desert. The workers lived a miserable existence and were treated like virtual serfs. Those who lived there year round lived in little shanties with dirt floors. Others lived in tents. It was usually brutally hot. Even in January when we arrived the temperature was in the eighties or nineties, and in the summer it was always well over a hundred. The growers provided no drinking water for the workers except for that in the irrigation ditches, and those ditches were used for everything, including washing and toilets. Driving into the valley you had the feeling of leaving the United States behind you. The ordinary legal rules and protections, imperfect as they were, no longer applied. The most horrendous things could go on, and did go on, and all you could expect was that perhaps months later the news would gradually leak out to the people who read the *Nation* and kept up with such things.[244]

The two green organizers stepped into this unforgiving arena and tried to launch a cotton workers' strike for a modest wage increase, drinking water, transportation to the workplace, and other bread-and-butter demands.[245] By their second day there, a warrant was issued for their arrests and they had to operate covertly, moving from safe house to safe house to avoid the police and vigilantes. They held meetings in Azteca Hall, where, as Healey notes, "the relations between the Filipinos, the Chicanos, and the few Anglos involved in the strike was also a remarkable thing to watch. All of them, in their own way, were initially afflicted with feeling of mutual animosity, and yet within a few days the suspicions and prejudices just evaporated . . . through sharing common experiences and hardships."[246] Their political fortunes were less sanguine, however, as the strike was crushed before it even had a chance. One of their meetings was discovered by a combination of cops and thugs and Azteca Hall was trashed by a mob that destroyed all of their furniture, typewriters, and other equipment in the process of savagely beating the farm workers and arresting fifty of them.[247] Healey and Hancock fled and were hidden by the workers for over a week, but they were eventually found by the police after being turned in by a reporter, put on trial for "disturbing the peace," and sentenced to 180 days in jail. During the trial, the jury foreman stood up and interrupted their defense, in which they sought to expose the working conditions and poor diets of the farm workers, by saying, "Your Honor, do we really have to listen to any more of this red agitation? I was in the war, and the soldiers had to eat plenty of beans, and if it was good enough for American soldiers, it's good enough for these dirty Mexicans!"[248] While Healey's stay in jail was uneventful, Hancock and other male organizers were sent out to a work camp, where they were harassed by vigilantes who dug a grave and burned a cross near it, leaving a cat-o'-nine-tails and a note that threatened, "If you reds come back, this is what you are going to get."[249]

San Diego Communists were also involved in other Imperial Valley strikes, as Hancock notes of the 1934 lettuce strike: "We were accepted into leadership by virtue of our previous activity but we had to be very circumspect about it."[250] An African American party member, Nathaniel Griffin, was sent out to help organize black workers in the valley, and East Indians, Japanese, and whites also joined with their fellow Mexican and Filipino workers to demand a wage increase to thirty-five cents per hour.[251] As with the earlier strikes, their meetings were broken up and Azteca Hall was trashed along with typewriters and mimeograph machines. Free speech was not to be permitted. Legal defense for strikers was also eliminated when their American Civil Liberties Union lawyer, A. L. Wirin, was kidnapped from his hotel in El Centro by members of the American Legion, who robbed and severely beat him before leaving the attorney barefoot and penniless in the desert eleven miles from town. Amazingly, Wirin made it back to El Centro, where he was again threatened by an armed band of two hundred vigilantes before he was "escorted" to safety by two deputies. As a result of his work, an injunction from the federal district court allowed the workers to have a meeting, but afterward many of the Mexicans were beaten, arrested, and deported.[252] Another attorney for the strikers, Grover Johnson, was badly beaten by Imperial Valley county official Chan Livingston and a mob of vigilantes on the courthouse lawn as police looked on passively.[253] These and numerous other atrocities led General Pelham D. Glassford, who was sent by the United States secretary of labor to investigate the terrorism in the Imperial Valley, to conclude:

> After more than 2 months of observation and investigation in Imperial Valley, it is my contention that a group of growers have exploited a "communist" hysteria for the advancement of their own interests; that they have welcomed labor agitation, which they could brand as "Red," as a means of sustaining supremacy by mob rule, thereby preserving what is so essential to their profits, cheap labor; that they have succeeded in drawing into their conspiracy certain county officials who have become the principal tools of their machine.[254]

Glassford's visit was denounced by the governor of California as a violation of state's rights, and he, like Weinstock during the free speech fight, received death threats from the vigilantes. Even generals were not immune to the fascist tactics of the lords of the valley. Nonetheless, while the 1934 strike was repressed, it and others to follow slowly achieved a few basic rights, if not revolution, for farm workers. As Dorothy Ray Healey remembers, by 1939, "Unionism was now legal in the Imperial

Valley."[255] Still, it would not be until the 1960s and 1970s that the Imperial Valley would again see the kind of commitment evidenced by the Red organizers of the 1930s.

In May 1969, César Chávez led a nine-day United Farm Workers (UFW) march across the desert from Coachella to Calexico to convince Mexican workers to honor a strike against the big vineyards in the Imperial Valley. The workers endured brutal heat, carrying the black-eagle flag of the UFW and a banner of the Virgin of Guadalupe proudly under the scorching sun all the way down to the border, where Father Victor Salandini held mass for them. The priest, who wore a UFW emblem on his vestments, was chastised by the bishop of San Diego but loved by the workers. They were joined by celebrities, politicians, and the media but would later have to struggle with a new generation of vigilantes.[256] The drama of events such as these brought their cause into the spotlight and the UFW, as Cletus Daniel tells us in "César Chávez and the Unionization of California Farmworkers," "compiled a record of achievement that rivals the accomplishments of the most formidable industrial unions of the 1930s."[257] Despite this, by the 1990s, 25 percent of the Imperial Valley's population still lived below the "official" poverty line, and today conditions are still bad for the worst paid and frequently undocumented workers who, in a few notorious cases, have actually been forced into slavery in Southern California.[258] The ghost of the Red thirties still haunts the valley.

On May 30, 1933, the Young Communist League (YCL) brought three hundred activists down from Los Angeles to hold a rally in Pantoja Plaza, or "New Town" Park. San Diego officials had denied them a permit as the young radicals would not give in to the city's demand that they not fly the red flag. When they began their parade, singing the "Internationale" as they marched, they were met by twenty-five policemen who charged into the crowd with billy clubs. What began as a Memorial Day protest against imperialism turned into a riot during which thirty Communists were injured and ten cops wounded when the protesters, unlike most of the Wobblies before them, fought back with the sticks from their placards. Eight Communists were arrested and the rest were "escorted" back to Los Angeles by the police.[259] In a 1983 article in the *San Diego Union*, headlined "S.D. Police Saw Red the Day the Communists Came to Town," retired newspaperman Arthur Ribbel playfully dismisses the Communists' "prattle" and warmly remembers how the police "cracked their heads together," specifically recording the wounds of the policemen but not those of the clearly unsympathetic protesters. More important, however, the article makes the argument that "Communist seeds of discontent didn't grow big in San Diego during the Depression" despite the "despair and poverty of many" because the city was not industrial and had the Navy and a thriving tourist trade. Ribbel goes on to mention that the police's "Red Squad" kept watch over the city's three hundred Communists, but that, other than the invasion from Los Angeles, not much else of note ever happened.[260] While elements of this story are accurate, it distorts the picture of San Diego in the 1930s by ignoring the work of Communists in the local unions and early civil rights struggles.

Interestingly, local elites during the thirties expressed far more worry than Ribbel's article would suggest they did. San Diego's Chamber of Commerce didn't just aid the fight against Communism in the Imperial Valley, it passed a resolution endorsing a local fight against the "rising menace."[261] City Councilman Roy Goodbody agreed, calling for the "suppression of communistic activities" in the city.[262] What these declarations show is that while San Diego was far from a revolution, it did have enough radical activism to rile the Chamber of Commerce and send a shiver down the spine of a city councilman. The city of San Diego did not see the historic strikes and open bloodshed that characterized the Imperial Valley, but it did witness a bitter struggle for control of the local labor movement, and, after the thirties, it saw many of its radical leaders persecuted by relentless right-wing witch-hunters.

As has already been noted, the San Diego labor movement's leadership, with its bias toward the crafts, nativism, racism, and generally conservative outlook, was frequently slow to open its doors to unskilled workers, women, and people of color.[263] The legacy of the free speech fight's repression, the elites' constant fear of even hints of "radicalism," the ever-present threat of open-shop drives by the Merchants and Employers Association, criticism from the American Legion, and the conservative influence of the national American Federation of Labor are probably all factors in the basic conservatism of the Labor Council in the twenties and early thirties.[264] Despite this, there were always more progressive elements in the San Diego labor movement and even on the council itself. In April 1912, the *San Diego Sun* reported that when an AFL official from the State Federation of Labor came to town and criticized Socialists and called the IWW "notorious liars" in an address at Germania Hall, "union men laughed and hissed." The official, Paul Scharrenberg, tried again and, according to the *Sun*, "several champions of both [organizations] arose and protested ... hot words were passed back and forth." After this, "Scharrenberg informed the audience that if they did not keep quiet he would cease speaking. The cheers were redoubled, apparently 90 percent of those present participating."[265]

In the twenties, Stanley Gue, an old Wobbly, was on the council along with Stanley Hancock, a Communist. There was also an active Socialist element. The Left together called for organizing the unskilled and promoting the cooperative movement.[266] Thus, while radicals never had control over the Labor Council or the overall direction of the labor movement, the seeds of the thirties' conflicts were present throughout the teens and the twenties.

In the late 1920s in San Diego, the unemployed were jailed as "vagrants" and, as Frederick Ryan points out, as the Depression hit San Diego's "well-to-do citizens seemed to have no concept of the forces that had been unleashed in the city by the large numbers who had lost everything in the Depression, including any hope of betterment under conditions as they were."[267] Indeed, during the depths of the Depression, the San Diego Tax Payers Association pushed for wage cuts for city employees, WPA workers were used as union busters in Balboa Park, and local ministers and politicians suggested setting up central labor camps for the unemployed in remote areas, out of sight but difficult to access.[268] All the while, the mayor of San Diego was on the take and would later be arrested for drunk driving.[269]

As if to add insult to injury for the city's struggling workers and unemployed, the theme of the 1935–36 California-Pacific International Exposition in Balboa Park was the "Culture of Abundance," and exhibits like the one in the Ford Pavilion presented a mythological view of San Diego's history, devoid of all race and class conflicts. As Matthew Bokovoy puts it: "The Ford vision of industrial and agricultural servitude resonated with the white and middle-class hopes for social control

over working-class militants during the 1930s." Worse than that, "The Ford vision
. . . indicated that working-class Californians were excluded from the culture of
abundance and relegated to the mean cycle of subjected labor in the state's fields and
factories."[270] Just as the boosters did when they used the fantasy of the "Spanish past"
for their Social Darwinist dreams of the future in the early teens, San Diego's current
crop of promoters proclaimed in the advance literature for the 1935 exposition that
the city was "open shop" and free from "labor troubles."[271] Other boosters like Edgar
Hastings, San Diego's county supervisor, crowed that "When I hear of Red riots,
grave unemployment crises and other economic disturbances in cities of the country,
I thank my lucky stars I live in San Diego. None is hungry here." And though some
may be "temporarily out of employment," jobs could be found.[272] Despite such self-
serving proclamations, the number of San Diego's unemployed soared from 5,800 in
1930 to 23,000 in 1933.[273] The *WPA America Guide* for San Diego was less sanguine
about the economic situation in the city than Supervisor Hastings, arguing that the
boosters' plans to "keep the town basically a resort area has resulted in a top-heavy
economic balance, with too sharp a dividing line between those who are economically secure and the large stratum of working people."[274]

The conservative AFL old guard in the San Diego Labor Council was slow to
respond to the new realities of the Depression. As Ryan points out, they restricted
the activities of unions, misread the economic and political situation, and were too
close to business.[275] More specifically, the policies of the Labor Council showed more
fear of radicalism than business take-backs. President O. C. Heitman and Secretary-
Treasurer Edward Dowell led the council and pledged no strikes or boycotts in the
hope that employers would not cut jobs or wages, but local businesses ignored this
and cut them anyway.[276] My survey of the *Labor Leader* in the 1930s before the
"radicals" took over reveals that the Labor Council was constantly fighting wage cuts
and complaining about new labor-saving technologies and immigrants.[277] As Ryan
observes, the Labor Council's program for dealing with the crisis of the Depression
was a "defensive" one and it opened the conservative leadership up to criticism from
the radicals.[278] The radicals, on the other hand, were calling for more decisive action.
The Christmas day edition of the *Labor Leader* in 1931 includes a statement by the

Unemployment Council of San Diego, led by Daisy Lee Worchester, a Communist and member of the teacher's union, which asserts that for the unemployed, "It is our moral right and our duty to our children to demand that the city, state, and national officialdom get busy immediately and create unemployment insurance by taking from the incomes of the rich and the millions of dollars that are spent on war preparations." The proclamation, entitled "Unemployed Council Prepares for March," went on to demand seven dollars a week, free clothing, shoes, milk for children, free streetcar tickets, and lunches at school for unemployed workers and their children. According to the Unemployment Council, there should be free rent (and no evictions), water, gas, and light for the city's dispossessed, and relief funds should be managed by a committee of workers.[279] The contrast between the conservative AFL faction and the radicals could not have been clearer, and as the Depression deepened opinion turned against Heitman, Dowell, and the old guard.

As the conservative-led Labor Council pursued a defensive strategy aimed at maintaining stability, Communist union members were quite active. Communist Lee Gregovich of the Cooks and Waitresses Union ran a successful strike against the Golden Lion Tavern that involved much picketing and a few stink bombs.[280] Gregovich was, over the years, involved in trying to organize virtually every nonunion restaurant in the city.[281] Leftists in local unions also organized a "hunger march," held "hunger hearings," and were active in many local unions, including the Carpenters, Painters, Retail Clerks, Cleaners and Dyers, Machinists, and others. As San Diego Communist and member of the Retail Clerks union Dan Taylor remembers: "There was a communist in nearly every trade union in San Diego."[282] Even though they never had huge numbers, the organizing work and activism of local Communists gained them the respect of many workers. Hancock remembers the reception given him on his return from jail in the Imperial Valley:

> Many people not at all sympathetic with communism were brought very close to us in their active resentment against [the repression of striking workers]. . . . That large segment of the population that calls itself liberal with radical offshoots, in this atmosphere, came more and more to identify themselves with the Communists. For example, the

night I came home from the chain gang, it was quite an event in San Diego. The reporters were there. I remember the reporters being violently upset at this series of events,
expressing sympathy.[283]

If the support of non-Communist workers helped the left faction of the Labor
Council gain power, their discipline and political savvy were also important. Taylor
remembers how "every week the Communist members of the union met in what they
called a faction meeting in which they discussed the aims and policies, plans, strategy,
and tactics, which the Communists were going to carry out at the next union meeting, or the next meeting of its board of officers."[284] Sympathetic non-Party members
also came to these meetings and, after the planning sessions, the Communists were
able to win the debate with "eight or nine people in a crowd of 300."[285]

More important than their organizational skills, the Communists in the labor
movement promoted an agenda in line with interests of the majority of San Diego's
workers. They were, particularly by the Popular Front period, interested in working
with other trade unionists rather than competing with them for members. Indeed,
in the mid-thirties, mass recruitment was not the goal. As Hancock puts it, "At no
time were hundreds of members recruited into the CP. It was not intended that way.
The CP rather carefully would select one, two, up to a dozen, set up a unit, then start
working on another unit. . . . People were selected on the basis of their leadership
capacity."[286] More than anything else, however, it was the organization and growth
of new unions that brought the radicals to power in the Labor Council. The organizing efforts of 1933 and 1934 brought the lumber handlers, Teamsters, gas station
employees, roofers, optical workers, agricultural workers, auto mechanics, domestic
employees, office workers, building service employees, dairy workers, and bindery
workers, among others, into the council and helped to radicalize it. As the labor
movement grew, the old guard's conservatism failed to appeal to the new unions.

In the spring of 1934, Alva C. Rogers beat longtime conservative leader Edward
Dowell in the election for secretary-treasurer of the San Diego Labor Council.[287]
He was joined by Communists and fellow travelers Daisy Lee Worchester, Harry
Steinmetz, and John Lydick in pushing for change. In 1935, Steinmetz won the

presidency of the council and the radicals were in charge.[288] Rogers and Steinmetz won support for new organizing drives, criticized the union-busting policies of the exposition organizers, more aggressively supported the Wagner Act, and championed radical causes like opposition to the criminal syndicalist law being used against union organizers.[289] As president, Steinmetz democratized the labor movement by pushing for lower initiation fees to help expand organizing efforts, changing the constitution of the Labor Council to bring in more delegates from the industrial section, and moving away from "closed session" meetings to wide-open exercises in participatory democracy. Steinmetz summarized the point of his "new deal" by stating that the goals of the labor movement must "lie beyond bread and butter; the goal must be social. We must be the welders of a new and better social order, even of a new civilization based upon production for use, competition of ideas, devotion to a classless society, peace."[290] This new broader social unionism led to some wage increases, more militant actions in the service of the unemployed, support for strikes, calls for free lunches for poor schoolchildren, and a significant increase in membership.[291] In advance of the Congress of Industrial Organizations (CIO), the Communist-led radical leadership of the Labor Council pursued a more democratic and effective form of unionism.

The radicals also criticized their conservative opponents in the *Trade Union News,* and, worse still for the old guard, garnered support and beat them on most issues. As Hancock recalls, "You could say 80 percent of what the Communists wanted done was accomplished."[292] Unable to win the debate democratically, Heitman and Dowell resorted to Red-baiting. As opposed to the days of the free speech fight, when union solidarity outweighed ideological differences for San Diego unionists, in the 1930s, conservative unionists persecuted their own members. In the midst of a battle over whether to pass a resolution supporting Leftist unionists on trial in Sacramento for organizing farm workers, Heitman lashed out at his enemies. He Red-baited his opponents, charged them with "disrupting and destroying" San Diego unions, and openly threatened that "We have the right to, and we will, protect our unions by eliminating any such disruptive influences."[293]

In January 1936, probably after complaints from angry San Diego conservatives,

AFL national president William Green sent a telegram to Pacific coast organizer Joseph Casey ordering him to revoke the charter of the San Diego County Federated Trades and Labor Council and appoint new leadership.[294] Casey came to San Diego unannounced, walked into a meeting, and declared his intention to revoke their charter for "unconstitutional, illegal, and subversive activities." Casey appointed a new council, with Dowell in a central leadership position, and pledged them to oppose San Diego's "Communist wrecking crew." It was not an easy purge, however, as the new AFL-approved Labor Council discovered that it did not have majority support among local unions, who ignored the existence of the puppet council and held meetings in the Labor Temple without them.[295]

In 1936, the dissident council elected John Lydick president and took legal action against Casey.[296] In February of that year, Casey returned to San Diego and assaulted Lydick, singling him out of a crowd in front of the Labor Temple and yelling, "You pink-faced baboon!" at his union brother before missing his head with an errant swing. Lydick noted that "He did knock my cigarette from my mouth. He swung a second time but couldn't connect; he's clumsy as an ox." Later, Casey turned on the whole crowd, declaring he would "take on any three of them." As he was led away by police, Casey waged a complaint rare in San Diego history: "What's the idea of these cops siding with these Communists?"[297] Casey's heavy-handed tactics failed and local unionists, led by Lydick, put together a compromise council to which most of the radicals returned.[298] Quickly afterward, however, Dowell set to Red-baiting again, using his seat on the credentials committee to refuse delegates he suspected were Communists. This was then followed with a thorough purge of not just Communists but also suspected CIO sympathizers, proving that the conservative Dowell-led AFL faction was not just anti-Communist but intolerant of any form of unionism that challenged their narrow, bread-and-butter approach.[299]

A postpurge Labor Day issue of the *Labor Leader* featured Walt Whitman's "I Hear America Singing" (a Popular Front favorite) on the cover and celebrated the addition of new unions and "the greatest progress in San Diego's Labor History" while it solemnly discussed the "Dismissal of disloyal and disruptive delegates" who were largely responsible for those gains in membership.[300] In the same issue is an editorial by a Unitarian minister, Howard B. Bard, who cautioned that labor was at a "crossroads," having "overstepped its justifiable bounds." The good minister then cautioned San Diego's working class that "If it is led into the position of the extreme left, it must expect to lose public sympathy."[301] In the Copley-owned *Union,* San Diegans were reading that their city council was preventing "Reds" from using schools for public meetings[302] and that their police were jailing them for distributing handbills.[303] The city's conservative mouthpiece also told San Diegans that the Communists were organizing against the GOP and that Steinmetz's arguments in favor of free speech for minority opinions at a local discussion group were specious.[304] By 1939, the *Labor Leader* cried out that "AFL Unionism Is Bulwark against Foreign ISMS."[305]

Along with the *Union,* San Diego's Labor Council was on guard against the Red Menace, even if that meant turning on itself. In the years that followed, the AFL returned to its previous conservatism, failing to actively recruit women and minorities and continuing Red-baiting and expelling its members, moving toward a nonthreatening business unionism.[306] By 1957, the *Labor Leader* decried the movement's lack of activism, asking, "Have labor members become tranquilized?" However, the leaders of the Labor Council, who were slower than most of the nation in reuniting with the CIO, had only themselves to blame.[307] Meanwhile, radical activists inside and outside the labor movement in San Diego were paying a heavy price.

The first local labor activist to be arrested under the federal Anti-Subversive Act was Luisa Moreno.[308] Born in Guatemala, Moreno came to the United States in 1916 to attend college in Oakland, California, and returned again in 1928 to New York City, where her experiences with racism and sweatshop labor radicalized her. She joined the Communist Party in 1930 and remained a member until 1935 when she left as a result of ideological disputes.[309] During the early thirties, Moreno worked organizing unskilled laborers around the United States, and she joined the CIO in 1934 after becoming disillusioned with the AFL's disregard for the plight of agricultural, cannery, and other marginalized workers.[310] Along with fellow activists, she organized the United Cannery, Agricultural, Packing, and Allied Workers of America (UCAPAWA), a Popular Front–period descendent of the CAWIU.[311]

As Vicki Ruiz explains in *Cannery Women/Cannery Lives,* "UCAPAWA provides a model for democratic trade unionism in the United States." As opposed to the local AFL, UCAPAWA encouraged local control of unions and "worker solidarity across occupational, racial, gender, religious, and political lines."[312] Moreno was the Southern California director of Spanish-speaking locals, a post that allowed her not only to organize workers, but also to fight for gender equality and the rights of the undocumented.[313] Her bilingual skills made her an effective organizer and defender of basic rights.[314] She came to San Diego in 1937 and began organizing in canneries and packing houses.

Both the working conditions and the spirit of the women in the plants Moreno was organizing in Southern California are well described in a letter written by Moreno's friend Carey McWilliams, about a meeting of nut packers:

> The employers recently took their hammers away from them—they were making "too much money." For the last two months, in their work they have been cracking walnuts with their fists. Hundreds of them held up their fists to prove it—the lower portion of the fist being calloused, bruised, swollen. They told of the hatred they feel for their miserable stooges who spy upon them, speed up their work, nose into their affairs. They were really wonderful people. You had the feeling that here, unmistakably, was a section of the American people. And you felt stirred, profoundly stirred, by their wonderful good sense, the warmth and excitement in their faces, their kindliness.[315]

The San Diego canneries were segregated, the women had to deal with frequent speed-ups, and workplace injuries were common.[316] Together with Robert Galvin, Moreno organized hundreds of workers in places like the Old Mission Packing Corporation, San Diego Packing Company, Van Camp Sea Food Company, and elsewhere. By 1939, they had established San Diego UCAPAWA Local 64 at Van Camp Sea Food Company, and, during the next few years, negotiated a contract that recognized the union, created a closed shop, and gave the UCAPAWA cannery workers the highest wages in the tuna packing industry.[317] As a result of gains such as these, McWilliams called UCAPAWA "the most progressive, best organized, most intelligently led CIO movement in the country."[318]

Civil rights work went hand in hand with Moreno's union organizing. In 1938 she helped create El Congreso de Pueblos que Hablan Espanol, which sought to coordinate Latino organizations in defense of civil rights.[319] She spoke out against the internment of Japanese Americans, fought racism in the workplace, and, in the forties, got a nondiscrimination pledge from the Royal Packing Plant, and supported Madres del Soldado Hispano Americano, which fought for the rights of Mexican American soldiers and their families.[320] Also in the forties, Moreno spoke out against the anti-Mexican hysteria that swept Southern California in the wake of the Sleepy Lagoon case and the zoot-suit riots in Los Angeles.[321] The racist violence hit San Diego in June 1943, when gangs of vigilante servicemen, both sailors and Marines, swept through the downtown streets in search of Mexican youths who struck them as hoodlums. When they found them, the servicemen beat them viciously and stripped many of them of their clothes.[322] Incidents such as this one were followed by many individual acts of violence, as the Mexican consul complained to Admiral D. W. Bagley. Moreno, who was also concerned about racism on the base, teamed up with San Diego Councilman Charles Dail and sought to bring the issue to the Navy, which, along with the local press, ignored it. It was Moreno's conclusion that "we will never know much about the San Diego civilian casualties. The Navy and the local newspaper ignored the violence since most of the victims were Mexican."[323] Dail dropped the issue under political pressure and Moreno soon learned the cost of organizing poor women and challenging the racism of the Navy in San Diego.

As Ruiz points out, Red-baiting was the main weapon used against UCAPAWA.[324] As early as 1938, Moreno's union activity, along with the activism of El Congreso de Pueblos, gained the attention of Congressman Martin Dies of the House Un-American Activities Committee (HUAC).[325] By the late forties, Moreno had accumulated a group of well-placed, powerful enemies. Old Mission Packing Corporation and San Diego Packing Company requested that their nemesis be questioned by the HUAC.[326] In addition, Admiral Bagley had allied himself with California State Senator Jack B. Tenney, who disliked labor and blamed the zoot-suit riots on Communist newspapers, as well as V. W. Kenaston Sr., who, as Larralde and Griswold del Castillo tell us:

. . . stayed active against Hispanic labor and civil rights activities. While a member of the Klan, he was on the Building Trades and Labor Council and also an affiliate of the Federal Mediation Service. Kenaston was well acquainted with the city's mayor and councilmen, and with local bankers and merchants. With the friendship of Senator Jack Tenney, head of the California Un-American Activities Committee, it put Kenaston in an ideal position to incapacitate Mexican-American civil and labor rights.[327]

In fact, as Larralde and Griswold del Castillo outline, the Klan had direct ties to the tuna packing companies. Specifically, California Packing Corporation, Marine Products Company, Van Camp Sea Food Company, and several other firms actually financed the Klan "to battle leaders like Moreno."[328] Thus, with the canneries, state and federal politicians, the Klan, racist labor leaders, and the local press against her, there was little the ever-defiant Moreno or her lawyer Bob Kenney could do.

On September 10, 1948, Moreno was asked to appear before the state senate Committee on Un-American Activities, which held a hearing in the San Diego Civic Center. The *Union* characterized her as a "defiant witness" as she invoked the Constitution's Fifth Amendment. When Senator Tenney threatened to send Moreno's transcript to the Immigration and Naturalization Service (INS) in order to foil her application for citizenship, Moreno shouted back at him, "Citizenship means a great deal to me but the Constitution means more!" Her spirited defense drew the applause of a middle-aged woman who was expelled from the meeting for violating a ban on "demonstrations."[329]

As she awaited action by the INS, Moreno's phones were tapped, her neighbors questioned, and her gardener paid to spy on her.[330] She was offered a deal for citizenship if she would testify against the famous Longshoremen's Union leader Harry Bridges, but, unlike Stanley Hancock and other local ex-Communists, she refused to betray her principles.[331] After that, the "Encanto grandmother," as the *Union* referred to her, was arrested under the Anti-Subversive Act and deported in 1950. From Mexico, Moreno made her way back to Guatemala in 1951, only to be forced to flee her native country when, in 1954, a CIA coup overthrew the popular democratic Arbenz government in favor of a U.S.-supported dictatorship leading to years of repression and tens of thousands of state-sponsored murders.[332] Moreno returned to

Mexico until her husband died in 1960 and then moved to Cuba to work as a translator for six months. After her time in Cuba, she moved back to Tijuana, where she ran an art shop on Avenida de Revolución for a time before moving to Guadalajara and finally back to Guatemala, where she died in 1992, forever freeing San Diego from the woman whom Senator Tenney called a "parasitic menace."[333]

After being purged twice by the Labor Council, Dr. Harry Steinmetz was followed by trouble for nearly two decades until he became the first employee of the state of California to be fired for "insubordination" and allegations of "subversion." The American Legion first went after Steinmetz in 1936, sending a resolution to the state Board of Education demanding an investigation of Steinmetz for "subversive activity."[334] Along with the *Union*, the American Legion criticized the professor with regularity, but they were unable to mount a serious threat until the 1950s. By that time, the local American Legion chapter was headed by Harry L. Foster, who was also chair of the San Diego County Counter-Subversion Committee and president of the Chamber of Commerce.[335] Foster made it something of a personal mission to persecute college professors whom he deemed "subversive." Questions of freedom of speech were not an issue for the hyperpatriotic Red-baiter, who had developed a polished doublethink on the matter. As Foster saw it, "The question of academic freedom is not now challenged. Dr. Steinmetz's thinking has been far from an open mind. His mind has been closed to the fundamental principles which most Americans believe are the soundness and whole-hearted structure of our educational system."[336]

With that thorny question dispensed with, Foster and the American Legion went after Steinmetz with a vengeance. After Steinmetz had spoken to an off-campus peace group, the Legion swung into action, requesting that State Director of Education Roy E. Simpson remove Steinmetz from his position.[337] After Simpson replied that he was legally unable to do so, the matter was brought to the legislature, where Fred Kraft of San Diego introduced Senate Bill 1836 allowing for the firing of state college employees for speaking at meetings sponsored by "a communist front organization." The bill passed easily in the legislature but was vetoed by Governor Earl Warren, who refused to sign a law designed to fire a "particular professor at San Diego State College."[338] Thus, much to the chagrin of the American Legion, Steinmetz survived for another two years.

In 1953, Steinmetz received a subpoena requiring him to appear before HUAC in Los Angeles. San Diego State College President Malcolm Love showed little of it, declaring himself "unsympathetic" to Steinmetz's dilemma.[339] At the HUAC hearing, Steinmetz was grilled about Communist infiltration of the American Federation of Teachers, but he invoked the Fifth Amendment and refused to cooperate. Years later, Steinmetz admitted he was an "undisciplined" Communist fifteen years prior to his questioning but that he had refused to answer on principle.[340] His defiance would cost him his job. After State Attorney General Edmund G. Brown announced that Steinmetz could not legally be fired for his refusal, San Diego legislators again swung into action.[341] When Senator Dilworth of Riverside introduced a bill that would help purge the state's educational system of Communists in the school districts, Assemblyman Luckel of San Diego introduced another bill that would include state college employees. Foster referred to the second piece of legislation as the "Anti-Steinmetz Act" and he was right.[342] In December 1953, Steinmetz gave a talk to an SDSC political science club and denounced HUAC as the "Un-American Committee."[343] His comments provoked the immediate rage of the American Legion, who yet again demanded his ouster.[344] This time they got their wish.

A. L. Wirin, who during the thirties was beaten by vigilantes who were likely members of the American Legion, was Steinmetz's lawyer and advised him to hold to his refusal. Bob Kenney, Luisa Moreno's old lawyer and Steinmetz's friend, advised that he take a different course.[345] When he appeared before the State Board of Education, Steinmetz took Wirin's advice and the board, which included Max Osslo of the Butchers' Union, who would later spend time in prison for conspiracy and assault against his union competitors, recommended his dismissal.[346] Steinmetz was fired on February 5, 1954, and few of his colleagues came to his defense. As opposed to the days of the free speech fight or the 1930s, when principled San Diegans risked life and limb to fight for free expression, liberals in the fifties were either too afraid or too placid to make much noise. Paul Eisloeffel puts it well: "Quite simply, intolerance of nonconformity bred from a reactionary climate dictated that Steinmetz the activist/educator must be silenced."[347] In the midst of his failed court battle against the Luckel Act, Steinmetz explained that it was his "feeling of responsibility as an educator charged with the duty of cherishing freedom and democracy" that fueled his struggle against the McCarthyites.[348] In an eloquent letter to the *Union*, he explained that: "The important question for me, as the first state employee summoned for public humiliation, is not how to answer police-state, one way questions. My problem derives from responsibility for the precedent I must set."[349] It was a brave and principled one.

After his firing, Steinmetz had trouble finding employment in academia and went to Europe, where, the *Union* gleefully reported, he didn't even have enough money to pay for his expenses for a visit to the Soviet Union.[350] Without Steinmetz and most of the other ex-Communists to worry about, the *Union* spent the rest of the fifties dealing with grave matters such as "wetbacks," "What an A-Bomb smuggler would find at the Mexican border," and the Reds who all "go to Baja" and had infested Mexicali "like a nest of wasps."[351] Steinmetz's son took up his father's tradition of rebellion by seeking conscientious objector status to avoid the draft.[352] The older Steinmetz did eventually visit Russia and then came back to San Diego where he managed to be reinstated as an unpaid professor emeritus after the Luckel Act was declared unconstitutional in the late sixties. He briefly wrote for a local progressive paper, the *New Gadfly*, and taught world affairs in the San Diego State University extension program until his death in 1981, living just long enough to see California's Red-baiting governor elected president of the United States.[353]

Racial Crisis, Tenured Radicals, and the Revolt of the Guards

> They would have you think that we are breaking the law, but I tell you that the Bank of America is the one that is breaking the law. And until Bank of America agrees to some type of conciliation with CORE, we will defy this injunction or any other injunction that they bring down. America is going to have to grapple with this, and the city of San Diego is going to have to grapple with this, because this is nothing but a denial of freedom of speech of millions of Negroes, and this is nothing but a refusal to recognize the deplorable conditions of racial discrimination in this city.[354]
>
> *Harold Brown, chairman of San Diego CORE*

Oh, a nigger lover, huh? I hope one of those black bastards moves in right
next door to you.[355]

A San Diego deputy sheriff, to Charles Collins of CORE

You know this is one of the most reactionary communities in the United
States, and they don't like a free university that tolerates radical opinion.[356]

Professor Herbert Marcuse, UCSD

Much of the *Union*'s coverage of the HUAC trials and the Red Menace focused on
race. Communism was seen as being just across the border, waiting to sneak in from
Mexico, or in the city's ghetto engaging in what the paper called "seductive crooning
to negroes."[357] Of particular concern was the Communists' argument that the United
States was a racist country. The HUAC testimony of an African American ex-Com-
munist from San Diego, Tony Smith, was front-page news as was the reason for his
initial membership: "I'm against discrimination and I thought this would help."
More disturbing than that was the testimony of another witness that "half the people
at the meetings of the Civil Rights Congress were Communists."[358] Framed in this
way, civil rights struggles were seen by many San Diegans as troublemaking and law-
breaking, the product of alien agitators rather than homegrown racism. Nonetheless,
notorious incidents of racist brutality sometimes came to the surface and exposed
San Diego's underbelly, such as the Elizabeth Ingalls case in 1947, in which a Coronado woman was convicted of keeping Dora Jones, her black maid, as a slave for
thirty-seven years.[359] As in the Deep South, sit-ins were one of the first forms of civil
rights protest. In 1949, San Diego's first black dentist, Jack Kimbrough, conducted a
sit-in at the Grant Grill in the U.S. Grant Hotel to challenge the restaurant's de facto
segregation. With San Diego State students serving as witnesses, Kimbrough and his
cohorts were successful at the Grant and other restaurants.[360]

By the early 1960s, San Diego police were worried about the city's civil rights
movement. As former chief Wesley Sharp remembers, "The number one problem
started in 1964 with the passage by Congress of the civil rights legislation. Minorities
thought that they had the right to do anything, and they had no respect for law and
order." Putting the unrest of the sixties into historical context, Sharp claims, "CORE

activity was the first indication of unrest in San Diego, starting with picketing and sit-ins. It was a troublesome time and we had no precedent, for nothing on this scale of unrest had happened in fifty-three years, not since the IWW riots in 1912."[361]

The horror with which Chief Sharp remembers CORE is indicative of the city's response to racial issues in the early sixties. As Harold Keen's reporting pointed out in a 1963 article on "San Diego's Racial Powder Keg," there was skepticism on the part of those in local government and in the Chamber of Commerce as to whether the city even had a problem with discrimination.[362] Leaders in the African American community saw things differently, with Reverend Dwight Kyle of the Bethel African Methodist Episcopal Church saying that San Diego in 1963 was "the worst place on the coast in discrimination practices. . . . The powers want to whitewash the situation, make everything appear ideal. Yet we have more unemployment among Negroes [than Los Angeles or San Francisco]."[363] The head of the San Diego National Association for the Advancement of Colored People, Hartwell Ragsdale, complained about discrimination within the labor movement as well, and some of the city's harsher African American critics saw it as "a redneck cracker town where the whites view the blacks as inferior."[364] Along those lines, Harold Brown, leader of San Diego's CORE, claimed that, "Through the years, no substantial steps were taken by the white leaders out of their own consciences. They had to be pushed and if we must hold demonstrations to obtain what is long past due, we'll demonstrate."[365] For many white San Diegans, this attitude, rather than discrimination, was the problem. Hence, Chief Sharp's disdain for protest, like that of earlier generations of conservative white San Diegans, grew out of a sense that people of color and poor people of San Diego were causing problems where none existed rather than responding to injustice.

CORE persisted in the face of opposition, picketing outside of the El Cortez Hotel, while the California Real Estate Association was inside devising ways to fight the Rumford Act and mounting a campaign against the Bank of America for its discriminatory hiring practices.[366] During the struggle against the Bank of America, CORE activists defied an injunction limiting picketing outside the bank's downtown building on Broadway. As Brown, an ex-Aztec (San Diego State) basketball star and then junior high school teacher, put it, "An injunction that limits to minimal expression any group working for the betterment of minorities is immoral because it makes this group's expression unheard."[367] Brown and future City Councilman George Stevens were arrested, as was Grossmont College Dean Charles Collins. Mayor Curran, members of the city council, judges, and police all condemned the protesters. Collins's jailors made their racism readily apparent, calling the white academic a "nigger lover" and asking him if he'd like his daughters to "marry a couple of niggers."[368] Nonetheless, protests continued and the Bank of America began to hire more African American employees.

In the realm of education, San Diego had much to improve as well. In 1966, the city's schools were less integrated than those in Little Rock, Arkansas, and they ranked among the lowest in the nation in the number of minority faculty hires.[369] San Diego's schools maintained de facto segregation and did not serve black and Chicano students well.[370] Indeed, as late as 1977, a Superior Court judge had to issue a desegregation Memorandum Decision and Order, which argued that the "Board has not yet demonstrated its commitment to the necessity of immediately instituting all reasonable and feasible steps to alleviate school segregation."[371] This resistance to desegregation and the improvement of inner-city schools resulted not just in CORE protests but also in a student walk-out at Lincoln High School in Logan Heights in 1969. The school district, which was already facing lawsuits, now had to deal with an outraged student body and an increasingly activist community in Logan Heights and elsewhere in southeast San Diego.[372] Dissent expressed itself in less orderly ways as well, as the rioting on Imperial Avenue in 1967 and in Mountain View Park in 1969 illustrates.[373] Radical groups such as the Black Panthers, US, and the Citizens' Patrol Against Police Brutality also had a presence in San Diego's ghetto in the late sixties and early seventies.[374] It was not action on the street, though, that most threatened the San Diego elite; it was the effort to bring dissent into the city's institutions and transform them from within.

In *The Year of the Monkey,* former UCSD Chancellor William J. McGill's self-serving account of his years in La Jolla during the student revolts of the late sixties, he reveals his genuine terror when protesting students threatened to bring in support from radical groups from "downtown":

The prospect of tough street people from Los Angeles and San Diego [like the Black Panthers and Brown Berets] appearing at UCSD to beef up the demands of our minority students was real enough and frightening. That was the direction the struggles with radical minorities had taken at San Francisco State, Berkeley, and in a number of other places. I made a mental note to call Walter Hahn, San Diego's city manager, to brief him on our new problem. It might soon be his problem, too![375]

McGill, who UCSD professor Reinhard Lettan remembers as "a very questionable, oily character" and an "extremely opportunistic, not very intelligent man," might more generously be described as a frightened white moderate, more afraid of radical students, especially black and brown ones, than of the city's reactionary power structure.[376] While he readily admits that he had "little sympathy"[377] for the New Left, McGill reserves his most condemning prose for the Lumumba-Zapata group that was seeking to transform UCSD's Third College into a revolutionary college specifically designed for students of color.[378] His first impression of them is revealing, as the ex-chancellor recalls the students' entrance into his conference room: "All at once they appeared, sixty of them, blacks and Chicanos filing silently and grim-faced into the room." Angela Davis, who McGill refers to as "a black Joan of Arc," is said to have read the demands with a voice "dripping with hatred."[379] Indeed, McGill shows a special fixation with Davis in his memoir, admitting to having fearful "visions of Angela Davis dressed as Joan of Arc surrounded by legions of Black Panthers and Brown Berets."[380] He describes Davis as "macho," with "violence" in her rhetoric.[381] Interestingly, he admits to the fear that the "snarling" students led by Davis were "pushing" and "threatening" the provost, who came from "a more golden era," in a quest for his "emasculation."[382] Clearly, in that golden era of the past, chancellors did not have to deal with dynamic black women or, for that matter, very many black women at all. By the end of the chapter on the "Lumumba-Zapata College," McGill is sure to tell his readers that "Angela Davis and her radical supporters had lost their bid for a revolutionary college preaching slavery and genocide as the goals of white society."[383] Civilization as it was known in San Diego had been saved.

Angela Davis, on the other hand, recalls the creation of Third College with a focus on students of color as a "victory—of which all of us were proud," despite the fact that it was not a "revolutionary institution." In fact, rather than "dripping with hatred," Davis sounds quite pragmatic: "Concessions were going to be inevitable, however, the creation of the college would bring large numbers of black, brown, and working-class white students into the university. And it would be a real breakthrough to have a college in which students would exercise more control over the education they received."[384] What McGill's somewhat hysterical version of the story shows is how anxious even "liberal" whites were at the prospect of an aggressive movement of people of color in San Diego. While he repeatedly laments "double-edged racism,"[385] McGill is remarkably unconscious of his own.

The "rude bombshell" of the Lumumba-Zapata paper was delivered to the UCSD administration in March 1969.[386] Rather than coming out of nowhere, as McGill recounts, the student uprising came after the moderate suggestions of the Black Student Council for improving the liberal arts curriculum by creating an Institute for Afro-American Studies and hiring black faculty were lost in the bureaucratic machinery of the university. Particularly upsetting to students was the failure of the university to recruit more than one black faculty member. As Dr. Joseph Watson, the lone African American professor on campus at the time, recalls: "The situation deteriorated from total trust and an attempt by the students to cooperate, to well-founded distrust, based on nonproduction and noncommitment by the University to whatever was relevant to the minority students."[387] Just as the student strike at Lincoln High came as a result of administrative inaction after a highly critical report by a faculty committee,[388] the demands for a Lumumba-Zapata College were triggered by institutional blindness to the needs of minority students. Hence, the students' statement asserted, "If the high schools and colleges are not devising more efficient techniques of mystifying the students with irrelevant inanities, then they are consciously subjecting them to a cold-blooded and calculated indoctrination into a dehumanized and unfree society."[389] The central demands included a guarantee of higher minority enrollment, student control over the college, and a radical curriculum that included a revolutionary canon of Chicano, black, and Third World writers and gave the students the tools they would need to analyze and transform their society.

If the revolutionary demands of the document were not enough to scare McGill, who remembers being "paralyzed by the possibility of racial conflict at UCSD," the students' revelation that their document was prepared with the support of members of the Urban League, NAACP, CORE, US, and the Black Panthers probably intensified the chancellor's deep-seated anxiety.[390] The FBI was also nervous and, as McGill tells us, agents requested the files of Angela Davis and other minority students.[391] All the tension came to a head on May 8, 1969, when the students occupied the registrar's office by shattering the glass door, and were convinced to leave only after a sympathetic faculty member, Silvio Varon, proposed a compromise solution in the faculty senate which the senate then passed.[392] What eventually emerged was a college with an expressed "dedication to the education of large numbers of minority youth" for the purpose of alleviating "contemporary social and economic problems." There would be more student involvement in the running of the college, more flexible admissions requirements, and Third World studies.[393] While it would be assailed for its "Leftist stance," investigated by the regents, and criticized in the *Union,* the college would survive, but, with enrollment of Chicano and African American students still well under the 35 percent level requested by the radicals, it remains a far from revolutionary, if noble, experiment.[394]

Angela Davis remembers that when the students wanted "to demonstrate the extent to which we were serious":

> We decided to occupy the Registrar's office. So we went to Marcuse and I asked whether he would come with us. There was no question about it—of course! We took over the building and we had to kick in the door, break the glass. The first person to occupy that building was Herbert Marcuse.[395]

Herbert Marcuse, who would later secretly pay for the door and argue that the students read Plato as well as Third World writers, was McGill's other problem and the center of the fears of the Copley press and the American Legion.[396] His work was widely read by an international audience of New Leftists, he opposed Governor Ronald Reagan's plan for the rationalization of education, and he inspired, as well as protested with, his students at UCSD. Born in Germany, Marcuse began his career at the Institute for Social Research, where he worked with Max Horkheimer, T. W. Adorno, Walter Benjamin, and other members of the Frankfurt School, one of the most important intellectual circles of the twentieth century. With other members of the institute, Marcuse, a Jew, fled Nazi Germany in 1934 for the United States, where the school was reconstituted at Columbia University in New York. Before he gained international notoriety, Marcuse joined the Office of Secret Services in 1941 and worked in the State Department until 1951 in order to fight fascism. After his decade of government work, he got a job at Brandeis University in 1958, which he later lost after reproaching the president's attempts to stifle academic freedom. Finally, in 1965, a year after the publication of his *One-Dimensional Man*, Marcuse was hired at UCSD.[397]

Marcuse's work fused Marx and Freud and argued that human beings had an inherent drive toward happiness and freedom that was blocked by the "surplus repression" imposed on human labor, social life, and sexuality. He was relentlessly critical of both capitalism in the West and Soviet-style communism, and came to believe that advanced industrial societies had created one-dimensional men who had been seduced into numbness by false needs. Such one-dimensional citizens had lost the ability to see beyond the reality of the existing society and imagine fuller lives and a better society. As he puts it in "An Essay on Liberation": "What is denounced as utopian is no longer that which has no place and cannot have any place in the historical universe, but rather that which is blocked from coming about by the power of established societies." Thus, "It is the task and duty of the intellectual to recall and preserve historical possibilities which seem to have become utopian possibilities." Importantly, for Marcuse, it was no longer the traditional Marxist proletariat who had revolutionary potential, but rather students, the Third World, and racial minorities. This utopianism was to earn him condemnation from both the East and West and admiration from young people around the world.[398]

It would be four years until "Marxist Marcuse" was hung in effigy from the flagpole in front of City Hall. For a while he would write, teach, and stroll the beaches of a town that was the living embodiment of his notion of the one-dimensionality of contemporary human consciousness, a utopia of impoverished imaginations. In his office he collected hippopotamus figurines because he thought the animal, as one former student recalls, "embodied the reality of the absurd and the possibilities of the imagination."[399] Perhaps writing utopian tracts in an affectless military-industrial complex/theme park was also an embodiment of both absurdity and the optimism of his will in the face of the pessimism of his intellect. What began his persecution was a trip to Europe in 1968, during which he visited Berlin and praised Rudi Dutschke of the German Student Socialist Organization just before a series of huge demonstrations during which Dutschke was shot. Marcuse was also in Paris celebrating the birthday of Karl Marx during the May 1968 student revolt that was later transformed into a general strike. These coincidences, combined with the rumor that Marcuse had invited Dutschke to come to UCSD while visiting the recuperating radical in the hospital, sent San Diego's right-wing leaders into action. The Copley press and Rep. Bob Wilson demanded that "Red Rudy" be denied a visa and the American Legion called for an investigation of Marcuse. All of this was despite the fact that both Marcuse and UCSD denied that Dutschke was coming to the university.[400]

The truth, however, was not of much concern to the rabidly anti-Communist retired military officers who edited the ultra-conservative Copley-owned *Union*. As McGill's memoir shows, Harry Foster had not even heard of Marcuse until he had read about him in the *Union*. Thus, when Foster went to McGill's home to extort from him a pledge not to reappoint Marcuse by threatening a full-fledged campaign against the chancellor's running of the university, he was only operating as a front man for the Copley interests. When this attempt failed, a meeting with the paper's editors sought to persuade McGill, but finally it was only a relentless, coordinated campaign waged by powerful San Diego interests in business, government, and the press that forced Marcuse out.[401] Interestingly, McGill does not use the same invective he favored when describing radicals in his portrait of the right-wingers who sought to impose their will on both the university as a whole and on himself. Indeed, he associates those power interests with the "community" versus the "university,"[402] and is careful to compliment the self-appointed vigilantes' military records and to call Copley "a nice man."[403] Apparently, radical *right* politics were seen as less of a threat to McGill.

Fueled by the vitriolic attacks of the "nice man's" newspaper, which also printed numerous hostile letters,[404] the death threats started to pour in to Marcuse from anonymous sources along with those from the extreme right-wing group the Minutemen, and the Ku Klux Klan. A letter he received in July 1968 from the Klan went as follows: "Marcuse, You are a very dirty Communist dog. We give you seventy-two hours to live [*sic*] United States. Seventy-two hours more, Marcuse, and we kill you."[405] After this letter was received, someone claiming to be Marcuse's wife called and had his phone service cut off. At his wife's pleading, the two fled to northern California and later to Italy before returning for the fall quarter. In August, the American Legion, following their old Steinmetz strategy, sent a letter to the University of California regents asking for Marcuse's ouster.[406] UCSD's academic senate then issued a statement supporting academic freedom and, while in Italy, Marcuse shot back at the Legion: "I'm not going to give in."[407] By the time Marcuse returned for the new school year, two San Diego Republicans, Senator Jack Schrade and Assemblyman John Stull, were pushing the regents for Marcuse's dismissal, and the American Legion had raised $20,000 overnight to "buy out" his contract.[408] In September, the Military Order of World Wars jumped on board the campaign against the professor and Foster was back at it too, explaining of the man who he had never read, "His teaching goes beyond Marxism, almost to violent revolution." The expulsion of Marcuse, Foster explained, would be followed by the "cleansing" of all higher education campuses.[409]

Unlike the San Diego State College faculty during the Steinmetz period, the academic senate at SDSC in the late sixties responded to the recent "incursion into academic freedom" and issued a statement in support of Marcuse's rights.[410] Marcuse also received the public support of his department chairman at UCSD.[411] Still, this, combined with the strong support of students as well as national sympathy from Left and liberal circles, was not enough to hold off the Right.[412] Marcuse's appearance at an anti-regents protest at the site of a meeting attended by regent and then governor Ronald Reagan, followed by his speech at a New York fund-raiser for the underground newspaper the *Guardian,* inspired the wrath of the *Union* anew. His New York speech, which had engaged in a complex analysis of the past failures and the possible future of the Left, inspired the *Union* headline: "Marcuse Calls for Sabotage of U.S. Society." This was followed by an editorial entitled "Doctrine of Rebellion Must Go," which engaged in a doublethink similar to Foster's 1950s justification of the Steinmetz firing by chastising Marcuse the Marxist for saying "nobody is free in this society" and then calling for his head, claiming that "The issue is not one of academic freedom."[413] This was followed by yet another letter from the American Legion and continued attacks from Stull and the *Union* in early 1969.[414]

When it came time for McGill's decision on Marcuse's reappointment, he split the difference between the right and left wings of San Diego, reappointing Marcuse for the 1969–70 school year while simultaneously announcing a new mandatory retirement age of seventy, which was Marcuse's age at the time.[415] While McGill argues at length that he was "defending" Marcuse, the terse summary of the event in UCSD's 1993 official history is more to the point, saying, "McGill technically reappointed the professor while denying him a job."[416] As Dr. Avrum Stroll, one of the original members of UCSD's philosophy department, argues in his response to McGill's memoir, the retirement policy was "not long afterwards suddenly forgotten," thus suggesting that McGill's action "abandons morality for expediency." In essence, according to Stroll, "Marcuse [and others] were innocent persons sacrificed by the administration to keep the public wolves at bay."[417] Marcuse himself eloquently expressed what had been on the line: "What is at stake is the right and the duty of the scholar and educator to teach the truth and expose lies."[418] Thus in the Marcuse case, San Diego's right-wing elite had once again successfully "cleansed" local higher education.

Back outside the walls of academia, things were hot as well with the emergence of an off-campus Black Power movement which included both US and the Black Panthers.[419] The Panthers sponsored the "John Savage Free Hot Breakfast Program" for poor children at places like the Christ the King Church at 32nd Street and Imperial Avenue, but they complained of persistent police harassment. Speaking at a rally at San Diego State, Walter Wallace protested that "Brothers have been harassed on their way to feed hungry children."[420] Later, the Panthers would sue the city of San Diego, seeking an injunction that would stop detentions without warrants, unauthorized searches, harassment, and surveillance.[421] There was also an intense conflict with US that resulted in the shooting of Sylvester Bell and another Panther as well as a retaliatory shooting of an US member.[422] Los Angeles and Oakland Panthers, however, generally thought of San Diego as "US territory,"[423] and by 1970, as Harold Keen wrote, the Panthers "have been virtually eliminated from the San Diego scene by a combination of police pressure and fatal shootings by the rival US organization."[424] Ron Karenga's US organization, which persisted in the city, was less leftist and more culturally nationalist in its orientation.[425] Angela Davis recalls of the battles of those years that, "Beneath the façade of unity, under the wonderful colors of the bubas, lay strong ideological differences and explosive political conflicts, and perhaps even agents provocateurs."[426] Thus ended the Panthers' stay in San Diego.

The Chicano civil rights movement was also gaining steam. Inspired by the example of the United Farm Workers of America union, young Chicanos formed local chapters of MEChA (Movimiento Estudiantil Chicano de Aztlán), and there was a small but active group of Brown Berets in addition to many sympathetic mainstream activists. As opposed to the feud between US and the Panthers, local Chicano activists, while not always agreeing, worked together to gain one of the most significant achievements of their era—Chicano Park in Logan Heights.[427] In the 1950s, Logan Heights was California's second largest barrio until new zoning laws brought in industry and junkyards. The barrio shrunk and the quality of life deteriorated drastically. Things got worse in the sixties when Interstate 5 sliced through the heart of the neighborhood, only to be followed by the Coronado Bridge in 1969.[428] As Logan Heights resident Salvador Torres put it: "Nobody came and said 'We want to build this huge bridge on top of you. We want to annihilate you once and for all with something so big your humanity will just wither up and die.' I can tell you everyone hated it."[429]

All of that pent-up anger came to the surface when, on April 22, 1970, Logan Heights residents woke up and discovered that bulldozers had been brought in to clear the way for a Highway Patrol headquarters on what was supposed to have been the site of a new neighborhood park. More than 300 people occupied the site at the foot of the bridge and stopped the work crew from proceeding.[430] After twelve days of occupation, the city agreed to negotiate with the Chicano Park Steering Commit-tee. By May 1971, the state had agreed to a land trade, but Mayor Pete Wilson was not pleased and lamented that the park had already cost San Diego "great sums of money."[431] Despite his opposition, the park was born, and in 1973, Salvador Torres and a group of other Chicano artists began what would become the largest set of Chicano murals in the world.[432] Now a historical site, Chicano Park is also a shining example of the reappropriation of public space by ordinary citizens lined up against powerful interests. Following in the tradition of Diego Rivera, these murals *détourne* the monumental ugliness of the underside of the Coronado Bridge and turn a state-ment about the city's racist planning into an affirmation of Chicano identity. In addition to the Chicano Park protests, Chicano activists occupied the Ford building in Balboa Park, picketed the San Diego police station, and marched into the city council with four nonnegotiable demands: to turn the Ford building into a cultural center, commit more money to Chicano Park, create a community review board to screen police officers assigned to the barrio, and reroute the 805 freeway away from San Ysidro.[433] While not all of these demands were successful, the gesture was proof of rising Chicano political consciousness in the city.

These events, as well as the first stirrings of the gay liberation movement, feminist critiques of men in the movement, welfare advocacy, the "LSD vs. TM" debate, Balboa Park love-ins, antiwar protests from North County to downtown, Cameron Crowe's analysis of the Beatles, and "erotic" film reviews alongside ads for Les Girls, were covered in the pages of San Diego's countercultural newspapers, the *Street Journal* and the *Door*, with the latter covering most of the drug and sexual libera-tion stories. More irritating for San Diego elites than all of those stories, however, were the *Door's* relentless attacks on C. Arnholt Smith, the Copley press, numerous prominent local politicians, and big-business leaders. As Smith snarled to his stock-holders about his enemies at the *Door*, "I wish there was a way to bomb them clear to the other side of the Coronados."[434] Thus, while the San Diego Left and countercul-ture were both quite small compared to their northern counterparts in Los Angeles and the Bay Area, they inspired the wrath of local elites, the police, and right-wing fanatics with alarming regularity. From 1969 to 1972, at least thirty-five separate incidents of terrorism were committed against the two alternative papers and/or local radicals or countercultural institutions. During that period, an alternative school was ransacked, bullets were fired into the office of the *Street Journal,* shotgun blasts were directed into a bookstore by the Minutemen, and $1,000 worth of equipment at the offices of the *Door* was destroyed. In addition to these incidents, the Minutemen waged a death threat against the SDSC Associated Students' president, and bombed the home of a socialist student. There was also a drive-by shooting of the Movement for a Democratic Military's office in Oceanside that wounded one, a death threat made to SDSC professor Peter Bohmer, a grenade thrown into the Peace House on Market Street, and yet another death threat phoned to Peter Bohmer, this one by the Secret Army Organization (SAO). Professor Bohmer's house was then shot up, wounding a woman, Paula Thorpe of the *Door,* inside. Another local radical had his brake lines cut, numerous others received death threats, and the car of a member of the San Diego Convention Coalition and the staff of the *Door* was firebombed in Ocean Beach. Even local Democratic Party chairman M. Larry Lawrence and future mayor Maureen O'Connor received death threats during the month before the Guild Theatre was bombed,[435] resulting in the arrest of members of the SAO, which brought out some of the bizarre connections between that group and the FBI.[436]

After the Guild bombing, the police arrested William Francis Yakopec, and, in a surprising twist, it turned out that the main witness against him was Howard Barry Godfrey, the local SAO commander and an FBI informant working under agent Steve Christianson. Godfrey, it was revealed, had been working for the FBI since 1967, had infiltrated the Minutemen, and had actually helped set up and run the SAO. He was driving the car when SAO member George Hoover shot into Bohmer's house and wounded Paula Thorpe, and he later hid the gun in agent Christianson's house.[437] After the Guild bombing trial, members of the SAO met with their old adversaries from the *Door* at a Jack-in-the-Box in Lemon Grove and began to spill the beans about Godfrey.[438] What the *Door* reporters learned was that SAO had a connection with the future "dirty tricksters" associated with Watergate and that Godfrey had cooked up some wild ideas for the then upcoming 1972 convention, including spiking the punch of antiwar groups with LSD or cyanide, bombing the headquarters of the Vietnam Veterans Against War, bombing the homes of antiwar leaders, kidnapping or assassinating activists, and firebombing the vehicles of activists. More interesting, in light of the September 11, 2001, events in New York, was Godfrey's idea to acquire a drone plane, fill it with explosives, and use it as a flying bomb that would hit Air Force One and kill then President Richard Nixon, who the SAO people saw as a traitor for dealing with Communist China.[439] Thus, the most insane ideas for acts of terrorism came not from the right-wing fanatics themselves, but from the agent provocateur supplied by the FBI. Local activists were convinced that the SAO spy served a dual function by helping to destroy the Left while infiltrating the Right.

If all of this was not bad enough, local police harassed the advertisers in the countercultural press, a sheriff's deputy infiltrated the press staff to spy on them, and the city of El Cajon fought a losing battle to ban newspaper racks specifically to censor the *Door*.[440] In addition to the assaults on the countercultural press, the police, mostly through the Investigative Support Unit, known as "the Red Squad," wiretapped, spied on, and infiltrated antiwar groups, the Brown Berets, the Convention Coalition, and nearly every activist group in the city, all of whom were engaging in legal, nonviolent activity.[441] In a blatantly political move, SDSC Professor Peter Bohmer was also fired because of his activism, despite having been cleared of "unprofessional conduct" charges. Freedom of speech and political assembly did not apply to the Left in San Diego during this period. Perhaps it was some form of cosmic revenge for the ghost of Red Emma that the 1972 convention was taken away from San Diego as a result of corporate and governmental scandal accompanied by fears of massive protests.[442] All the while, the *Union* printed little on such matters other than City Manager Walter Hahn's denials of police brutality.[443]

With no GOP festivities to crow about, Mayor Pete Wilson came up with the pathetic, compensatory idea of having "America's Finest City Week" to help nurse the wounded pride of conservative San Diegans. The label endures as a perpetual symbol of contemporary San Diego's inferiority complex despite the fact that most San Diegans don't know the origins of their self-aggrandizing nomenclature. Since the demise of the alternative papers in the mid-seventies, San Diego has yet to regain an aggressive, progressive alternative to the wholly conservative local media.[444]

On May 10, 1970, George Winnie walked into Revelle Plaza at UCSD, poured gasoline over his body, and burned himself to death like the Buddhist monks in Vietnam. He left a suicide note that said, "In the name of God, end the war." In addition to Winnie's stark, ultimate statement of conscience, San Diego saw significant antiwar protests on all of its major college campuses and on the streets from downtown to Oceanside. In November 1969, 5,000 protesters marched through the streets of downtown San Diego.[445] A May 1972 protest, which also drew thousands, demanded that the city council adopt an antiwar resolution. The marchers later stopped traffic by crossing the freeway.[446] Also in 1972, protesters in Del Mar were arrested as they sought to stop trains filled with munitions heading to Los Angeles and eventually to Vietnam.[447] The wave of protest was unlike anything seen in the city since 1912, but perhaps the most startling dissent came from the ranks of the military itself. As McGill points out in his memoir, the city of San Diego was transformed by the decision of Washington officials "to liberalize Navy regulations and to proceed with the full integration of the U.S. Navy."[448] This transformed the military and brought in a much more diverse group of enlisted men. Later it would help change the shape of the city, but its first effects were seen in a revolt of the guards in the midst of a war.

As early as 1967, US was trying to build support for Ed Lynn, a black serviceman who was protesting racial discrimination at Balboa Navy Base.[449] By the late sixties and early seventies, resistance to racism, to Navy discipline and working conditions, and to the war in Vietnam exploded into open defiance on the part of many servicemen and veterans. In October 1969, the *Door* published the "Eight-Point Program of the American Servicemen's Union [ASU]," which demanded collective bargaining, the election of officers, the end of saluting, a minimum wage, an end to racism, rank-and-file control of court-martials, the right of free political association, and the right to disobey illegal orders.[450] By December, these demands had been picked up and expanded in the mission statement of another group, the Movement for a Democratic Military (MDM). In addition to the ASU goals, the MDM added a preamble calling for the "ending of the suppression of the American serviceman" as part of a "larger struggle for basic human rights" and openly called for the "pull out of Vietnam now."[451] The MDM's first major protest in Oceanside on December 14, 1969, was extraordinary in that 25 percent of the marchers were active-duty Marines. As the *Door* put it, "One felt that even the military is rebelling, and indeed it is." The MDM servicemen were surrounded by their allies, as well as a large number of Black Panthers. The marchers chanted, "All we are saying is bring the war home!" as they were heckled and threatened by a smaller crowd of 200 Marines. Angela Davis gave a fiery speech at the end of the rally and as the crowd dispersed, skirmishes broke out pitting protesting servicemen and their civilian cohorts against angry prowar Marines.[452] Camp Pendleton was getting hot.

In February 1970, thirty Marines were injured in a riot in the barracks at Camp Pendleton. Upset over what they felt was harassment by two white corporals, thirty-five black servicemen went through the barracks smashing windows, overturning beds and lockers, and picking up sticks, mops, and brooms to fight the other Marines quartered in the barracks. No one was arrested for fear of sparking even more unrest. Commanding officer R. R. Miner blamed the riot on the MDM and the "Green Panthers."[453] On February 2, the shore patrol and San Diego police occupied the block of J Street between 4th and 5th Streets downtown and broke down the locked door of MDM's headquarters without a warrant, arresting one serviceman inside and everyone who left the building that evening without reading them their rights or stating the charges.[454]

That same month, two shore patrolmen were involved in an altercation with off-duty GI's and MDM members in downtown San Diego after they were caught taking down numbers from the military decals on cars parked near MDM headquarters. Six people then rushed out of the building with cameras, flashbulbs, and microphones and proceeded to survey the shore patrolmen, following them up and down the street until one of the cameras was smashed by an officer.[455] This incident forced the shore patrol to retreat to their vehicles for surveillance, perhaps making "absent without leave" arrests, of which there had been twenty-two in two months, more difficult.[456] In March of that year, the MDM protested outside the court-martial proceedings of an enlisted man charged with desertion at the 32nd Street Naval Station, claiming the man was denied due process. Aggressive actions such as these led Marine Commandant General Leonard Chapman to say that "the Movement for Military Democracy is a serious threat to the defense of the country." Local terrorist vigilantes agreed as they showed by hitting the Oceanside MDM headquarters with machine-gun fire, injuring one Marine deserter inside.[457]

Despite military and police harassment of legal meetings, as well as struggles with the city of Oceanside for parade permits, MDM's organizing continued. In May 1970, it held a peaceful antiwar march of 5,000 people that ended in Oceanside's Beach Stadium. As in the earlier marches, this one was met with threats and heckling from angry Marines.[458] Nonetheless, these remarkable protests from within the ranks would continue. In August 1970, the *Door* published a statement by the "Concerned Officers Movement," a fledgling group of twenty-five officers "who have all served honorably in the armed forces," calling for freedom of expression for military men and an end to the war in Vietnam.[459] Antiwar protests, it seemed, would not be silenced.

Vietnam veteran Peter Zschiesche came to San Diego in 1971 and remembers that "If you were here in San Diego in the 1970s, to be in the antiwar movement was quite a deal. It really set people apart given the conservative nature of the town. It wasn't a big antiwar movement, but people were committed."[460] There was, according to Zschiesche, a distinct difference between the countercultural segment of the antiwar movement and the GI protesters:

> A lot of people in the antiwar movement who were countercultural or at the university tended to be more middle class. . . . Then you had people in the GI movement who were not part of that at all. They still had short hair. They were anti-counterculture people. They were very political but their idea of politics was to do whatever they needed to do to relate to GIs. So they kept their hair short, dressed conservatively. They were the heavies, they were more working class . . . there were more people of color. The Center for Serviceman's Rights was the group I knew of. They had various storefronts they operated out of. Probably the biggest and most successful was the one in the heart of the belly of the beast—in what is now the Gaslamp Quarter downtown—which at the time attracted a lot of off-duty servicemen to funky rows of shops, bars and "adult"

theatres. They advised people of their rights to become Conscientious Objectors while they were in the service. And they'd leaflet the bases. They weren't roundabout about it—everybody knew who they were and where they were coming from, and they had big campaigns. One of the big ones was advertised on a poster with beautiful multicolored graphics of the Veterans' graveyard at Point Loma with the *Connie* [USS *Constellation*] steaming out of the harbor. So you had the picture of the ship with the backdrop of the cemetery. It was a powerful message.[461]

On the USS *Constellation,* nine sailors got the message. On September 29, 1971, four sailors walked off the aircraft carrier and went to several churches asking for sanctuary. Initially, a number of churches refused to shelter them, but they eventually found sanctuary at Christ the King Church at 32nd and Imperial, where Father James Gallas and other Jesuits took them in. Later, they were joined by five more men. Once inside the church, the sailors put together a joint "conscientious objector statement," which said, "We as men will no longer take part in war; and we are ready from within to suffer every persecution that our abstention from war will bring us."[462] The defiant sailors were arrested and taken back to the ship where, once on board, they began a hunger strike that lasted for fourteen days. They were sent to the brig for the hunger strike and refused to work in jail. As San Diego sailor Scott Flanagan put it, "I have laid my life on the line . . . and it's up to the Navy what happens. I figure if my beliefs are worth anything then my life should definitely be part of them." Their principled, persistent refusal worked and on December 9, 1971, eight of the nine men were honorably discharged.[463] A statement issued by the men after the discharge read, "The Navy is totally unable to deal with a man's individual conscience. It can only react blindly with its own antiquated regulations." Flanagan, who claimed that "as a human being" he could no longer support the military machine that killed in the name of his country, sought to reframe the meaning of patriotism: "As a patriotic American . . . I must refuse to take part in my ship's mission. I have a conscience to live with. I could not live with the deaths of thousands of human beings knowing I was in any part responsible for those deaths."[464] This time it was not a Communist who shocked San Diego, but one of its cherished Navy men. The guards had revolted.

In May 1972, the Vietnam Veterans Against War were denied a permit to march in the Armed Forces Day Parade but marched anyway as an unofficial part of the San Marcos Drum and Bugle Corps and were booed roundly.[465] Other events in 1972 were more serious, as evidenced by the October 10 revolt at sea on board the USS *Kitty Hawk,* when black sailors, outraged by the racism, job discrimination, lack of free assembly rights, and unequal justice on board the Navy vessel, rebelled. Particularly onerous was the captain's order to the Marine detachments on board to break up any group of blacks walking more than two abreast. According to the Black Servicemen's Caucus, twenty-five black sailors went to the captain to air their grievances, and after dispersing they were set upon by Marines with nightsticks. Other black sailors who were not part of the group of protesters then came to the aid of their fellows, swelling their ranks to over two hundred. Black Marines refused to fight them, but on a ship with only 600 black servicemen out of 5,000 sailors, they were heavily outnumbered by gangs of white sailors. Only a threat to destroy the sick bay unless wounded blacks were treated along with wounded whites kept many of the injured from having to wait until all the whites were treated first. After it was all over, twenty-one black sailors faced a court-martial, while no whites did. In San Diego, a *Kitty Hawk* Defense Committee was formed, which held a support rally on March 11, 1973, in Mountain View Park. In April, an article in the *Union,* "Early Survey on Kitty Hawk Didn't Spot Rising Tension," cited a Navy psychologist who blamed "stress" along with the long tour and miserable working condition as the sparks of the riot, but did not mention racism at all.[466]

Another revolt in the fleet occurred on March 30, 1973, when twenty-three men aboard the USS *Ogden* LPD-5 refused to go to work. The men claimed that the ship was unsafe and that the officers would not listen to them. A petition was given to the commanding officer, who refused to discuss the problems with the men and ordered them back to work. Thirteen of the sailors refused and were sent to the Philippines to be court-martialed. Back in San Diego, members of Concerned Military called for a congressional investigation.[467] Clearly, news of such a "navy strike" was probably making San Diego's original boosters turn in their graves. The master plan for keeping the city white, middle class, and conservative was founded on the Navy and now San Diego was witnessing some unforeseen circumstances.[468] The new sailors and Marines were more racially diverse and working class and they would slowly come to change the face of the city. As for San Diego's famous martial spirit, while it would not disappear, it would never be quite the same. In 1982, the *Union* would report a "draft crisis," with only 66 percent of eighteen-year-old men registering with the Selective Service.[469] Indeed, in 1980, San Diegan Benjamin Sasway became the first person in the nation to go to prison for violating President Reagan's "sign-up" order.[470]

During the eighties, there were weekly protests against the Reagan administration's Central America policy in Balboa Park as well as on college campuses and in front of the *Union,* which supported those polices.[471] On the eve of the Persian Gulf War in 1991, thousands of antiwar marchers again flooded the streets of San Diego, and weekly vigils took place in Balboa Park.[472]

The buildup for a second war in Iraq in 2003 inspired similar dissent, with well-attended teach-ins at City College, San Diego State University, and UCSD, and rallies that drew anywhere from several hundred to as many as 7,000 in Horton Plaza Park, Ocean Beach, Balboa Park, and the Federal Building downtown. Even in the midst of the wave of patriotism accompanying President George W. Bush's "war on terror," flag decals on SUVs abound but there has been no rise in enlistment in the armed forces in San Diego County. Like the vast majority of Americans in the 2000s, San Diegans neither volunteer to fight nor protest. War has become a spectator sport, a problem for somebody else's son or daughter.[473] Perhaps the "Vietnam Syndrome" the city caught in the late sixties and early seventies still haunts San Diego like its other troubling ghosts.

"Behind the Steel Curtain" and Other Tales of Fear, Loathing, and "Si Se Puede!"[474]

> We do the dirty work, the dangerous work. They were friends of ours. And the next morning, they wanted me to help clean up the blood on the ship.[475]
> *Gloria Canisalez, National Steel and Shipbuilding Company*
> *worker, in 1988*

I used to believe in the system, but I don't believe in the system any more.[476]
Tony Hernandez, drywaller, in 1992

People are getting richer and we're getting poorer.[477]
Ignacio Quinones, janitor, in 2000

On May 4, 1973, Teamsters President Frank Fitzsimmons was enjoying himself at a $50-a-plate charity dinner at the Kona Kai restaurant with "Mr. San Diego" C. Arnholt Smith and Desert Inn Casino owner Irvin Kahn, who was rumored to be linked with the mob. In addition to his control of the U.S. National Bank, Smith, through Hollis Roberts, was one of the biggest produce growers in the country. Roberts Farms had an unlimited credit line at U.S. National Bank, which also handled some $10 million of the Teamsters' Central States Pension Fund, money that was being used by Irvin Kahn to fund a north county land boom that included places like Rancho La Costa, where John Alessio and James Copley were charter members, as well as projects in University City and Los Peñasquitos. Both Smith and Fitzsimmons were close personal friends with Richard Nixon and, along with Roberts, bitter enemies of the United Farm Workers, who were angrily picketing outside the swank gala.[478] Thus, when César Chávez linked his enemies with the White House during a speech at the National Press Club in May of that year, he was drastically understating his case.[479]

The Teamsters' efforts to raid the UFW were indeed strongly encouraged by both the Nixon administration and the American Farm Bureau Federation, an industry group. Einar Mohn, director of the Western Conference of Teamsters, shared the growers' disdain of Mexican farm workers and questioned how effective a union "composed of Mexican Americans" could be. He openly speculated that mechanization might make jobs "more attractive to whites" with whom it would be easier to "build a union."[480] In the midst of the battle between the Teamsters and the UFW, a *Union* editorial predictably condemned César Chávez and the UFW for engaging in "senselessly disruptive activity," while it ignored Teamster corruption and violence.[481] Hence, the interconnections that the Kona Kai event revealed are a graphic illustration of the totally compromised and corrupt business unionism aligned with powerful interests that the UFW and other rank-and-file organizations challenged in the early seventies.

The Teamsters started raiding the UFW in 1970 by signing sweetheart contracts with the growers that dealt only with wages rather than the much broader agenda of the UFW, which had been pushing for power sharing, grievance procedures, and checks on pesticide use.[482] Ignoring the fact that the majority of farm workers were still aligned with the UFW, the growers used the Teamsters as strikebreakers in Coachella and elsewhere by signing contracts with the Teamsters once the UFW contracts expired.[483] In 1972, the California Supreme Court ruled that the relationship between the growers and the Teamsters was collusion and lifted an injunction against UFW picketing.[484] AFL-CIO President George Meany also condemned the Teamsters' union busting as "intolerable."[485] Nonetheless, the Teamsters sat back in a La Costa resort and planned to expand their raiding activities.[486] By September 1973, after 3,500 arrests, countless assaults, and the killing of two UFW activists (one by police, another by a Teamster goon), the UFW was forced to withdraw from the fields and resort to boycotts.[487]

The farm workers' boycott received no support from the Labor Council in San Diego because of opposition to their fight from the Teamsters, Culinary Workers, Retail Clerks, and the Amalgamated Meat Cutters Union.[488] Only the relentless efforts of Chavez and the farm workers, with their boycotts and political lobbying, would overcome the reprehensible tactics of the Teamsters and their allies in the farm industry. During this period, the UFW received support from the students of City College, who demanded of President Gorton that the cafeteria stop selling nonunion lettuce. They then marched to the offices of the deputy superintendent of schools to demand the same thing of him.[489] Mesa College students also boycotted their cafeteria.[490] In 1973, over 400 UFW members and supporters marched from store to store in downtown San Diego demanding that the proprietors stop selling wine made with nonunion grapes.[491] There were also UFW victories in the fields of San Diego County—in the Imperial Beach–Brown Field area—as well as in San Ysidro.[492] In 1974, with the election of Governor Jerry Brown, things began to turn around. California passed the Agricultural Labor Relations Act, which guaranteed the rights of organization, collective bargaining, and secret-ballot elections in 1975 and, within two years, the UFW became the dominant farm labor force in the state, effectively beating out the Teamsters.[493] By October 1975, the UFW held a 9–0 lead over the Teamsters in San Diego County elections.[494] Specifically, the UFW won several elections in Chula Vista, as well as in San Ysidro, San Luis Rey, and Encinitas.[495] On September 16, 1975, Chavez spoke to a crowd of 800 jubilant farm workers in San Ysidro who clapped their hands, stomped their feet, and sang in celebration of their victory.[496] By 1977, the farm workers had new contracts at seven of the San Diego farms and in March of that year, the Teamsters signed an agreement with the UFW, handing over jurisdiction over all of the state's field laborers.[497]

As one local ex-Teamster recalls, when his Local 481 gave out coupons for Safeway in order to help bust the UFW, "I thought, hey, I'm in the wrong union!"[498] The UFW had that effect on a lot of people in the labor movement in the seventies. Chavez's union grew up, in many ways, outside of the traditional structure of the AFL-CIO and represented a movement in flux.[499] The genuine democracy, antiracism, and socially minded unionism of the UFW were also seen in the American Federation of State and Municipal Employees (AFSME) garbage collectors' strike in 1969 that brought together black and white blue-collar workers to fight for union recognition, the right to strike, some fringe benefits, and an end to discriminatory promotion procedures. After two weeks out, they won most of their demands.[500]

Similar militancy was seen in the Machinists' Union sixty-three-day strike at Rohr, where another unified multiracial group of workers was joined by students and other community members who helped them picket and eventually win.[501] Successful strikes were also undertaken in 1972 by taxi drivers, bakers, construction workers, and workers at Electro-Dynamics.[502] Interestingly, some local unions even became involved in the antiwar movement, and a 1971 march was attended by the United Auto Workers; the American Federation of Teachers; the United Federation of Postal Clerks; the UFW; and AFSCME.[503] In 1973 a rank-and-file revolt occurred in the Retail Clerks Union as several members started an alternative union newsletter called *Checkout* that sought to expose corruption and lack of democracy in the union.[504] While their local was put under trusteeship, the rebellious spirit of the workers in San Diego did not die, as the following example illustrates.

Workers in the National Steel and Shipbuilding Company (NASSCO) do the dirtiest and most dangerous work in San Diego. NASSCO has frequently been cited for safety violations by the federal government and, over the years, a good number of workers have died in the yard as a result. As if the nature of the work was not tough enough, over two decades the company's union-busting activities have managed to turn what was once a thriving yard of 7,000 union workers into a shell of its former self, employing under 2,000 workers whose wages, benefits, seniority, and union security have been pillaged by the company. NASSCO workers, however, did not go down without a fight. Indeed, their struggles with the company from the late seventies to the mid-nineties is a story of heroic perseverance in the face of overwhelming forces at one of the most difficult times for labor in the history of the country.

At its height, the shipyard was a vital place populated by a tough, multiracial workforce with a long tradition of rank-and-file rebellion. As Peter Zschiesche, a member and eventually president of the Machinists' Union and later business representative and one of the chief negotiators for the yard's seven unions from the mid-eighties to the mid-nineties, recalls:

> The shipyard was a great place to be because it was so open. When Cherokee [Ironworkers' union presidential candidate Reynaldo "Cherokee" Inchaurregul] first started running, you'd be walking down the yard in the morning and there'd be huge chalk things saying "Cherokee's Coming" written in huge letters all over the side of a ship. The political expression of the artist was totally out front. It was such an anarchistic place. There were 7,000 people wandering around this yard. And there was every kind of political banter, political writings, flyers.[505]

In the midst of this environment, militant rank-and-file activism began to grow in the mid- to late 1970s. Radical publications like the *Waterfront Worker* were circulating among the unionists on the waterfront, and men and women from the New Left and antiwar movements had filtered into the yard and had taken up union work, mixing in with an already solid trade union tradition.[506] In 1977 five men died in the shipyard, and this helped radicalize the workers, particularly members of Ironworkers Local 627, which elected a slate of progressive young union officers led by Reynaldo "Cherokee" Inchaurregul and union business agent Miguel Salas.[507] The new group negotiated a contract that improved upon the previous one in 1978, but many were still unhappy with the cost of living formula, and safety issues continued to be a hot button as well as the subject of numerous flyers and petitions.[508] In 1979, conflict increased as the union sought to reopen negotiations on the cost of living (COLA) formula and angrily protested the laying off of 350 workers as a result of subcontracting in a year in which NASSCO made a record profit.[509] The workers held huge lunchtime rallies with as many as 3,000 workers venting their frustrations at the company and, at times, roughing up managers who dared to spy on them.[510]

Much of the anger came to a head in August 1980 when a mass demonstration disrupted the ship-launching ceremonies for the *Cape Cod.* Two hundred NASSCO workers booed company officials, chanted "No more lies! We want a raise!" interrupted the speech of the undersecretary of the Navy, and then took control of the podium to give their own speeches with bullhorns, denouncing the working conditions in the yard, low wages, and the suspension of a shop steward.[511] NASSCO responded by firing twenty-eight employees, an action that prompted a three-day wildcat strike during which workers scuffled with police on National Avenue, sang blues songs over a bullhorn, and hung NASSCO president Larry French in effigy.[512] While the "illegal strike" was not endorsed by the Ironworkers International or the San Diego Building Trades Council, other local workers largely honored the picket lines against the wishes of their leaders. After three days, the strikers met in Chicano Park and voted to "bring the war inside" the shipyard.[513] Both Inchaurregul and Salas were fired as a result of the wildcat strike but continued on in their union posts.[514] NASSCO officials soon learned that they could not escape the consequences of the firings anywhere when the Shelter Island home of NASSCO vice president Joseph Flynn was picketed soon afterward.[515]

Just when it seemed that tension on the shipyard could not get any higher, two men, Michael Beebe and Kenneth King, died in yet another fatal accident.[516] There were more lunchtime rallies and NASSCO workers sought to turn their grief into solidarity by attending the arbitration hearings for the fired employees en masse. It was clear to the workers in the shipyard that the firing of shop stewards who had aggressively filed safety grievances was a sure sign that NASSCO cared more about union-busting and productivity than safety.[517] Most of the activists were never rehired, but the militancy in the shipyard continued nonetheless. In September 1980, conservative San Diegans' age-old fantasies of bomb-toting Reds finally came true when fired NASSCO workers and Communist Workers Party (CWP) members Rodney Johnson and Clyde Loo were arrested along with fellow worker David Boyd for plotting "various acts of sabotage and violence at NASSCO."[518]

Interestingly, two of the "NASSCO Three" came out of the ranks of San Diego's beloved military. Johnson, an African American Navy veteran, claimed that one of the factors that led to his radicalization was the time he spent in the Navy where he had the humiliating experience of being assigned to clean toilets. This, combined with the poverty of his Chicago childhood and the difficulty he had supporting his wife and three children on his NASSCO salary, made him willing to die to end capitalism.[519] Boyd, a white Air Force veteran of the Vietnam War, told reporters that he had been transformed from a racist reactionary who wanted to come home and "punch a hippie in the mouth" to a militant activist by the indifference of NASSCO for the safety of its employees. While never a Communist, Boyd, the father of two sons, came to see that corporations had too much power and needed to be challenged in order to bring about sweeping change. Loo, a Chinese college graduate and father, joined the Communist Workers Party, which was a small group that grew out of the New Left, after his work experiences and reading pushed him in that direction.[520]

The three men were arrested and eventually convicted as a result of the work of an agent provocateur, Ramon Barton. Barton worked with NASSCO, local police, and the FBI to help set up and convict the radicals. While Johnson, Boyd, and Loo did discuss bombing the transformers at NASSCO, their lawyers and supporters in the shipyard pointed out that Barton had always been one of the most aggressive, angry activists. During the trial, Barton was forced to admit that he disliked the defendants, had suggested a day for the attack, told NASSCO about unrelated union strategy, and had been paid more than $5,000 by the police and the FBI.[521] The tapes from the trial also revealed that Barton was an active participant in the plot, leading NASSCO activists as well as many outside observers to question whether or not the whole thing was a frame-up.[522] Other witnesses revealed that Barton had suggested bomb plots to other employees, bought the materials for making the bombs, and tried to get NASSCO officials to give him a job as a payoff for his activity as a spy.[523] Nonetheless, the jury convicted all three men, who then served four months in prison.[524] As with the SAO investigation in the early seventies, the line between police surveillance and active participation was perilously thin.

Throughout the trial, the NASSCO Three received strong support from many of their colleagues. As one of their fellow employees put it, "Who cares if they are communists or socialists or vote for Reagan or Carter. We know who the real enemy is. That's NASSCO."[525] Miguel Salas, who himself was linked to the plot but not charged, went further: "We have to stand by these individuals who have fought to build our union and spoken up to the company. The real criminals sit behind desks in the front office and other fancy corporate offices. We indict them for union-busting. We charge them with the deaths of Beebe and King and the countless injuries in the yards."[526]

Company officials, on the other hand, continued to go after activists, even suspending an ironworker for passing out literature sympathetic to the NASSCO Three.[527] The intense publicity surrounding the arrest of the CWP members obscured the fact that the militancy in the shipyard was not the result of Red infiltrators as much as it was the workplace issues that persisted there. While the coroner's final report left the cause of Beebe's and King's deaths a mystery, after a thorough investigation of the details, the Occupational, Safety, and Health Administration (OSHA) cited NASSCO for two safety violations on the ship.[528] Hence, radicals who fought the company hard gained the support even of the rank and file who were very unsympathetic to their ideology. One such worker quoted in a *Union* article on the shipyard, "Radicalism Confuses Labor Unrest at NASSCO," said, "There are a few too many radical Commies. The majority of us don't favor their political philosophy but we're stuck with it. They're the only ones who're fighting for us." Interestingly, the largely unsympathetic story claims that "fewer than two dozen" members of "radical fringe groups" were active in the shipyard, hardly a majority of the 6,000 workers.[529] Consequently, it seems implausible to suggest that militancy at NASSCO was the product of anything other than grassroots anger and activism with a solid foundation among the rank and file.

While NASSCO was fond of Red-baiting, the union election of 1980 shows that the most radical slate had the support of enough workers to win an election.[530] Miguel Salas, who had been fired by Inchaurregul from his post as an organizer for the International and business agent for the local because of his links to the bomb plot, beat Inchaurregul in the following union election and his slate of supporters took a majority of the other offices.[531] Unable to tolerate the democratic election of Salas, the International set aside the results and declared Local 627 under trusteeship: an action applauded by the editorial page of the *Union*.[532] After a bitter struggle against trusteeship, more factionalism, and a failed effort to start a new union, Salas and his supporters were finally defeated.[533]

After all of this, however, the NASSCO workers who remained were still ready for a fight with the company and went out on strike for three weeks in October 1981. With NASSCO president Larry French talking about eliminating 70 percent of the workforce over the next two years, the seven unions went into the talks with a hardened attitude.[534] Thus, in October 1981 they struck when negotiations stalled.[535] The legacy of the radical activism of the previous leadership was still there. As Peter Zschiesche remembers:

> The tenor of the yard when I came back in 1981 was that if you were an activist union member (I got active on the Health and Safety Committee), you were a communist. That was the residue of the struggle. The flavor of everything that happened in 1979 and 1980 was still there. There were all these different leftist groups. My politics were a "pox on all your houses." It was tweedle dumb and tweedle dee to me. And still, the fact was, in 1981, there came this huge strike. Even with all the Red-baiting that was going on, you couldn't deny the fact that for the average worker, they weren't getting COLA, health and welfare stuff. So you had this huge strike in 1981 when everything all sort of came back together and coalesced. In the 1981 strike they silk-screened shirts. These were beautiful shirts and were a link: people learned to silk-screen shirts in the antiwar movement and brought what they had learned to NASSCO.[536]

The strike resulted in a pay increase of $2.31 over three years. Another gain was the incorporation of OSHA language around a joint health and safety committee. This was noteworthy because, as Zschiesche puts it, "There were a lot of accidents before that—and it was always quick and it was always gruesome. And it would always be covered up."[537] As important as these gains were, however, the hostile political climate of the Reagan years, combined with the race to the bottom for cheaper labor abroad, would continue to put pressure on the NASSCO unions as they faced the hard edge of the new global economy.

By the time of the 1984 one-week strike over wages, COLA, and job classifications, the workforce was down to 3,400.[538] There were over 1,000 more layoffs in 1986 and the workforce was pushed down to 2,300.[539] In 1987, workers at both Solar and General Dynamics had unsuccessful strikes and the owners of NASSCO smelled blood. Thanks to the Reagan administration, the specter of permanent striker replacements gave management most of the cards when it came to negotiations. As the union business agent at the time, Zschiesche recalls, "Coming into '87 there were dark clouds on the horizon. The company was going through rock bottom times. They were going to lowball the contract, which would be big takeaways in '87."[540] The "dark clouds" soon turned into a proposed pay cut in January of that year, followed by one of the worst accidents in NASSCO history when a steel basket carrying twelve men plunged to the deck of a ship, killing six and injuring the others.[541] OSHA would eventually exonerate the crane operator and cite NASSCO for the deaths.[542] Later the company would even seek to bar federal safety inspectors before it was again cited for an additional 451 safety violations.[543] Nonetheless, NASSCO ruthlessly proceeded to implement the pay cuts on their grieving workers after the union rejected the proposal. Specifically, the pay cuts reduced worker pay by 22 percent on average, 17 percent for journeymen, and up to 50 percent for more experienced workers.[544]

Rather than striking in an unfavorable climate, the unions decided to play the "inside game" by working to rule and giving the company as much trouble as they could without risking being replaced by strikebreakers.[545] In addition to this, NASSCO workers sought to raise public awareness through protests such as the one in which striking Chargers linemen visited the shipyard to show support for the unions.[546] One of the more significant events was the Veteran's Day march composed of NASSCO workers who had been in the service.[547] As the crowd of several hundred men reached the gates, Zschiesche recalls, "It was one of those times when I really realized how powerful that kind of thing can be, because at that point, those guys would have climbed that fucking fence. Those guys would have physically charged the gate. The guys at the gate, who were ex-Navy guys, were frozen. Everybody was totally silent." As one guard later said, "If you guys had wanted to march into the plant, we couldn't have stopped you."[548]

Another powerful event was the picketing of the homes of NASSCO executives in December by workers, some of whom were dressed as Santa Claus.[549] As Zschiesche explains, the purpose of these "mind-blowing events" was to show "the contradiction between our lives and their lives." At one of the homes in La Jolla, Juan Vargas, a newly elected city councilman from a largely Latino district, spoke to the Latino workers in the crowd in Spanish and told them that "the only people who come up here are the people who make their beds and mow their lawns."[550] In February 1988 there was a twelve-day hunger strike at the shipyard by NASSCO worker John McClusky. McClusky, who lost twelve pounds before his union brothers voted for him to stop, was fired by NASSCO because of his protest.[551] That July, the unions again rejected a company offer that failed to restore their pay, and the managers declared NASSCO an open shop.[552] On August 10, the workers, by now down to 1,000, walked out, but, after the longest strike in company history, they were forced to come back and accept a contract that retrieved some but not all of what had been lost.[553]

As part of the 1988 strike settlement, a profit-sharing program was established with the workers, which raised hopes that a less antagonistic relationship was on the way.[554] Unfortunately, the opposite was true. The company's managers, with the help of some outside funding, bought NASSCO from the owner, Morrison-Knudsen, and put in place the Employee Stock Ownership Plan that gave the new owners some tax benefits and a company-dominated concept of "worker ownership" of the yard.[555] As Zschiesche recalls, the new management caused the Machinists Union to "appreciate the old [Morrison-Knudsen] rules because these guys had no rules. The rule they lived by in business [was] that there are no rules. What we didn't understand was that the people on the other side of the table had no boundaries."[556] Thus the 1992 strike was over "job security and the survival of unions."[557] Yet, after twenty-five days, NASSCO workers broke the 1988 record for the longest strike, but they were nevertheless forced to come back to the shipyard with no contract.[558] It was all down hill from there. In 1993 the workers rejected another company offer, but by 1994 there was still no deal.[559] With seniority and union security lost, the seven internationals took over the local unions but did not do much better.[560] In 1996, there was yet another strike, but, with no cards left to play, it failed.[561] In 2001, the Machinists Union signed an "open shop" contract and, presently, there is an effort to organize a new union at NASSCO, but prospects for success there are dim.[562] The once-fearsome waterfront militancy is gone, a victim of global economics. In the end, it was not the Communists who destroyed the solid blue-collar jobs but NASSCO managers and capitalism itself.

In addition to the major bleeding at NASSCO, San Diego also saw significant job loss and deunionization at companies like Rohr and General Dynamics. Tellingly, a column by Don Bauder in the *Union-Tribune* in 1983 celebrated San Diego's lack of unions and the "excessively high wages" that they bring as a huge boon for local business. The low level of unionization that Bauder was crowing about in the early eighties was 18.4 percent.[563] By 1989 an article in the *San Diego Economic Bulletin* noted that the level of unionization had fallen to 13.6 percent, but by 1995 the *San Diego Business Journal* outlined labor's losses in industry while noting new gains in the public and service sectors.[564] With the disappearance of so many of San Diego's best-paying industrial jobs, the labor movement has declined in numbers, but it is far from dead.

In the 1990s there were dramatic signs that new sectors of the San Diego working class were ready to wear a union badge. An August 4, 2002, front-page story in the *Union-Tribune* touted labor's "new clout in town."[565] This "new clout" is a product of the energetic new leadership of Jerry Butkiewicz since 1996 and labor's more recent political successes, such as the 2002 election of prolabor environmentalist

Democrat Michael Zucchet over Kevin Faulconer, a Republican supported by large amounts of money from developers and endorsed by the city's conservative mayor, Dick Murphy, as well as the editorial page of the *Union-Tribune*. Heavily outspent, Zucchet's grassroots campaign beat the money put up by San Diego's right-wing elite and, as Donald Cohen of the Labor Council pointed out, "fractured the old guard lock on San Diego politics."[566] Zucchet's election spurred much whining by the editorial page of the *Union-Tribune* about labor's threat to the "interests of taxpayers" if the city's "priorities shift,"[567] but as a letter to the editor by Allen Shur of International Brotherhood of Electrical Workers (IBEW) Local 569 put it:

> Working people have become very active in San Diego County over the last few years. There are several reasons for this "new activism." One, and probably the most important, is that up until the last few election cycles, working people and their interests have been ignored by the media and most local politicians. This evolution of this new activism is the natural result. . . . If "priorities shift" to consider working people, the majority of San Diego's citizen's and taxpayers will be well represented.[568]

Other factors support the possibility of an even stronger labor movement in years to come. The city's demographics have changed dramatically over the last twenty years. Foreign-born residents, who now represent a United Nations–like range of ethnicities—from Africa, Asia, the Middle East, Eastern Europe, and Latin America—comprise 25 percent of San Diego's population. More important, the number of foreign-born San Diegans has grown six times as fast as that of native-born residents.[569] In addition to this, 58 percent of the population below eighteen years of age is now comprised of people of color, indicating a much more diverse San Diego in the future.[570] These statistics, combined with the growth of the service sector, an expanding gap between the rich and the poor, a closing education gap, and a rising cost of living, speak of a fundamentally changed San Diego in the years to come.[571] The Anglo bourgeois utopia that the boosters envisioned is on the run, pushing the suburbs farther to the north and east. An old bumper sticker in San Diego used to declare, "There Is No Life East of I-5," but such a mind-set will become increasingly difficult and dangerous to maintain. The voices of those who live "east of I-5," and, for that matter, "south of I-8," where most of San Diego's increasingly diverse working class live, have begun and will continue to make themselves heard and, in the process, transform the city. In doing so, however, they will have to deal with a long, enduring legacy of top-down class war and an utterly naturalized system that maintains white privilege through city planning, politics, economics, and the media.

Some of the stories that show the face of the new San Diego include the struggles of recently organized workers, socially minded unionists, community-based environmentalists, and bicultural activists working in both San Diego and Tijuana. One of the first such struggles, in the 1990s, was the drywallers' strike of 1992. Reviving a militancy not seen since the NASSCO strikes of the early eighties, the predominantly Latino drywallers sought to reunionize a profession that the industry had busted in the 1970s. Under the leadership of Tony Hernandez, who saw the drywallers' movement as similar to the struggles of the early UFW, 500 laborers engaged in a bitter months-long struggle to gain union recognition, a wage increase, and health benefits for the men who earned $300 for a sixty-hour week.[572] When the drywallers walked out on June 1, 1992, things quickly became contentious, since the San Diego subcontractors fought the strike more fiercely than builders elsewhere in Southern California. There were altercations between strikers and scabs in Coronado, Lemon Grove, Rancho los Peñasquitos, and elsewhere.[573]

One of the strike's more compelling events came in October when Father Victor Salandini, who had ministered for César Chávez and the UFW in the Imperial Valley, held a protest mass for the drywallers outside a church that his Superior was building with nonunion labor in Poway. "The bishop cannot practice unbridled capitalism," Salandini declared to his impromptu congregation of picketers.[574] By November 1992, the strike was won everywhere in the southland but San Diego, where the subcontractors resisted a lawsuit that would have compelled them to accept the union, choosing instead to sue the Carpenters Union for "orchestrating and directing acts of violence." In the face of this stiff opposition, the drywallers rallied in Pantoja Park, picketed newly built homes to scare off buyers, held a sit-in at a drywall firm, and engaged in a nineteen-day hunger strike. "This is our final plea to the community of San Diego to help us," Hernandez said during the fast. "I hope no one has to die, but we're willing to go that far."[575] Finally, in July, the drywallers signed their first contract.[576] Their struggle was important in that it demonstrated the possibility of strong grassroots activism among San Diego's unorganized, lowest paid workers—the very population the Wobblies sought to organize almost a century before. The drywallers' Southern California struggle was the first successful grassroots union victory in the building trades since the 1930s. Unfortunately, widespread permanent gains did not materialize in San Diego.

Other previously unorganized groups also sought to unionize in the 1990s in San Diego. Local strippers at Pacers were the first group of dancers in the state to organize, winning a vote in 1993 and later signing an open-shop contract.[577] Unfortunately, their union didn't survive, but women in San Francisco followed their lead, establishing a closed shop at the Lusty Lady in the mid-nineties. Teaching assistants (TAs) at UCSD were more successful, winning the right to collective bargaining in 1996 and engaging in a successful strike in the mid-nineties.[578] At San Diego State University, nonunionized TAs, along with faculty and undergraduates, staged weeks of protests over proposed budget cuts in the early nineties and held several rallies that drew thousands and were a contributing factor to the resignation of President Day. Outside of the four-year schools, primary and secondary school teachers struck successfully in the nineties and, more recently, at the community college level, the American Federation of Teachers Local 1931 stopped the privatization of their food service workers, won gains for office employees and part-time professors, and had success electing sympathetic candidates to their board of trustees. All of this comes in the face of mounting pressures on educational institutions to adopt a more instrumentalist "business model" that values cost efficiency and dumbed-down "measurable outcomes" over quality instruction.[579]

Other local union successes include the participation of San Diego Teamsters in winning a nationwide strike against the United Parcel Service in 1997, and the successful struggle of the Hotel Employees and Restaurant Employees (HERE) against the Hotel del Coronado.[580] In Coronado, twenty-four workers were arrested during a march in which they were joined by some Japanese tourists who chanted: "The Hotel Del is cheap as hell!" with the protesters.[581] Only after a lawsuit charging the Del with racial harassment and a one-day strike did the workers win a fair contract.[582] HERE also grabbed headlines when twenty-six unionists were arrested at a December protest at a hotel in Mission Valley after they sat down around a Christmas tree in the lobby and chanted union slogans.[583] In August 2002, HERE protested the Acura Classic tennis tournament at the fancy La Costa Resort and Spa. Unionists picketed outside, wore union T-shirts inside, and rented a plane to fly a banner over the event.[584]

Born in César Chávez's backyard in 1977, the United Domestic Workers (UDW) is the first labor union founded exclusively to represent domestic and other home-care workers and only the third union in the history of the United States, after the Sleeping Car Porters and the UFW, to be founded by blacks or Latinos. The UDW, which signed its first contract in 1980, is 90 percent women and driven by a philosophy of bottom-up unionism.[585] As President Ken Seaton-Msemaji put it, "The problem our union faces is that we must build an organizational culture that works against the concept of leadership."[586] In 1994, UDW merged with AFSCME, and from there the San Diego–based union went on to conduct massive organizing campaigns across the state. In 1999 it sponsored legislation that brought collective bargaining rights to 200,000 home-care workers in California, and in 2000 and 2001 it lobbied the state for millions of dollars for increased wages and health insurance for home-care workers. In October 2001, the UDW won an election to represent 12,000 home-care workers in San Diego.[587] The gains of the UDW in organizing the unorganized in San Diego and elsewhere are historic and represent hope for the future of unionism for some of the city's poorest workers. Equally important, the UDW's socially minded unionism is a clear break with the failed business unionism of the past.

Perhaps the shining example of what a new socially minded unionism can accomplish in contemporary San Diego was the janitors' strike of 2000. In April of that year, the Service Employees International Union (SEIU) Local 2028 began a series of rolling strikes against the six contractors who supply janitorial service to most of downtown's high-rise buildings.[588] When they struck at Symphony Towers, Emerald Plaza, and elsewhere, the several hundred mostly Latino janitors were threatened with permanent dismissal and stonewalled by their employers.[589] Undaunted in their quest for a living wage and health benefits, the janitors, who made only $7.05 an hour with no benefits, persevered for two weeks. On April 16, four of them, along with SEIU executive director Mary Grillo, went on a hunger strike to dramatize their plight. As Grillo put it, "Do they buy food or pay the rent? Do they buy enough food or pay for medicine for their children? Do they buy food or fix their cars so they can get to work?" Grillo was joined by Susana Rivera and several others as they fasted for ten days. "We want to pressure the companies," she said of their effort. Dick Davis, lead negotiator for the contractors, responded glibly to the hunger strike: "If they want to starve themselves that's up to them." Ignacio Quinones, a Vietnam veteran, was ready to endure hardship; as he put it, "I've done a lot of hard things in my life."[590]

As the days dragged on, it became clear that many San Diegans supported the janitors, who cared less about the money than the health benefits.[591] Teachers, students, labor leaders, and San Diegans from many other walks of life helped them picket buildings and joined their Workers' Memorial Day march chanting "Si se puede!" along with the janitors as they made their way toward City Hall.[592] Finally, after a month, the janitors reached a tentative deal with the contractors that gained them a modest pay increase and, more important, money for health benefits.[593] Although the gains in San Diego were less than what they would have wanted, theirs was a historic victory in San Diego and a sign that the poorest workers in the city could fight and win. Mexican immigrant workers had stood up to be counted. At the meeting at which the pact was approved, the janitors cheered and chanted "Si se pudo!" reveling in the dignity that came with victory.[594]

While the *Union-Tribune*'s coverage of the janitors' strike was fair, its treatment of its own unions in the 1990s was less than sporting. Ironically, the birthplace of the city's first labor union has always been ambivalent at best, shrilly critical at worst when covering progressive activism. In 1982, William McGill, the victim of a few *Union* broadsides himself, argued that after the death of James Copley, Helen Copley had "moved the paper into the mainstream of professional journalism."[595] This assessment may seem accurate to the superficial observer, but an investigation into the paper's tactics during its war on its unions reveals the same old penchant for heavy-handed crusades against the paper's enemies as well as a disturbingly hypo-critical attitude toward free speech. At a 1990 Newspaper Guild rally, César Chávez criticized employers like the *Union-Tribune* for having "no qualms over using con-sultants—I call them industrial soldiers of misfortune—to threaten workers and bust their unions."[596] This is precisely what the paper did in the nineties when it hired a union-busting law firm, King and Ballow, engaged in a strategy of ignoring rather than negotiating with the unions, and, as former assistant business editor at the *U-T* James Kellenher puts it, "stripp[ed] the union of its power as a collective bargaining agent for the 900 workers in the newsroom and advertising departments."[597]

In addition to stonewalling the union, the *U-T*'s managers manipulated workers by taking them to lunch on company time in order to give them an antiunion pitch and "inviting" them to dinners and ball games to do the same. The *U-T*'s union-busting crusade also involved spending large amounts of money (union supporters suspected millions of dollars) on a well-orchestrated campaign that included giving every employee an antiunion videotaped pitch. Some of the less seductive tactics included sending employees letters informing them that: "You have probably heard that the company has been training striker replacements. That is true. These replace-ments would be used only for positions where employees opt not to work during a strike. If you decide to work during a strike, you do not have to be concerned about being replaced."[598]

In other cases, the *U-T* simply fired workers sympathetic to the union, as it did with Allan Sundstrom, who later sued the paper and won $790,000 in damages. "It's hard to imagine how a jury could decide a company owes someone a job for life," said *U-T* Publishing Company President and CEO Gene Bell of the verdict. Unfazed, the *U-T* pressed on, giving the unions the cold shoulder from 1995–98, setting the groundwork for the decertification votes, which, by very close margins, ousted the Newspaper Guild and the Communications Workers of America from the paper.[599] As Rick Dower of the *San Diego Business Journal* reported, several sources at the *U-T* believed the hardball tactics employed by management were the result of Helen Copley's anger over the unions' boycott of one of her Christmas parties and a sign held by a picketer outside the Mission Valley offices that said, "She has the gold mine while we got the shaft."[600] This may be true, but the total elimination of the unions would also give the paper the "flexibility" it needed in the future without having to worry about any unruly overpaid workers with job security. The *U-T* employee of the future will surely pay for the shortsightedness of the employees who voted out the union.

When it came to ridding itself of the pressmen's union, the *U-T* had a tougher time. After "imposing implementation upon impasse," the paper sought to use the same strategy it had used against the other unions but was met with stiff resistance as Local 432-M of the Graphic Communications International Union (GCIU) started a campaign of its own. The pressmen printed up flyers, t-shirts, bumper stickers, and signs featuring a skunk that proclaimed "Something Stinks at the *Union-Tribune.*" These materials in hand, they picketed advertisers, waged their own public relations battle, and started a successful subscription boycott of the paper.[601] Union activists claimed that *U-T* management responded by harassing them on and off the job and doing everything it could to break their spirit.[602] The most despicable tactic used by the *U-T*, however, was the effort of its lawyers to get the National Labor Relations Board to bar the pressmen from publicizing their dispute even while they were not on the job. As GCIU President Jack Finneran put it, "They're trying to deny our First Amendment rights, which are the very rights that enable them to make the tremendous profits they do. I mean, Helen Copley is worth close to $800 million, according to *Forbes Magazine*. She made that money on the First Amendment. It is incredibly hypocritical."[603] Hence, the Copley press was no more tolerant of the free speech of its union opponents than it was of the free expression of radical professors back in the Red-baiting days of the anti–Steinmetz and Marcuse propaganda campaigns.

When one remembers the paper's editorial condemnation of César Chávez and its praise of the Ironworkers International's decision to void a democratic union election, it is clear that the *U-T* always had and continues to have a different standard for free speech for its enemies than it holds for itself. Not surprisingly, the *U-T* gave no coverage of their legal efforts and very little coverage of the campaign against them. For example, a protest of 300 people in front of the Mission Valley headquarters of the *U-T* that included the secretary-treasurer of the Labor Council, who came to give the paper the Lemon Award for poor labor-management relations, was barely reported and buried in the middle of the paper.[604] Nonetheless, Local 432-M held out with the help of other unions and the community at large and finally settled in August 2002, nearly a decade after the previous contract had expired in October 1992.[605] The contract was not perfect, but it saved the union, an accomplishment in itself given the odds the pressmen were up against. Even more problematic for public discourse in the city of San Diego is the fact that the *U-T* remains the only game in town, dominating not just its own pages, but also the weekly political forum on San Diego's only public radio station.[606] There is no "other side" to challenge San Diego's conservative media hegemony.

Outside of the labor movement, San Diego also has a small but vital community of activists. Founded by Steph Sherer in the late 1990s and currently directed by Martin Eder, Activist San Diego is, according to its mission statement, "a social justice organization that promotes and facilitates the development of an active, interrelated, progressive community in San Diego through networking, culture and electronic technology." Member organizations include the American Friends Service Committee, Compassionate Living, the City Heights Community Development Corporation, the Environmental Health Coalition, North County Forum, the Peace Resource Center, the San Diego and Imperial Counties Labor Council, the San Diego Foundation for Change, the Utility Consumers' Action Network, and the World Beat Center.[607]

Environmental groups are also quite active in San Diego. At the beach, the Surfrider Foundation is debunking the *Baywatch* stereotype of vapid tanned surfers and beach bunnies by energetically fighting the degradation of the coastal environment. Specifically, they call for conservation measures such as keeping houses and roads away from the beach, avoiding quick fixes for beach erosion that hurt the coast in the long run, keeping rivers natural so as to maintain natural cleansing processes, and ending poor city planning that encourages the destruction of the local ecology. Some of their activities include beach cleanups, stenciling environmental warnings on storm drains, water testing, and educating the public on environmental issues.[608]

The Environmental Health Coalition (EHC) is one of the oldest grassroots environmental justice organizations in the United States. For over twenty years, it has been alerting the public to the nasty environmental realities that San Diego's tourist mythology has swept under the rug. For instance, there are over 150 million pounds of toxic waste generated each year in America's Finest City, 3 million of which are released into the air. San Diego's beloved Navy is one of the city's worst polluters, as evidenced by the twenty-two contaminated sites on North Island and the fact that San Diego Bay is one of the most polluted harbors in the United States. In fact, the bay is second only to Newark Bay in its pollution level, with 56 percent of its sediments registering as acutely toxic and 74 percent of the area exhibiting chronic toxicity. As opposed to freeing the city from polluting industries, the Navy has turned out to be the local environment's worst enemy.

On the border, the over 800 maquiladoras are also pumping toxins into the air, earth, and water. In response to these realities, the EHC has helped secure the preservation of coastal wetlands, successfully pushed for the banning of the use of the toxic pesticide methyl bromide near exposed Latino communities, persuaded the EPA to fund the relocation of polluting industries out of residential areas, and engaged in an intensive public education campaign about lead poisoning and other environmental threats to the San Diego–Tijuana region. Some of the EHC's most vitally important work takes place in Barrio Logan, where the mostly Latino residents have been victims of environmental racism as city planners have allowed a disproportionate number of polluting industries to operate there. Things like chrome-plating plants next to schools have exposed children in the community to the cancer-causing substance chromium 6. By going to court to shut down or relocate such plants, the EHC is doing some of the most important social justice work in the city. As Nicole Capretz of EHC puts it, "We want to reduce the amount of toxic pollution in San Diego. We focus mainly on low-income communities of color because those are the communities that are most burdened by toxic pollution."[609] Many San Diegans like to favorably compare their city to "smoggy" Los Angeles, but it is only the activism of groups like EHC that protects San Diego from the same devastating environmental problems suffered by its northern neighbor.

The Globalphobics are a binational network of activists who have sarcastically adopted former Mexican President Ernesto Zedillo's dismissive name for critics of neoliberal economic policies. Seeing the Tijuana–San Diego region as a microcosm of globalization worldwide, the Globalphobics proclaim:

> Those of us who live on the border or who live in the two Californias have been the laboratory and guinea pigs for the globalization experiment. First came the maquiladoras, then came the North American Free Trade Agreement (NAFTA), and now we have the proposal for a Free Trade Agreement of the Americas (FTAA) to take effect by 2005. The World Trade Organization (WTO), the International Monetary Fund (IMF), and the World Bank, as well as the governments of Mexico and the United States, have been instrumental in establishing this model of corporate power on the border that is its home.[610]

In response to this reality, in October 2000 the group held the "Festival of the Globalphobics: Cry of the Excluded Ones," which brought together organizations and individuals to analyze the effects of neoliberalism on the border region. For four days, 250 environmentalists, advocates of the rights of women, migrants, and labor, as well as artists and people concerned with children's issues, met in Tijuana and formed the Globalphobics Network of the Californias. They committed themselves to struggle against the authoritarian version of globalization that undermines democracy and human rights. Specifically, Globalphobics resolved to promote a constitutional salary in Mexico and a living wage in California, campaign for the rights and self-sufficiency of indigenous peoples on both sides of the border, create a binational front in defense of the environment, work for the demilitarization of the border and an end to Operation Gatekeeper, and fight for just legislation concerning education, respect for cultural diversity, environmental justice, and other matters.

On April 21, 2001, 1,500 to 2,000 people gathered for a peaceful protest against the FTAA in César Chávez Park in San Ysidro. Buzzed by police helicopters and surrounded and surveyed by officers on horseback, the protesters listened to speeches by San Diego union activists, day laborers, farm workers from San Quintin, Mexican and American environmentalists, and members of the Frente Zapatista. After the rally, 500 protesters marched past hundreds of heavily armed police to the port of entry and met 500 more people gathered on the other side at Playas de Tijuana near the border fence. At this gathering, they heard more from maquiladora workers and others who outlined the negative impact that globalization was having on their lives. Today, the Globalphobics continue to act on behalf of maquiladora workers, farm laborers, indigenous peoples, migrants, and others who have been left behind by the corporate globalization that continues to be pushed by the Bush administration even as evidence of the costs multiplies. They stand as a local microcosm of a better future driven by grassroots democracy, international cooperation, and cultural reciprocity that might save us from the current apocalyptic dialogue between the institutionalized economic terrorism of authoritarian globalization and the reactionary fundamentalist terrorism of certain of its enemies. At present, such thinking may seem naïvely utopian, and pessimism about the future is warranted in light of San Diego's history of reactionary politics and shortsighted city planning, but hope, as Percy Bysshe Shelley once said, is a moral obligation.[611]

Antiwar body bag installation art (UCSD, 1970)

Better believe it (northeast San Diego, 1970)

Don't go near the water (Mission Beach, 1976)

NASSCO strike (1981)

Pentagon mall (Fashion Valley, 1988)

A motto for the nineties (1996)

Solidarity with maquiladora workers (1997)

Chain-in by Han Young maquiladora workers (Tijuana, 1997)

Life in Vacationland:
The "Other" San Diego

Kelly Mayhew

The rush to California . . . reflects the greatest disgrace on man-
kind. That many are ready to live by luck and so get the means of
commanding the labor of others less lucky, without contributing
any value to society—and that's called enterprise!
Henry David Thoreau

When you take a cab in San Diego, your driver will likely be Somalian, Eritrean,
Ethiopian, Ghanian, Afghan, or Pakistani. This, of course, is not unusual in many
large cities. It does, however, run counter to the image San Diego's boosters have
worked hard to promote of their sunny city. With its pristine sandy shores, tanks
of jumping Shamus, strolling mariachis, and bougainvillea-covered adobe houses
with red-tiled roofs, the tourist version of San Diego is meant to conjure up a hybrid
picture of relaxing sunshine glinting off an azure ocean and a romantic *ranchero* past.
Such a chimera is very much at odds with the reality of the place. Your cabdriver, for
instance, may have been questioned or even detained by the Immigration and Naturalization Service (INS) as part of "Operation Gameday" during the 2003 Super
Bowl game, played in San Diego. With its growing Latino population and waves of

immigration from Africa, Asia, and the Middle East, contemporary San Diego offers up a paradox in which the "real" city is all but eclipsed by the tourist Mecca. Because many of its communities are isolated from one another by a labyrinth of canyons, freeways, and class divisions, a lot of the city's own residents don't know how multifaceted and multicultural San Diego has become. And those sandy beaches might not be so pristine if there has been a recent sewage spill or storm water runoff. All of these contradictions make the United States' seventh largest city an interesting place to watch.

As San Diego becomes more Democratic in its politics, the gap between the rich and the poor continues to grow. Communities in the South Bay area between San Diego and Tijuana, such as Chula Vista, National City, Bonita, San Ysidro, and Imperial Beach, have become largely working- and middle-class Mexican American. Meanwhile, downtown San Diego is witnessing a high-end building boom that is pushing out those who can't afford a $600,000 condominium. In line with the city's history, these developments are just another attempt by business leaders to promote their interests by re-creating the downtown as an elite playground for gentrifying urban pioneers. Coupled with the city's marketing of itself as a vacation paradise, such urban renewal, vaunted as it is on glossy flyers and full-color magazine ads, obscures what it is like to actually live and work in "America's Finest City" (the feel-good moniker coined by then-mayor Pete Wilson after San Diego lost the 1972 Republican National Convention). As the portraits that follow show, the reality of "vacationland" is not always perfect sunshine and endless summers.

So what is the "other" San Diego like? Beyond the beach, the biotech industry, Sea World, and the zoo, San Diego is a city characterized by extremes. There is gorgeous weather; the landscape is beautiful; and tourism and the military produce jobs. However, the cheery sunshine does not prevent one from falling behind on the exorbitant rent or mortgage: Tourism and the military don't pay a living wage. There is also the city's exploitative and exclusionary relationship with Mexico. From its past as a debauched drinking and gambling outpost to the current era, with its maquiladoras churning out a wide range of consumer goods on its outskirts, Tijuana exists as San Diego's Mexican alter ego. In many U.S. citizens' view, Tijuana is merely a gateway for countless illegal migrants crossing over into the Promised Land. And yet, ironically, San Diego's economy depends on this migrant labor force to work for a pittance. This constant migration is so much a part of the fabric of everyday life that "Migrant Crossing" signs featuring a silhouette of a running man, woman, and child line Interstate 5 near the border just below the INS checkpoint on the northern edge of San Diego County. The American greed for new TVs and fashionable blue jeans keeps the maquiladoras humming along while tourists and military personnel roam Tijuana's *Avenida de Revolución* looking for cheap souvenirs and plentiful tequila shots. But beyond the gringo vision of Tijuana, as Enrique Davalos points out in his portrait, is a cultural crossroads to which more and more people are moving from all over Mexico and Latin America to create new lives for themselves. Many who migrate to San Diego note the rich border culture that exists in this region, and the city's growing Latino population attests to the fact that Anglo hegemony will be challenged in the future.

The portraits that follow are an attempt to capture an emerging San Diego. How do people experience the city? Why are they there? How are they helping to change San Diego? Their stories represent a loose cross section of an overlooked San Diego made up of people involved in labor, environmental, and community activist movements, as well as those who challenge the "fun in the sun" stereotype. Some, like San Diego Congress of Racial Equality (CORE) founder Harold Brown and University of California at San Diego (UCSD) professor of literature Carlos Blanco, have participated in some of San Diego's seminal political movements, including the civil rights movement and the founding of UCSD's Third College in the early 1970s. Others, such as Employee Rights Center director and Machinists' Union president Peter Zschiesche, Service Employee International Union (SEIU) Local 2028 executive director Mary Grillo, San Diego–Imperial Counties Labor Council political action director Donald Cohen, and Graphic Communications International Union (GCIU) president and former *San Diego Union-Tribune* pressman Jack Finneran, have been active in some of the most volatile labor struggles of recent local history. I have also tried to show the various ways environmental issues play out in San Diego by including portraits of Marco Gonzalez, an environmental-rights lawyer and chair of San Diego's Surfrider Foundation chapter, and Sonia Rodriguez, a former maquiladora employee who now works for the Environmental Health Coalition (EHC) as a Barrio Logan activist. Finally, there are the people who are not so easy to categorize. Roberta Alexander is a longtime activist and professor of English at San Diego City College. Enrique Davalos helped to found the binational activist group Globalphobics. Geraldo M., an undocumented student, is trying to go to San Diego State University. Binh Hue Truong, a Vietnamese refugee and Canadian immigrant, also participates in San Diego's peace movement. Jenniffer Chase is a Home Start program manager who helps young women. Jane Collins surfs and owns a hair salon. And Iris Blanco has been a bilingual educator and mentor to young women in Barrio Logan.

The following narratives came out of interviews that took place over a six-month period from the summer of 2002 to early 2003. Each person speaks for himself or herself, with only slight editorial intervention for readability. What emerges from these stories is a more complex view of the types of people who live in San Diego, as well as of the various efforts people have made over the years to alter the city. It is my hope that these narratives will inspire readers to think of ways to counter the prevailing power structures they inhabit—be it through activism, political engagement, or even surfing.

Harold Brown: Founder of CORE San Diego, Director of The Center for Community Economic Development Program, San Diego State University

I came to San Diego in 1953 as a transfer student from Penn State to San Diego State University—I was an athlete, and I was recruited by the basketball coach at San Diego State. My impression of San Diego when I arrived was that it was a nice, warm, and friendly place to go to school—and that was all I planned on. I had no intention of making my home here. Since being black in America was a primary concern to me because it had the most impact on my life, more than anything else I was very much aware of and concerned about the conditions of living here as a black person. For example, at San Diego State, I counted twenty-five black students out of probably 11,000 students total. But it was similar to where I came from: there were the same problems of segregation and discrimination.

My impressions have changed, however. San Diego is a different city now in terms of black-white relations; the opportunities that exist for a black American living in San Diego are much different than when I first came here. Now the society is generally open. Back in those days, it was specifically or individually open, which meant that you had to have some help from a white person in order to move up and so on. We fought to have blacks and other people of color work as tellers in banks and even to get jobs to bag groceries in stores. Those were examples of entry-level things that were not open, much less the higher positions in those areas. So those conditions were really poor. Now those things are open.

Another example of how closed the society was is that blacks lived primarily in Logan Heights and southeast San Diego after that—we all lived in those areas. We could not buy a home in another area, nor could we rent apartments in other areas. The conditions back then were pretty much closed to blacks—jobs, places to live, and other areas were all closed. Now it is different. You have blacks working as a result of the work that the civil rights movement and the Congress of Racial Equality (CORE) did. When I say civil rights movement, I mean as a result of the movement in San Diego and in the United States, around the country, but also of the work that CORE did here specifically, leading all of those efforts, mostly by itself—there was no help from other black organizations.

Now we have black people who are teaching in schools all over the place. In the past, you didn't have black principals in schools, and you didn't have black teachers teaching all over. They taught primarily in the black areas. Law firms were in the black areas. Dentists and doctors were all in the black areas. There just wasn't this mass participation, this freedom to participate in this society economically and politically. It was just not available then. For instance, there were no black elected officials back in those days. Now we have had some. They may be regarded as tokens, but we have black elected officials in San Diego and around the country. So a lot has really changed. I'm not so sure about attitudes of people. And most of us who came out of the civil rights movement weren't concerned about attitudes; we were concerned about behavior and visions of opportunity and so on. We wanted to change the conditions that prevented blacks and other so-called "minorities" from being able to live the life of a first-class citizen.

As another example of how things have changed: my wife and I live in Del Cerro, which wasn't even in existence back in those days. And when my wife and I returned to San Diego [from New York] in 1971 after being away for four years, I was surprised to find that we could rent an apartment in Point Loma. I had found a nice apartment in Point Loma and I was sure that they were not going to rent it to me. When we left in 1967 that would have been the case. But they rented it to us. That was the beginning of integrated housing for me. In the mid-sixties, CORE had demonstrated against the California Realtors Association over their stance on the implementation of the Rumford Act [which desegregated housing, in effect].

In 1961, I had been asked to help organize a CORE chapter by Jim Stone, who is now deceased. I was involved at that time with the El Cajon Open Housing Committee, and when we were working on getting whites in El Cajon to accept blacks who wanted to live there, we circulated petitions and went door-to-door and stuff, talking to whites about it. So Jim talked to me about CORE and about helping him form a CORE chapter here.

One of the first things we did, if not the first, was to hold a demonstration when President Kennedy came out here to San Diego. The purpose of that demonstration was to send a message to President Kennedy that conditions in San Diego were just as poor in terms of its racial situation as they were in other places that he may have visited in America. We knew that that information would not get to him any other way, so we held the demonstration. And of course we were accused of all sorts of stuff. Harold Keen interviewed me to explain why we were doing what we were doing. But then after that, we held a lot of demonstrations. Over the years we demonstrated against food markets—one of them was in southeast San Diego, where we demonstrated to try to get blacks hired there. We demonstrated against the real estate associations—the San Diego Real Estate Association and the California Real Estate Association—and against banks, San Diego Gas and Electric Company, and the zoo, and we also held mass marches on issues. There were some demonstrations where we challenged the "separate but equal" practices that were going on around the United States. Unfortunately, there is no record of all the things that we did back then. Generally, it was a protest movement that especially protested the conditions in which blacks were living.

One of the things about CORE membership is that in the chapter in San Diego, the majority of members were white, and people don't know that. They think that the Congress of Racial Equality was a black organization. It wasn't: it was black and white. In fact, the black numbers were in the minority, and it wasn't until we held demonstrations next to the Bank of America that we got a large number of blacks at all. We were constantly recruiting members by word of mouth, encouraging people to join, and the membership grew. I can't recall the top number that we reached, but our meetings used to be pretty full in number and in expression—all that feeling of anger and everything else.

As far as other civil rights and political movements in San Diego in the sixties go, the Black Panthers and US were not in San Diego at the time of our demonstrations, so it was more of a question of what was CORE's relationship to the other black organizations in San Diego, like the NAACP and the Urban League. And the answer to that is that there was a very restrained relationship. The other organizations did not participate in almost any of the activities with CORE. The NAACP, the Urban League, the Black Muslims, the black church, and CORE were all the organizations dealing with race during this time. The Black Muslims didn't believe in integration, so they wouldn't participate with us. The Urban League and the NAACP thought that we were too militant, so of course they didn't want to participate with us. So CORE did it on its own. And any other participation from those groups was very minimal.

The only time that there was any semblance of "unity," as we used to talk about it back in those days, was when I organized a march which was sympathetic to either the march on Washington or the march from Montgomery to Selma. I forget which one it was. CORE organized a demonstration where we marched down to the County Administration Building on Pacific Highway. That was the only activity during all those years in which the other organizations participated with us. We were regarded as *persona non grata* by the people, and—for years I've always hesitated to really say this, or to say it strongly—it was quite hurtful in those days and painful to go through that experience of being hated and disliked by so many people in the white community and ignored by those in the black community. It was a very lonely position. And I was at the forefront of that position, so I received much of the abuse. There's no need, at my age, to say that it wasn't that way or pretend that it wasn't that way, because it was. And out of all those other organizations, none of them participated with us other than at that one march. I don't know how to describe how it felt. It took a lot of strength on the part of CORE members to endure that sort of thing. The most hurt, of course, came because the other organizations were our own people and they did not demonstrate real support. That's a very general statement, I know. I don't mean to imply that there weren't supporters. Most blacks in San Diego agreed with what we were doing and supported what we were doing, but they didn't participate. And I don't know why that was. I've thought about it for thirty years or more. I just don't know. Some people disagreed with my analysis and they may be more right than I, I don't know. But my analysis is that there was a tremendous amount of fear of repercussions, as there was around the country, particularly in the South, where the repercussion could be death.

So blacks in San Diego had a lot of fear of what could happen to them if they protested. I think some people were content to let other people do the work and they would benefit from it—which is the case everywhere. Sometimes they would realize more benefits than the person actually doing the work. I watched many people go forward in protesting inequalities; meanwhile, the ones behind them got the jobs and the political positions and all those things. None of us were going to get those positions because what we were doing wasn't too great for those organizations. The thinking was: "Break the individuals, especially the leaders," which was demonstrated in terms of the jail sentences that were handed out. I always got the most time because I was the leader. Maybe I was actually arrested six to seven times, and the jail sentences came as a result of two demonstrations, at SDG&E and Bank of America. The jail sentences handed out were for "trespassing." Those were some tough times and they're still kind of raw for me.

I eventually left San Diego and CORE in 1967 to become a deputy director in the United States Peace Corps in Africa, and I'm not sure how much longer the San Diego chapter of CORE survived after I left—not that long, I think. Even though it was there at that time, there was not much going on. There was still a lot to do, but there was a lot of internal strife, which forced me to resign. Although it doesn't sound good when I say it, when you take leadership away from an organization, that leadership is missed. Sometimes the organization doesn't survive and move forward. It's not the only time that's happened, either. Even the organization nationally became defunct after a while, although there are other organizations that did survive those times—the Urban League and the NAACP. People had stopped making donations to CORE, though, because we were so "militant," as they described us. So it was a combination of things that led to CORE's demise in San Diego.

I had applied to the Peace Corps because I had this strong desire, this longing, to visit Africa. The opportunity came in the form of the deputy director's position. I was asked if I would be interested in it, and I said yes. It was a fabulous experience and did so much for the soul. It was also good for me to get away at that point.

After returning to the United States and living in New York for a few years, San Diego State University was particularly interested in my coming to SDSU as an administrator to help them with their Afro-American Studies program. That was very interesting to me. So I accepted the position, and from 1971 to 1973 I organized the Afro-American Studies program along with performing my other duties as an administrator. I also served as the director of the program. We formed a major and a minor [course of study], hired the teachers from different parts of the country, and really created a good program that still exists today.

Eventually I moved to the College of Business Administration as the associate dean and organized the external relations office. I did that until I proposed that we establish a program in community economic development. That is something that has also been near and dear to my heart over many, many years because I'd realized at some point after the civil rights movement, or maybe even before, that economics was where we should be focusing our attention. Not that we shouldn't have done what we did—that was very necessary—but we needed to evolve into attaining economic clout that commanded respect. So that was the area which I felt was the next step for the civil rights movement. I decided "Here I am, associate dean in the Business School; why not do it here?" The college agreed and that's what I've been doing since 1995.

There were other organizations that were very important in my life in this whole process. In 1987, we formed a Black Economic Development Task Force. The purpose of that organization was to introduce economic development into the African American community. I served as president of that organization for close to ten years. And another organization that I and two other very prominent and successful white business leaders created here in San Diego is Community Leaders Undoing Biases—CLUB. We started that organization in 1995; this is our seventh year.

So, there's a lot of work to be done, and I think it's going to take some really strong leadership from the business community and from the political and the civic organizations. The Community Economic Development program is important because it helps people who are out there in the community understand what this country is all about: how the economy works, how business and economics fits into the goals that we have socially, and so forth, and how to meld those and bring them together. That kind of intelligent leadership is in our communities, and if we can get intelligent leadership from politicians and businesspeople, then we've got a really great thing going, where maybe someday we will actually become "America's Finest City" (although I have a mental block about that term!). San Diego has such great potential. But no one's addressing the economic development issue that I'm aware of. It certainly wasn't on the list of things that the mayor said he was going to do when he got into office.

Roberta Alexander: Teacher, San Diego City College

For the most part I grew up in Los Angeles, California. My parents were always very active: my father was a trade unionist for most of his life. He was a mixture of what we used to say back then was "Negro" and white—his mother was Scots-Irish and his father was black. My mother was Jewish. Her father came from Russia and her mother came from Poland. During the 1950s, I remember, anti-Communism was rampant, and my family was actually sympathetic to the idea that socialism could give working people a better life and that the wealth in this country should be distributed in a different way. I was involved in the civil rights movement in Los Angeles when I was in high school, and when I went to school at U.C. Berkeley, I participated in the Free Speech movement in the 1960s. I went on a study-abroad program to Spain and got kicked out for participating in a demonstration against the war in Vietnam. When I went back to the Bay Area and graduated with a B.A. in Spanish, I joined the Black Panther Party for a short period of time. It's interesting to me that I got my B.A. in Spanish, because, while my father was black and my mother was white, I grew up largely in an immigrant neighborhood, or a neighborhood that was changing from being mostly black to being predominantly Latino immigrant—that's South-Central Los Angeles.

I didn't have an official position in the Black Panthers—only men had official permanent positions at that time. My "unofficial position," when they found out I could type, was to work on the newspaper. I didn't do the "female" things. In fact, Bobby Seale always cooked for us. When they found out I had a B.A., I also ran some of the study groups for the Panthers. And I was sent to Seattle and Japan as a spokesperson; I think I became known as an orator after my speech about women in the Panthers at the United Front Against Fascism conference that the Panthers held in 1969.

After I left the Black Panther Party, I was trying to figure out what to do. I went to see a mentor, Carlos Blanco, whom I had met in Spain because he was the director of the University of California Abroad program, and he encouraged me to come down and get involved in the Third College at UCSD, which was going to open for the first time in the fall of 1970. So I came down and had an interview to become the resident dean of Third College. After I actually got the position (at the age of twenty-two or twenty-three, believe it or not!), I moved down and had my own little house near the dorms in the grassy area on the edge of campus.

The experience was very interesting. It was a wonderful project initially. Third College had been organized by Chicano, African American, and white students at UCSD who wanted to have a college that would both serve students from ethnically diverse backgrounds and also emphasize the study of people who do not share in the power structure of this country—namely, Chicanos, blacks, and working people in general. But what happened right from the beginning, from the first meeting that we had in the fall of 1970, when everyone was there and all the students were trying to make some decisions, was that a lot of very divisive things were said. There were some African American students who immediately started to attack Chicano and white students, saying that they were racist and that they were trying to get all the resources. It really set the tone for the college for the whole first year and caused problems for a great deal of time after that. It set up a situation in which people were fighting with one another rather than working together, which was very unfortunate. It was indicative of what was happening at that time in the late 1960s. There just seemed to be people who were very provocative who ended up not doing things in the most constructive kind of way, which would have been sticking together rather than working apart.

My involvement in political movements in the late '60s and early '70s in many ways ended up being very painful for me because they involved identity-based politics, and I didn't fall into any of the categories. I crossed the categories. So the Panthers, to some degree, and UCSD's Third College, where you were being forced artificially to choose an allegiance between one or another ethnic group, were impossible dilemmas for me. So that part of it was extremely painful. The antiwar stuff was different, though. I will never forget the two demonstrations I participated in that were ostensibly going to stop troop trains. One was in Berkeley in the spring of 1966, and the other was at UCSD in the early 1970s. In Berkeley, we thought we were going to sit on the train tracks to stop them. Well, a lot we knew about trains! The train comes slowly, with steam coming out the top, and guess what? We got up off the tracks as fast as we could because it wouldn't stop. The demonstration in '72 in Del Mar was similar. But I think some students set something on fire on the tracks. We said we were having a picnic down there so that it would not be considered an illegal gathering. There were a few thousand people protesting. I also remember the police came in large numbers and surrounded the area. We were able to get out on the sides, but some people were arrested.

After one year of being the resident dean of Third College, I decided that administrative work, especially at that age and in that particular capacity, was not very good for me. So I applied and was accepted to the Ph.D. program in the literature department at UCSD. From 1973, I had been teaching adult school in Logan Heights, which turned into a contract. I didn't want to deal with the tenure thing, and I didn't see myself as the kind of academic who wanted to publish or perish, so I ended up staying in adult education. I taught English as a Second Language for many years. I worked with Vietnamese students when they first came in 1979. And in 1977–78, I worked with a lot of students from Iran, because that was when there was a lot of trouble with the Shah in Iran at that time.

It was very interesting to work with Vietnamese students because these were the students who left after the National Liberation Front (the Communists) was successful and had won the war. These students were people I thought I wasn't going to like because I thought they were going to be a bunch of rich people who were just anti-Communist and unreasonable. This was my first real contact with people from Vietnam; when I got their individual stories, I could understand the other side of the story there, too. Many of them did not come from wealthy families, but explained to me what their experiences had been—having to be refugees and boat people. Some of them became very good friends of mine. In east San Diego and, until lately, in Linda Vista, there are large Southeast Asian communities. Many of them work very hard and have become pretty successful—especially the Vietnamese and the Chinese from Vietnam who had done business in Vietnam as well. But then I got more and more involved in and enjoyed working with Spanish-speaking students, mostly from Mexico, and I was able to use my language history with these students more.

In the time I started teaching ESL to now, there have been many different waves of immigrant populations. The first students I worked with in adult education were immigrant students in Logan Heights, and they were from Mexico. The next group of students I worked with, when I taught in Mira Mesa, actually had come from a variety of backgrounds, but many more of them were from Asia, even Japan and China, and many were from Iran, as I mentioned earlier. And then, in 1979 and 1980, I worked with a large influx of students from Vietnam, from Laos—Hmong students from the mountains of Laos, a minority population from that region—and a few Cambodians, but not very many. Toward the mid- to late 1980s there was the amnesty program that affected mostly students from Mexico and Central America. That program required that students study English, so we had a huge influx of Mexican and Central American students at that point. We were teaching in elementary school cafeterias and all over the place to accommodate the large numbers of students.

In the late 1980s, I transferred over from adult education to organize the ESL program at San Diego City College, which, beginning in the late 1980s, had an influx of students from the Horn of Africa, mostly from Somalia. Those students lived primarily in East San Diego. So when I started teaching at City College I had students from Somalia, Ethiopia, and Eritrea at the beginning of the 1990s.

City College is a particularly unique institution of higher education in San Diego. Because it is downtown, bordering Golden Hill, Sherman Heights, and Logan Heights, City College serves largely working-class people and a number of ethnic minorities. However, what's important about City is that there is no one majority group, which makes it a very interesting atmosphere to teach in. We have a lot of students who are in the military and a lot of other places, but I think people choose to go to City College because they get along there. They have other alternatives if they want to be someplace else.

I don't see San Diego as a real cohesive city but as a bunch of enclaves, each of which has its own culture. And those cultures don't necessarily communicate with one another. San Diego in general is, and has historically been, a very conservative city. We have a large influence from the military presence here. There appears to be a lot of protest activity in other cities north of here like Los Angeles or in the Bay Area. The African American community is somewhat smaller here, although it certainly does exist, but it's really pretty much located in southeast San Diego and in East San Diego, where the community is more mixed.

My son lives on 50th Street in East San Diego, which is a particularly interesting place because there is a three-block area that shows how immigration is transforming the city. This is so because the area is an important center of spirituality. There is a mosque with a Buddhist center right next to it, and about three blocks away, there is a Buddhist temple that looks like you're in Thailand or Laos. There is also a Russian Orthodox Church within a few blocks of that area. This single street, 50th east of University Avenue, used to be called, and still is called, "Little Mogadishu" because of the number of Somali people who live there. But it's changing a little now because there are a lot of Mexican families who live there as well, and there are a couple of Pakistani families and families of Muslims, including my own daughter-in-law, who is from Gujarat, India, and my son, who practice Islam. So there is an incredible variety of languages that are spoken in this area. If you are there around 2:30 in the afternoon, you see a pack of what looks like fifty kids of all colors walking home from middle school, though they divide up into their little groups pretty quickly. Five times a day you hear the call to prayer from the mosque and you see people—men only—coming from several directions to pray there.

So, they're all from many different countries. There's a delivery truck that comes twice a day with produce for Mexican people who don't speak English; it honks its horn and people come out of their apartments. They sell produce and eggs and little things for people who are stuck at their houses. Mostly Mexicans, but a few Somalis, know what's going on. The Somali women walk around with their big scarves in bright colors on their heads. A disproportionate number of men have canes or something else that's happened to them. The other day, in my house, I had a cane and my grandson, who's three, said, "What's that, Grandma?" I replied, "Well, that's a cane for someone who's having trouble walking." And he said, "Oh, like the *musjit masjid*?" So often he sees disabled people go into the mosque.

My grandchildren stand on the trash cans next to the fence to see the street because they live in a house or compound with a big gate so that nobody can see their mother. When they're fidgety, we set them up on these big trash cans so that they can look over the fences and they say hi to everybody because there's always something going on in the street—especially when the men are coming to the mosque. The men all know them and say, "Hi, Abdullah! Hi, Hassan." There is a sense of community. People know one another and, among Muslims, the men know one another. I'm kind of this oddity, though. Everyone knows who I am, they know who my son is, and half of them know that I teach at City College. In many ways I cross over because the men know who I am as well as the women. A lot of the Muslim women come from all kinds of places, like Turkey, India, and parts of Africa, and they often visit my daughter-in-law's house.

After the events of September 11, from what I understand, women have been attacked more than the men. They feel more threatened than the men do; apparently they get more comments on the street than the men do, and there is some discussion among the women who wear veils that cover everything but their eyes that they are much more worried about things now than in the past. So they've restricted themselves. There is a story I heard about an Ethiopian cabdriver who grew up in Somalia, which is the case for a lot of the people because the border or distinction between Ethiopia and Somalia is sometimes blurred by the circumstances of the area. He said that a couple of days earlier, he had delivered three guys from the Navy to the 32nd Street station, and when he dropped them off they said "'Bye, slave." He didn't expect this sort of thing from people in the Navy.

At the same time, though, perhaps ironically, the presence of the Navy integrates the city in ways where it would otherwise not be integrated. The whole Murphy Canyon area in Tierrasanta, where I live, is very integrated because of the presence of the military, and in some ways, that's really positive; otherwise, much of that community would be white and middle class. So it brings different things.

Carlos Blanco: UCSD Professor of Literature; and
Iris Blanco: La Jolla Resident/Bilingual Educator/Mentor

Carlos

I came to San Diego in 1964 to found UCSD. It was a beautiful experience, with good work.

The story of UCSD, roughly speaking, begins with Scripps Institute of Oceanography, which had very good scientists of all kinds—mathematicians, physicists, biologists, and so on. In Clark Kerr's master plan for founding the different University of California campuses for the expansion of the student body, the regents had to pick the places for the campuses. They decided that San Diego would be a very good place simply because Scripps was already here. So there was already a bunch of scientists. In 1963, they brought in more scientists, not associated with Scripps, necessarily. And in '64, they brought the rest of us because they couldn't have the kind of university that was cultivated without us."

And so they began to bring in the humanities people, and the first ones they brought were the literature people, and a couple of philosophers. We planned Revelle College and the scientists loved it because they were the kinds of scientists who were not like these guys today; they were the kinds of scientists who were humanists, too. They knew literature, they knew something about philosophy, and some of them played instruments, so they loved to have humanists around. The humanists loved to talk about Picasso or theories about Melville or whatever. The physicists were all theoretical physicists; none of them were like these guys now who only work in a lab. They were really cultured. We had three Nobel Prize winners on campus and about six guys who thought they were going to be Nobel Prize winners. So it was very hot, very high-powered stuff.

The first students came in in 1965, I think, and there were maybe 500 of them, with not a single black or Mexican. They were all Anglo and all had 4.0 GPAs—the best in the state system. Herb York, who was then acting chancellor, a physicist, totally committed to economic development, had a social consciousness, so he initiated the idea of having some black students and some Mexican students in the next year. (By the way, there was not a single Chicano professor, nor a single black professor at that time, either.) To recruit nonwhite students (provided their grades were reasonably good), we went to high schools in the area. So we were doing Affirmative Action without Affirmative Action. And by 1968 there were about forty black students and forty Chicano students. This was all in Revelle College, which had this very strong humanities sequence that was supposed to go on for two years while students did all the sciences, too. What were the humanities courses? The Bible, Plato, the Greeks, the Romans, the English middle ages, the nineteenth to twentieth centuries, the great French and Russian novelists. At a point, shortly after the death of Martin Luther King Jr., in April 1968, the black students began to demand that the humanities sequence have some African American or African relevance.

I had been in Spain, and when I came back in 1968, this was going on. By then, these forty to fifty black students and forty to fifty Chicano students had organized their clubs: the Black Student Council (BSC), which later became the Black Student Union, and the Mexican American Youth Association (MAYA), which later became the Movimiento Estudiantil Chicano de Aztlán (MEChA). They didn't have much against each other because there were so few of them. The black students began to ask for changes: a text or a novel here or a picture there in the humanities sequence. They did this with the help of a wonderful Jamaican professor, who, when he went back to Jamaica for a vacation, wasn't allowed to come back into the United States, and with Angela Davis, who had come in 1966 to 1967 to work with Herbert Marcuse, who had arrived in 1965. The first graduate student we had in Spanish Literature was a woman named Graciela Molina de Pick. One day she walked into my office and asked me: "Well, how can you be sitting here while all these poor Mexicans are wandering around campus not knowing what they're doing? And you claim to be a Mexican." Shortly afterward came one of the Chicanos who says, "Would you be the advisor for MAYA?" Clubs and organizations needed advisers from the faculty. So what could I say? I said yes.

Immediately the Chicanos began supporting the BSC students, who wanted some changes. By October or November 1968, as fast as that, the plans were laid. The second college had been founded, and Muir was what it was going to be called. There was also going to be a third college, the provost of which was going to be a guy named Rappaport, who was a historian. (By then, we had historians.) And to respond to the demands of the black students, who had been supported by the Chicano students, the faculty decided to have something in the third college (which was going to be a historical college) relevant to blacks and Chicanos.

I was on all the committees, and I had all the information, so I reported to MEChA. And through the influence of Angela and myself, we began to have joint meetings between MEChA and the BSC for over a year. We had all sorts of meetings. And somebody said it first, at one of these meetings where we were debating what we wanted in this third college: "Well, why don't we just get the whole college?" We all said, "Wow! Yeah, let's get the college!" A year later, in March 1969, it was approved, and in September 1970, it started. And of course it was not enough to say we wanted the college; we had to say what's going to be in the college. So hour after hour, night after night, we worked and the students drafted the program. First, it would be called Lumumba-Zapata College (after Patrice Lumumba, the democratically elected, CIA-assassinated president of the Congo, and Mexican revolutionary Emiliano Zapata). It was then very obvious: there would be Third World Studies. The college would also have Communications because the establishment lied to us, so it was not how communications machinery worked, but rather the ideology of communications. And, we thought at the time, blacks were mostly urban and Chicanos were mostly rural (which may have been true at one point, but by then it wasn't quite true anymore, but we still thought that way), so we had Urban and Rural Studies. And then, of course, we would have Science and Technology. And we wrote all this out—these were the basic courses for the first year. They were compulsory: everyone had to take them.

To get this through we had sit-ins, occupations of buildings, demonstrations, speeches by Angela, marches, speeches by Marcuse, the total support of Students for a Democratic Society (SDS), and things were happening all over the place. Everybody was for it. We would have these meetings in Revelle Plaza in the center of campus with a microphone and Angela would come in, then Marcuse would come in and say a few words, then we'd march. And the administration was scared shitless. As I was writing all this down the other day, I began to check dates and what was going on: of course they were scared. Things were happening all over the place: at Kent State things had taken place; People's Park in Berkeley had seen a big conflict; there was violence all over the country. And in 1964, there had already been the Free Speech movement in Berkeley. So they were scared. Jorge Mariscal, one of my colleagues, has found a letter from then-Chancellor William McGill to me saying, "Dear Professor Blanco, I understand from a good source that you were one of the people occupying Building 3-F. . . . I know that on your honor you would tell me if you were." Jorge also has the answer, which says: "Dear Chancellor McGill, I don't know 2-F or 3-H. [Because the buildings in Muir didn't have names yet, they had only numbers.] How could I know if I was occupying it?" He thought, by the honor code of the profession, that I would say, "Yes, I was there!" And I didn't. I didn't read

McGill's book on his time at UCSD as chancellor. I looked at a few pages and it's all lies. Not only is he a racist, he lies.

By the time the final debate was taking place in our academic senate about Third College, Joseph Watson was around, and he was the adviser of BSC. Watson was the only black professor; he was very young, and because he was an assistant professor, he had no tenure. The only guy with tenure in the whole Chicano movement in California was me. All the other young Chicano professors had no tenure. That's why I have such affection for Joe Watson: Who would get involved like that? He was a young, promising chemist with parents from Jamaica who were immigrants to New York. He was raised in Harlem, became a chemist, and then he came to this fabulous institution and he got mixed up in the revolution. Joe and I were always together, and he's tall, so we were like Mutt 'n' Jeff. We were sitting in the senate meeting, and we thought, "This is going to be very exciting." All of a sudden, Dean Murphy comes in and says, "Gentlemen, the students are surrounding the Administration Building, and I would beg you to make a decision because things are very bad." Some assistant of his comes in and tells him that the students are taking over the Administration Building. Joe and I shot out the door and ran to the Administration Building. Sure enough, students were taking over—they had knocked the door down. So we came back and they approved the college.

In the process of the discussions in the senate over several days, our students had presented the case. Azzan Davis would get up and explain why there would be Science and Technology, someone else would get up and explain why Third World Studies, and so on. The faculty listened to these nineteen-year-old kids explain what the new college was going to be about. In the meantime, we were having rallies with speeches, and some people were walking around with guns. Some jerk came into the senate meeting one day with a gun. He didn't do anything, he just gestured with it. So the senate approved the proposal for the college. And then the Regents had to approve it. And they approved it with U.C. President Kerr in favor from the start.

The college opened in September 1970. We had gathered a faculty that was pretty respectable and even included some eminent people like Herb Schiller. We had recruited the administration, too. The students had interviewed every possible candidate for everything in the college. It sounds like science fiction, especially when you see the students now. It was so science fiction that they invited me to talk about it in New York. I went to New York to explain how to found a Third World college. People from Germany came to visit—"How was it done?" It was done because they were scared and because of the times. There was the Vietnam War, the civil rights movements, the murders of the Black Panthers—everything. It was just the right moment. After all, we had figured it out. In terms of what was happening, we spent days and nights and hours figuring out tactics and the strategy. For instance, one May 1 we said, "Let's do a May 1st thing." All of a sudden comes Angela and says, "Let's have a party." So we had a rock 'n' roll party in Revelle Plaza. There were police and everybody was waiting. They sent the secretaries home because they thought there would be trouble and instead we had a big dance. We violated regulations because we brought beer. So instead of a revolution, we had a dance. We did figure things out. And that, I think, we should take credit for. We were not so dumb.

And after that, it was all downhill. Actually, before that, it had begun to go downhill. The last time I saw Angela for several years, I met her at a gas station and she was beginning to be on the run. The last words she told me were: "Watch out, be careful, because now the nationalists are going to take over the BSC." Which is exactly what happened. Even though she was in Los Angeles during this time, she still had connections and some control over the BSC, so she knew what was going to happen.

One day I was in my Third World Studies office (I guess this must have been '71, the following year), and somebody knocked on my door. This big guy came in—an ex-con—and he said, "Are you Professor Blanco?" And I said, "Yes." And he said, "My name is Sonny Ali and I'm a new student here. I just got out of prison. And I've been told that you are the leader of the Mexicans, so I'm going to play it straight with you. I want you to know that all cooperation between the two groups is over. We're going to do our thing." Just like that—directly. And I said, "O.K." He had to be one of the provocateurs. There was all this FBI presence around at the time. I mean, a guy like Sonny Ali shows up who must have been, what? Thirty-two years old, coming straight out of jail.

Then, things got very bad at about that time, with fighting in the dorms. Joe

would call me or I would call Joe, and he or I would say, "Are you ready? Let's go."
He and I would walk along the dorms just to show that the solidarity had not been
broken. We did this at least two or three times a week; we would walk along the halls
and say, "Hello, hello, hello." Maria, my daughter, who was going to UCSD and
living in the dorms at the time, has told us stories that we as faculty didn't know.
They would be having a little dance in one dorm with four black students, and the
Chicanos would come in and say, "What are you playing?" And another guy would
say, "Get out." Or vice versa, with Chicanos having music and the blacks coming in.
Or the ones coming into a mixed room and putting the Mexican record on and the
other guys taking it off and back and forth. This apparently started going on every
night.

The whole thing got resolved in a very dicey fashion. Third World Studies was
nearly eliminated—not quite, but nearly. And that was that. Fortunately, it's still
the college that has the most minority students. What is amazing to me is that until
it became Thurgood Marshall College in 1992, from 1970 to 1992 the college had
no name. The students kept voting no to various names. It could not have been
Lumumba-Zapata College, so it was called Third College. Students kept refusing to
name it. They had a referendum every year. Shall we give this name or that name?
They always said, no, Third College. Until '92! Some of the myth remains, but that's
the reality.

Iris

La Jolla, where we live, also had racial issues going on. The Mexican community
ran into all kinds of problems in La Jolla several years ago because Clinton, the guy
who was the owner of one of the local newspapers, threw everybody out of the low-
income community. He said: "You have to leave the place." At that time (I don't
remember what election it was), La Jolla people gave permission to build higher
buildings, so everybody saw the opportunity to build condominiums. All the people
who owned property in that part of La Jolla, in the minority community, they got
very upset. Clinton sent his men to scare the people at night by saying: "If you don't
get out . . ." So we had sixty or sixty-five people, along with children, who were going

to be thrown out of their houses. We called a meeting. The developers had said, "We are going to bring the bulldozers in." We said, "If you bring the bulldozers in, we shall bring the Chicano community in from Logan." They got sort of scared. This is what's interesting: the white liberal women in La Jolla who were employers of these Mexican maids all of a sudden said, "Gee, we'd better do something, otherwise we're never going to have our maids." From one day to the next, they found houses for all the people who were going to be thrown out—in a day. The most interesting part is that they were city houses—in downtown La Jolla—that had incredible rents like $135 to $150. So all the families were accommodated in very nice houses.

I also worked with the Chicano community to create the first bilingual day-care program in La Jolla. And then we said bilingual education should be in first and second grades. People started saying, "No, it's not good for the children," and so on. But we already had proven that all the kids who went through the bilingual day care did well when they went into kindergarten. Children were not very common in La Jolla, so the school was in danger of closing because they didn't have enough students. They decided to bring students from Logan into La Jolla to go to school. I was there teaching a class on basic things. They sent me all the Mexican kids who were in trouble. I was working in two areas: in the morning, I was working with the kids in the school, and then the Logan kids started coming, so I took over the day care after school as well. I cooked in the day-care center at UCSD at the time as well.

Finally, though, I said to myself, "Why don't I go to the source of everything? Why don't I go to Logan?" So I started working in the elementary school there. It was a great experience for me because I felt immediately that it was the right thing. But then there were cuts that affected teachers' aides. They also cut art, and all kinds of other programs. I saw that the bilingual kinds of programs were shrinking, and I figured that very soon I was going to be cut. And that happened.

But I had been working with a group of such bright students, mostly girls, that I went to the junior high and said to the woman who is in charge of personnel there: "I have a dozen or so young girls who are very bright and I would like to keep on working with them." She said, "Only if you can find two or three teachers who would like to work with you." I was lucky because I found three teachers who were very interested in the girls. So we organized our club, which began in 1992.

I worked with the girls for so many years that I moved with them from elementary to junior high and then on to high school, and I think I did a very good job, because half of them went to college. The important thing is what Irma Castro, who invented the program, said: "We have to grab them. We have to get them when they are in the fourth grade. We need to be very sincere, very brutal. We have to talk to them like they are older." And I see how this works. You get three or four teachers in the elementary school, you get three or four mothers, and you get the girls. And then you start moving. If we can get more mothers, more teachers, we make a solid group. Never does a woman say, "No, I cannot do it." I have never found a mother (and I have a good eye) who didn't say, "Yeah, we have to do something for those girls." It was a feminine group—a group of women for many years—and it was beautiful to work with them. So, we didn't change the system, but we did change some lives.

Carlos

Let me tell you something about these girls. They're from San Diego, right? Which is by the water, right? They're from Logan, which is right there at the docks, where they construct ships and whatnot. The first time Iris brought them all over here—this was a few years ago—they came in and they had never been to the beach! Can you imagine that? They had never been to the beach. So, what does the establishment do? Well, it does things, of course, but then they close these programs. So what are you left with? An individual here, and an individual there, trying to make things better.

Jenniffer Chase: Young Women's Advocate for Home Start, San Diego

I came to San Diego when I was two, so I'm one of the only people I know who actually grew up here. I think probably I was extremely isolated from life—I went to school in Ramona, which is not a very diverse place. But I was determined to get out. I got my bachelor's degree, took a semester off, and then went right into my master's degree program in Communications from San Diego State University.

My first semester of graduate school was horrible and wonderful at the same time. My professor, Dr. Geist, had everybody do some volunteering for her course.

She said, "Go and volunteer. You must do so in order to be in this class." My idea when I got into graduate school was that I was going to be a consultant to hospitals and doctors. Instead, I got an internship with the YWCA helping women get out of abusive relationships, or get off drugs, or get off of the street. I ended up staying there for four years as both a volunteer and a paid employee. I also worked in a domestic violence shelter. My first research, my first passion, and my passion still, was to help the people who actually work with the public—the direct service staff. They so often don't get the support that they really need and then they can't give support to the people they're working with. I did one of my first research projects on the hot-line workers and the trauma that they experience. San Diego, in my opinion, has a big problem with domestic abuse. Most places do.

After I got my master's, I eventually worked for the Center for Community Solutions for a year and a half. The center is approximately thirty-two years old now and had been part of the women's studies program at SDSU until it broke off from the university. I was an educator and community developer, and my favorite part was working with kids in the high schools talking about sexual harassment, sexual assault, and relationship violence. I worked all over mostly eastern San Diego: in East County; in Lakeside, which has a huge problem with racism; in El Cajon; and all the way out on the Indian reservations. I also worked a lot in Lemon Grove, which is a great community. They really want to do the best they can do for kids. I worked in the schools, and I would work with kids. In East County it was and still is very difficult to talk about sex or diversity or anything like that in the schools. The kids, though, knew so much about what I was talking about, and the teachers knew so little, that it was a surprise to the teachers. I would teach the teachers more sometimes than the kids. And the kids would teach me more often than I would teach them.

I left the CCS to work at Home Start, where I've been employed for almost two years now. When I started, I got to work in the best program ever: the WINGS program, which means Working to Insure and Nurture Girls' Success. That program was about a year old when I got there, and my office mate and I had the same division; we were team leaders. We each had five home visitors, which is a case manager in social work who works primarily in the home with the family and the primary client, who was a teenage girl between the ages of twelve and eighteen, referred to us through probation. Sometimes they came in for having a knife at school that they never used, and sometimes they came in for battery, prostitution, stealing—sometimes large sums of money. We had a client who stole $100,000 from a school financial aid office. I don't know why they had $100,000 lying around, but it was $100,000 that she and her two friends were arrested for. We had all sorts of girls, and all sorts of families. We had specialists in drug and alcohol abuse and victimization and abuse; we had delinquency specialists, a nurse on one team, a parent advocate, and a parent educator. Each of the home visitors had up to twenty clients, which is a lot, given the cases that they had.

We had some really good success stories. We had a girl who had lost her mother to obesity while the home visitor was working with her. They were a poor black family. The girl was really shy at first and dressed very inconspicuously. Then, about four months into working with her, the home visitor and a lot of the other people noticed a huge change because she started wearing small, flashy clothing, with lots of make-up. We immediately suspected that she was prostituting herself, which turned out to be true. It took us a long time to get her to admit that. It was through our trust and compassion for her and her situation with her family that she finally said, "I've got to tell you something," to the home visitor. So many of the girls—and she actually admitted this in a group of girls—just want to be wanted. And while a few of the girls knew about her, a lot of them didn't know that she was prostituting. Each one of them had their different answer. Some said other things, but she said, "It's because you want to be wanted, you want somebody to love you." She ended up speaking to groups on three different occasions for us and stayed in the program longer than she was supposed to. But she was wonderful, and I'll always remember her.

Prostitution is a huge problem now in San Diego. I would say it is in San Diego because of the changing economy and because the line between well-off and extremely poor people is getting wider and wider; more people are just not able to make it here. And so the girls have this, quote-unquote, "opportunity" to be "loved," to be "wanted" in very skewed ways, to make money, and to have a little bit of what they think is power. They have somebody giving them something that they want for doing something that after a while they say isn't very difficult. So the prostitution in San Diego is really bad and it's directed at all men and not just some groups, like the military. What the police officers would say is that it's because more men have access to afternoons and lunchtime, and have Internet access. A lot of the prostitution right now is on the Internet, so there are a lot of avenues of access.

There was another case, a girl who was born in Ethiopia. Her parents, her younger sister, her older sister, and she came here as refugees. The girl herself also has a two-year-old daughter that she had when she was in Ethiopia. The family came here because of the upheavals in their country. The minute they got here she was picked up by a prostitution ring. This is a very heavy, very violent nationwide Ethiopian prostitution ring. Her little sister was either in it or being recruited into it, and the girl stepped up (it's just amazing what these girls will do sometimes) and got her aunt to report it to the police, with the help of the home visitor and a parent advocate. At a big interview with about four police officers, and after a lot of questioning, the younger sister told them, "Well, they gave me a pager." And that was the cue that she was being manipulated, being sold, and was doing something she didn't want to do. She also had to tell the police what she had to go through. This was one of our girls, who wasn't one of the higher-level probation girls; she was a low-level probation girl.

Currently, I'm working in North County, a new area of San Diego for Home Start. Home Start has two programs there. I help two other managers coordinate the operations of the building. I miss WINGS, though, because it was an awesome program. All the women (and it was all women—we weren't against having men, but they just weren't as qualified to interview the girls) worked, as the drug and alcohol abuse expert said, as women should work together. We were very nurturing, very close, and very open. There was none of the competitive stuff. But the state budget cut us off, so that was it. I worry about what will happen because we helped a lot of girls and we won't be able to do that as much anymore.

My impression of San Diego as a city is that it's way too money-driven, way too conservative, and blind in many aspects to what people need here. There are so many people who are just being forgotten.

Binh Hue Truong: Vietnamese Refugee, Student, Peace Activist

I was born October 3, 1974, in Vietnam, which shows you why my name, Binh, means Peace. This was probably what my mother was thinking when she had me: "I wish this war would end!" I am Vietnamese of Chinese extraction: Truong is the Vietnamese version of Chong. My living immediate family is my father, my mother, my two older sisters, and a younger sister and brother. My sisters and I were born in Vietnam, but my baby brother was born in Malaysia in a refugee camp. That was when we took off, in 1979, and there were several hundred of us on the boat. We were boat people. My memories of all of that are sketchy: enough to traumatize, but not enough to put together a full story without my parents saying, "Oh yeah, that did happen." I know that I lost my aunt and two of my cousins in one of the boats, but I'm not certain if that was one of the boats that went out with us or if that was a boat that went before us. And I remember the really stupid details, like it smelling so bad. That's how refugee camps are—the toilets are these pits. There are thousands of people and it was summertime in Malaysia. But it was on a beach, and we were little kids running around naked. And I remember crying so badly because they had to take pictures of us for identification purposes or to figure out who people were. I remember thinking, "I have to put on a sweater!" It was a bright red sweater, and it was so hot. I was being a brat. It's kind of a silly memory, considering everything else that was happening. I remember that you could trade on water. We would take anything we had when it was raining—bottle caps, pots, pans, bottles—to collect it and hope that some other desperate family didn't steal it. Our family had to drink from something like a bottle cap, and there were seven of us.

We were in the refugee camp for nine months. After that, we got really lucky because when my brother was born, the international community, which at this point was composed of mostly churches in the United States, Canada, and Australia, was sponsoring families. My mother had a newborn, and several other kids, so we got sponsored to go to Nova Scotia, Canada. We were flown to Montreal in January or February 1980, and, getting off the plane, I had never seen so much white in my life. Everything was white! I wondered, "What is this place?" I had never seen anything like that. Then we were brought to Halifax, Nova Scotia. We lived in a really small town, but there were two Vietnamese families at that time—my family and my friend's family—out of a community of about 200 people. So that was traumatizing because we were refugees and also really poor.

The reason we left Vietnam is because my uncle was a very prominent person in the community—he was a cross between the principal and supervisor of the Chinese School. He controlled the Chinese school system, and he owned several bakeries that my father and mother worked at and managed for him. There were a lot of restrictive laws placed against the Chinese when the Communists took over Vietnam. So my uncle was sent to prison for a year and the Communists took over the house and the business. I remember hating the Communists because I was thinking that my parents still had to work—that they weren't paid for it and if they had money, they couldn't buy us food or else they'd be accused of stealing the money. So we were eating stuff like raw sugar. As an adult, this is really strange, looking back, because I don't hate communism. As an idealist, I make a very distinct line between the idealism of Ho Chi Minh and the subsequent Communist government and those policies. So basically, I separate the ideal from the policies. But, if I was part of the older generation who had that happen to me, who had everything taken away, and who were brutalized like that, I might not be able to make that distinction. I feel that I speak from a privileged vantage point. So I don't blame people for being angry, but I think it's hard for me to be angry because the way that I see it, instead of victim/victimizer, there were all these desperate people trying to make this work.

After my uncle got out of prison, my family decided to leave Vietnam. I think he was the one who got the boats together and got the money. This was all totally illegal and really scary because even if you did this, even if you pooled all your money, what you were pooling your money for didn't cost that much to make—these rickety things that fall apart. But what you were actually doing was bribing the soldiers to look away from what you were doing. One of the most awful things happened. Parents would choose to send their oldest child off first because they thought this might be their only chance rather than have them stay in Vietnam and starve. My parents were going to send my two oldest sisters in a boat, but I'm so glad they didn't.

About an hour or so before they were supposed to get in the boat, my mother got this feeling. She said, "We can't put them on this boat." So she pulled them off. A little bit later, the boat blew up. Somebody had squealed. It's one of those things I think about: wow, to not have my sisters.

It's really disconcerting going to a Canadian school or going to an American school and to hear people talking about war and peace in these abstract terms. For me, you know, people die. It's hard for people because they don't connect; they can't possibly understand what that means. So this is a really odd time for me to be living through right now. We are re-creating the Cold War. I don't care what other labels you put on it, terrorism could be communism. We're just interchanging the villains.

I came to San Diego a year ago. Two years ago, my husband got a postdoctoral fellowship at Stanford University, so we moved to northern California. Then my husband got this phone call saying, "Would you like to move to San Diego and start up a biotech company?" He was asked to make his decision and call them on September 11, 2001. So I really remember that day because it's when we decided to move to San Diego. It's a strange marker for me, especially since I did not watch TV at all that day. I got home and found that my mom had been frantically trying to call me all day. She's in Nova Scotia, and she has no idea where New York is, so she freaked out. Regardless of what political side you're on, it was devastating.

My impression of San Diego is that it's warm. I really like the weather. It is a strange city because we're on a border. We have one of the most multicultural populations, and yet it hasn't managed to reach our representation in power and who has money and who doesn't. It's just disproportionately odd.

I live in Hillcrest. We had a month to move down here from the Bay Area. We got on the Internet, and the Internet said Hillcrest is the most walkable area of San Diego—you can walk out the door and you can get a cup of coffee. There are a couple of things about Hillcrest that I do like: (a) It's considered a very gay area and I just like that. I'm bisexual—I came out in high school. The gay and lesbian community—not everybody, but specific people—has usually gotten me through some of the worst times of my life. So I really value them, and I'm much more comfortable living around them. And (b) Hillcrest is walkable. It's very different than the rest of the city. It's a very multicultural neighborhood, which I think might have to do with the fact that once you reach a certain economic level, race ceases to matter as much. So, you either live in the ghettoized, ethnic communities, or you live in the white upper-class neighborhood, or you live in the middle-class mélange. Middle class is O.K., you're not breaking that glass ceiling. I think that's why we like it: it's kind of neutral.

Currently, I am a full-time student. My major is political science and I'd like to get into law school. And while there are a lot of things I'd like to do in the future, right now I'm thinking that I'd like to get into the international court. I'm really interested in human rights issues—things like getting rape included in international law. It's interesting because rape has been used as a primary tool for so long, partly because devaluing women devalues the community, since in most communities women are highly valued. Rape wouldn't be such a powerful tool if women weren't powerful. So I'm interested in the international criminal court and also, in general, I want to get involved in international law and refugee rights.

When my family was in the refugee camp, I was hanging out with my baby sister—I was four, so she must have been about two—and this woman comes by. She goes to my mother and says, "You have so many children. Let me help you and give you some money to feed your children. Let me just take this youngest daughter." Slave trading is pretty common. The refugee community is the most desperate community in the world. They are easy victims for slave traders, as is anybody in an impoverished community. My mom said, "Of course not!" I was so upset, even though at the time, I didn't really know what was going on. But I started crying and told my mom not to let her take my sister. I still have nightmares about this. So from a very young age, I knew slavery was still happening. It's one of those things most people don't believe because they're not closely tied to poverty—they're very far away from it. It's an interesting thing when you look at our media today, when it focuses on Western and First World experiences, because it allows us to completely ignore the fact that many people are experiencing this as a reality and that all these other things are happening. It's a strange thing. My dad was a taxi driver in Canada before he retired, so any time labor issues and immigrants come into question, I think of how my dad's a former taxi driver and my mom's a former janitor. I remember how hard they worked and how much less their work was valued by society.

I don't really know much about the Asian or immigrant community here in San Diego. I got here and started school immediately, so I'm not really connected. What I do know is that there is an organization of Chinese Americans here. There was one Chinese American student who decided to educate his fellow students about a certain type of academic testing that was optional because students weren't being told that they could opt out of it. He got suspended but took the school to court, and he won. He got an apology and all of that. This was in San Diego, believe it or not. And a whole bunch of students opted out of the test. I thought this was great not only because he spoke up, but also because we tend to ghettoize ethnic communities to ethnic issues, and this Chinese guy brought up this broad issue that affects everybody and that's what we really need to start to deal with—to make those connections to those broader freedoms beyond our personal communities.

These days, my own activism tends to be limited to going out to protests or to educational forums (in the past I did a lot of stuff around gender and queer politics and training immigrant and refugee youth for leadership roles), which is one of the reasons why I'm going back to school. It's important to realize what you don't know—you think you're on the side of good, but you have to know what that is. I've been involved in peace issues as well—protests against a war with Iraq and marches about the illegal occupation of Palestine. My husband and I feel that this is extremely important. He's Jewish and one of the things people like to believe is that it's a holy war and not an economic one. My impression of the activist community in San Diego is that it's old in age. I don't mean that derogatorily at all, it's just that I've gone to the meetings organized by the San Diego Coalition for Peace and Justice, and I think a lot of the people are members of the college communities or the Unitarian Church. They're great, they do really good peace work, but I feel so weird going in there because I swear I'm the only one under fifty. That is not to make fun of them because they are doing what I believe the young people should be doing, and it really shocked me that more young people aren't there. For some reason peace has become this passé idea: "Peace was O.K. for the hippies way back when, but it's not O.K. now." I think the idea of peace has become marginalized recently. There are definitely groups here—Activist San Diego being one of them. They're trying to organize people. It's just less active down here. But things do happen.

Geraldo M.: College Student, Undocumented Immigrant

I am a twenty-four-year-old student who has been here for eight years. I immediately started taking English classes like crazy when I got here, and I have been in school ever since. I've also tried to assimilate into the culture and to get an education. I came from a state in the northwestern part of Mexico. I was born in the area of the country where the capital is located.

I was starting the *prepatoria* in Mexico, what you would call the tenth grade in high school here. I was going to study law, but I always wanted to have English as part of my repertoire. And I wanted the opportunity to actually live in the United States and learn the language from the people. I had taken English classes in Mexico, but it wasn't the same thing. You never really learned how to speak because you didn't hear it from people's conversations. So I thought I'd go on a vacation and take courses in the United States and go back and continue in my law studies. But since I came here, I ended up staying for practical reasons. There are a lot of professional people in Mexico who, after they finish their educational careers, try to get work and there are no jobs—no place for them to work. It's not easy to say, "I'm going to school, and I'm not going to make it." You want to say, "I'm going to have a degree and have a good-paying job." I've seen a lot of people who finish their careers and take a job at the corner stand. So my brother said to me, "Why don't you stay here and try it out in school, and then you can finish in Mexico and come back here."

My brother really influenced me. He came here about three years ago, I think it was. I've had a lot of support from my family. I have about eight family members here—there are eleven children in my family, plus my parents, so a lot of my family is already here. My parents go back and forth between here and Mexico. Currently they are residents; with so many kids here and some of them are already U.S. citizens, they were able to get resident status. They go back and live in Mexico because they don't want to give up their citizenship in their homeland, but they also live here with us. We are a binational family.

I just hopped into this country. Unexpectedly. It was much easier to do it when I came in July 1994. My niece and I went up to Tijuana. It was before Operation Gatekeeper was in existence, which means there was not as much driving back and forth by the border patrol. We ran across the border, jumped the fence, and we were in San Diego. We ran into the street on the other side and someone picked us up. So we jumped the fence in San Ysidro and that's how we came into this country.

My illegal status has caused me some problems. For example, since I was here illegally, I couldn't drive a car because I couldn't get a license. So I flew to Oregon and got a driver's license. It was much easier to do it in that state because, since it is not a border state, they pay a lot less attention. It is impossible to be without a driver's license here in California, and when you drive without one, you get a $1,000 fine. There is nothing you can do because that is the law. Another thing about my status is that I had a lot of concern for when I had to make the jump from high school to community college. I took the risk on my own, because I was hoping that something would allow me to go to the university some day.

I was able to go to high school in San Diego because they basically don't ask for any documentation. I just brought in my transcripts from the *preparatoria* in Mexico and proof of vaccination shots for the protection of other children (so I wouldn't bring disease from the tropical place I came from). But that was as far as it went to get enrolled in high school. My first semester of high school was very stressful for me because I could not speak the language. But also the need to feel like I fit in was very strong. The first couple of years I tried to hang out with as many English-speaking students as I could because I was determined to get the language down. That helped me absorb other cultures as well. There were a lot of white kids, Somali kids, Chinese, and of course my Mexican friends. But I tried to communicate more with the ones who did not speak my language. I don't know if it was my personality—that I had to meet as many people as I could—or what.

After I graduated from high school, I let one semester go by because I was afraid to enroll in community college. I was hearing from everyone that it would be impossible for me to go to college here. I talked to a guy who became a very good friend of mine and he said go ahead, so I did, and it worked out O.K. I stayed away from applying to other colleges, although now I think I will be able to go to San Diego State University. However, all of this I have to finance myself, since, as an undocumented immigrant, I don't qualify for financial aid. I've been working ever since I got out of high school, and even in high school in my senior year I started working. I got a more stable job when I got out of high school, as a busboy in a restaurant. And I've been working there ever since. It's how I can afford to go to school, afford food, and afford to help out my relatives, since I live with them and don't pay rent.

The recent legislation that Governor [Gray] Davis signed into law allows undocumented students to transfer to the University of California and California State University systems and not have to pay out-of-state tuition. As long as you went to high school for three years in the United States, you can pay as a resident, which I'm glad for since that really helps my situation. But as far as financial aid goes, that is something I cannot get. I'm lucky that I have a lot of family members here, but I know a lot of high school kids who are the eldest in their family and their parents have a construction job or a cleaning job and they are barely able to pay for food or other necessities. So I've had a lot of advantage since high school. I know a lot of these people are very smart, very bright, but the reality is that their families can't afford for them to continue their education. And without being able to qualify for financial aid, they can't go on to school. The system is more flexible than it used to be, but it still keeps people out who want to go on to another level.

I come from a farming family, so I came from the bottom. It's tough to get an education coming from where I did. First of all, there aren't many universities in Mexico. Because of the high demand for classes, you don't even know if you're going to appear on the next semester's enrollment sheet. If you're the child of a politician or an ambassador or an entrepreneur, it's much better. It's a corrupt system because it only works for those with special interests. That is why I decided to stay here. And I feel I am going to do a lot because of my brothers. They paved the way for me here. I'm lucky that my family is supportive. The brother I live with went to some college too, but he didn't have any financial aid. He went from working on the farm to currently taking classes at City College to get a two-year degree. He wants a career in computer programming.

I have mostly lived in the east part of San Diego. I've compared the conditions living here to where I came from. The quality of life is much better here. But when I go to other areas of San Diego, like La Jolla or other places where the upper classes live, I can see a big differences in San Diego. It's much better up there. So it depends here on what position you have in society. I would say San Diego is a pretty conservative city. I read a lot of stuff from New York and Los Angeles, and it's not like those cities.

My people don't tend to mingle with the first-class citizens. I don't see a lot of my people going to the theater, or going to nice restaurants. Why? There are not a lot of us who have the careers that would allow us to do these things. You have white people who don't like school and just drop out of high school. There are a lot of us who don't have school and there are things that stop us from going. It's like when they show you a candy and you can't have it. I can be part of it. I like a good lifestyle, but, in reality, I don't know if I can make it, if I can get a visa to stay. I don't know what will happen to me. I might have to go back to Mexico. It feels very strange.

There's been a big change at the border since September 11 [2001]. There was a piece of legislation that would have allowed people living here illegally to get their driver's license and also food stamps, but after what happened on September 11, the bill was not passed. I see on the news that the security along the border has become much more tight. I don't go down there—I can't—but I have watched it on the news. I understand about the desire to be more secure, but it has negative effects on us, especially on those who come over every day, who live in Tijuana and come here to work. The government now keeps a close watch because there are a lot of us. We're spoiled here in the United States. We can pay for someone who has more need to do a job that people here don't want to perform. When it comes time to give recompense to those people who bring the food to our table, then it gets political.

Enrique Davalos: Activist, Part-time Community College Teacher

Before immigrating to the United States and San Diego, I went to the largest Mexican public university in Mexico City. I majored in pre-Columbian Mexican history with a focus on gender and sexuality in pre-Christian cultures in Mexico. While I was in school, I became active in social issues. In Mexico City, there are always a lot of demonstrations—especially during that time period of the eighties. In doing activist work, I felt I could not only follow my beliefs but also establish some sort of identity for myself: I made my circle of friends around activism, and I got married to an activist. The people I was involved with were all leftists in the university. We mostly supported the struggles of workers such as truck drivers and elementary school teachers. Then a crisis occurred in the communist world. The Soviet Union collapsed, and I had a personal crisis as well, so I decided to stop participating in the group I had been with. I didn't return to activism again until the Zapatista movement of the mid-1990s. In the meantime, I got remarried to Lisa, who is a *gringa,* and that's how I ended up in San Diego.

To elaborate a little on what I said earlier, in the late 1980s, after five or six years of spending all of my free time doing activist work, I began to feel disappointed because my general sense was that we weren't going anywhere. The conditions for activism at school were becoming more and more difficult as well. On top of everything, the group I was involved with began to transform itself and it became more like a sect rather than something that was open to new developments and responsive to what was happening in the country. The people in the group no longer enjoyed their lives while working at doing something to change things—they became more and more like a radical, closed, and in some ways pain-filled sect. I didn't want to be there anymore. In addition to that, when the Soviet Union collapsed—we knew that they were not real Communists, of course—it was a turning point in society in general that made everything more difficult. And the process of China's emerging alliance with the United States was a little bit disillusioning as well, so I decided that a break from everything was needed. I decided to go to the past to learn about the Aztecs and to learn about history. That was when I went to graduate school. I also wanted to do something that I didn't usually do, which was travel: I went to the United States, Cuba, South America, Europe. This time away from being an activist ended with the Zapatista Revolution and partially with discussions with my wife, in which, in talking about world events with her, I rediscovered my positions and my interests.

I came to San Diego in 1997–98. My wife and I lived in Mexico for several years after we got married, but she had a cultural crisis because she missed her country. She suggested I move here with her. Since I was already becoming a little disappointed with Mexico City at that time and not sure what to do with myself, I agreed to move with her. After a brief stay in San Antonio, Texas, the only place we found where we could both be comfortable was San Diego–Tijuana. In this place, we could live in both countries and also, on both sides of the border, there is a city. That's why we ended up here.

Probably the most important aspect of this city for me is that I never think about it as just San Diego, but always as San Diego–Tijuana. So actually I spend my time both there and here in San Diego. I teach on both sides of the border and I can't really be in one city without having something to do with the other one. When my Mexican American students come to Tijuana, they say that Tijuana is really ugly (actually, that is the impression they have of Mexico as a whole). They put the two together: Mexico is Tijuana; Mexico, then, is a very ugly place. What I find interesting about Tijuana, however, is that it is the combination of many Mexican cultures, so you have migrants from all around the country as well as people from Central America in this part of the country, which is unique for the Mexican culture. As far as San Diego goes, something interesting for me is that I can't really feel that I'm in the United States.

In fact, I can't really generalize at all about the culture in the United States because my contact with the country is very minimal. I never have a chance to be in an environment where everyone is white because most people speak Spanish in the places I occupy, and there are always many different cultures around me. So in this way, I find San Diego beautiful. I know the city contains many sophisticated racist groups, but I haven't had the misfortune of having any contact with them except for when I had to teach at a community college in the East County, where the students were more sensitive to some of the questions I had about the concept of "Western Civilization"—if they understood the implications of that term. But in general, I am very lucky to have very good friends and to be able to inhabit many different environments. In this way, I think that San Diego is an interesting place.

My wife, son, and I live in Chula Vista, which is just south of the city of San Diego, somewhat near the border. The neighborhood has two worlds. The western section is older, poorer, and has a downtown, four trolley stations, and some personality. I like it because you can see people walking on the streets even during weekends. On the other hand, eastern Chula Vista is just a typical new urban development in Southern California and in the United States in general: sterile, uniform in styles and colors, expensive, and everything is designed for driving instead of walking. It is equivalent to a McDonald's hamburger in the housing business. This second area is the one where we live. Here, everything is easy, nice, fast . . . and boring and soft—one would say *blando*. The good thing is its cultural diversity and the many Mexicans who make me feel at home. The bad thing is that they have to work themselves to death in order to pay their mortgages. However, I like the place because it is close to Tijuana, and this is a big priority for me. We can see Tijuana's lights at night from our dining-room window. Also, the area has nice and diverse schools, with Filipino, white, black, Latino, and other students, which is a priority for my wife, Lisa. Finally, the home we bought was affordable for us, which was a big priority.

In order to support my family and in addition to my activist work, I teach at sometimes two, sometimes three, community colleges in San Diego and one public university in Tijuana. I teach Mexican, Mexican American, European, and world history. I have never worked as hard as I work here in the United States. I used to be an adjunct university instructor in Mexico, and I taught history in a high school there, too, to about twelve different groups. But even though that meant many hours in the classroom, it was nothing in comparison to how many hours I have to work here. My working week here is fifty to sixty hours on average, both in-class and out-of-class, teaching, grading, and preparation. It's just amazing. It is an interesting job and a privilege that I was able to get jobs teaching even though I come from another country, spoke very little English at first, and didn't know very much about the

United States. I am aware of how privileged I am in that regard. On the other hand, it's really interesting to learn how advances in capitalism in the United States impact all of its systems. It's amazing the labor instability you have here. I don't ever remember feeling something like that. This exploitation makes me feel that very soon all work as a teacher will be completely unstable. An answer to some of these problems is unionization, I believe. After living in Texas a couple of years, I almost forgot the meaning of unionization [because Texas is a "right-to-work" state that doesn't have collective bargaining rights for workers], so when I got here I was happy to find out that at least in public education, the unions are real and can be powerful. Some of them are, in fact, excellent. The American Federation of Teachers in the San Diego Community College District is one I like a lot. I began to be involved by getting elected to the executive board, because basically it's the only thing we workers have to defend ourselves collectively and to defend ourselves individually. The union positively affects my labor relationship with my workplace. Also, it allows me to create something collective in the college.

As I said earlier, once I became established in San Diego–Tijuana, I began to be active again in social movements. I decided that my contribution here, however, would be as some sort of bridge between the U.S. and Mexican cultures. Even though the people in San Diego and Tijuana are very close geographically, the cultures, the history, are very different. People don't believe they have much in common. There are a lot of misunderstandings; people don't always believe each other and there's a lot of mistrust. So I thought that something I could do would be to facilitate understanding between people from the north and people from the south; therefore, this is what I am trying to do and, in this process, I work on both sides of the border trying to be involved in any kind of project that involves something binational.

The first thing I did here in San Diego was to participate in a demonstration in front of the Mexican consulate in support of the Zapatista Revolution. We also gave presentations, showed films, and generally tried to get the word out on what was happening in Chiapas and what people could do about it in San Diego. The Zapatista movement really captured my attention and the attention of a lot of people in Mexico. The Zapatistas came into being at a moment when things looked very dark. The Mexican president at that time, Ernesto Zedillo, had plans for Mexico to become a First World country, while everyone knew that that was a complete lie. Also, the Mexican government seemed so powerful to people because of the North American Free Trade Agreement (NAFTA) with the United States. It was amazing that, overnight, a group of Indians coming from one of the most remote areas of Mexico, the poorest people in Mexico, the people with the least power, in only one to two months, could just completely destroy the lies the Mexican government was putting out and show the country's real face in a way that was impossible to predict. So it was a show for everyone, and it was also a demonstration of what was possible to do. It would have been difficult not to become inspired. The Zapatista movement is an incredible combination of Mexican indigenous tradition with Meso-American cultures, modern or postmodern ideologies, and a combination of Marxism and Christian liberation theology, which have created some very original ideas about revolution that have captured the attention of people worldwide.

After that, I also got involved in a coalition of more than twenty different progressive movements that tried to address several key issues important to California and Baja California, San Diego, and Tijuana—human rights, immigration, maquiladoras, and moral issues—in one single framework, or one coalition, called Globalphobics. We felt that globalization could be the issue to unite all of these things. We saw that more and more people were talking about globalization and that the movement was becoming stronger. As we put in our mission statement, our "principal objective is to construct bridges which promote communication, respect and understanding, and to generate reciprocal support between progressive individuals, groups and movements of both sides of the Mexico–United States border in the California region." The name "Globalphobics" or *Globalifobicos,* is an ironic use of former Mexican president Zedillo's term that he came up with to dismiss critics of neoliberalism. We use it to show that we reject the neoliberal form of globalization. We organized a conference in October 2000 that was very successful, and we saw that there was a lot of interest in these issues. We wanted to create something global *and* binational—something about Baja California/South of California.

A few months after this conference, on the weekend of April 20–22, 2001, we held a big demonstration on the border against the FTAA (the Free Trade Agreement of the Americas). Thousands of people participated in the seminars held in both San Diego and Tijuana. We had one rally on the U.S. side with many speakers and then another rally on the Tijuana side later that day. Between 1,500 to 2,000 people showed up in César Chávez Park in San Ysidro for a rally with speakers from many different organizations around the area. At the end of the rally, over 500 people tried to march across the border but were stopped by U.S. police, who aimed guns at the protesters. A lot of people did manage to cross the border and were able to join the demonstration in Tijuana, which was followed by a binational cultural event later that night. It was a pretty successful event.

After these actions and others, I now realize that trying to do this kind of work is very difficult. When the euphoria that comes from doing a successful specific action wears off, it is difficult to maintain something so big. One needs to choose something more concrete that one can work on every day and be successful at. So I chose the issue of maquiladoras to focus my attention. Now I am trying to be instrumental in supporting groups of workers in Tijuana that are protesting maquiladoras every single day. In most of the cases, we are trying to do something to help. Every day a group arises which may be destroyed, but then a new group springs up in its place. The corporations know exactly what to do to destroy these movements. We try to support these people in their efforts to protest and to take action against these companies, and we try to make their activism more successful.

Sonia Rodriguez: Barrio Logan Environmental Activist

Help with Spanish/English translation by Hays Witt (EHC policy department)

I'm a single mother originally from Tijuana, and I've been in San Diego on and off since 1978. When I lived in Tijuana, I worked in a maquiladora, so I know what the maquiladora process is like. It's very hard work for low pay. I was an inspector in the maquiladora I worked in which put together Sony televisions. The people who operate the maquiladoras don't treat the employees very well. When you work in one, you lose touch with your family, and you work long hours, far away from home. You have a long way to travel to work and you have to go in early. And when you leave, you have a long way to return home. So you have very little time to be with your family.

From 1988 until now, I've been living in Barrio Logan. I like to live there in spite of its bad reputation. People shouldn't just criticize a community, they should also try to change it—to help change it. Yet if I'd known what the environment is like in Barrio Logan, I wouldn't have moved there. However, I do like San Diego as a city because it's a slower, calmer place than Los Angeles. One can live pretty well here. I say I'm from Tijuana, but I don't feel the difference between San Diego–Tijuana because we'd come up here when I was a girl, and all my life, I'd come and go. Barrio Logan has changed a lot in the last eight years, which I'll come back to later. There are not as many gangs, and it's a lot safer. I now feel that it's like anyplace. I would say it's now as safe as Chula Vista or National City—but not eight years ago! Barrio Logan is comprised of Latinos and African Americans. The groups get along very well and are clustered in various places. There's mixing, but the groups are some-what separate, although they have issues that they will work together on. My group works with other groups, like with a Baptist Church from King-Chavez. So there's mixing.

After I came back to San Diego in 1988, I worked at night as a tortilla maker at Porkyland, so I had to leave my three kids with my sister. I didn't sleep—I'd come home during the day, I'd get the kids ready for school, take them to school, make food. If I got three hours of sleep, that was good. I lived like this for two years. After that, I worked for twelve years in the cafeteria at Perkins Elementary School. In spite of my schedule, I also volunteered at my kids' school so I could know what was going on with them. That's where I got involved with volunteering and community meet-ings. This all got started because they built the Mercado Apartments, which is where I live. And that's where Salud Ambiental, Latinas Tomando Accion (SALTA) comes in, which is a program that the Environmental Health Coalition (EHC) started that had been working in San Diego for a long time. Translated, it means Environmental Health, Latinas Taking Action.

People from SALTA showed up at the Mercado Apartments and invited us to get involved. There were twenty of us when it started. The Environmental Health

Coalition became active in Barrio Logan through the SALTA program—the EHC started bringing information into the neighborhood about SALTA. I'd go to protests at the port as a volunteer. So when EHC needed community activists, they looked to us because they knew we were already very active. That's how I got started on a part-time basis in 1997.

As community members in Barrio Logan, we're not very informed as to how to solve problems. People who don't go to school, people who aren't informed, have a hard time knowing what to do about issues. That's why I was attracted to the SALTA program because one of the things they brought to us were practical strategies for how to get toxic chemicals out of our community. They showed us how to make multiuse household cleaning solutions that don't have toxic chemicals in them. For cleaning glass there's water and vinegar, and for cleaning other things, just soap and water. That way we don't use chemicals in the house and it's cheaper. This program opened a lot of people's eyes. We also started learning who our elected officials were, which is something we didn't know before. Originally we were very fearful when we didn't know who these officials were. The organization has shown that we have a right to live in a community that is as clean as other communities. Now we demand it—things have changed a lot. As I said to someone yesterday, we know we can go to our elected official because we know what his name is and what his job is. Before, we asked if maybe he would do us a favor, but now we demand it, because it's our right to do so. We learned not to ask, but to demand. We have the right to live as safely as anybody, anywhere. To live like that we have to work together and the residents have to do their part too. We're not just waiting to let them worry about it themselves because we know they won't. So we go knock on their doors and ask. That's the difference today.

The Environmental Health Coalition has been around for twenty-three years and was cofounded by Diane Tavkorian, the executive director. It was a small group back then; now there are a lot more of us. The other projects EHC works on right now are: the Clean Bay Campaign; a border campaign that works with community members on problems with maquiladoras and social and justice issues related to them; and a shipyard campaign. I've gotten involved a bit in the border campaign since I know

Tijuana, and I worked in a maquiladora. So if they need me, sometimes I help them. As far as the shipyard campaign, to get them—NASSCO, for example—to clean up their toxic sediments, we want a good-neighbor agreement. We are not just trying to close the shipyards down for the sake of closing them down, but we're thinking about the employees, about their safety, about their security. We want the shipyards to clean up their problems, but we recognize that they are a source of jobs in the community. We're also worried about worker safety. We have a good relationship with labor.

Other organizations that come to the community, arrive, take what they want, and leave. Or, if they're still there, they're not doing anything for the neighborhood. The EHC is an organization that's like a school for the neighborhood, so it's very unique, I think. It's educating us and we know that it's about the health and well-being of our families. They know, too, that we're also residents and that we understand people's problems because we live them. That's the difference between EHC and other organizations. We're not getting rich working here—just the reverse. I see people working late, and on Saturdays and Sundays. We're working hard because we have to; if we have something to do, we do it. But I see other organizations that go and say they're doing their work, but it's for their own benefit only. People here think EHC is different as well. As Latinos, when we met Diane Tavkorian, we saw an American, but we also saw a difference in the way this organization treats us. We were housewives—we were volunteers, but also housewives. And we have had a lot of opportunities opened up to us to learn by working here. We work on computers, we do a lot of things we didn't know how to do. So, we've grown a lot as human beings. I'm very happy here.

One of the big reasons I started getting involved in EHC was because of the environment in Barrio Logan, as I mentioned earlier. Eight years ago, there was a lot of gas in the air; smells would emerge and we didn't know where they were from. There were several kinds of health problems people were having. We had a lot of asthma, respiratory problems, a lot of allergies, including those of the eyes. Wherever you would go, there would be asthma and allergies. The people who live there have more of these ailments than other people. We realized that we have more because we live close together and we can share information about these things. So we hear, "Oh . . . so and so's daughter is sick." The environment makes all of these illnesses worse—so it's not one in twenty people, it's one in five. It's terrible.

Research was done to find out where the smells were coming from. We found that there was a sewer pump that was ancient, and they hadn't cleaned it for years. So we demanded that they clean it. All the industries that are on Harbor Drive along the coast put their waste into this sewer and it goes out into the ocean. So we started fighting for them to clean it up by doing protests and other actions. We were willing to fight however far we had to go for them to pay attention to it. It was only because of these sorts of actions that they would respond to us and do something about it. The smells were only the beginning. The problems had been there for a long time, but as a community we didn't know about them. If it's in your house, you don't find out about it. It wasn't until EHC started showing us that it's not just about complaining, but it's about working to change the problems.

The bay also causes health problems in Barrio Logan because it's completely dirty. We have a bay where we can't fish and we can't swim. It's been contaminated by the shipyards. So what use is this bay? I live under the Coronado Bridge. The noise and the smells are terrible. I'm next to the CalTrans maintenance yard, and it's the same thing: they run diesel trucks, so it's a constant odor that we're invaded by. I-5 cuts through my neighborhood. There are small shops, like the ones that do painting, that also contribute to the problem. There's a lot of injustice in the community because of the zoning. It goes house-business-house-business, and the city doesn't do anything about it. They don't care about this community.

So we did a survey with SALTA participants. There were five community health activists and each of us worked with fifty families. We did 250 surveys that asked questions like how was someone's health, where did they work, if anyone had had cancer, etc. That's when we realized how common these problems are. But we didn't just do the survey, we also kept in contact and are still in contact with all those families. Some have moved, but when somebody moves we get in contact with the new people who moved in. And the new people tell us that they came here in good health and have gotten sick since they came to our neighborhood. That's how we know it's the neighborhood. Whatever happens, I have to keep in touch with those fifty families—and more, really—because I always felt that being a community organizer means it's not just a four- or eight-hour day, it's a twenty-four-hour job. People have me identified as the one to contact. It might not be just for environmental things; people look to you for anything. And you've got to help them. You have to give people whatever information they need—help them fill out a form, etc. And you have to be ready twenty-four hours a day. That's what's nice about being an organizer. Maybe people like our work because we're not organizers from a different neighborhood or a different community; we live there and we know that the problems are true because we experience them like everybody else does. The good thing is that I can now tell people, "Hey, if you don't like it, let's get to work on it." Then they can't just complain.

I feel a lot of trust among the people I'm trying to help. I'm actually more intimidated when I have to go work in another community. We've gone to Chula Vista with petitions, and I see that the people there aren't that informed. They don't stop to take the time to get informed either, because that's a hard thing to do. The community members here in Barrio Logan are more interested, more willing to be involved. They are more interested in getting informed. There are more problems in this neighborhood than in richer neighborhoods because, politically speaking, we haven't had someone there who has done their job, who really worries about the neighborhood. When our former representative was there, he was somewhat more accessible. I say "somewhat" because I feel that he's more of a politician. He helped and he had the press there to see what he was doing, so he was doing something. I don't believe that the people in more affluent communities are more active; it's just that they've had better political representation than we've had. We've been to other places and there's not such a community presence, but there's better representation and they get things done. Our representatives don't do their jobs. They do it for other communities, but for Barrio Logan, no. Whatever other people don't want, they push it to Barrio Logan. We need somebody who will do their job better. We get frustrated when we see that the politicians aren't doing anything or that the county agencies aren't following through. To get them back in there we almost cry. These aren't losses, but they're constant frustrations, especially when politicians don't do their jobs. I ask them: "What are you here for?" If nobody is going to do this, who do we look to?

Some of the issues we've been dealing with in my time have been very challenging. The methylbromide fight with the Port of San Diego, for example, was a victory for EHC. It took years and years because they were fumigating fruit down at the port, and they didn't have any kind of equipment to capture the fumes, so they were fumigating us too. It was a great fight because it was a powerful opponent, and people were really satisfied with the outcome. It wasn't easy: we would walk and do vigils from the Mercado Apartments to the entrance to the port. We did a lot of those. We went to meetings at the Port District. We'd take our kids, and it was tough because we had to find time to do it in between picking up our kids, taking them with us, and so on. People were very happy with what happened. It was a joint effort with the EHC and the community of Barrio Logan. We've had a number of other victories. What I like is that when I talk to people, they don't say, "Ah, that's what you guys did." They say, "That's what *we* did. We got that done, we won." That's the nice thing about this work—we all win, not just organizations, but everybody.

The chrome-plating plants fight, on the other hand, has been a very frustrating one. We know that there are pollution problems in the neighborhood but the agencies always say, "We don't know who's causing the problems." They come in, put in a monitor, and that is that. The first monitors they put in were at Memorial School, and they didn't find a whole lot of worthwhile data. We thought this wasn't capturing what was really going on in the community. The EHC went to a committee meeting of the Air Resources Board (ARB) and our representative lobbied for monitors in the community. They would listen to us, but they wouldn't do anything about it. We invited them to come down here, we took them on a tour, and we had a lunch where we invited all the residents so they could air their problems. When we sat all these people down with their problems so they could talk with each other, the committee members saw that there was a problem. They agreed. Again, they put monitors in, but the results weren't really conclusive. We asked again for them to put in different monitors—we thought maybe the wrong monitors were in the wrong places. They put them in. They realized that they needed our organization because when they would go in the community and knock on people's doors, people wouldn't open the door. But when we would go and introduce them, people would let them in and allow them to put a monitor in their yard. So they put them in again. Same thing, no conclusive result. But we kept them in because we knew there was something going on. So we got the residents back together. The ARB committee wanted to keep the monitors in for just a short amount of time but we asked if they would please let them stay in longer. So then they said they would put in a different kind of monitor. That's when all the results showed up, and they realized that there was pollution. The emissions were twenty-seven times above normal. Now the problem was: What's the source? It ended up being these two chrome-plating plants.

They found these high levels of emissions and said, "Now we're going to do something." We decided we really needed to get their attention, so we protested at the State of the County Address. The politicians were trying to say everything was fine, but we were outside protesting. The next day, the county supervisor called—"How can we help? Let's get together." We went to a meeting and the county was there, the city was there, all these lawyers—now everybody wanted a piece of it. So they did another round of monitoring and that showed what and who was polluting. They put monitors inside the plating shops, but you could tell which one was the big polluter just by looking at them. The Master Plating shop just had a fan up in the ceiling; the other guy had a whole system to control the emissions. So all the elected officials started meeting with the community—now everybody was in on it. That's when they set up a committee and said, "What are we going to do about it?" So the county sued Master Plating, and now they're in settlement talks. In the meantime they've been prohibited from working with chrome. They're operating but not working in chrome plating. So that's a victory.

One of the keys to this victory was our work with the Martinez family—the family that owns and lives in their home between the plating shops. They have a son who they're worried about because of his severe asthma. What we like about them is that they want to make changes. They ask why they have to leave their home and want to get the plating shops to change their ways or leave. [In November 2002, Master Plating was ordered to shut down permanently as a result of the lawsuit and these actions. Barrio Logan and the EHC threw a big block party to celebrate the outcome of this struggle.]

Personally, I've seen the way my kids' way of thinking has changed. My eleven-year-old has a calendar and is involved in all these different programs. That's really positive. People think that our neighborhood is no good, but my daughter is really active and that satisfies me. My other daughter is too. Each of them is different, but both ways are positive. My goal is to have more people involved. We have a right to live like anybody else does.

Marco Gonzalez: Surfer/Environmental Lawyer, Chair of Surfrider Foundation, San Diego

I was born the son of an immigrant Mexican field worker who had begun to make his way in the used furniture business in Oceanside, San Diego, in 1970. My mother is a nurse at Tri-City Hospital in Oceanside, which is where I was born. I spent about the first nine years of my life in Oceanside, in elementary school. My parents got divorced when I was young and my mom raised us and was always very liberal, which meant a lot. I have one older brother and one younger sister, both following in the same progressive political direction as I am. My sister, Lorena, has made quite a name for herself in San Diego. She's a senior policy adviser for California's lieutenant governor, Cruz Bustamante. She runs his office here in San Diego and was named as one of the top fifty people to watch in the state.

We moved from Oceanside to Vista at a time when Vista wasn't quite as diversified as it is now. That opened up our eyes coming from Oceanside, which was heavily diversified. Full time, around 1982, I started surfing a bunch and being in the water. I felt this environmental ethic, since I was always in the water surfing, or going fishing and camping, so it's been more than an academic interest from day one. I started recognizing this and I also came to the realization that the world is not infinite—that there are finite boundaries to it. That kind of directed me in that way. Then, of course, I can look back at how my parents influenced me—that my mom always felt this way.

After getting a degree in environmental law and moving back to San Diego, I recognized what the global problems are and what San Diego's are, specifically. We have two major problems as I see it: we have growth issues and we have clean-water issues. So that's what I focused on. My practice is very much split between land-use and smart-growth issues, both on the coast and inland. We do a lot of work in the backcountry—there are a lot of environmental and community groups out there. And then there are the clean-water issues, from storm water to sewage spills to discharges out in the deep ocean. You can't imagine how big the problems are in these quick-growing suburban areas in the coastal south—not just in San Diego, but in the whole Southwest: Phoenix, Albuquerque, Los Angeles, Riverside. It's just mind-numbing how huge the problem is. This is all exacerbated for me, personally, because my family's from Mexico. And coming back here, being on the border, I had an epiphany that we can do whatever we want here on this side, but unless we start attacking the problems that exist thirty miles south, it's all for naught. And so I've focused some of my more recent stuff on border issues and transborder water issues.

In addition to my law practice, technically I'm also chair of the San Diego chapter of the Surfrider Foundation, which is a volunteer position. Surfrider is an international volunteer grassroots organization that has more than fifty chapters around the world. Our mission statement says we're an environmental organization dedicated to the preservation and enjoyment of the world's ocean's waves and beaches, using the acronym CARE: Conservation, Activism, Research, and Education. We have eighteen to twenty chapters here in California, the oldest of which is in San Diego. We are in about our eleventh or twelfth year, and we're the chapter that's the most active as well. Surfrider Foundation itself was founded by three guys up in Malibu: Tom Craft, Glenn Henning, and former professional long-boarder Lance Carson. And basically, it was the three of them looking at the beach where they had all been surfing, seeing that it was horribly polluted, and that no one was doing anything about it. Surfers are in the unique position of actually being in the water more than any other recreational group that uses the ocean; they are actually submerged. The number of surfers who are in the water day in and day out is phenomenal. These guys recognized an avenue for people to do something. As their message spread up and down the coast, they formalized it in a nonprofit group, and chapters started popping up. Ours was the first. I don't know who actually came down and started the San Diego chapter. I've been a member of Surfrider since the early '90s, but being in school, I was kind of tramping around. So when I came back down here to San Diego, I really got involved. Now I run the chapter and its programs as a volunteer, but I represent the national organization in lawsuits as well, usually on behalf of the San Diego chapter, but sometimes on a statewide or federal issue.

I'm also involved in San Diego Bay Keeper, doing much the same work. And both groups are very active members of the San Diego Bay Council, a consortium of the more active clean-water groups in town, which includes San Diego Bay Keeper, Surfrider, the San Diego Audubon Society, the Sierra Club, and the Environmental Health Coalition. For about two or three years now, we've been meeting monthly and coordinating strategies on our regional policy issues as well as local developments that affect San Diego and Mission bays and our waterways.

The single biggest challenge facing us is to find a solution to the Tijuana River and the Tijuana–South Bay–border sewage problem, and to the South Bay ocean outfall. For many years, there has been a fight going on about how and where to build a secondary treatment facility for the water coming out in Tijuana. We believe a plant should be built in Mexico, and there's a plan on the table and we've got a bunch of supporters of that going forward. The federal government, for a number of reasons, is making that difficult. That, I think, is the biggest issue, because the area has got so much history, and if it works out, that would be significant.

The second big policy issue is the sewage from the city of San Diego, and that really has two prongs. The first is that San Diego has a deep ocean outfall where the city has a waiver to discharge untreated sewage. San Diego is now the single largest entity to obtain one of these waivers in the United States. It just looks really bad. But what we're fighting is [the] Scripps [Institute] and scientists telling us that the discharges that are occurring right now don't show any harm. The question that I have is, Why should we have to wait until we see harm to start taking steps to protect the ocean? We know that putting stuff in there isn't good, so we should be doing something about it and we're not. The second prong has to do with infrastructure for sewage conveyance. San Diego has expanded so much over the last five years that there have been an obscene amount of sewage spills, both in numbers and volume. It makes sense that these things have occurred. We have pipes that are fifty to seventy years old, and they're just reaching the end of their life span. The city hasn't committed to the level of funding that it needs to in order to deal with the problem. Not only that, but institutionally, they haven't had the procedures in place to respond adequately.

We've had two large spills in particular in the last couple of years that have brought this issue to a head. One of them, out in Alvarado Creek, spewed thirty-four million gallons of sewage into the San Diego River and out into Ocean Beach for nine or ten days before it was discovered. There's no excuse for a system that doesn't get alerted to that size of a spill. The second was more than a million gallons that spilled into Mission Bay. The interesting thing about that was that the spill was identified by an employee of the State Regional Water Board. It was a holiday weekend and the phone call that was made to the city was not responded to for three days. Actually, an employee who was checking messages deleted it, and it took a second call for them to follow up to see what they were doing about it before they found out about it.

Those are our big sewage challenges right there: the discharges in the ocean and the illegal discharges on land. From there we go to storm water. Probably the biggest single problem is storm water and urban runoff to our near-shore environment. These are discharges that go right into the places that we swim and surf in every single day. San Diego has come a long way. We currently have the strongest storm-water permit in the nation—or one of them. But the building industry is fighting that. We are working with the state to defend that permit. We were involved in getting this permit through in 1995, which was a long seven years. Now that the permit's in place and the cities are starting to do what they have to do in terms of planning to come up with ways to deal with their runoff, we have to be right there saying here's how you do it and keep their feet to the fire.

The last issue that I would put on that same tier is, in general, how we deal with growth and density, especially near the coast. Right now, our major transportation corridors exist on the coast, in terms of rail and freeways. Our I-5 corridor is our major north-south corridor in the county. We have to interject our voice in the discussion of how we place density in a way that gets people out of their cars, gets communities more livable and more walkable, and does so in a way that protects our open space and really maintains our quality of life. So that's kind of overarching, but it really has a lot to do with housing, transportation, runoff, wetlands preservation, species preservation, and general habitat stuff. That's the big regional picture that connects everything together. And of course, from that, you get all the offshoots of taxation: How will our transportation taxes be spent? Will we have a portion of those allocated to environmental issues and open space acquisition? That also brings us to things like hotel developments and how we preserve our park space along Mission Bay. Do we allow Sea World to expand to a point where they're a theme park with roller coasters taking over least tern nesting sights? The fight that we've been having right now with Sea World is absurd. We talk about whether we should put a roller coaster in a public park, and everyone else is saying that if we don't let them do this, they'll close the park and take dollars away from our economy.

Finally, do we advocate any development of low-cost visitor service facilities on our public parklands so that everybody can enjoy them? This last issue brings us into fights with people like Doug Manchester, who is trying to build a four-star resort on public parkland in Oceanside, which we've hopefully defeated now with the Coast Commission, but those things are coming up daily. And those are all growth-related issues.

Then there are the challenges facing Surfrider. You can talk about projects and policy initiatives that we work on, but fundamentally what it also comes down to is that the history of San Diego is such that we have an entrenched conservative establishment, and we're one of the biggest cities in the country that runs like a small hick town in Arkansas. The politics in this city really are still the good ol' boys network, but I would say in the last five years that I've been really involved—maybe the last three—we've seen a really big change. We have a new city council, and Mike Zucchet's recent election means a humongous change in terms of possibly swaying environmental votes over to him and fellow council member Donna Frye. It's interesting from a political and sociological perspective to see how this is happening. It's all linked to the economy. We're moving away from a military-based economy. We have seen, with the biotech firms and then the traditional tech and telecom firms, a change in the ethnography of the region. There has been a change in the number of high-paying jobs, and we've seen more of that Silicon Valley politics regarding environmentalism making its way down here, with the yuppie or socially conscious young family coming in. Those people are motivated, not only with their checkbooks but with their feet and their mouths, to go out and help us change the paradigm.

There are a number of things that we've done that were successful. Recently we reached a settlement on our lawsuit on the Tijuana River issue—not on the secondary treatment, but on trying to find the source of pollution to the south bay. There had been a lot of speculation that the effluent from the Tijuana River has been causing problems at Imperial Beach and Coronado. We and our experts feel that actually what we have is a return to the beach of the sewage that is being discharged into ninety feet of water through the south bay ocean outfall. There's also the possibility that the outfall just south of the border in the Rosarito Playas region is getting caught in northern out-currents and being recirculated up in the south bay and around Point Loma. As a result of that lawsuit settlement, we're going to get about $2 million from the EPA to do some in-the-water studies to try to determine what's going on, where the currents are moving, and whether that sewage is coming out of the outfall and back to shore. That's a huge success in terms of the acquisition of money. As I said, we were able to help the state pass one of the strongest storm-water permits in the country. On a federal-legislative front, San Diego Surfrider chapter volunteers were at the center of drafting and trying to pass the federal beach bill that would apply water-testing standards to all the coastal areas in the United States. That was one of our biggest successes as an organization.

One of the reasons I do what I do is because I don't see another Mexican doing it, and I think we need to have our Latino role models in every element of society that we can. One of the things that we care about in San Diego County, from Surfrider's perspective, in addition to our fight for clean water, is our fight for beach access—making the beaches available for all people. What we saw up in Oceanside with Doug Manchester's hotel proposal was that right now we have a county that is book-ended with Imperial Beach and Oceanside, where we have our most diverse coastal communities existing on a resource that's wide open: we have beaches, piers, fishing, and anybody can come down to the beach on any given day and find parking, lay out their blanket, have their picnic, and enjoy their day. With the Manchester hotel proposal, they were looking at a significant avenue of access to bring it up to their so-called "four-star level." And of course when they did that, they said that the facilities would be open to the community and anyone could partake in them. In reality, though, the socioeconomic barriers to beach access that they would have created would have taken an entire piece of the community and said to the local people, "You're not welcome."

From Surfrider's perspective, and maybe it's because I took it as personally as I did, that was just not what we're about. We recently amended our mission statement to say that we're for the protection and enjoyment of beaches for all people. That element has to come in. It's not just for all surfers, it's for all beach users, whether you swim, ride a surfboard or boogie board, kayak, fish, or just go there and look at the sunsets. In an urban or largely suburban environment, what is our connection to nature? The fact is that I can still go out in the water and, if I paddle twenty yards out past the next person, I've just got the expanse of the ocean with nothing else before me. If I stand on top of Palomar Mountain, and I look in any direction, I don't get that same sense. I can see Tijuana, I can see the Anza Borrego desert; there's nowhere else you can go in an urban environment and actually still see that endless horizon. You cannot create barriers in any form, whether it's excessive parking fees, loss of parking altogether, or a four-star resort that, quite frankly, makes the lower-income fishermen feel uncomfortable taking their gear through on their way to the pier to fish. We're trying to take this issue statewide in terms of how Surfrider looks at issues, trying to interject environmental justice into our issues.

One of the other things that's starting to make it onto my radar screen is that, being from Oceanside and North County, I'm starting to see the patterns that we would have seen had we been in Huntington Beach, Newport Beach, Laguna Beach, and San Clemente back in the 1940s on up. Essentially, our coastal communities were farming communities at one time—they have really good soils and as a result of the migrant farmer population in Southern California, we have large settlements of minorities on the coast. But what we've seen in Orange and L.A. counties, and what we're starting to see here now, is the gentrification of those coastal environs. Whereas Oceanside was once the culturally diverse area and Vista was largely white when I moved there, when you go anywhere now in that North County inland area, you just have this migration from the coast of the Latino population. And when you match that to property values—not so much Oceanside, but starting in Carlsbad and moving to Leucadia, Encinitas, Cardiff, Solana Beach, Del Mar, La Jolla, Pacific Beach, Mission Beach, and Ocean Beach—in all of those places, Mexicans are getting swept out.

So, I've found myself in a unique position because I'm the son of an Italian mother and a Mexican father, and out of everyone in my family, I got the genes that make me appear least Mexican. My brother and my sister look much more Mexican than I do. Thanks to my dad's hard work, and my mom's intelligence in making me bust my ass in school, I'm now in a position where, economically, I can live on the coast and I can maintain a surfing lifestyle that really hasn't been that open to Latinos or less-represented ethnic groups in the past. It's a really interesting perspective to view from the inside. People look at me when they come out of Mexico and they rarely believe that I'm Mexican, that I speak Spanish, and that my cultural roots and identity are Mexican. They assume that because I look white, because I speak in an educated tone without an accent, that I don't have that cultural bias, but I do. And so that's one of the things that keeps me going at what I'm doing. I can provide a voice for my cause from the inside that I don't hear a lot of other people doing.

As far as the surfing community here in San Diego goes, a lot of people see the work that our foundation does and they think that, as a lot, surfers are really out there and really cool. I am someone who's very, very committed to the surfing lifestyle and understand how it all works from the industry side and the social side. Surfers are largely an apathetic lot. We like to go out and surf and come in and relax, drink our margaritas and beer, and enjoy that casual lifestyle that is either rooted in Hawaiian culture or in Baja California. It's very much an "I'm going to give up on the real world and I'm going to spend my life on the beach—live the surf and just be happy" lifestyle. One of the things we're seeing industrywide in surfing is an increase in female participants. It started out more from the economic side: the women's styles in surf clothing were opening up the sport to a lot of people. But now as the mainstream media has taken advantage of that, we're seeing more women enter the sport at a younger age, which not only translates into demographics in the water, but also we're tapping into these people as volunteers, since women typically are more willing to volunteer, sacrifice their time, and are possibly more passionate in caring for their causes.

But we also love to bitch about the problems in the world around us, and at Surfrider, we hear all the time surfers come to us and say, "Hey you need to be doing more. What are you doing for us?" It is a constant struggle to mobilize that faction beyond just yelling at you to actually do something. Yeah, we have 4,000 members here in San Diego County, but there are maybe about twenty of us who do any work. Sometimes we can get people to come out to a bar for a fund-raiser and drink some beer on our behalf. Out of those events, every once in a while, we pull one or two people in who have it—who have not only the heart for it, but who are also willing to make the sacrifices to put in the time. Right now, we have a better group of environmentalists and surfers in San Diego than we've ever had. We're more sophisticated, more educated, and a little bit younger than some of our activists in the past generation. And I think that gives us a little bit more energy and that comes out in our passion and how we express it. Everyone likes to believe in the old *Fast Times at Ridgemont High* Jeff Spicoli burned-out-surfer stereotype, but you go look at people who are in Surfrider and see lawyers, engineers, Ph.D.'s and master's degrees of all forms, coastal geographers, oceanographers, marine biologists, etc. We're not just a bunch of burnouts anymore, which is kind of cool.

Jane Collins: Salon Owner, Surfer/Artist

I was born in San Diego in 1968. I grew up in Pacific Beach, but then when I was fifteen, I moved to Hillcrest with my mom. Hillcrest was a lot different than Pacific Beach, where our house was sort of a beach hangout. Growing up at the beach wasn't the typical San Diego beach experience because I really didn't go to the beach that much, even though I lived there, since I never really cared for the ocean. I wouldn't even put my feet in the water. I was a kind of antistereotype girl for a long time, partially because I was very modest and didn't want to wear a bathing suit.

Some of the kids I knew at the beach were some of the worst punk rockers around, and they became my friends. I had been the youngest person in my punker group, so I felt like I was coming into it very late. I didn't feel like I was in on the early scene, although looking back, I guess I was. It was interesting to see the different scenes from the beach to the inland areas—downtown, North Park, and Hillcrest—and how different the people were from one another, and how they knew each other or knew about each other. There were the real hard-core punk rocker types with Mohawks, which was really cool for my scene. And there was one place I went where there were a lot of bikers, kind of cholo punk rockers. We listened to all the usual suspects: GBH, Black Flag, TSOL, PIL, when they came to town. Everyone thought the biker cholo guys were really cool, although also pretty awful and scary. They had me run drugs for them—and I didn't even know it because I was fifteen and very naïve. I would have a bunch of money on me. . . . I was just dumb—not to mention that they abused women and all of that. They were called the San Diego Skinheads, which didn't have any reference at the time to anything racial. It was just more of a punk thing. So, they were a real tough bunch and they would go to the beach and start big fights. They got a lot of respect.

All of that changed when I started working at Sea World when I was seventeen for about a year. It was a teenager job, so of course everybody complained because it was really excruciatingly boring. You had to do the same routine every day: for example, we had to go to the polar exhibit and watch people in line, or pick up trash, or do other equally mindless things. I do think that they hire so many kids because kids don't ask questions or think about how they're treated.

When I was eighteen, I got pregnant. After I had my daughter, I was on and off welfare for about six years. I did a lot of different jobs, like I worked at the NASSCO shipyard in the early nineties. Before that I went to welding school through City College. I wasn't at NASSCO for very long. Even though there was a strike there during the time I worked in the shipyard, it wasn't part of the sheet metal area where I worked. I was only there about six months and it was awful. I would work on a metal platform, so I think I must have sweated the whole summer. It was hot every day. We used to wear hard hats with cardboard boxes to put over them for shade because the sun was blazing. The heat would just come up and radiate off of the planks or big metal slabs. There was definitely a strong criminal element, and I felt that way all the way up until I left. I think there were a lot of drugs and basically nobody cared about their jobs. There seemed to be hundreds and hundreds of supervisors—the bureaucracy was just crazy. What people wanted to do was to waste as much time as they could all day. I worked with a couple of guys, and we would put together these giant bolts in the sheet metal department. I would get a different job description of things to put together to put on the ships every day. So we would get these big packages on cranes, move them over, and bolt them. Everyone's thing was that they would pretend to seem busy and when a supervisor would walk by, they would pull out their tapes—that was the joke, to pull out your tape and pretend to measure something. You know, you're talking shit, but with your measuring tape, you act like you're talking about something. People would do drugs on the ships, take naps, and hide all day. There was basically only one girl in the whole sheet metal department—me. In fact, there weren't a lot of women at NASSCO at all. I had only two girlfriends there.

I got laid off from NASSCO. I went back on welfare for a while, and then looked through the City College catalogue. What I had wanted to do was weld, be artistic, and make furniture. And that didn't happen. As soon as I decided to become a hair stylist, everything changed for me. Not only was this going to be a job where I could make a decent income, but it was also something that I could like and be good at.

I started surfing about two years ago when my daughter and I went to Hawaii. I loved it because after we went back to the hotel room that day, I took a nap, which I hadn't done in years. I realized that I could relax when I surfed. So it made me less materialistic and more focused on my family and on things that are important to me. Almost every surfer I've ever met feels the same way. Maybe it's a meditative thing that's happening when you're in the water, seeing dolphins and other things. I don't know what it is—you have an interest that has to do with your body and the waves. It's such an independent thing, and it's just for yourself. You can't be bothered out there, so it's a break, too. But I think people would feel that way even if they just paddled out.

The surfing culture here is a lot of the stereotypical stuff that you see on TV—a lot of beach bums. It can happen to many people, especially if you throw alcohol on top of it. People get unmotivated and just want to hang out at the beach. Every beach I've ever been to my entire life has beach bums, so it's there. But there's also definitely the culture that I see that is more of a healthy life where you take care of your body and your mind, and you try to make time for things that you like to do with your family.

As far as the environmental aspect of surfing goes, you can go on the Internet and usually you can look up the water quality. The Surfrider Foundation does a lot of great work in that area. I also have some friends who sample water and know a lot about the environment of the ocean, so I already know which beaches to stay away from or the ones I'm supposed to stay away from, which are my two favorites. I used to go to Tourmaline north of Pacific Beach all the time, and they have a lot of runoff. I live in Cardiff where the beach is connected to the San Elijo lagoon, which is an estuary. When that floods out the first time of the season, the water goes back and forth, and it gets really disgusting. The environment the lagoon has provided for the birds is beautiful, though.

When I first started surfing here in San Diego, I used to get sick—I'd say, maybe six times a year—an ear thing or a stomach thing. And I knew it was caused by surfing. I think my body has gotten used to it now, and I hardly ever get sick. I've heard of a few cases where people have had an open cut, then had a serious blood disease, and they can never go back in. Or people who've all of a sudden had an allergy and they could never return to the ocean. But I can tell you, just paddling in the water, I might pass a nylon or a piece of trash; I see broken balloons all the time. We've had a lot of changes recently. There've been a lot of dead squid and it could be El Niño, but there are a lot of odd things happening. So it could just be weather-related.

In terms of the future, I'm very optimistic about living in San Diego. I feel like if I'm connected with nature and I can stay out of traffic, then things are fine. I know the county is growing—in my immediate neighborhood, especially, which I'm not happy about. Anyone who was born here would have to say that the city is changing in a negative direction. There's too much stress and too much traffic, too many people.

Peter Zschiesche: President of Machinists' Union, San Diego Community College District Board of Trustees Member, Director of the Employee Rights Center

We moved to San Diego in the winter of 1970 from Detroit. I came here because I wanted to go back to school on the G.I. Bill. We lived on the G.I. Bill and whatever Pam, my wife, made as a waitress. We picked San Diego because, originally coming from Syracuse, which has the least number of sunny days, we wanted to live somewhere where the weather was nicer. Detroit's weather wasn't that great either. So coming to San Diego for me was a whole new life. I had met Pam in Detroit. Before that, I had gotten out of the army in 1969, and my friend Vince and I had been reading books about Vietnam while we were in the service, so we sort of had an idea that we were against the war when we got out.

The thing that got me when I came home on leave from the service in 1968 was when I was on a flight with two guys who had served in Vietnam from Cleveland and they said they were more scared—this was right after the riots—to come home to Cleveland than they were to stay in the war. I thought, "How could it be that these guys are afraid to come home?" I mean, coming home from overseas was the big thing. I was away from 1967–69, so it blew my mind about what was going on in America while we were all 10,000 miles away. I had signed up for the ROTC before the war, so when I got out of graduate school for my M.B.A., my time came to go overseas and luckily I went to Korea. After I read the biography of Ho Chi Minh and *The Fall of Vietnam*, I decided to accept the opportunity to go there for my last two months of service. I saw what was going on there and it seemed more real to me.

I knew I was against the war, and this is when I got involved in the antiwar movement and joined Vietnam Vets Against the War. I immersed myself in Detroit and just lived there, experiencing it. There were people who were giving a critique that was new to me. There were also black nationalists who came down very heavy on young, white activists. Those guys would just blow our minds. Then there were the activists in the UAW who were totally turned against the war and were overwhelmed by what they were up against in their union. It was just an amazing place to be to find out what was wrong with America. And of course, Detroit's a hard city. There was none of "Hi, welcome, white liberals." There was none of that shit. If you were on the street, it was like, "I think you're on the wrong block."

When we decided to move to California, we thought about San Francisco, but it seemed too easy. In one of the underground newspapers here in San Diego, they had a big center section called "The Belly of the Beast," and that sort of became one of the local movement's mottoes. After we got here in '71, we found an antiwar movement. If you were here in San Diego in the 1970s, to be in the antiwar movement really set people apart, given the conservative nature of the town. It wasn't a big antiwar movement, but people were very committed. Early on, I went to a demonstration at North Island Naval Station and found out that the air war in Southeast Asia was being run out of the electronic system out at Point Loma. All the bombing missions for the B-52s and that stuff were being programmed out of Electronic Naval Headquarters at Point Loma. And this was one of the big exposés that started to come down: it wasn't just ships, it wasn't just troops, but it was the whole thing. It was important to expose the level of what was going on. The early antiwar stuff that we went to in '71 was very small but it was ardent and it was combined with the youth culture that was going on in Ocean Beach. Ocean Beach was a big connection because you had a large segment of the antiwar movement that was youth culture.

Then you had people in the G.I. movement who were not part of that at all. They still had short hair and they were the anticounterculture people. Then there was the Golden Hill contingent, which is where we lived, that did a food co-op, a child-care center, and stuff that tried to relate to the community and be community-based. It wasn't that big of a political movement in Golden Hill, but there was a collective process of deciding what we were going to do in the neighborhood. There was enough variety going on at the time that you could live your politics.

Some of the things we did in the antiwar movement were really powerful. We did a big demo down at the 11th Naval District Headquarters. At that time, one of the "Peace Houses" that related to the G.I. movement in the Navy was over on

Market Street. The 11th Naval District had glass doors, and there were around 500 people down there and all of a sudden the heavies decided that they were going to go inside. Well, the Navy never fathomed that there would be any radicals trying to get in through the glass doors. I mean, glass doors, how easy can that be? It became this heavy-duty confrontation. There were conga drums and marching in front of the door. I think eighty-eight people got busted after they did a sit-in there. It was one of those things that was right in the heart of San Diego that focused on the military. It was very disciplined and when it was over people felt like they had accomplished something.

I was also involved in the anticonvention coalition that opposed the Republican Convention coming to San Diego in 1972. My friend Vince, whom I went to graduate school with back in Michigan, was the office staff person for the group. During this time I was going to graduate school at SDSU, and I joined with several faculty members who started this thing called the Center for Radical Economics (CRE). The coalition basically decided that we were going to try and stop the [Republican] convention from coming to San Diego. It was really neat because it united all of these different groups. Whatever your beef was, you could come here. There was actually this plan by someone on the other side to kidnap the leaders of the convention coalition and take them to Tijuana to get rid of them. When they didn't end up having the convention here, a bunch of people got in their cars and went to Miami to protest the convention there. A friend of ours who lives down the street still has an ashtray that says "GOP Convention, 1972, San Diego" that they made for the convention before they moved it.

As far as the Labor Support Committee goes and labor's involvement in the antiwar movement, there were several key people who were activists in their unions: Terry Christian was at Rohr (he also organized the protests in Balboa Park in 1991 against the Persian Gulf War), Mike Sweeney was in the Retail Clerks, and there were people in the Center for Servicemen's Rights who were working during the week. They were blue-collar guys and they wore it on their sleeves—and they were antiwar. There was a big Rohr strike I think in 1971. At that time Rohr was huge and the Machinists' was a big union in town with a lot of muscle and, in a certain sense, a militant unionism that conducted a lot of strikes.

So the Machinists' Union would have these militant strikes at Rohr. Here's what happened: the convention coalition and the antiwar movement were drawn in to participate in the Rohr strike—to do strike support stuff like walk the picket line. I'd have to say that Mike Sweeney and people like that brought labor politics into these movements, which brought Marxism and prolabor politics to the antiwar movement.

I stopped going to graduate school, took a machinists course, and got a job at a little machine shop out in Spring Valley, in 1974–75. After that, I had an opportunity to work at NASSCO. A lot of stuff was happening at NASSCO; they'd had a lot of strikes. There were a lot of politics going on in that yard among Latino workers, although I had no relationship to that. By 1976 Pam and I were both at NASSCO, both in the Machinists' Union, and we were both active in the rank-and-file stuff going on there. The whole waterfront was part of the Machinists' Union. There was stuff going on at these places. And Campbell's was actually the hotbed of activism in the Machinists' Union, whereas NASSCO was kind of the backwater. Then, when Pam and I lived in Chicago between 1978 and 1981 it just so happened that this was a superintense period at NASSCO—there were the NASSCO Three, the alleged bomb threat, the PLP, Cherokee, and the Communist Worker's Party. Every political faction in the city came out of the woodwork at NASSCO during that time.

When we got back from Chicago, I got active on the union's Health and Safety Committee. There was this huge strike in '81 that made people come back together, and it all sort of coalesced. It was the first time that activists in different unions actually brought the unions together. Up until and including 1975, they struck every three years. In 1975 all the unions bargained separately—it was like, "Fuck you, I'm an ironworker, you're a machinist, you're a carpenter." In 1978, the Ironworkers were the militants at NASSCO. They decided to break off and wouldn't negotiate with anybody else. And then after '81 those guys were gone, so it was moderate politics in all the unions and the activists in each union resolved that they were going to keep all the unions together. One of the best things about all this was the way the activists worked together. One person was bilingual and she would go down and rap with the workers every day. You had activists organizing the picket lines, you had others doing soup kitchens, you had others on the bargaining committees who were coming back to the yard and reporting on what was happening. The business agents did their thing in negotiating and in doling out the strike money, but basically it was the activists in the yard who ran the strike. There were significant gains from the contract: health and safety rules. Also, the activists became fully legitimated in most people's views.

So out of the 1981 contract came several significant things. One was that they incorporated the OSHA language around a joint Health and Safety Committee. There were a lot of accidents before that. It was always gruesome, and accidents would always be covered over, even by the union. There were two guys who got killed in 1981. I can't remember their names, but they were machinists. These guys were found dead in the space down at the bottom of the ship. The shame of it was that the families of those two guys got bought off by the company before the union even got wind of it. The families got virtually nothing out of it. And the union never opened up. This is when, in the Machinists' Union, we started saying how fucked up it all was. Nobody could account for how these guys died—it's like all of a sudden they got lost.

Eventually, I got to be president in 1985, and then, at the end of the year, Bud, another guy, decided he wanted to run for business agent, and I decided I wanted to run, too. Business agents are elected. This was really unusual for a lot of people because I had to be elected by the rank and file. By the way, that's one of the things I really like about the Machinists' Union—they don't often hire any staff people from the outside. The advantage to that is that leaders are really a part of the people they represent. It turns out, I won business rep.

That was in December 1985. It really gave me the opportunity to lead. Nine reps were elected in the Machinists' Union district here, and four out of nine people were people who'd been in the antiwar movement. I didn't know them at all but there we were in office. The problem was, though, that the shit in the plants was really hitting the fan. My first negotiations took place after I was only a month into office. I walked into the room and a guy said, "By the way, we're closing the plant. We're closing in thirty days, so what would you like to negotiate?" Within the first four months, I was confronted with negotiations that were really terrible. I had my first strike negotiations that fall with about 130 people, half of them women and half of them young Filipino men who usually disliked each other. But the Filipino men liked to party, so they wanted to come out and do the pickets at night and the older ladies wanted to do the days. So we had a great strike because we had everything covered. And in the end, they came out and said they actually respected each other.

I don't care what your politics are, if you don't know how to do this stuff, it doesn't mean shit. I had to learn how to get stuff done and to keep people from getting hurt. Even in 1986, before I got into office, NASSCO was telling the guys who were in office before me that they were going to do cuts. If they got this one contract, they would have to cut wages in order for them to stay open in 1987. They didn't tell me, but the business agents had been schooled that they were going to low-ball this contract and that was the way the company was going to cut back. At that time there was a huge recession in defense spending and ship building. So all of a sudden this wonderful place, the yard, was going to shit. When I took office there were 3,000 people there, but by the end of 1987 there were 1,700 [the high point in the late 1970s–early 1980s had been 7,000 people]. In early 1987, I figured out that we better get our shit together. The company was going through rock-bottom times. But by the spring of '87, I knew, and the activists knew, that there was going to be a strike. My main goal was to make sure I kept tabs on the other unions. The Machinists' Union had a strike fund. None of the other unions had strike funds. We were much more organized.

We got to the fall of '87 and NASSCO came in with a big take-away offer, which was a killer thing for the, quote-unquote, Left to take. We opened negotiations and we couldn't shake it. At that time our union had been active in the shipyards up and down the coast and this yard in Portland had had a strike and they did something called the "inside game." Because the Navy would just pull all their work out and there'd be no work to stop, these guys decided that they wouldn't go on strike. Instead, they would work "inside" to make their point. Somehow we decided in 1987 that we would not go out on strike, so we had to play with what we had. That's when we decided we weren't going to strike and we figured out we were going to have to play the inside game.

Who was going to tell the workers? We had a big rally in front of the yard. I got up there to speak in front of 1,000 workers and I said, "We're not striking." I looked at their faces and it looked like every one of them would have beaten the shit out of me if they could have come up there. It was a trial by fire to tell these guys the truth because the only thing that was going to get us through was if we did it together. So we didn't strike and we started learning how to improvise the inside game. It was really neat because most of the people in the yard were veterans—they'd been there ten years or more—so we didn't have to spell it out for them. All we had to do was to give them the idea and then they'd just do their thing. So we said there'll be no sabotage, no fucking up the Navy. In fact, I sent a letter to the 32nd Street commander because I didn't want to have the Navy as our enemy. The Navy was sort of cool about it; they said, "Hey, you're getting screwed." We conducted that struggle for eleven months. It was a year out of my life—I just ate and slept it for a year.

Through the summer we did that and then we more or less got the elements together. We had some negotiations, we put some stuff on the table, the company still wouldn't give us enough, and we were trying to squeeze out our last pennies' worth. So we went on strike for three weeks and we got nothing more at the table. But we went along with the Ironworkers. Afterward, the Ironworkers explained it to me: they didn't think their guys would go along with the settlement without a strike. So that left a real bad taste in my mouth: number one for the Ironworkers' International, and number two, because I couldn't really tell my guys the truth. But everybody was finally ready to settle. It was a wonderful victory because nobody had done a major struggle for eleven months down there like that. It blew their minds in the company that we could hold out for that long. That whole year took whatever happened in the late '70s and put it at a much higher level. There were still concessions made to the company, and there were things we couldn't have changed. As far as I know, no one in San Diego had played the inside game like that. Nobody had marched on an executive's house in La Jolla with a police escort, and nobody had involved the rank and file in that way.

A big thing that happened after that was the *Exxon Valdez* coming to San Diego in 1989 for repairs after the spill in Alaska. I knew Jay Powell from the Environmental Health Coalition. The gist of it was, when they got the ship down outside the San Diego harbor, could they get permission to bring it into NASSCO for repairs or not? Was it going to pollute the harbor? We were meeting with the head of Exxon and the state because the ship was falling apart. The ship was sitting outside the harbor and its bottom hull plates were going back and forth and at some point they would open up and the ship was going to sink. Since I knew Jay, I sat down with him and said, "What can we do to satisfy you guys to get it in the yard? It's got to go somewhere and we'd like to have the work." Jay told me what had to be done and what the EHC wanted. So then I went back to the company and we set up a meeting with Exxon. The state attorney general at that time wasn't going to cut a deal unless he knew that everything would be done right. So we set up the conditions among Jay Powell, the attorney general, and Exxon, and we all worked out a deal. We got the ship inside the yard without polluting the harbor and NASSCO got a lot of work. For me it was important to join hands with the Environmental Health Coalition.

Between '88 and '92 there were good things and bad things. The good things were that the unions were working together on a number of things. On the other hand, there were some real schisms, and one of the issues was around how to deal with the company. The Machinists' Union had a different approach than the Ironworkers during this time. The Ironworkers were real standoffish. That was a problem, but I didn't think it was of any consequence at the time. In '91 I got reelected, and I began doing other stuff. I started working with Economic Conversion, which is how I got involved in local economics and city politics. Now people would ask me for advice. And I lobbied. I got to know some city politicians. Part of getting jobs back was doing legislative stuff. So I was breaking out of just the trade union stuff and getting involved in other issues.

Coming into '92, the Ironworkers were doing their thing, we were doing ours. In spring of that year, though, we brought Bill Clinton to the NASSCO shipyard. They wanted me as a union representative on the platform. It really pissed off the company, though. The company had a really cogent view of what they wanted to do in negotiations that fall and part of it had to do with the Ironworkers. We got to meet with Clinton beforehand, and our line to him was that he had to say something about the workers' right to strike. I said this to him in a room of eight people where I was the only union guy. And sure enough, in his speech, he said, "I support the right of workers' to strike and not suffer consequences." But I didn't understand then how the company was viewing us. Therefore, I and everybody else were totally blown away by the company's proposal in 1992 where we walked away from those negotiations with no seniority, no fully paid health care, no cost of living increase, and no significant economics. The whole fucking thing was a mess. I couldn't figure it out. My only read is that they were trying to fuck around with us with all the contract language as a way to scare us a little and then come back with just a minimal economic proposal and the other stuff would come back on the table. It never came back to the table. In the end we were stuck with nothing, and I didn't know what to do. So then the debate was between going on strike and doing the inside game.

We decided to go on strike, and the strike was very good for a week or two. But then, typically, as happens with strikes, nobody else had a strike fund except us. Because of the seniority issue, we had a lot of the senior guys out there. And one of the things I noticed was that the younger guys wanted the economics the company was not putting on the table. For them, seniority was what was in their way. In other words, why should they get laid off when there were older, less able guys to lay off? Seniority was good, but the problem was that only half the yard bought into it. The newer guys weren't interested in it.

The seniority thing didn't come back. I have to say, I couldn't believe that the company could do that. Then, at the end of April 1993, they took away union security. We figured then that we had to do some stuff. In May and June we came up with a plan in which we were going to try and do rolling strikes. Each union was going to do a strike. You can do intermittent strikes under the Labor Relations Board, but you can only do so many before it becomes illegal. We were trying to create spontaneous strikes inside the yard that would meet the conditions of protected concerted activity. After the third one, the company basically called the board and they filed charges so there'd be no more strikes. Then we did some marches, but frankly, I was still at a loss as to how we were going to regain seniority. Seniority, at that point, became the key—otherwise, what was the point? The nonunion yards paid the same money, so the only difference between us and them was seniority and job security. In the summer, the company got a bunch of new contracts. By this time, the Ironworkers International had taken over negotiations.

Then, at the end of the summer, all of a sudden, the company started real negotiations again. By October 1993, I could see a possible contract. On the other hand, there was a long way to go. The company did actually come back with some stuff we could live with, including modified seniority. Then the company put union security back on the table. For the next two months there was all this tit for tat over union security, and slowly you could feel the whole thing unraveling. My problem was that there was nobody I could trust to get through this situation. For all the unions, the bomb dropped when management jerked union security off the table in April or May of 1994. When we finally recovered, we put together a union proposal to have a vote in the yard and we told the company we'll put union security on the line and we'll let the members decide. If the members vote "yes" for union security, then we accept the final offer with union security. If they vote "no" for union security, then we accept the final offer without it. We'll go by what the yard says. We figured if we could do it quickly enough, people would either see it as a yes or a no for the union. We would just say, "Hey, if you want a powerful union, vote yes. If you want a weak union, vote no." But we pissed away the summer and the fall arguing over it and my international would not allow me to conduct the vote in the yard. By December 1995, they took me off the bargaining team. It was probably a good thing but very frustrating because I couldn't talk about what was going on to the guys in the yard. For me, then, it was over. I saw that move as one that severed my relationship with the yard for several years.

When we unionists conducted the struggle at NASSCO we did not reach out very much to the labor movement in San Diego. And by and large during the inside game and the stuff in the '90s, we only reached out to the labor movement for rallies and stuff like that. But basically, I didn't consider what the labor movement had to offer us. The problem with NASSCO, though, is that they don't answer to anybody.

We tried the community, we tried the corporate community, we tried Representative Bob Filner, we tried the Navy—and the Navy wasn't going to do anything. That's why we engaged in the Clinton campaign, because we thought if we got someone like him in office we could affect the Navy's relationship with NASSCO and then things would be easier. But that didn't work out either. We were on our own.

The great thing that's going on in the labor movement right now, and this is happening under Jerry Butkiewicz, the current secretary-treasurer of the Labor Council, is that no one has to go it alone anymore. Whatever they have internally can be multiplied by what's going on in the labor movement as a whole. I don't know what it would have done for us at NASSCO because the Navy is its largest customer. But after what happened in the '90s, people have a lot more solidarity. What's important now in the labor movement and community-based organizations is the way public pressure can be used and the ways it can make the difference. Because UPS has a consumer product and because the janitors do a public service and because the hotels serve people, those struggles engage the whole community. In that sense, they have more impact on the labor movement. These are struggles that link the labor movement to the community. They ended up being more significant than the NASSCO strike because of this. We were the best and the last of an old era of industrial struggles in San Diego.

I've just been elected to the board of trustees of the San Diego Community College District. I was interested in this because I've lived with education issues in my life. When I became a union business representative, Pam became a schoolteacher. So we really do live education at home. The other thing is I felt that labor people need to have a better connection to education. I have a lot to offer in bringing these two areas together. And I know the district could use some of my skills, especially those having to do with labor conflicts. I figured here's an opportunity on a lot of levels to test myself. I know people in the education community, and I know I can do all of this. In terms of mettle, there's nothing I haven't seen going into this position. When I left my position in the Machinists' Union in 1995, I felt like I had run my course with that life. I feel comfortable trying my hand at this board seat. Everybody in town knows I'm a labor person. For me, it's time to apply my skills and values in a new way.

Mary Grillo: Executive Director, Service Employees International Union, Local 2028

I was born in 1960 and grew up back east, mostly in Massachusetts. I basically got interested in labor by virtue of waitressing in a resort area during the summer. I kept figuring my rights were being violated and in the restaurant industry, you just don't have that many. And so, I decided pretty early on that I wanted to be in the labor movement. When I was in school at Wellesley College, I got an internship my sophomore year with the Service Employees International Union and just stuck with it. After I graduated, I volunteered for District 9-5 Working Women on a strike and worked for four months or so. And then after that, finally, SEIU hired me full time in 1983.

I've been in San Diego since January 1987 and have stayed here ever since. As far as living in San Diego goes, my friends say, "What, are you crazy? Going to San Diego to organize a union?" San Diego is very different than other parts of the country. It's much more focused on enjoying life than it is on political activism. I'm not saying that's a bad thing, but it makes it difficult because there's just so much to do here recreationally. The other thing about San Diego is that it's easy. The neighborhoods are nice, and the community people are nice. Part of it, too, is—to be a weather wimp—you can't live anywhere else. I also really like the border culture and the diversity of San Diego. Those aspects make the city very attractive, and I think the other aspect is that you can make a dramatic difference in workers' lives here because there is a vacuum of advocacy and because for the very same reason, the establishment doesn't know how to deal with any kind of community organizing, so pressure tactics work. So I think the determined minority can run this city; it's just a question of who's going to be the determined minority—the political activists or the conservative right wing—because everybody else is out playing. It's a tough culture to overcome in terms of politics because it's conservative. But although it's conservative, people aren't innately selfish. I would say it's just that there's a total obliviousness to how working people live. And that's the thing I noticed the most in the Justice for Janitors campaign. So it's really a question of awakening people.

I came to SEIU Local 2028 as a field representative. The local had gone through a very bad eight years, so I came in at a time where we had hit bottom, basically. We were down significantly in membership. So we started organizing one of the first Justice for Janitors campaigns in the country. The janitors, though, are now over with the statewide local in Los Angeles. SEIU Local 2028, at the time of the Janitors' strike and before July 31, 2002, had six divisions: Janitorial; Public Events, which is composed of the racetrack, the convention center, and those types of places; Public Schools; Cities and Special Districts (we're in seven cities and one district); Health Care, where we have a couple of areas; and then the County, which is the vast majority of who we represent. So this is what's called an "amalgamated" union, an old-style amalgamated union. Post–July 31, 2002, we are now at 10,000 members. Pre–July 31, we were at 12,000, which represents a lot of work. We have about forty-five different contracts. There are three big service locals in San Diego: United Food and Commercial Workers (UFCW), us, and now the United Domestic Workers (UDW). SEIU is shifting toward industry-based unions, and we specialize in health care, public sector, and building services.

Clearly the struggle for the janitors was one of SEIU's biggest gains. What we accomplished there was a raising of consciousness in the community. I think that was important for everyone. When we did our first demonstration on César Chávez Day, we heard from people who didn't think it could be done in San Diego anymore. They were all from the farm worker days in the '60s, and I just missed all that—I'm forty-two. So I didn't live through those days. It was seeing that, seeing some activism, and some people willing to go to the line for workers that really woke people up. People didn't understand that the janitors didn't have health insurance. What were they thinking? It really changed the nature of the fight, and it became a moral fight as opposed to just an economic fight, although I think they're one and the same.

The Janitors' strike was not something we initially planned to do—we did it in support of the local in L.A. It was really the scariest thing I've ever had to do because of the sacrifice you're asking people to make. The responsibility of it, the load of it, was just more than I could imagine. But it was such the right fight to have and the timing was perfect. It's the accomplishment I'm proudest of at this point in my career. It was a humbling experience—that's how I'd describe it. The sacrifices these people made who had so little to begin with just blew my mind. The media were unbelievable—the newspaper reporter assigned to the story was great and the TV media were phenomenal. The settlement was far better than what they wanted us to get, and it set a standard for a lot of the contracts throughout the country. In Cleveland, they didn't even have to go on strike because they saw from what San Diego went through what would happen there. Again, because we're so conservative, not predominantly union, our success was magnified. It was incredible.

We ended up doing a hunger strike because it had gotten very far into the Janitors' strike with no resolution in sight. We had talked about hunger strikes at the beginning of it and a lot of people advised us against it. Personally, I wasn't prepared to do it. I talked to someone who said you had to be spiritually prepared to do it. I am not a religious person—that's just not my thing. But then, as we got into the strike, we had to keep raising the bar. So I think it was the third week into the strike that we had to do something. At that point, then, I was prepared. I said, "O.K., I'll do it." So we launched the hunger strike around Easter 2000. We had the janitors agree to do it. The people who did it—I could not believe it. Ignacio was on pain medications for his back. He had to leave one day to go get an MRI because he wasn't taking his meds. I tried to prep the janitors about fasting. I knew a little more about it than they did, so I cut down the caffeine intake and ate lighter as the fast got closer. They did the opposite. They're like, "Well, we're going to fast, we've got to eat!" So the morning of the fast, we did the Twelve Stations of the Cross, then I took them to breakfast, and I said, "This is it." And they ordered *machaca* burritos, and I got oatmeal and orange juice. And they were pissed at me. I was wondering how we would get through this. We lived in the SEIU office. Susanna quit smoking and caffeine at the same time she quit eating. Dolores got into it because Susanna was going to do it, so talk about not being prepared! She had a tough time with the caffeine headaches—they were brutal for her. I just didn't know if we would make it through. We did the fast for ten days. We had some kind of juice three times a day—that's what we would do. But the janitors who did the fast were incredible. They never wavered. Dolores had a granddaughter in the middle of it. She went to the hospital for the birth, came back, and hadn't eaten. It was interesting to me because Dolores and Susanna only spoke Spanish; Ignacio was bilingual; and my Spanish was lousy. We did get along, though.

In retrospect, I, as the chief negotiator, probably should not have done this. It was hard for me to negotiate at times during the hunger strike. I would probably rethink that strategy in the future. It did, however, certainly make a statement. And I'm glad I did it, because I can't ask members to do something that I'm not willing to do. It bound us all together. It also had a huge impact and really galvanized the community. And it held the strike together. That's the thing about a fast—you do it as much for the workers who are sacrificing as you do it for the public attention. It helped conclude the strike and it got the mayor's attention to help end it. The result of the strike was very good. We would have liked more—you always like more. But it was a good victory.

As far as membership goes, the majority of our members in SEIU, and I think in most unions except for maybe the trades, are women. I think that women are the foundation, quite frankly, because they're willing to work hard for change and don't need to be the leaders of it, which unfortunately is why we don't have a lot of women leaders. And we, as women, definitely bring a different perspective, and I see it within my own international. But it throws people off. When you're dealing with the male establishment, they don't know how to deal with you as a woman, and you don't always know how to deal with them, so it's just a very different dynamic. With women, though, it's different. You can understand why it ended up being almost all men, but to break through that is going to take an awful lot of work and sacrifice for women. I think a lot of women choose not to lead because of those sacrifices. When they weigh it, they choose balance in their lives, which is quite understandable.

I think that if there's anything we can do for each other in this community, it's to connect somehow. We're all swamped like this. It gets very isolating to do this work. So I am encouraged with the labor movement. I think the changes in the future will result in a much broader community, which will help all of us do a better job.

Jack Finneran: Former *Union-Tribune* Pressman, President of GCIU Local 432-M

I was born a poor white child in a place called the Bronx, New York, a couple of miles north of Yankee Stadium. I moved to San Diego in 1991. I actually moved here for a couple of reasons: one, I'm a bike racer and the idea of riding a bike twelve months out of the year appealed to me; and two, the prospect of working at the *Union-Tribune* at the time was a really good opportunity for a good job with decent pay, and working conditions that appeared to be favorable. My immediate impression of San Diego was that it was summer all the time. I always liked living by the ocean. As I've spent some time here, I just came to like the city more and more. Pretty much all the time I've lived here, with the exception of a brief stay in North Park, I've lived entirely in Ocean Beach. Right now I live in south Ocean Beach, on the ocean, which is not a bad place to be.

To me, there's a huge distinction, however, between the city of San Diego and Ocean Beach. I would love to consider my address an Ocean Beach address and not a San Diego one. I find Ocean Beach to be more progressive than most if not all other areas of San Diego. There's a real sense of community; people are more proactive there. I had more support for my struggle with the *Union-Tribune* from Ocean Beach. When I told OB People's Market about our issues with the *Union-Tribune,* they abruptly stopped selling the *Union-Tribune* at the store and they're not going to sell it. When I tried to get other stores to do that, I got a very cold shoulder. But I think if I had pushed the issue in Ocean Beach, other small businesses would have done the same.

My impression of San Diego as a city is that it is a wonderful place. Politics here are really odd, though. I find the average San Diego resident to be complacent, bordering on lethargic. I think people here like to whine about certain issues, but ask them to do something about it, something as simple as voting, then you're asking too much. You ask them to take a stand on clean water, or pollution in the bay, or jet skis and what they're doing, and they don't give a damn. I can remember when I was living here for a short time, and there was a rally by the beach that Surfrider or one of those groups put on. It was just a rally for clean water. There might have been thirty people there when there were a hundred-plus people surfing. One would think that someone out surfing would be concerned about the sewage pipe that's directly underneath them with holes in it. But then, to me, that summed up San Diego: "Don't bother me with clean water now, I'm surfing." It's kind of like that sick Carl's Jr. ad: "Don't Bother Me, I'm Eating." But it's a great city—and could be, should be, a better place. I think if people had a better sense of community, they could make things happen, and they could make this place what the city fathers claim it is, "America's Finest City." But it's not just something you can say: "O.K. it's 'America's Finest City.'" Well, why? Because of the climate? It's a better place to live in than I've ever lived, and I'd like to continue to live here. My only issue with that is, can I afford to live here? Do I have to become a union-busting attorney to afford to buy a home here? If so, I'd rather live in Hoboken, New Jersey.

I started working for the *Union-Tribune* in January 1991 as a journeyman newspaper pressman, which is the top wage scale for a pressman worker because I came in as a qualified worker, having been in the industry for a number of years. I left the *Chicago Tribune* to get a better position at the *San Diego Union-Tribune*, which at the time was paying $20.64 an hour. So at the time, in 1991, a twenty-dollar-an-hour job was good here. I got into print production a long time ago, in 1977, and I've been running printing presses or doing something in the graphic arts industry ever since.

Shortly after taking the job with the *Union-Tribune* in 1991, I was informed that there was a union there representing workers and that it would be to my benefit to join Graphic Communications International Union (GCIU) Local 432-M. Sometime in 1994–95, David Rubi, who was then president of the union, nominated me to be vice president. A month later, I was voted in. A year or so later, David Rubi lost his job. He developed carpal tunnel syndrome and they said, "We can't have you here." Two and a half years later, after a long and expensive legal battle, we got him his job back. By that point I had taken over the leadership of GCIU. David Rubi has fortunately remained active in the local, and in a strange turn of events, he is now my vice president. I'm delighted to have a guy there with thirty-plus years, a guy who should be respected by management. It's a lot of work, but it's good work. It's work that you don't resent. It's something you can look back on with a real sense of pride. I'm really goddamn proud of what I did at the *Union-Tribune*.

I was terminated by the *Union-Tribune* in August 2000, which was, to a great extent, a relief. I had wanted to leave there for quite some time. It was only my job as president of the local and the responsibility that went with that kept me working there. I found that I was actually able to be more effective after being terminated because, as a nonemployee, I didn't have to worry about things like disparaging the company. I could disparage them all I wanted, as long as I didn't slander them. I had no reason to. I felt that my message was clear and honest, and I did everything I could to bring it to the public's attention. When people started to hear what type of employer the *Union-Tribune* had become, our campaign started to pick up steam. They fired me, they fired Jeff Alger (who was secretary-treasurer) in November 2001, and they also tried to fire our previous president, David Rubi, in '97. I think it's worth showing that they fired two union presidents and the secretary-treasurer who was next in line, so you're not just saying that they fired union activists; they fired consecutive union presidents and the secretary-treasurer who was the most active among us. His grandfather was in the sit-down strike in Flint, Michigan, with [film-maker] Michael Moore's dad.

So what happened to the good job at the *Union-Tribune*, and how did every-thing lead up to my termination? The earliest beginnings of problems at the *Union-Tribune*, from my understanding, started with the involvement of King and Ballow, the union-busting law firm of Nashville, in 1978. But they were kind of on the sideline for a long time. I don't think it was until about 1992 or 1993, when Gene Bell became president and CEO of the *Union-Tribune,* that the real trouble started. Bell had previously been vice president of operations at the *Chicago Tribune*, and, to a great extent, orchestrated the strike there, and later worked and orchestrated the forced strike at the *New York Daily News*. Gene Bell's job is to break unions, and he gets paid a lot of money to do that. One person that should also be mentioned here, who has been a huge part of the problem, is the *Union-Tribune*'s manager of labor relations, Patrick J. Marrinan. He's the company's lawyer. He is the go-between for

King and Ballow and Gene Bell and is the guy who we had to develop a contract with. He must stay up late at night thinking of these creative ways to screw working families; that's his job.

And that's where the *Union-Tribune* is headed, and I'm glad there are enough people there to put up a fight and put some roadblocks in the way of that. It's far from over. We've got a contract now, but two years from now, we're going to be right back where we started. Our next contract proposal from the *Union-Tribune* is going to result in worse working conditions than those that the employees are working under currently unless something happens, and unless the *Union-Tribune* is sold or other management people in the *Union-Tribune* decide that Gene Bell is doing something to hurt the company, but I don't see that happening. The Copley family is 100 percent behind Gene Bell and his tactics. What they look at is the bottom line. Why pay someone $20 an hour if you can get someone for $10? And why pay someone $10 if you can get them for $7?

So the newspaper did a lot of things to realize their ambition to get rid of the unions. The single worst union-busting thing I saw was during the campaign to oust the Communications Workers of America, CWA Local 9400. What the *Union-Tribune* did there, prior to going into an election to get rid of the union, is they went out and hired literally hundreds of part-time employees. I'm sure they did a great job of screening them to see what their union background was, if they had any union affiliation. These were mostly part-time students with no union background and the *Union-Tribune* had a fair idea of how they were going to vote in an election. So they hired these people in, knowing that within two months, they would be eligible to vote in a Labor Relations Board election and that their vote would count as much as a full-time employee that had been working there for thirty years. They brought these people in, worked them a couple to three days a week, and used them to vote the union out. That's exactly what happened: they stacked the deck.

There were a lot of other incidents. What I found the most difficult through this whole struggle—it was more difficult than being fired, more difficult than seeing my friends get fired—was being up in the *Union-Tribune*'s cafeteria the day the newspaper guild got voted out. To see women up there in tears with their kids when they tallied those votes was the saddest thing I've ever experienced. It was worse than funerals I've been to. Those of us on the right side were just stunned. You couldn't believe it was happening and that the company could have manipulated people so much that they would go the other way. But this is what happens. The workers were six or seven years into a situation where they had had no pay raises. How many years do you go without a pay raise? GCIU went ten years. Had we gone eleven, I don't think we could have done it. You just go on and on, and you can succeed in convincing people that the only way in hell you're going to get a pay raise is if you get rid of this goddamn union. A lot of people that don't have the convictions of union leaders are going to say, "Fuck the union. A pay raise to me comes first. My family's first, my family's more important than the union." So they got rid of the union and they didn't get their pay raises anyway. The *Union-Tribune* made promises, but what they ended up getting is roughly 3 percent a year—same thing we're getting now. Three percent a year is less than the cost of living, and food goes up maybe 5 percent a year. And rents have doubled in the last five or six years, and the price of housing has doubled in the last five years. So what the hell does 3 percent a year do for you? Ten years ago at the *Union-Tribune*, a working family could afford to buy a modest home from the wages they made. I don't know of anyone working there now who has bought a house lately.

They did several bad things to GCIU as well. The single worst thing was stringing us along for ten years without a pay raise. Then they posted working conditions in March 1999 and effectively lowered the wage by $5 an hour. The top wage was $20.64 at the time, and they lowered it down to $15.48. We had an apprentice program, and after every six-month period, you were reviewed and you got periodic pay raises, so every six months, your wages went up 5 percent. After a four-year apprenticeship, you were at the top of the wage scale. When the newspaper posted working conditions, they scrapped that program, and instituted lower wages. What had happened was that they implemented everything in the contract that we were currently negotiating that was favorable to the company and omitted all the parts that would have put more money into the pockets of workers. So although we had agreed to terms and conditions on health and welfare, when they posted working conditions, that went away. We had agreed to a production bonus, which would have put more money in people's pockets, and that went away. We had a union pension plan that paid $4 per shift to a GCIU pension, and that went away. So they started hiring people for lower wages, had them topping out at a much lower wage—25 percent lower—and just made it more difficult for senior employees to continue working there. They would do things like give favorable daytime shifts to brand-new employees, while people who had been working there for twenty years (and they're still doing this today) worked three different shifts in a workweek. And it changes from week to week to week. They'll actually bring people in, have them work third shift one day, come back after eight hours and work second shift, and come back after another eight hours and work the first shift. So you literally work, try to get enough sleep, go back to work, sleep, go back to work. They do this regardless of your years of service, your commitment to the company—none of that means anything, because what they want is these higher wage earners to go away. They want to create a situation to force those people to quit because they don't respect or appreciate these experienced and skilled workers and because they can now get people in at lower wages to replace them. So they can fire or force those people out by making the situation harsh and give the quality day shifts with weekends off to the people they just hired in the hope of maintaining those employees. They're hiring them at $12 an hour as part of the effort to get rid of the people at $21 an hour.

They have at least four times the number of supervisors they used to have. If they want to harass you, as they did with me or with Jeff Alger, they would often have a supervisor assigned to you for an entire shift, to the extent that even if that supervisor went to lunch, they would have another supervisor watching you for that time. They would just follow you around, watching everything you did, hoping that you would make a mistake. And if you ever worked in a situation like that, where someone is looking over your shoulder and asking you stupid questions like, "Why did you do that?" or "Couldn't you do it this way?," you're a whole lot more likely to make a mistake, not to mention that you get edgy, when you're working on a big, ugly, dangerous piece of equipment. It's nerve-wracking. It's amazing that those tactics didn't force somebody to get hurt on the job.

The other thing that happened through the course of not getting a pay raise for ten years, and the implementation of working conditions including lower wages, was that every increase in health insurance was passed directly on to employees. So where other *Union-Tribune* nonunion employees might have been paying $10, $15, or $20 a week for health insurance, GCIU people were paying over $50 a week. The company's line is always something like: "If we didn't have the union, we could deal with you directly. If we didn't have this third party that we have to go through that mandates that these are the wages, maybe things could be different for employees like you that are doing an exceptional job. But since we have to pay you the same thing that we pay everybody else because of the *union,* there's really nothing we can do. We'd like to pay you more, but we can't." Show me a union anywhere that turned down a wage increase! It just doesn't happen.

What helped us hang on to membership during this time, more than anything else, was the fear of part-time work. People were really afraid of being cut back to part-time wages. They felt that that was one area where the union could offer them some protection. They saw what happened to the people who were just on the other side of the wall from us in the packaging department, who were represented by CWA. When those people were cut back, new people were hired in as part-timers. Our people didn't want that. We did have a good, solid base of people who had been there for many years, through the course of several contracts, and they saw that there was something very valuable in having a union. These are people who had been union members for many years and recognized clearly that their wages and working conditions wouldn't be as good were it not for the union. To some extent we were successful in conveying that message to new employees. As new people came in, we got them to join the union by telling them, "This is where we are: the wages you are making are from our negotiations because we have had a strong union in here for a lot of years. Without a union, the company can pay you whatever they want; they can bring you in and work you part-time, like they're doing next door. Is that what you want?" Most of these people come in and say, "No, that's not what I want. You guys have been working here for ten, twenty, thirty years. We think this union's a good thing. It's something we can believe in." If it was just a small group of union officers with that message, it wouldn't have gone over. But since it was the veteran people who new employees were working with on a day-to-day basis, saying, "Yes, this union's a good thing, because of the union I was able to buy a home, because of the union, my kids are in college now," the message was much more credible. And that's how we were able to get them to join with us rather than join with the company against us.

Currently we represent 148 employees, but it changes all the time. They're constantly bringing in new people. And there are always people leaving. For a long time, after the posting of the working conditions, when they started bringing people in at lower wages, 75 percent of these people were quitting. So the company was then bringing in a lot of undertrained people and it was a revolving door. On numerous occasions I confronted the company and asked if this was the situation they were looking for where you have people working here for two or three months. It's just a matter of time before people would start getting hurt. And that, in fact, did happen: we had a huge increase in injuries, and many of those serious. We had a woman who lost part of her hand, a new employee working by herself who had been there for just under three months.

There are people very willing to work for lower wages. If the *Union-Tribune* wanted to hire people for $8 an hour and offer no benefits, there would be people in this city willing to take those jobs. And what they would do then is take advantage of less fortunate people with poor educations, mostly immigrant workers. Fortunately, a lot of the people the *Union-Tribune* has hired are very proficient in English, and we've been able to communicate well with them. And we've gotten a big percentage of those workers now as members of the local. But it doesn't always work that way. Very often these workers feel very committed, and feel they owe a lot to the company. If they get word from the company that "Well, we'd rather you not join the union," they're not going to join the union, and there's no way we can convince them to join, because when you get that paycheck, it says *Union-Tribune* Publishing Company. It doesn't say GCIU Local 432-M. The only check that's going to say GCIU 432-M is a check they would be writing to us for their union dues. So you have the company on one side saying, "Here, we're giving you money. The union wants to take your money." And put in those base terms, it makes it really difficult and it's a major hurdle for unions to overcome. How do you get your message out to these workers who have already been sold a bill of goods by the company they've been hired by and that's where their allegiance is? That's one I can't answer.

What were effective strategies in winning a contract from the *Union-Tribune*? In May and June 2002, we labeled David Copley a "corporate pig," and actually made up the pig costume and paraded around the corporate headquarters to let his employees at Copley Press and area businesses know that David was a corporate pig. I don't think he liked it. It's hard to say, given the years that the struggle went on, what was effective and what wasn't. I'd be inclined to think it was a combination of everything that happened. It probably cost them a million dollars, the National Labor Relations Board decisions didn't go their way, and we embarrassed them through two trials. The corporate campaign "Something Stinks at the *Union-Tribune*" seemed to settle in much more than their campaign that they paid several millions dollars for, which was "How Will You Be Changed?" And we didn't have any multimillion-dollar ad agency working for us; it was just a couple of undereducated pressroom grunts doing what we did. It's hard to say what's effective and what isn't. Was it hassling the *Union-Tribune* advertisers? Or was it getting information to the public? Or was it articles in the *Reader* and other publications that were sympathetic to us? Roger Hedgecock slammed them, and there were a lot of other things going on as well. So a lot of things helped. When they tried to build circulation through a very expensive telemarketing campaign, the circulation was just dead flat. If anything, it started to go down at a time when they were spending tons of money to bring it up. Yet, if the *Union-Tribune* was willing to be reasonable and say, "O.K., if you're willing to help us build circulation, then we're willing to work with you. Show us that you can bring circulation up 10,000, and we'll throw your guys a small bonus," that's all it would take. They could make money by doing that. But they're just so set on the idea that a union's a bad thing, so the whole concept of the union doing something in conjunction with them is not something they're willing to entertain.

If I had known years ago that taking on an officer's position in GCIU would have taken this much away, I probably still would have done it, but I would have given it some real serious thought. I've learned a lot through the process, but it's taken its toll. Between the time spent, aggravation, lost sleep, depression and stuff that goes with it, how much was that worth? I've developed ulcers in recent years, and I know it's not because of anything that's happening now; it's because of what happened six years or so ago at the *Union-Tribune*. I'm especially proud of doing things my way and of seeing the union stay alive. It's something I'll take to the grave with me. And it's something I'll be able to tell my grandchildren—that when push came to shove, I stepped forward and took a stand and didn't just shy away from it like most others did. Instead, I chose to get involved. There's great value in that.

Remaining active in the labor community is important to me because it's something that becomes a belief—although I'm not a very religious person. Some people are capable of doing a little; I'd like to think I'm capable of doing a little bit more. When you see what corporations like the *Union-Tribune* are capable of doing, having done some research in the area, having studied some labor law, and having dealt with the NLRB and things like that, I would like to use some of this hard-earned experience I've gotten through the struggle with the *Union-Tribune* to benefit other workers who may not know how to go about doing this type of corporate campaign. We won a total of twenty-eight NLRB charges against the *Union-Tribune* and dragged them into court a couple of times. When they don't want to sign a fair contract, those are the things that can push them in the right direction.

Donald Cohen: Political Action Director of the San Diego–Imperial Counties Labor Council, Co-Director of Center on Policy Initiatives

I came to San Diego in 1979 because my sister lived here. I had graduated from college and was living in Ann Arbor. I didn't want to go back to Ann Arbor, so I stayed here where my sister was. When I first got here, Three Mile Island, the nuclear power plant, had just blown up, in March 1979. A number of us in Ann Arbor had been active in that stuff. So then when I came to San Diego, I joined an antinuclear group, which was called the Community Energy Action Network.

The movement here had big marches and all that. Then I hooked up with some folks who decided to open a cultural center, called the Grassroots Cultural Center, which was right next to the Big Kitchen in Golden Hill. It was a progressive book-store and cultural space where we had forums and concerts and stuff. We would produce bigger concerts elsewhere. Then I went to central Mexico to learn Spanish, and on the way, too, met a lot of Central Americans. Once I came back, I decided that I would do anti-intervention in Latin America work. So I did anti-intervention in El Salvador politics—CISPES—for a while.

Eventually, I got recruited by the labor movement here in San Diego. People knew I was a good organizer and here was an opportunity to be in the labor move-ment with some political power. We had been trying to do that in the community for quite some time, and it wasn't going anywhere, so I decided to try it. I actually wasn't working, so the timing was good. I had done consulting for nonprofits, unions, and churches, and actually did a retreat for the Labor Council, and then I was doing health care. A bunch of us wanted to create a Canadian-style form of health-care system, and we got our asses kicked. That was '94, the year of the Gingrich revolu-tion. It was a dark time for the country: the Contract on America. Joe Francis was the secretary-treasurer at the time and Jerry Butkiewicz had decided to challenge his leadership. I wasn't around then, but some of the central complaints people had with the old leadership was that nothing was happening. A whole new labor movement needed to be built because the old guard was passing the torch. The Cold War gen-eration of labor leaders were on the ship as it was declining and really didn't know how to turn it around. So there was this big changing of the guard. People decided that it was time for them to go and Jerry got to be the one to do it.

So, in terms of what was happening at the Labor Council, people decided that they were going to try to elect a new leader and infuse new energy, and one of the consequences of that struggle was that people said they needed programs here if this thing is supposed to go on. I got hired to put together a Labor to Neighbor program, which was bringing labor issues into the community, and I worked for Joe. It only had an eight-month budget, and it was slow-going, trying to piece it together. While I was here during my first year, Jerry's campaign was happening. It was a pretty mean campaign, and so I just did my work. I wasn't going to do it for very long, but I'm still here.

The Labor Council and Labor to Neighbor have had some tangible accomplishments. Recently, the *Union-Tribune* wrote an article about labor's new power. We've been able to elect people to political offices. In 1996, we elected Dede Alpert, Susan Davis, and Howard Wayne to the statehouse. So we've got a pretty good record of electing people to state [legislative] offices. And we got Susan Davis in at the federal level, which, even though it ended up being disappointing, was a fairly significant accomplishment. I think we can get a lot of credit for that. The campaign was good and her staff was outstanding, but we did a lot as well. We've elected people to the city council as well. And now we're getting close to a labor majority on the city council. We've elected people in other surrounding cities also—municipalities like Imperial Beach, National City, Chula Vista—we pay attention to all the cities and try to move our agenda. And we've helped with the community college district. So we've got a track record now of electing folks.

Another accomplishment is that huge numbers of people who want to run for office really want our endorsement. And they're not just Democrats; they're Republicans as well. People are now seeking our help in their campaigns. We have clout, and we have members who vote, so people come to us. That's important because if they come to us, we're pretty good at saying what it means to get us—it's about the issues. We hand them a questionnaire: "Where are you on this? Where are you on that?" We're not for sale, and we stay really true to that. Our endorsement process has been a powerful thing: we get all the unions to sit around the table and discuss the candidates. A lot of the unions used to really hate each other; now, they're all sitting around the table on an endorsement, trying to work it out together. So when a candidate comes in, they come to a labor movement with clout because, in fact, we can deliver 100,000 members. It used to be that the unions worked against each other. Such disorganization worked against us, number one, and number two, we failed to pay attention to our own. We don't work for the candidates anymore; we work for our members, and we've talked to them about the issues. They're not campaign issues, they're our issues. So we get Democrats to vote for Republicans and we get Republicans to vote for Democrats because it's about labor issues. The goal was to synchronize the labor vote—that was my goal—so that it would be a labor vote and not a partisan vote. And we've made a lot of progress there.

One of the most important things we do actually is to support organizing, and we use politics to support these efforts. So, for example, the United Domestic Workers represent 10,000 people, which is a big accomplishment; Service Employees International Union (SEIU) had a great accomplishment in organizing the janitors; and Hotel Employees and Restaurant Employees (HERE) is poised to make great strides. The stuff that the American Federation of Teachers has done with the community college board elections has been notable. Those are a few of the ways we support organizing, so it's a complicated movement.

As far as the future goes, we want to have influence in the city and the county—a goal that is pretty impacted by the current county board of supervisors. Their policies on services like welfare and other really important stuff to people are in the hands of fascists, so that's a long-term plan. Also, you have to change the politics of the town and change the attitudes so that people will not just be socially progressive, but will support things like taxation, increased regulation, and union organizing. You have to move the electorate that way, too. It's a little bit of a different fight, but it's crucially important. If you can't raise taxes, you can't pay for stuff. If you can't pay for stuff, you can't provide services. The key to that is supporting collective bargaining and unions. That's essential: the most important thing we can do is support that and elect politicians that support that. It gets to economic justice faster than anything else when people can negotiate. There's just nothing more important.

Another thing I'm involved in is the Center for Policy Initiatives (CPI), which Mary Grillo and I cofounded. It is a hybrid organization that does research to be able to frame and to describe, from our perspective, what *is* for people, so that the people who are describing what *is*—what living conditions are like, what the problems are—can be the first in line to describe what the solutions are. Part of political conflict is being able to describe the problem first. The second thing you've got to be able to say is that our solution is the right one. CPI does that. We also want to win things, which means policy and organizing drives. You institutionalize gains such as living-wage policy, low-wage and inclusive housing, which is the policy side of things. The organizing side is helping the janitors downtown get health care by supporting the strike—we helped get the media and the community on the strike. So that's what we want to win—and then organizing people to their community and then to issues. If we want more capacity, then we have to do that kind of stuff. We have these sub-projects that have to do with linking economic justice to strategic constituencies, such as the faith community, students for economic justice, etc.

Generally speaking, my impression of San Diego is that it is an awful place. It's not just that it's conservative, it's like it's on another planet. There are more Democrats on the city council now than Republicans for the first time in the history of the city. Now, they're not always the greatest Democrats, but it's the first time nevertheless. But that's just a sign of the mushiness of San Diego politics and the shitty Democratic politics of America. Even the strongest ones aren't very ideological. I can't really put my finger on it. America is a relatively apolitical nation—not that it's right or left, it's apolitical. And San Diego is even more so. It's not very polarized, not very active, not very sharp politically. And so it's a pretty suburban place.

But it's shifting: the demographics are shifting, and so that begins to shift the politics. It's far more open than it used to be. Environmentalists actually have a little bit of juice these days, and that's a big thing. Labor has much more juice in town. There are also a few community-based organizations emerging. These are all hopeful signs.

Notes

Foreword

1. I commend Goldfarb Marquis as the author of an excellent biography, *Alfred H. Barr, Jr.: Missionary for the Modern* (1989).

2. Consider the following names, all taken from David L. Ulin's splendid *Writing L.A.* (2002) in the Library of America: Vachel Lindsay, Louis Adamic, Aldous Huxley in the 1920s, H. L. Mencken, Edmund Wilson, Cedric Belfrage, William Faulkner, Nathanael West, F. Scott Fitzgerald, Bertolt Brecht, Chester Himes, Rayner Banham, Cees Noteboom, Jan Morris, Simone de Beauvoir, Truman Capote, Evelyn Waugh, Octavio Paz, Tennessee Williams, Jack Kerouac, Gary Snyder, Tom Wolfe: all literary vagabonds, journalists on assignment, passing debunkers, scholars on grants, professional travel writers, exiles and internal émigrés, and as a group more numerous and on the whole more distinguished than the occasional native or more common born-again Californians until about 1980, although the latter groups include such notable figures as M.F.K. Fisher, Christopher Isherwood, Budd Schulberg, Joan Didion, out of Sacramento and New York, and John Gregory Dunne, out of Providence, R.I., and New York, both now returned to New York, somewhat blur the distinction I am trying to make. After 1980 the natives and the born-agains predominate: Carolyn See, Robert Towne, Wanda Coleman, Rubén Martínez, Walter Mosley, Mike Davis, Lynell George, and James Ellroy (alas). Another fine collection, *L.A. Exile: A Guide to Los Angeles Writing, 1932–1998* (1999), edited by Paul Vangelisti and Evan Calbi, whose thesis is announced in its title, adds among other unassimilable aliens Theodor W. Adorno, Robert Craft, Edward Dahlberg, Malcolm Lowry, Thomas Pynchon, and Dorothy Parker. Only Wilson and Pynchon wrote substantially about San Diego.

3. In 1944, FDR accepted his fourth presidential nomination by radio from an "undisclosed location," in fact a railroad siding in Camp Pendleton, where he paused on his way to a conference in Hawaii with General Douglas MacArthur, to settle strategy for the rest of the Pacific war.

4. San Diegans will remember the bizarre episode of May 1995 on which the film is based, in which, as described by Scott, "an Army veteran stole a sixty-ton tank and ran amok over surface streets and freeways until police shot him." *Cul de Sac* sets Shawn Nelson's "rampage" against the background of suburban decay and the drug-addled second-generation suburbanites he interviewed in the Clairemont–Linda Vista area.

The Next Little Dollar

1. *The Pacific Slope,* Lincoln 1965, p. 151.
2. See Alan Harding, "Elite Theory and Growth Machines," in David Judge, Gerry Stoker, and Harold Wolman (eds.), *Theories of Urban Politics,* London 1995.
3. Glenn Dumke, *The Boom of the Eighties in Southern California,* San Marino 1944, p. 135.
4. The Derby map is in the California Room of the San Diego Public Library. (For Derby's "legendary" career, see William Goetzmann, *Army Exploration in the American West, 1803–1863,* Austin 1991, pp. 253–60.) According to Gerald Kuhn and Francis Shepard, "in the fall of 1821 . . . a flood changed the river channel in one night, and the greater volume of the flow was diverted into what was then known as False Bay." The river reverted to San Diego Bay around the time of the American conquest. (Kuhn and Shepard, "Dana Point to the Mexican Border," in Gary Griggs and Lauret Savoy (eds.), *Living with the California Coast,* Durham 1985, p. 368.
5. Goetzmann, p. 293.
6. Professor Goodyear (1872) quoted in Richard Pourade, *Gold in the Sun,* San Diego 1965, p. 49.
7. Roger Showley, *San Diego: Perfecting Paradise,* Carlsbad 1999, p. 51.
8. Julius Grodinsky, *Transcontinental Railway Strategy, 1869–1893,* Philadelphia 1962, pp. 58–59.
9. Showley, p. 64.
10. Grodinsky, pp. 58–59.
11. Hubert Bancroft, *Chronicles of the Builders of the Commonwealth,* Vol. 7, San Francisco 1892, p. 394.
12. Clarence McGrew, *City of San Diego and San Diego County,* vol. 1, Chicago 1922, pp. 154–60.
13. Dumke, *The Boom of the Eighties,* p. 140; Don Stewart, *Frontier Port: A Chapter in San Diego's History,* Los Angeles 1966, pp. 105–7.
14. Cited in *San Diego Transcript,* March 1981.
15. Pourade, p. 246.
16. H. Austin Adams, *The Man John D. Spreckels,* San Diego 1921, p. 163.
17. This detonated a plutocratic version of the Hatfields versus the McCoys. As Gray Brechin writes, "The vendetta begun at that time between the de Young and Spreckels families persisted for decades." The Spreckelses bought the *San Francisco Call* in 1895 largely to publicize scandal allegations against the de Youngs. Originally under John D.'s thumb, the *Call* would later become the pulpit for brother Rudolph's Progressive crusade against civic corruption and too-powerful unions. (*Imperial San Francisco,* Berkeley 1999, p. 177.)
18. *Memoirs of Ed Fletcher,* San Diego 1941, p. 205.
19. Richard Dodge, *Rails of the Silver Gate,* San Marino 1960, p. 17.
20. See Mary Marston, *George White Marston: A Family Chronicle,* 2 volumes, Los Angeles 1936; and John Nolen, *San Diego: A Comprehensive Plan for Its Improvement,* Boston 1908.
21. Generations later, donations of choice pueblo land on Torrey Pines Mesa would be crucial to the city's success in attracting both the world-famous Salk Institute and a new campus of the University of California.
22. Amy Bridges, *Morning Glories: Municipal Reform in the Southwest,* Princeton 1997, p. 79.
23. Oscar Cotton, *The Good Old Days,* New York 1962, pp. 111 and 145.
24. Scripps's creed was "Obey the Ten Commandments and make 15 percent cash divisible profit each year." As a dynastic biographer notes, "Only the brash William Randolph Hearst rivaled E. W. in this wide swath of character contradictions." (Jack Casserly, *Scripps: The Divided Dynasty,* New York 1993, pp. 5 and 30. Also Walter Swanson, *The Thin Gold Watch,* New York 1964, p. 120.)
25. Fletcher, pp. 55–58; and McGrew, pp. 227–28.
26. Fletcher, p. 178.

27. Fletcher, p. 109; and Pourade, p. 245.
28. Abraham Shragge, "Boosters and Bluejackets: The Civic Culture of Militarism in San Diego," Ph.D. thesis, UCSD 1998, pp. 178–80
29. Fletcher's partner was Montana millionaire James Murray, and together they began to aggressively buy up water rights downstream from the Cuyamacas, acquiring the strategic El Capitan site in 1911. (Fletcher, pp. 109 and 170.)
30. Pourade, pp. 42–48.
31. Ibid., p. 166; Adams, pp. 263–82.
32. Philip Foner, *The Industrial Workers of the World, 1905–1917*, New York 1965, p. 205.
33. On the sectional conflict and the crucial anti–San Francisco alliance between Oakland and Los Angeles, see Franklin Hichborn, *Story of the Session of the California Legislature of 1911*, San Francisco 1911, pp. 284–323.
34. Pourade, p. 164.
35. Ibid., pp. 297–314.
36. Grace Stimson, *Rise of the Labor Movement in Los Angeles*, Berkeley 1955, p. 335.
37. Frederick Ryan, *A History of the San Diego Labor Movement*, San Diego 1959, p. 19.
38. There was also the 32,000-acre Compania del Rancho de San Isidro near Tijuana, an exclusive hunting and fishing club whose members included both Ed Fletcher and Harry Chandler. See John Mason Hart, *Empire and Revolution: The Americans in Mexico since the Civil War*, Berkeley 2002, pp. 364–65.
39. The *San Diego Union* had denounced Otis's and Chandler's "chronic hatred of San Diego." See Pourade, p. 5.
40. Ryan, p. 21.
41. Austin, p. 77.
42. Pourade, p. 31.
43. See Doug Porter and Larry Remer, "The Sordid Saga of the Copley Press," *Door,* April–May 1973.
44. Pourade, p. 166.
45. Showley, p. 93.
46. Pourade, p. 172.
47. Ibid., pp. 172–73.
48. Roger Lotchin, *Fortress California, 1910–61,* New York 1992, p. 29.
49. Bruce Linder, *San Diego's Navy,* Annapolis 2001, pp. 35–37.
50. Shragge, "Boosters and Bluejackets," p. 266.
51. Ibid., p. 228.
52. Linder, pp. 54–58.
53. Ibid., p. 58.
54. Ibid., p. 47. Pourade adds that the rivalry between Los Angeles and San Diego over a major Army training camp "became so bitter . . . that the War Department eliminated Southern California from consideration." Los Angeles's elites, fearful of losing the regional revenue, subsequently abandoned their claim and supported Kettner's successful campaign to create Camp Kearny (p. 225).
55. Schragge, p. 420.
56. "Transforming itself into a military theme park, San Diego found a Progressive middle way between the untrammeled capitalism of Los Angeles and the restrictive aestheticism that was even then relegating Santa Barbara to the permanent status of a semi-resort." (Kevin Starr, *The Dream Endures*, New York 1997, p. 113.)
57. California State Reconstruction and Reemployment Commission, *Planning Pays Profits: The Story of San Diego*, Sacramento, May 1945, pp. 12–13.
58. It should be noted, however, that San Diego employers have always capitalized on the labor reserve

army constituted by service retirees (many in early middle age) and Navy wives.

59. Cotton, p. 130.
60. McGrew, pp. 169–77.
61. Ibid., pp. 172–73.
62. For a self-commemoration with dozens of appended testimonials, see William Kettner, *Why It Was Done and How*, San Diego 1923.
63. See Fletcher, pp. 320 and 345.
64. According to Glenn Rick, San Diego's original planning director, Senator Fletcher "had a way of becoming involved in real estate commissions on public land purchases such as the site for a new post office on E Street and the Agricultural Department race track at Del Mar." (*San Diego, 1927–1955: Recollections of a City Planner*, San Diego 1977, p. 88.)
65. Cotton, p. 121.
66. Ibid., pp. 121–23.
67. Ibid., p. 123.
68. Ibid., pp. 130–31.
69. See Table 6 in LeRoy Harris, "The Other Side of the Freeway," Ph.D. thesis, Carnegie-Mellon University, Pittsburgh 1974, p. 40.
70. Rick, p. 82.
71. Walter Swanson, *The Thin Gold Watch*, New York 1964.
72. Hart, p. 255.
73. Roberta Ridgely, "The Man Who Built Tijuana," *San Diego Magazine*, September 1967. Ridgely's long series on Coffroth, like her later serial profile of C. Arnholt Smith, are small masterpieces of diligent research.
74. William Wagner, *Reuben Fleet and the Story of Consolidated Aircraft*, Fallbrook, 1976, p. 281.
75. Reprinted in Edmund Wilson, *The American Earthquake*, New York 1958, p. 420.
76. Schragge, p. 413.
77. Rick, p. 106.
78. *San Diego Union*, 7 May 1935.
79. *San Diego Herald*, 7 November 1935.
80. *Time*, 10 June 1935.
81. Quoted in Ryan, p. 86.
82. Irving Holley Jr., *Buying Aircraft: Materiel Procurement for the Army Air Forces*, Washington, D.C., 1964, pp. 28–29.
83. Ibid.
84. Lotchin, p. 122.
85. Holley, p. 249.
86. Fred Rohr, a production manager at Ryan, left in 1940 to manufacture the "power package" assemblies that mount engines to planes.
87. According to the Chamber of Commerce, in 1940 the Navy and industry (80 percent aircraft) each generated $30 million in city income, while tourism and agriculture each contributed $20 million. See the chamber pamphlet *Postwar Opportunities in San Diego*, San Diego 1945.
88. Mary Taschner, "Boomerang Boom," *Journal of San Diego History*, Winter 1982, p. 7; and James Vaughan, "Introduction" ("War Comes to San Diego"), Ibid., Winter–Spring 1993, p. v.
89. Schragge, p. 494; and Christine Killory, "Temporary Suburbs: The Lost Opportunities of San Diego's National Defense Housing Projects," *Journal of San Diego History*, Winter–Spring 1993, pp. 36 and 41.
90. Taschner, p. 3.
91. Linder, p. 141.

92. Ibid.
93. Wagner, p. 223.
94. Killory, pp. 36 and 41.
95. San Diego had adopted a "Long-Term Program of Capital Expenditures" in 1938 in rough conformity with the second Nolen Plan. See California State Reconstruction and Reemployment Commission, *Planning Pays Profits: The Story of San Diego*, Sacramento 1945, p. 4.
96. Lotchin, p. 122.
97. Wagner, p. 242.
98. Lynne Doti and Larry Schweikart, *Banking the American West*, Norman 1991, p. 152.
99. Wagner, Ibid.; and *San Diego Union,* 17 June 1973.
100. Letter to Congressman Bob Wilson, quoted in Lotchin, p. 229.
101. *Planning Pays Profits*, pp. 5–8; and Lotchin, p. 157.
102. See San Diego Chamber of Commerce, *Summary of Day & Zimmermann Report*, San Diego 1945.
103. Ryan, p. 104.
104. Linder, p. 141.
105. Bill Yenne, *Into the Sunset: The Convair Story*, p. 45.
106. Russell Weigley, *The American Way of War*, Bloomington 1973, p. 377.
107. On de facto segregation in 1960, see Table 2 in Le Roy Harris, "The Other Side of the Freeway," Ph.D. thesis, Carnegie-Mellon University, Pittsburgh 1974, pp. 29–30.
108. Special El Cajon issue, *San Diego Magazine*, July 1958.
109. Chamber of Commerce, *San Diego Business Survey–1959*.
110. Nancy Scott Anderson, *An Improbable Venture: A History of the University of California, San Diego*, La Jolla 1993, p. 38.
111. When he was a council member in 1954, Mayor Charles Dail (1955–63) was accused before a grand jury of accepting a payoff in return for helping obtain a liquor license. In 1961 another grand jury investigated allegations that he owned property near Brown Field, where he was advocating a new municipal airport.
112. Roberta Ridgely, "The C. Arnholt Smith Story," parts 3 and 4, *San Diego Magazine*, September and October 1976.
113. Ibid. See also Ric Reynolds, "Industrialists Monopolize Tuna Industry,' *Door*, 10–24 February 1972.
114. On the illegal expansion of Hazard Yards, see Rick, pp. 67 and 134. On the Big Four's monopoly, see Lionel van Deerlin, "Favoritism Again on the Board of Supervisors," *San Diego Magazine*, June 1959.
115. See "Herb Klein's Old Paper," *Newsweek*, 5 January 1970.
116. Also key to this second tier, although not San Diego nobility, were Graydon Hoffman of the Bank of America and Walter Ames, a probate lawyer who represented the investments of the Putnams and Timkens, scions of Eastern millionaires who had retired to San Diego at the turn of the century.
117. See Harold Keen, "The Industrial Power Structure," *San Diego Magazine*, November 1970.
118. *San Diego Union,* 6 March 1957 (headline); Lochin, p. 305; and Linder, p. 149. The Navy also successfully blocked plans for a Coronado bridge in the 1950s, thus prolonging the lifetime of the obsolete but picturesque Coronado ferries. (See Linder, p. 157.)
119. Although supposedly an underwater test, shock waves from the detonation broke the ocean surface and ship crews—as well as, later, all San Diegans—were exposed to possibly carcinogenic radiation doses. For the widespread belief among veterans that naval personnel were used as secret guinea pigs, see the Wigwam page at the Atomic Veterans History Project Web site (link via www.nav.com).
120. What follows is summarized from Nancy Anderson's excellent official history, *An Improbable Venture*.

121. Lochin, p. 314.
122. Anderson, p. 78. The two key GD advocates of a San Diego campus, Convair's Biron and General Atomic's de Hoffman, later became, respectively, UCSD's vice chancellor in the mid-1960s and the president of the Salk Institute.
123. *San Diego Magazine,* August 1958.
124. James Britton, "Mission Bay," *San Diego Magazine,* June 1959; and Rick, p. 15.
125. See Rick, p. 153.
126. See historical account in *San Diego Union,* 23 March 1973.
127. Showley, p. 126.
128. "'Corruption!' is not a charge that we would lightly make against our city officials, but it seems that no milder term will do to explain the posture of lying down like a carpet for the May Company to enter town on." (*San Diego Magazine,* November 1957.)
129. See *San Diego Magazine,* November 1957 and March 1958. For Dail's controversial Industrial Development Committee, originally opposed by the Chamber of Commerce, see Frank Widham, "What's Going to Happen Next?" *San Diego Magazine,* October 1957, p. 31.
130. Ibid., July 1958.
131. Ibid., August 1958.
132. Ibid., July 1958.
133. "Valley of Our Discontent," *San Diego Magazine,* July 1980.
134. "Bust Town?" *Time,* 17 August 1962.
135. *Fortune,* 26 December 1961; *San Diego Union,* 26 December 1961.
136. *San Diego Union,*1 February 1962. A new management team was also brought south from GD's successful Canadair subsidiary.
137. Bob Adelizzi of Home Federal, in Sanford Goodkin, "A Hero," *San Diego Magazine,* Feburary 1992; *Time,* 17 August 1962; also Security Pacific Bank, *Monthly Summary of Business Conditions in Southern California,* November 1975 (for out-migration statistics); and SANDAG, January 1992 (aerospace job loss).
138. For a detailed discussion of the constraints on downtown, see *San Diego Union,*30 January 1949.
139. Cotton, p. 302.
140. The new malls, of course, had even more devastating impacts on the traditional town retail centers in El Cajon and Chula Vista—neither of which had recovered forty years later.
141. Reiner Hof, "San Diegans, Inc.," *Journal of San Diego History,* Winter 1990.
142. Harold Keen, "Would You Invest in This Town?" *San Diego Magazine,* January 1977.
143. Ibid.
144. Keen, "Curran and His Critics," *San Diego Magazine,* November 1963.
145. Harold Keen, "Stampede," *San Diego Magazine,* January 1965.
146. Harold Keen, "The Crisis That Broke Walter Hahn," *San Diego Magazine,* December 1971.
147. Byron Calame, "Self-Dealing Tycoon," *Wall Street Journal,* 16 April 1969.
148. "Crime in the Suites," *Forbes,* 15 August 1975, p. 19.
149. Harold Keen, "A City Led Down the Garden Path," *San Diego Magazine,* May 1968.
150. Kellog's lawyer promptly sent a telegram to Hoover denouncing the "reprehensible mobocracy and governmental domination which is sweeping the land and encroaching upon our basic American concept of private property." Harold Keen, "The Politics Behind La Jolla's Highrise War," *San Diego Magazine,* August 1965.
151. *San Diego Union,* 7 September 1967.
152. The phrase apparently originated with Glen Rick (see Anderson, p. 57).
153. Rick, pp. 80 and 106–09.
154. See Frank Rhoads's column, as well as Kahn's obituary, *San Diego Union,*12 September 1973.

155. Gus Russo, *The Outfit: The Role of Chicago's Underworld in the Shaping of Modern America*, New York 2001, esp. pp. 315–16, 350–51, 427, and 467–68. See also Sally Denton and Roger Morris, *The Money and the Power: The Making of Las Vegas and Its Hold on America*, New York 2001, esp. pp. 232–33; William Roemer, Jr., *The Enforcer*, New York 1994, pp. 182–83; and Dan Moldea, *The Hoffa Wars*, New York 1978, p. 317.

156. La Costa Land Company also became a major player in county politics. One of its chief beneficiaries was Sheriff John Duffy, an right-winger whose campaign promise was to round up the Black Panthers "*before* they can go into action." Harold Keen, "The Candidates and the Issues," *San Diego Magazine*, October 1970.

157. In 1957, Smith purchased Martinolich Shipbuilding Co. from Dalitz. Moreover, Smith's attorney and political henchman John Donnelley was the former executive director of Dalitz's Desert Inn. See "Crime in the Suites," *Forbes*, 15 August 1975, p. 19.

158. For reprise, see Gary Warth, "Spa versus Skin," *North County Times*, 2 January 2000.

159. Roemer, p. 316.

160. Quoted in "The Saint Louis Family," www.crimelibrary.com.

161. Ovid Demaris, *The Last Mafioso: The Treacherous World of Jimmy Fratianno*, New York 1981, p. 309.

162. Lowell Bergman and Maxwell Robach, "C. Arnholt Smith and the San Diego Connection," in Steve Weissman (ed.), *Big Brother and the Holding Company: The World Behind Watergate*, Palo Alto 1974, p. 197.

163. *San Diego Union,* 12 Feburary 1971.

164. Roemer, pp. 238–39.

165. See Frank Rhoads's interview with Kahn shortly before his death (*San Diego Union*, 24 April 1973) and his subsequent obituary (*San Diego Union,* 12 September 1973). On the frequency of heart attacks in otherwise healthy men who "knew too much" about the mob in Las Vegas, see Denton and Morris, p. 346.

166. The Teamsters claimed $180 million against the Kahn estate. See *San Diego Union*, 22 and 23 March 1974.

167. *San Diego Union,* 7 September 1967. In 1975 there were simultaneous but ultimately unsuccessful investigations of Shenker by grand juries in Las Vegas and St. Louis as well as by the FBI in San Diego. Investigators focused both on the use of Teamster monies in northern San Diego as well as on a jointly owned Shenker-Kahn venture, BAI, which had sold fictitious Swiss bonds to the pipefitters' union pension fund. (See *San Diego Union,* 15 January 1975.)

168. Denton and Morris, p. 317. Ex-FBI agent Roemer explains it this way: Glick "had gone to school with one of the sons of Frank Balistrieri, the LCN [La Cosa Nostra] boss in Milwaukee. Milwaukee being subservient to the Chicago LCN. The son recommended Glick to his dad, his dad contacted Chicago and suddenly Allen Glick was the ostensible owner of a multimillion-dollar property. Due to his clean record, he was quickly granted a gaming license by the Gaming Control Board. . . ." (p. 108).

169. See "New Leads in Unsolved San Diego Mob Murder," www.KFWB.com, 1 April 2002.

170. Roemer, p. 256.

171. "Arnie Smith Exposed by IRS Idealist," 30 March 1972.

172. Bergman and Robach, p. 186; and Roger Morris, *Richard Milhous Nixon*, New York 1990, pp. 370–71.

173. Roberta Ridgely, "The King Takes a Queen," *San Diego Magazine*, November 1976.

174. Peterson quoted in *San Diego Union* profile, 15 May 1983.

175. Harold Keen, "People Power versus the Megalopolitan Frankenstein," *San Diego Magazine*, September 1970.

176. Richard Popkin, "The San Diego Coup," in Weissman (ed.), *Big Brother and the Holding Company,* p. 63.

177. See *Door,* 9–13 March 1971.

178. *Wall Street Journal,* 16 April 1969.

179. Angelo Alessio, *Only in America: The Story of the Alessio Brothers,* San Diego 2003, p. 48.

180. Dennis Walsh and Tom Flaherty, "Tampering with Justice in San Diego," *Life,* 24 March 1972. The Alessios' lease was revoked.

181. Bergman and Robach, pp. 190–91. In 1972 the *New York Times* reported: "Mr. John S. Alessio, true name Giovanni Sevano Alissio, is well known to law enforcement agencies. Over the years his activities and associations have resulted in his being included with other known members of organized crime" (10 September 1973).

182. In 1968 vice detail sergeant Russ Ormbsy admitted that before 1961 (the statute of limitations) he had regularly accepted bribes while under the command of Wesley Sharp, later chief of police. Harold Keen, "City on Trial," *San Diego Magazine,* December 1970. See also *San Diego Union,* 24 January 1970.

183. Castanien, p. 91.

184. Walsh and Flaherty, "Tampering with Justice in San Diego."

185. David Stutz, the IRS special agent investigating Alessio, was ordered to secretly transfer the Alessio files to the White House. He refused. (Begman and Robach, p. 193.)

186. The custom of bribing officials would continue even in federal prison. A Lompoc prison administrator was fired after it was revealed that, in exchange for various Alessio gratuities, he had allowed John and his brother Angelo to cavort outside the walls with women friends and even go deer hunting. (*San Diego Union,* 22 March 1972; and *Life,* 24 March 1972.)

187. Harold Keen, "A Classic and Crucial DA Primary," *San Diego Magazine,* May 1970.

188. Ibid.

189. Keen, "City on Trial," December 1970.

190. The cab franchise was lucrative in a number of different ways. When Smith was a major investor in Yellow Cab it purchased all of its cabs from Guarantee Chevrolet, another one of his partnerships. Smith then sold his one-third share in 1967 to his friend and fellow Nixon-backer Ogden Bryan-Armour. Yellow Cab subsequently bought all of its gasoline through Armour Oil at higher prices than elsewhere (p. 5).

191. *Door,* 13–27 January 1972.

192. The atmosphere of crime and decay in City Hall was only reinforced in May 1971 by the arrest of Curran's chief assistant, George Lynch, for molesting a six-year-old. (*San Diego Union,* 22 May 1971).

193. *Life,* 29 March 1972.

194. Harold Keen, "Post-Mortem: The Trials," *San Diego Magazine,* April 1971.

195. Bergman and Robach, p. 204.

196. "Crime in the Suites," 15 August 1975.

197. Harold Keen, "The City Dumped," *San Diego Magazine,* June 1972.

198. *Door,* 10–24 Feburary 1972; also Bill Boyarsky's investigation in the *Los Angeles Times* (22 March 1972).

199. Walsh and Flaherty, "Tampering with Justice in San Diego."

200. On Barnes-Champ as Smith's conduit to finance Curran, see *Door,* 30 March—13 April, 1973.

201. Stutz explained to *Life* that Smith would have Barnes-Champ bill one of his companies for fictitious services. "Smith would have these bills paid, knowing them to be false, and the money used in political campaign." In effect, he was transferring the cost of the contribution to unsuspecting shareholders of Westgate or other entities (p. 36).

202. *New York Times,* 20 March 1972.

203. Ibid., 21 March 1972.

204. *Door,* 24 May–13 June 1973.

205. *Forbes,* p. 18.

206. *New York Times,* 10 September 1970.

207. Ibid.

208. "Crime in the Suites," pp. 17 and 20. Smith was eventually tried again, this time in 1979 for grand theft in the embezzlement of $8.9 million. He served eight months in a minimum security federal jail in 1984–85. He died, at almost a hundred years old, in 1996, survived by "Marie Antoinette," who still lives, in some extravagance, in Rancho Santa Fe.

209. *San Diego Magazine* Web site.

210. Profile in *Door,* 24 July 1973. Among these friends, the publicly stiff Wilson was able to let his hair down. One of his favorite pastimes was reportedly telling jokes "in a New York Jewish accent." (*San Diego Union,* 29 August 1982.)

211. Wilson profile in *Los Angeles Times,* 7 March 1976.

212. Showley, p. 138

213. Harold Keen, "Change at the Top," *San Diego Magazine,* January 1973.

214. The classic analysis is David Dowall, *Suburban Squeeze: Land Conversion and Regulation in the San Francisco Bay Area,* Berkeley 1984.

215. Harold Keen, "The Financial Power Structure," *San Diego Magazine,* January 1974.

216. Ibid.

217. For Gruen's talk at a Grant Hotel luncheon, see *San Diego Union,* 12 September 1973.

218. Raynes was a loyal Nixonite who gave the dishonored former attorney general Ed Meese a Rohr job in 1975. But Raynes and Meese were pushed out the following year when his diversification strategy proved a bust.

219. Harold Keen, "Mr. Button-Down Unbuttons City Hall," *San Diego Magazine,* July 1972.

220. Castanien, p. 99.

221. *San Diego Magazine* 2000 (52), p. 132.

222. Matt Potter, "All in the Family," *San Diego Reader,* 22 July 1999.

223. Harold Keen, "The Great Triple Alliance," *San Diego Magazine,* May 1977, p. 69. A study of "Who's Running San Diego?" by the La Jolla–based Western Behavioral Sciences Institute produced slightly different results, substituting Gordon Luce for Silberman in the top triumvirate and defining a second tier that included Burnham, Fletcher, Silberman, top cop Kolender, Chamber of Commerce head Clayton Brace, and Solar's Morris Sievert. (*San Diego Union,* 2 October 1977.)

224. *Los Angeles Times,* 12 October 1982.

225. *San Diego Union,* 17 September 1975.

226. *Los Angeles Times,* 7 March 1976.

227. Harold Keen, "Desperate Del Mar," *San Diego Magazine.*

228. "One of the most controversial sales was the secretly negotiated purchase in 1979 by the Signal Companies Inc. of a choice La Jolla industrial park site for a price estimated at half the value of the land. Signal Companies chairman Forrest Shumway is now one of the Wilson campaign's state finance chairmen." *Los Angeles Times,* 12 October 1982.

229. Ibid.

230. Interview, *Los Angeles Times,* 27 December 1982.

231. Donald Appleyard and Kevin Lynch, *Temporary Paradise,* San Diego 1974, p. 17.

232. *San Diego Tribune,* 16 December 1977.

233. Ibid., 20 August 1976.

234. Ibid., 9 June and 16 December 1978.

235. Ibid., 4 Jaunary 1982.
236. *San Diego Union,* 31 August 1982.
237. *Los Angeles Times,* 21 August 1981.
238. Ibid., 12 October 1982.
239. Donald Bauder, *Captain Money and the Golden Girl,* San Diego 1986, p. 110.
240. Harold Keen, "A War Without Proper Sides," *San Diego Magazine,* October 1976, pp. 45–46.
241. *Los Angeles Times,* 21 September 1984.
242. See profile in *San Diego Reader,* 25 August 1977.
243. Mike Bowler, "Roger Hedgecock and the Politics of Inclusion," *San Diego Magazine,* July 1983.
244. Matt Potter, "Big Money Boys," *San Diego Reader,* 22 November 2000.
245. Ibid.
246. *Los Angeles Times,* 3 January 1983.
247. Bauder, p. 171.
248. Potter, "Big Money Boys."
249. Bauder, p. 187.
250. Ibid., pp. 187–205.
251. See Bill Manson, "Roger Hedgecock and His Vegas Lawyer," *San Diego Reader,* 6 August 1998. Goodman is now (2002) mayor of Las Vegas.
252. "Thousands of welfare checks go to post office boxes in San Ysidro and are picked up each week by mothers living in Mexico." Roger Hedgecock and Rancine Phillips, *If We Say It Enough We'll Believe It,* La Mesa 1992, p. 37.
253. Ibid.
254. *San Diego Union,* 7 September 1990.
255. Cover text of Oakley Hall, *Mardios Beach,* New York 1955.
256. *Los Angeles Times,* 8 April 1995. In fact, she moved to Malibu.
257. *Los Angeles Times,* 4 September 1986.
258. *San Diego Tribune,* 30 September 1985.
259. Thomas Arnold, "The Four Freshmen," *San Diego Magazine,* December 1987.
260. See retrospective on O'Connor, *San Diego Union-Tribune,* 6 December 1992.
261. Ibid.
262. O'Connor in fact alienated all sides. Fred Schaubelt, the Libertarian who led the fight against Proposition A, bitterly claimed that O'Connor, although personally opposed to the initiative, had been pressured by her friend Helen Copley to stay neutral. See Paul Kreuger, "The Inside Story," *San Diego Reader,* 1 October 1983.
263. Hedgecock, p. 22–23.
264. Martin Hill, "The Great San Diego Land Rush," *San Diego Magazine,* November 1985.
265. Leonard Bernstein and Barry Horstman, "Making Sense of Maureen," *Los Angeles Times Magazine,* 10 December 1989.
266. *Los Angeles Times,* 6 October 1988.
267. For the *Union's* balance sheet of her mayoralty, surprisingly bleak in the face of her well-known friendship with Helen Copley, see *San Diego Union,* 6 December 1992.
268. Quoted in Peter Navarro, *San Diego Confidential,* San Diego 1998, p. 7.
269. *San Diego Union,* 9 April 1989.
270. Potter, "All in the Family."
271. Ibid. FBI diaries of the Yuba tap reveal Silberman's continuing role as middleman between Mexican maquiladora investors, Japanese corporations, and the San Diego establishment. See Jamie Reno, "The Silberman Factor," *San Diego Reader,* 9 April 1992. For more on Yuba (renamed Western Water after Silberman's conviction), see "Breaking Stories," *San Diego Reader,* 20 May 1999.

272. Silberman, like C. Arnholt Smith, didn't suffer unduly. He served his 46-month sentence at the notoriously comfortable "Club Fed" prison at Boron, with six furloughs for rest and recreation in San Francisco and Big Bear Lake resort. (Potter, "All in the Family.")

273. On Copley, see Matt Potter, "David Under the Influence," *San Diego Reader,* 31 May 1990.

274. Mani Mir, "Homegrown S&L Failures," *San Diego Reader,* 8 August 1996.

275. Mike Bowler, "Power Shift?" *San Diego Magazine,* October 1982.

276. *San Diego Union,* 10 June 1990.

277. Bowler, ibid.

278. *San Diego Union-Tribune,* 13 April 1998. The *San Diego Business Journal* claimed 25,000 manufacturing jobs lost (25 July 1997).

279. Linder, p. 161; and Keith Taylor, "Our Military Might," *San Diego Magazine,* April 1996.

280. Obituary for Bill Otterson, CONNECT online newsletter, 8 December 1999.

281. Stowley, p. 167.

282. *San Diego Magazine,* June 1996, pp. 52 and 122.

283. Ibid., p. 122; and *New York Times,* 6 November 2002. Geographers may prefer to see northern San Diego and southern Orange County as a single spatial-economic complex: the two areas are virtually mirror images of each other and UCSD/UCI function as a technology dipole, particularly in medical and biological research.

284. *San Diego Magazine,* p. 123.

285. Remark during talk.

286. Larry Remer, "The Democrats in Disarray," *San Diego Magazine,* June 1982.

287. *San Diego Union-Tribune,* 4 February 1999.

288. Nancy Williams, "A Housing Scorecard," *San Diego Metropolitan Magazine* Web site (April 1997).

289. Matt Potter, "Why Is Spanos Such a Heavy Hitter?" *San Diego Reader,* 30 January 1997.

290. "Back in Houston, Moores was known for his close alliance with a cadre of wealthy and powerful attorneys who helped launch the presidential candidacy of Clinton." See Thomas Arnold, "Clinton-and-Brown-Loving, Rich Texas Liberal Seeks Date with Padres," *San Diego Reader,* 3 November 1994.

291. Potter, "Why Is Spanos Such a Heavy Hitter?"

292. *Los Angeles Times,* 17 May 1992.

293. *San Diego Tribune,* 21 August 1984.

294. Navarro, pp. 8, 12, and 192.

295. Ibid., p. 192. Navarro's book—candid, spiteful, poisonous, and funny—bares the Darwinian competition of egos and the bonfires of principles that passed for politics, Democrat as well as Republican, in 1990s San Diego.

296. Matt Potter, "Golding's Tainted Money," *San Diego Reader,* 2 April 1998.

297. Ibid.

298. Dr. Theodore Bardacke, "Breitbard's Got Chutzpah," *San Diego Magazine,* December 1971.

299. *San Diego Union-Tribune,* 30 March 1997.

300. Potter, "Why Spanos"; "Mayor, City Council, City Attorney—Recall Them All," *San Diego Reader,* 27 February 1997; and "Why McGrory Quit," *San Diego Reader,* 3 July 1997. See also *San Diego Union-Tribune,* 24 June 1997.

301. The San Diego judiciary was rocked by scandals during the 1990s, with three Superior Court judges eventually convicted of corruption.

302. Thomas Arnold, "Fine Print Sell-out," *San Diego Reader,* 27 March 1997.

303. Joel Kotkin, "San Diego: A City for the New Millennium," *City,* Winter 1987 (7:1).

304. Potter, "Why McGrory Quit."

305. *San Diego Union-Tribune,* 24 June 1997.

306. Thomas Arnold, "Susan and Pete's Bay Area Money Machine," *San Diego Reader,* 10 August 1995.

307. Matt Potter and Thomas Arnold, "Why Golding Won't Debate," *San Diego Reader,* 15 Feb. 1996.

308. *Los Angeles Times,* 23 September 1997.

309. Potter, "Golding's Tainted Money."

310. For background see *San Diego Union-Tribune,* 2 May 1986. "We think it's the next major opportunity area downtown" (SDI leader speaking about "eastern downtown"). The largest landowner in the area is SDG&E (Sempra).

311. Ron Donoho, "Some Ballpark Figures," *San Diego Magazine,* 1998, p. 30.

312. *San Diego Union-Tribune,* 26 August 1997; and 9 and 24 July 1999. Dynes' father-in-law was wealthy San Francisco investor F. Warren Hellman, a close friend of Moores and his associate on the board of the Qualcomm spin-off Leap Wireless.

313. *San Diego Reader,* 3 September 1998; Potter, "Big Money Boys."

314. PEVA leaflet in vertical file, California Room, San Diego Public Library.

315. *La Prensa,* 3 April 1998.

316. *San Diego Union-Tribune,* 2 March 2000. "The poll showed a powerful negative reaction to the use of public funds. . . ."

317. *San Diego Union-Tribune,* 9 and 24 July 1999.

318. The *Union-Tribune's* usually laid-back Neil Morgan was incensed. See his column: *San Diego Union-Tribune,* 16 June 2000. One of McMillin's goldmines has been new home construction in Chula Vista. For his roughshod domination of that city's politics, see Susan Luzzaro, "Octopus Devours Chula Vista," *San Diego Reader,* 10 October 2002.

319. *San Diego Business Journal,* 2 September 2000. For a retrospective analysis of how the city council was bought, see Justin Wolf, "Corky's Game," *San Diego Reader,* 3 July 2002.

320. John McNab of "Save Our NTC" quoted in the *San Diego Union-Tribune,* 2 November 2002.

321. Herbert Asbury, *The Gangs of New York,* New York 1928, p. v.

322. Burgener, a true mummy of Republicans past, was the local 1950 campaign manager for Nixon, then served on the council in the 1950s, the state assembly in the 1960s (where he fought open housing), and, finally, ascended into Congress in the 1970s.

323. Typical Roberts quote: "I'm not saying bulldoze everything, but you can't look to discover on every project something unique to keep it from going ahead." (*San Diego Union-Tribune,* 26 July 1992).

324. *Fortune,* September 2002. Moores and "entitites associated with him" netted more than $630 million from sales of overvalued Peregrine stock before it collapsed to nothing in fall 2002. (See "Just How Much Did John Moores Know?," *Business Week,* 14 October 2000.)

325. See story by Caitlin Rother in *San Diego Union-Tribune,* 20 November 2002.

326. *CityBEAT,* 31 December 2002.

327. See *San Diego Reader,* 24 October 2002.

Just Another Day in Paradise?

1. Kelly Mayhew, who worked in Libros bookstore in Old Town from 1986 to 1992, remembers that tourists visiting the store frequently asked about the location of "Ramona's marriage place" without knowing that Ramona was a fictional character from Helen Hunt Jackson's novel of the same name.

2. Susan Davis, *Spectacular Nature* (Berkeley: Univ. of California Press, 1997), 44–45. Davis points out that "the space available for the reproduction of the species and the basic biological process of the wetlands was reduced by 99 percent" (44–45).

3. Jean Baudrillard, "Simularcra and Simulation," *Jean Baudrillard: Selected Writings* (Stanford: Stanford Univ. Press, 1988), 172.

4. Ibid., 170.

5. Susan Davis, 19

6. Michael Sorkin, Introduction, *Variations on a Theme Park: The New American City and the End of Public Space* (New York: Noonday, 1992), xi–xv.

7. Mike Davis, "Fortress Los Angeles: The Militarization of Urban Space," *Variations on a Theme Park,* 154–80; Neil Smith, "New City, New Frontier: The Lower East Side as Wild, Wild West," *Variations on a Theme Park,* 61–93.

8. Susan Davis, 47

9. Ibid., 36

10. Ibid., 89. Davis points out that 65–70 percent of Sea World's "operations employees" are part-time.

11. *Union-Tribune,* 6/2/02.

12. Susan Davis, 25.

13. Gregory Montes, "Balboa Park, 1909–1911: The Rise and Fall of the Olmstead Plan." *Journal of San Diego History* 27, no. 1, Winter 1982: 58–59.

14. *San Diego Union,* 1/10/15, quoted in Montes, 59.

15. Matthew Bokovoy, *San Diego's Expositions as "Islands on the Land," 1915–1935: Southwestern Culture, Race, and Class in Southern California,* diss., Temple University, 1999. According to Bokovoy, "A good portion of San Diego's ruling booster oligarchy maintained a liberal public culture in the face of conservative backlash" (85). While it is true that some of the exposition's cultural fare was not Social Darwinist in content, this made little difference in the city's political landscape. Social progressives existed in San Diego's elite, but they were never a dominant force. Hence, despite the liberal elements of the city's public culture, the ideological hegemony of Social Darwinism persisted.

16. Bokovoy, 340.

17. Douglas Monroy, "Brutal Appetites: The Social Relations of the California Mission," *Working People of California,* ed. Daniel Cornford (Berkeley and Los Angeles: Univ. of California Press, 1995), 52.

18. Abraham J. Shragge, *Boosters and Bluejackets: The Civic Culture of Militarism in San Diego, California, 1900–45,* diss., University of California, San Diego, 1998, 269.

19. Monroy, 39.

20. Ibid., 49.

21. Daniel Cornford, editor's introduction to Monroy, "Brutal Appetites: The Social Relations of the California Mission," 29.

22. Ibid., 29–30.

23. Peter Redfield and Pamela Cheek, *Frontier Gallery Storyline,* Museum of San Diego History, San Diego Historical Society, 1988, 139.

24. Ibid., 145.

25. Ibid., 145–46.

26. Bokovoy argues that the Indians who worked in the exposition were "free laborers" who "exerted their own unpredictable autonomy frequently on their employment sites" (151). This, however, does not negate the fact that a large range of other opportunities did not exist for Native Americans.

27. Carey McWilliams, *Southern California: An Island on the Land* (Salt Lake City: Peregrine, 1973), 63.

28. Ibid., 60.

29. Redfield and Cheek, 66.

30. *San Diego Labor Leader,* 2/12/26. In this edition of San Diego's labor paper (put out by the San Diego Labor Council) the editors bemoaned the fact that 75 percent of the county's indigent funds were expended to "aid Mexicans" (1).

31. *San Diego Magazine*, July 1967.
32. Redfield and Cheek, 66.
33. Shragge, 102.
34. Ibid., 103.
35. Ibid., 522.
36. Ibid., 521–22.
37. Leroy Harris, *The Other Side of the Freeway: A Study of Settlement Patterns of Negroes and Mexican Americans in San Diego, California,* diss., Carnegie-Mellon University, 1974, 193.
38. Ibid., 183. See also *Union,* 12/12/44, for a story about the efforts of whites in Golden Hill to kick black residents out of the neighborhood for fear of their driving down property values.
39. Ibid.
40. Harold Keen, "The Moral Dilemma of California Realtors," *San Diego Magazine,* January 1964, 39–40.
41. Ibid., 39.
42. Harris, 187.
43. *Union,* 11/10/65.
44. Roger M. Showley, *San Diego: Perfecting Paradise* (Carlsbad: Heritage Media Corp, 1999), 133.
45. Douglas L. Lowell, "The California Southern Railroad and the Growth of San Diego, Part II," *Journal of San Diego History* 32, no. 1 (Winter 1986), 7. Some *JSDH* articles are available online at www.sandiegohistory.org.
46. Elizabeth C. MacPhail, "San Diego's Chinese Mission," *Journal of San Diego History* 23, no. 2 (Spring 1977), 10.
47. Lowell, 8.
48. Ibid., 10.
49. MacPhail, 10.
50. Ibid., 13.
51. See Donald Estes, "Before the War: The Japanese in San Diego," *Journal of San Diego History* 24, no. 4 (Fall 1978), 425–56, and "'Offensive Stupidity' and the Struggle of Abe Tokunosuke," *Journal of San Diego History* 28, no. 4 (Fall 1982), 249–68.
52. Wilbur Jay Hall, "Just Like Dixie Land," *Sunset Magazine,* February 1910, quoted in Bokovoy, 72.
53. Estes (1978), 429.
54. *San Diego Labor Leader,* 7/8/32.
55. Estes (1978), 452–54.
56. San Diego Chamber of Commerce resolution, quoted in Shragge, 527.
57. Quoted in Shragge 300.
58. Ibid., 300.
59. San Diego Chamber of Commerce advertising affiliate, the San Diego–California Club, quoted in Shragge, 539–40.
60. Shragge, 554.
61. Susan Davis, 45.
62. Center on Policy Initiatives, "Prosperity and Poverty in the New Economy: A Report on the Social and Economic Status of Working People in San Diego County," December 1998, 52–53.
63. Ibid., 53. These numbers represent what CPI calls "realistic" poverty estimates rather than the "official" estimates, which don't factor in the cost of living in expensive regions like San Diego. See footnote 17 of the report for more on the difference between official and realistic poverty estimates.
64. Lowell L. Blaisdell, *The Desert Revolution: Baja California, 1911* (Madison: Univ. of Wisconsin Press, 1962), 131, 181.

65. Philip S. Foner, *U.S. Labor Movement and Latin America, volume I, 1846–1919* (South Hadley: Bergin and Garvey, 1988), 112.
66. Blaisdell, 148.
67. Ibid., 187.
68. Ibid., 10.
69. Ibid., 13.
70. James A. Sandos, *Rebellion in the Borderlands: Anarchism and the Plan of San Diego, 1904–1923* (Norman: Univ. of Oklahoma Press, 1992), 36.
71. Blaisdell, chapter 1; Sandos, chapter 1.
72. Blaisdell, 124–25.
73. Ibid., 27–28.
74. Ibid., 36, 54.
75. Ibid., 38.
76. Richard Griswold del Castillo, "The Discredited Revolution: The Magonista Capture of Tijuana in 1911," *Journal of San Diego History* (Fall 1981); Lawrence D. Taylor, "The Magonista Revolt in Baja California: Capitalist Conspiracy or Rebelion de los Pobres?" *Journal of San Diego History* 45, no. 1 (Winter 1999); Blaisdell, Foner, and Sandos also address this point.
77. Shragge, 52, 218.
78. Blaisdell and Taylor address this point.
79. Melvyn Dubofsky, *We Shall Be All: A History of the Industrial Workers of the World* (Urbana and Chicago: Univ. of Illinois Press, 2000), 85.
80. Griswold del Castillo, 261.
81. Ibid., 263–65.
82. Both Blaisdell and Griswold del Castillo address these problems thoroughly.
83. Blaisdell, 39; Griswold del Castillo, 258.
84. Blaisdell, 213.
85. Ibid., 213.
86. Griswold del Castillo, 258, and Blaisdell, 47.
87. Blaisdell, 77, 82.
88. Ibid., 99.
89. Ibid., 118–19.
90. Ibid., 120.
91. Ibid., 121; "Writing History with Postcards: Revolution in Tijuana," *Journal of San Diego History* 34, no. 1 (Winter 1988).
92. Ibid.
93. Blaisdell, 62.
94. Ibid., 63.
95. Ibid., 88.
96. Ibid., 131–36.
97. Ibid., 148.
98. Ibid., 146–58.
99. Ibid., 178–79.
100. Ibid., 180–81.
101. Ibid., 171.
102. Ibid., 195.
103. Ibid., 204.
104. Ibid., 202.
105. Ibid.

106. Sandos, 175.

107. Ibid., 174.

108. Blaisdell, 201.

109. Roberta Ridgely, "The Man Who Built Tijuana," part V, *San Diego Magazine*, September 1967, 88.

110. Ibid., 2.

111. Ibid., part VIII, 113.

112. Ibid.

113. Ibid., part V, 57.

114. Ibid., part VII, 102.

115. Ibid., part II, 129.

116. Ibid., part X, 106.

117. Ibid.

118. Ibid., part X 88.

119. *San Diego Labor Leader,* 9/10/20.

120. Ridgely, part VII, 111.

121. Ibid., part X, 88.

122. Ibid., part X, 103.

123. Philip S. Foner, *History of the Labor Movement in the United States, Volume 4: The Industrial Workers of the World 1905–1917* (New York: International Publishers, 1976), 199–200.

124. Ibid., 195.

125. *San Diego Metropolitan,* 8/00.

126. Frederick Ryan, *The Labor Movement in San Diego: Problems and Development from 1887–1957* (San Diego: State College Bureau of Business and Economic Research, 1959), 8.

127. *Evening Tribune,* 9/28/59.

128. Ryan, 136.

129. Ibid.

130. Ibid., 135.

131. Ibid., 22.

132. Michael McKeever's cursory coverage of the IWW in *A Short History of San Diego* is typical of local history "lite." More serious treatments can be found in Kevin Starr's *Endangered Dreams: The Great Depression in California* as well as the already noted Foner and Dubofsky books. Two other good sources are Heyman Weintraub's thesis, "The IWW in California, 1905–1931" (UCLA, M.A. thesis, 1947), and Charlotte Benz Villalobos's "Civil Liberties in San Diego: The Free Speech Fight of 1912" (SDSC, M.A. thesis, 1966). The *San Diego Reader* has also published some excerpts of M.A. theses.

133. San Diego Historical Society IWW vertical file.

134. Cornford, 4.

135. Rosalie Shanks, "The I.W.W. Free Speech Movement, San Diego, 1912," *Journal of San Diego History* (Winter 1973), 25. This essay was the award-winning paper presented at the San Diego Historical Society 1971 Institute of History.

136. Shanks, 33.

137. Roland Barthes, *Mythologies* (New York: Noonday, 1972), 42.

138. Shanks, 26.

139. Robert Warren Diehl, "To Speak or Not to Speak: San Diego 1912," M.A. thesis, University of California San Diego, 1976, 88–123. Cited in Bokovoy, 31.

140. Shanks, 26.

141. Ibid., 29.

142. Ibid., 28.
143. Ibid., 30.
144. Ibid., 32.
145. Ibid.
146. Kevin Starr, *Endangered Dreams: The Great Depression in California* (New York: Oxford Univ. Press, 1996), 29.
147. Ibid.
148. Foner, 194.
149. Ibid., 205.
150. Ibid., 203.
151. It is important to note that some prominent San Diegans such as George Marston and E. W. Scripps dissented from the fascist tendencies of the boosters who supported the vigilantes. Unfortunately, they did not hold the day.
152. Bokovoy, 18.
153. Ryan, 20.
154. Dubofsky, 77, 84.
155. Ibid., 32.
156. Ibid., 86–87.
157. Ibid., 84–85.
158. Sara Harris, *Skid Row U.S.A.* (New York: Doubleday, 1956), 180, 181–82.
159. Dubofsky, 98.
160. Ibid.
161. Ibid.
162. Ibid., 99.
163. Harris, 190–91.
164. Ibid.
165. Dubofsky, 109.
166. Foner, 195.
167. Bokovoy, 36.
168. "The History of the San Diego Free Speech Fight" (San Diego: San Diego Branch of the Industrial Workers of the World, 1973), 117. This pamphlet is actually a reprint of issues of the *New York Call* Sunday editions beginning March 15, 1914.
169. Harris, 185.
170. Foner, 195.
171. Ibid., 194.
172. Ibid., 195.
173. Pliny Castanien, *To Protect and Serve: A History of the San Diego Police Department and Its Chiefs* (San Diego: San Diego Historical Society, 1993) 27–28.
174. *New York Call,* 118.
175. Foner, 200.
176. *San Diego Sun,* 3/26/12; Foner, 201.
177. *New York Call,* Starr, Foner, and Dubofsky all recount this protest.
178. McWilliams, 289.
179. Harris, 187.
180. Foner, 200; Starr, 35.
181. Foner, 199.
182. Diehl in Bokovoy, 31.
183. Starr, 38.

184. Diehl in Bokovoy, 31.
185. *Sun,* 8/29/10.
186. *New York Call,* 126, 128.
187. *Sun,* 1/10/12 and 4/22/12; an article in the 4/3/12 issue of the *Sun* dismisses complaints about bad jail conditions.
188. This compromise, while allowing free speech, would have marginalized it much like the "free speech zones" created by police to make it easier for government officials and corporate elites to avoid the wrath of protesters. The way space was policed at the most recent Republican National Convention in San Diego is a good example of this practice in more recent times.
189. *Union,* quoted in Foner, 196.
190. *Union,* 1912, in vertical file at San Diego Historical Society.
191. *Sun,* 4/6/12.
192. *Sun,* 5/16/12; Foner, 198.
193. *Tribune,* quoted in Foner, 196.
194. *Union,* 1912, in vertical file at San Diego Historical Society.
195. *Union,* "The Vigilantes," 4/12/12.
196. Dubofsky, 110.
197. David Helvarg, "How San Diego Took Care of Its Wobblies," *San Diego Reader,* 8/10–18/77.
198. Foner, 198.
199. Dubofsky, 110.
200. Helvarg, 1.
201. Dubofsky, Foner, and Starr all recount this incident.
202. Emma Goldman, *Living My Life* (New York: Meridian, 1977), 496.
203. Ibid.
204. Ibid., 500–1.
205. *Union,* 1912, in San Diego Historical Society vertical files.
206. Goldman 510.
207. Ibid., 514.
208. Foner, 200.
209. Dubofsky, 112.
210. McWilliams, 289.
211. Foner, 204.
212. Dubofsky, 112.
213. Ryan, 73, for "Communist Wrecking Crew," which was California State Federation of Labor head Joseph Casey's name for S.D. Labor Council leadership in1935; Carlos Larralde and Richard Griswold del Castillo, "Luisa Moreno: A Hispanic Civil Rights Leader in San Diego," *Journal of San Diego History* 41, no. 4 (Fall 1995), 10 (online version), for State Senator Jack Tenney's name for Luisa Moreno.
214. Carlos Larralde and Richard Griswold del Castillo, "Luisa Moreno and the Beginnings of the Mexican American Civil Rights Movement in San Diego," *Journal of San Diego History* 43, no. 3 (Summer 1997), 2 (online version).
215. HUAC, *Hearings,* 1954, 4567.
216. Starr, 159.
217. Carey McWilliams, *California: The Great Exception* (Berkeley and Los Angeles: Univ. of California Press, 1998), 303.
218. John Steinbeck, *The Harvest Gypsies: On the Road to the Grapes of Wrath* (Berkeley: Heyday, 1988), 53–54, 61.
219. Starr, 158.

220. McWilliams, *Great Exception,* 302.
221. Starr, 160–61; McWilliams, *Great Exception,* 302–7; Carlos Larralde and Richard Griswold del Castillo, "San Diego's Ku Klux Klan," *Journal of San Diego History* 46, nos. 2–3 (Summer 2000) (online version); Dorothy Ray Healey and Maurice Isserman, *California Red: A Life in the American Communist Party* (Urbana and Chicago: Univ. of Illinois Press, 1993), 44–55.
222. Larralde and Griswold del Castillo (Summer 2000), 3.
223. Ibid., 4.
224. Ibid., 5.
225. *Union,* 8/8/34.
226. *Sun,* 1/16/34.
227. Larralde and Griswold del Castillo (Summer 2000), 2–3.
228. *Union,* 4/28/34, 5/1/34, and 5/4/34.
229. Paul Scharrenberg, quoted in Anne Loftis, *Witness to the Struggle: Imaging the 1930s California Labor Movement* (Reno: Univ. of Nevada Press, 1998), 94.
230. Starr, 73.
231. Vicki L. Ruiz, *Cannery Women/Cannery Lives: Mexican Women, Unionization, and the California Food Processing Industry, 1930–1950* (Albuquerque: Univ. of New Mexico Press, 1987), 48.
232. McWilliams, *Great Exception,* 148.
233. Ryan, 64.
234. Ibid., 44.
235. Ibid., 49.
236. Frank Spector, *The Story of the Imperial Valley* (New York: International Labor Defense, 1930), 24.
237. Ibid., 29.
238. Starr, 66–67.
239. Healey and Isserman, 44.
240. Starr 82.
241. Toby Terrar, "The San Diego Communist Party's Trade Unionism Role During the Great Depression," unpublished manuscript, 11. Terrar's paper is a thorough survey of the Communist Party's role in San Diego in the 1930s. He relies heavily on House Un-American Activities Committee hearing transcripts for information. It was written for a class at UCSD.
242. HUAC, *Hearings,* 1954, 4566–67.
243. Healey, and Isserman, 43.
244. Ibid., 44–45.
245. Starr, 80.
246. Healey and Isserman, 47.
247. Ibid., 4; Starr 81.
248. Healey and Isserman, 53.
249. Ibid., 54.
250. HUAC *Hearings,* 1954, 4567.
251. Terrar, 13–14.
252. Starr, 18; Healey and Isserman, 48.
253. Starr, 159.
254. "Report to the Board of Supervisors of Imperial County," June 1934, quoted in La Follette Committee hearings, Part 55, p. 20148.
255. Healey and Isserman, 79.
256. William deBuys and Joan Myers, *Salt Dreams: Land and Water in Low-Down California* (Albuquerque: Univ. of New Mexico Press, 1999), 182–83.
257. Cletus E. Daniel, "Cesar Chavez and the Unionization of California Farmworkers," *Working People*

of California, ed. Daniel Cornford (Berkeley and Los Angeles: Univ. of California Press, 1995), 373.

258. William Langwiesche, "Invisible Men," *California Dreams and Realities,* eds. Sonia Maasik and Jack Solomon (New York: Bedford/St. Martins, 1999), 99–107. For more on the estimated 27 million people living in slavery worldwide today, see also Kevin Bales, *Disposable People: New Slavery in the Global Economy* (Berkeley and Los Angeles: Univ. of California Press, 1999).

259. *Union,* 5/1/83; *Reader,* 2/13/92; Castanien, 60.

260. *Union,* 5/1/83.

261. Ibid., 4/28/34.

262. Ibid., 5/1/34.

263. Ryan 40, 43–4, 49.

264. Ibid., 29–30, 35, 48.

265. *Sun,* 4/20/12.

266. Ryan, 45, 47.

267. Ibid., 58.

268. Ibid., 58–59, 69.

269. Ibid., 67.

270. Bokovoy, 192, 247.

271. Ibid., 202.

272. Ryan, 54.

273. Ibid., 55, 61.

274. Quoted in Bokovoy, 195.

275. Ryan, 51.

276. Ibid., 52, 59.

277. *San Diego Labor Leader,* 8/25/31, 7/8/32, 7/15/32, 3/3/33.

278. Ryan, 57–60.

279. *Labor Leader,* 12/25/31.

280. Terrar, 20; Ryan, 71.

281. Terrar, 20.

282. *Union,* 5/1/83, Terrar, 14–15.

283. HUAC, *Hearings,* 1954, 4567.

284. Ibid., 4691–92.

285. Ibid.

286. Ibid., 4572.

287. Ryan, 64–65.

288. Ibid., 68.

289. Ibid., 65–68.

290. Ibid., 69.

291. Ibid., 66, 70–71.

292. HUAC, *Hearings,* 1954, 4532.

293. Ryan, 65–66.

294. Ibid., 72.

295. Ibid., 73.

296. Ibid., 76.

297. *Union,* 2/6/36.

298. Ryan, 79.

299. Ibid., 78–79.

300. *Labor Leader,* 8/28/37.

301. Ibid.

302. *Union,* 10/9/36.

303. Ibid., 8/5/38.

304. Ibid., 2/12/35 and 12/29/39. During this period, Steinmetz attacked the *Union* during a public lecture, saying that "San Diego's newspapers were giving their readers propaganda instead of news."

305. *Labor Leader,* 9/1/39.

306. Ryan, 92, 107, 121; *Union,* 4/16/47. As late as 1963 the AFL-CIO's Arthur McDowell was participating in the "Greater San Diego Evening School of Anti-Communism" at the U.S. Grant Hotel. The fact that labor was actively participating in Red-baiting while ignoring the activities of CORE speaks volumes about the problems of the city's conservative business unionism. To see the original pamphlets for the Anti-Communism school at the U.S. Grant, go to the vertical file on Communism in the California Room in the downtown San Diego Public Library.

307. Ryan, 107, 122.

308. *Union,* 10/26/50.

309. Larralde and Griswold del Castillo (1995), 1, 2, 13.

310. Ruiz, 42.

311. Loftis, 95; Starr, 81–82; Starr explains that "the Communist Party itself put the CAWIU out of business. In early 1934 Moscow reached a decision, which the Comintern communicated to the national parties. The struggle against fascism was intensifying, ran the communique. National Communist parties could no longer afford to go it alone. Communists should seek, rather, to align themselves with anti-fascist popular fronts. In terms of union movements in the United States, that meant the dissolution of independent unions such as the CAWIU and the scattering of its cadre into other organizations" (81).

312. Ruiz, 41, 45.

313. Ruiz, 97; Larralde and Griswold del Castillo (1995), 2.

314. Ruiz, 77–78.

315. McWilliams, quoted in Ruiz, 135–36.

316. Larralde and Griswold del Castillo (1995), 4.

317. *Union,* 6/25/39 and 6/29/39; Larralde and Griswold del Castillo (1997), 2; Ruiz, 81.

318. McWilliams, quoted in Ruiz, 57.

319. Larralde and Griswold del Castillo (1995), 3.

320. Ibid., 3–4; Larralde and Griswold del Castillo (1997), 7.

321. Larralde and Griswold del Castillo (1997), 3–4.

322. Ibid.; *Union,* 6/10/43, 6/11/43, and 6/12/43.

323. Larralde and Griswold del Castillo (1997), 5.

324. Ruiz, 115.

325. Larralde and Griswold del Castillo (1995), 3.

326. Ibid., 9.

327. Larralde and Griswold del Castillo (2000), 6.

328. Ibid.

329. *Union,* 9/11/48.

330. Larralde and Griswold del Castillo (1995), 7–8.

331. Healey and Isserman, 43.

332. Larralde and Griswold del Castillo (1995), 10; Noam Chomsky, *Deterring Democracy* (London: Verso, 1991), 69.

333. Larralde and Griswold del Castillo (1995), 11.

334. Paul J. Eisloeffel, "The Cold War and Harry Steinmetz: A Case of Loyalty and Legislation," *Journal of San Diego History* 35, no. 4 (Fall 1989), 2 (online version).

335. *Union,* 1/28/51.
336. Ibid., 2/5/54.
337. Ibid., 7/28/51.
338. Ibid., 7/25/51.
339. Eisloeffel, 4.
340. Ibid., 4, 12.
341. *Union,* 7/22/53.
342. Eisloeffel, 5–6.
343. Ibid., 7.
344. *Union,* 1/11/54.
345. Eisloeffel, 7.
346. Ibid., 8; *Union,* 1/29/54; *Tribune,* 8/27/56.
347. Eisloeffel, 10.
348. *Union,* 8/29/54.
349. Ibid., 1/18/54.
350. Ibid., 7/3/59.
351. Ibid., 8/29/54.
352. Ibid., 7/2/59.
353. Eisloeffel, 11; copies of the *Gadfly* are in the archives of the San Diego Historical Society.
354. *San Diego Magazine,* 12/64.
355. Ibid.
356. *Union,* 8/14/68.
357. Ibid., 7/7/47, 8/29/54.
358. Ibid., 4/22/54.
359. Ibid., 7/19/47, 7/20/47, 7/30/47.
360. Ibid., 5/13/43; *Tribune,* 4/23/90; *Voice and Viewpoint,* 4/16/92.
361. Castanien, 86.
362. *San Diego Magazine,* 7/63, 67; see also "San Diego Whites Deny Racism," *Christian Science Monitor,* 4/23/68.
363. Ibid., 90.
364. Ibid., 90–91; see also "Negroes' Problem Held Labor Ban," *Union,* 9/12/65.
365. Ibid., 67.
366. *San Diego Magazine,* 1/64; Harold Keen, "Why CORE Breaks the Law," *San Diego Magazine,* 12/64.
367. Ibid., 12/64.
368. Ibid.; *Union,* 5/29/64, 8/13/64, and 8/14/64.
369. Harold Keen, "De Facto Segregation in San Diego," *San Diego Magazine,* 8/66, 53.
370. Ibid., 8/66, 7/68, 7/69, and 6/77.
371. Ibid., 6/77.
372. Ibid., 7/69.
373. Ibid., 8/67; Castanien 91–92; *Union,* 8/25/65.
374. *Union,* 8/17/65, 8/19/65, 3/18/67, 3/3/68, and 3/4/68; see also *Door,* 5/2–15/68 and 7/17–30/69. *Door* was one of San Diego's countercultural newspapers in the late sixties and early seventies. Copies can be found both at the San Diego Historical Society archives and at the California Room.
375. William J. McGill, *The Year of the Monkey: Revolt on Campus 1968–69* (New York: McGraw Hill, 1982), 127.
376. *Marcuse in Paradise,* Paul Alexander Juutilain, producer, writer, and director. KPBS, 1996.
377. McGill, 39.

378. Patrice Lumumba was an African nationalist and Emiliano Zapata was a Mexican revolutionary.

379. McGill, 9, 123.

380. Ibid., 146.

381. Ibid., 124, 135.

382. Ibid., 135, 124, 126, and 128.

383. Ibid., 150.

384. Angela Davis, *An Autobiography* (New York: International Publishers, 1988), 197–98.

385. McGill, 55.

386. Ibid., 116.

387. Harold Keen, "UCSD's Third World College," *San Diego Magazine*, 9/69.

388. Harold Keen, "The Hard Lesson of Lincoln High," *San Diego Magazine*, 7/69, 47.

389. *San Diego Magazine*, 9/69.

390. Ibid.; McGill, 139.

391. McGill, 259; McGill claims that he denied this request, but former Third College resident dean Roberta Alexander suspects that the school was in fact infiltrated by agents from the beginning. Alexander interview, 7/8/02.

392. Ibid., 147–48; *Union*, 11/22/71.

393. *Union*, 12/5/69.

394. Ibid., 11/23/71, 11/18/71, and 11/26/71.

395. *Marcuse in Paradise*.

396. Ibid.

397. A. Buick, "Marcuse: The Professor Behind the Sixties Rebellion"; Michael J. Horowitz, "Portrait of the Marxist as an Old Trouper"; and Douglas Kellner, "Herbert Marcuse," all on www.marcuse.org; Herbert Marcuse, *Herbert Marcuse: Towards a Critical Society*, ed. Douglas Kellner (London and New York: Routledge, 2001); *San Diego Reader*, 9/11/86.

398. Ibid.

399. *Marcuse in Paradise*.

400. Harold Keen, "The Threat to Marcuse," *San Diego Magazine*, 8/68.

401. McGill, 71–72, 88–90, 248.

402. Ibid., 65.

403. Ibid., 248.

404. *Union*, 9/5/68, 9/6/68, 9/18/68, and 9/19/68.

405. *San Diego Magazine*, 8/68; *Union*, 9/29/69.

406. *Union*, 8/3/68.

407. Ibid., 8/10/68 and 8/14/68.

408. *Union*, 8/31/68; *San Diego Magazine*, 8/68.

409. *Union*, 9/23/68; *San Diego Magazine*, 8/68.

410. *Union*, 10/9/68.

411. Ibid.

412. As professor of literature Carlos Blanco, who was on the budget committee when Marcuse's promotion came up, recalls in an interview dated August 19, 2002, that the committee, in order to make it crystal clear that Marcuse was more than qualified to not only continue on at UCSD, but be promoted as well, asked for assessments of Marcuse from all over the world. Jean-Paul Sartre, for example, wrote: "Why are you asking me about Herbert Marcuse? Don't you know *who* he is?" Blanco also reports that Chancellor McGill showed up at this meeting and told committee members that they could not promote Marcuse. This action was a violation of university policy, as chancellors were not allowed to go to these meetings.

413. *Union*, 12/7/68 and 12/12/68.

414. McGill, 88–95; *Union,* 1/31/69.

415. McGill, 93–94.

416. Nancy Scott Anderson, *An Improbable Venture: A History of the University of California, San Diego* (La Jolla: UCSD Press, 1993), 120–21.

417. Avrum Stroll, "Taking Exception with Dr. McGill," *San Diego Magazine,* 10/82.

418. *Marcuse in Paradise.*

419. *Door,* 2/12/70, 2/26/70.

420. Ibid., 7/7–17/69.

421. Ibid.

422. Ibid.; *Union,* 6/6/69.

423. Alexander interview.

424. *San Diego Magazine,* 8/70.

425. *Union,* 3/18/67 and 3/3/68; *Door,* 5/2–15/68; *San Diego Reader,* 1/31/02.

426. Angela Davis, 159.

427. *Door,* 5/2–15/68; *San Diego Magazine,* 8/70.

428. Kevin Delgado, "A Turning Point: The Conception and Realization of Chicano Park," *Journal of San Diego History* 44, no. 1 (Winter 1998), 2 (online version).

429. *San Diego Magazine,* 12/73.

430. *Tribune,* 4/23/70 and 4/25/79.

431. *Union,* 5/21/71; *San Diego Magazine,* 12/73.

432. Delgado, 5.

433. *San Diego Magazine,* 8/70.

434. Lowell Bergman and Maxwell Robach, "C. Arnholt Smith and the San Diego Connection," *Big Brother and the Holding Company: The World Beyond Watergate,* ed. Steve Weissman (Palo Alto: Ramparts, 1974), 188.

435. The Guild was then an adult theater. "Adult" theaters and strip joints were some of the only advertisers the *Door* could get.

436. *Door,* 1/1/70, 1/15/70, 1/29–2/11/70, 8/17–9/7/72; Richard Popkin, "The San Diego Coup," *Big Brother and the Holding Company,* 64.

437. Popkin, 66–67.

438. Ibid., 70; *Door,* 8/17–9/7/73.

439. Popkin, 70–71.

440. *Door,* 6/19–7/2/69, 2/26–3/11/70, and 8/17/–9/7/73.

441. Ibid., 1/17–31/73, 2/10–24/73, and 6/18–7/1/73.

442. Vincent Ancona, "When the Elephants Marched Out of San Diego: The 1972 Republican Convention Fiasco," *Journal of San Diego History* 39, no. 4 (Fall 1992).

443. *Union,* 2/19/70.

444. As of this writing the *City Beat,* whose first several issues are encouraging, presents some hope for addressing this imbalance. Still, despite the editor's claim that their weekly leans "so far to the left that we walk in circles," San Diego's fledgling "alternative paper" is put out by Southland Publishing, parent company of the Ventura County *Reporter* and Pasadena *Weekly,* and its publisher Charles Gerencser proudly proclaims: "We're busting our ass to serve our advertising client base, and I think that will be appreciated"—a boast never made by the editors of the *Door* or *Street Journal.* Only the future will tell. *San Diego City Beat,* 12/31/02; "Slamm Reincarnating as San Diego City Beat: Targeting Young Readers in Central City," Association of Alternative Newsweeklies News, www.aan.org, 7/23/02.

445. *Los Angeles Times,* 11/16/69.

446. *Door,* 5/25–6/8/72.

447. Ibid., 2/7–3/7/73.

448. McGill, 73.

449. Angela Davis, 157.

450. *Door,* 10/9–22/69.

451. Ibid., 12/18/69.

452. Ibid.

453. *Union,* 2/13/70.

454. *Door,* 2/12/–25/70.

455. *Union,* 1/13/70.

456. Ibid., 2/19/70.

457. Ibid., 4/30/70.

458. Ibid., 5/16/70, 5/17/70, and 5/18/70.

459. *Door,* 8/27/70.

460. Peter Zschiesche interview, 8/6/02.

461. Ibid.

462. *Door,* 9/13/–27/71.

463. The ninth sailor chose to stay in the Navy.

464. *Door,* 12/923/71.

465. Ibid., 5/25–6/8/72.

466. *Union,* 4/15/73.

467. *Door,* 1973.

468. As Howard Zinn notes in *A People's History of the United States 1492–Present* (New York: Harper, 1999), the wave of revolts inside the military led the Navy to purge the ranks of the Pacific fleet in the wake of Vietnam. Specifically, Zinn tells us that "Pentagon officials in Washington and navy spokesmen in San Diego announced, after the United States withdrew its troops from Vietnam in 1973, that the navy was going to purge itself of 'undesirables'—and that these included as many as six thousand men in the Pacific fleet, 'a substantial proportion of them black.' All together, about 700,000 GIs had received less than honorable discharges. In the year 1973, one of every five discharges was 'less than honorable,' indicating something less than dutiful obedience to the military. By 1971, 177 of every 1,000 American soldiers were listed as 'absent without leave,' some of them three or four times. Deserters doubled from 40,000 in 1967 to 89,000 in 1971" (496).

469. *Union,* 12/7/82.

470. *Tribune,* 10/4/82.

471. *Union,* 12/9/84.

472. Ibid., 1/15/91.

473. *Los Angeles Times,* 10/26/01. In this article, "The Military: Lots of Interest, Little Action at Recruiting Office," Tony Perry reports that there has been no significant rise in actual enlistments after 9/11. This trend is consistent with the post-Vietnam trend of the volunteer military, which has allowed the majority of Americans to watch someone else go to war without the unpleasant anxiety provoked by the draft.

474. "Behind the Steel Curtain" is the title of an 11/80 Harold Keen article about NASSCO in *San Diego Magazine,* and "Si Se Puede" (Yes We Can) is the SEIU slogan that originated with the UFW.

475. *San Diego Union-Tribune,* 3/20/88.

476. Ibid., 8/23/92.

477. Ibid., 4/10/00.

478. Bergman and Robach, 196–99.

479. *Union,* 5/12/73.

480. Daniel, 397.

481. *Union,* 7/24/73.
482. Daniel, 397.
483. *Union,* 4/15/73.
484. *Door,* 12/20–1/10/73.
485. *Union,* 4/19/73.
486. Ibid., 7/20/73.
487. Ibid., 4/16/73; Daniel, 398.
488. *Union,* 4/30/73.
489. *Door,* 10/23–11/4/72.
490. *Union,* 2/28/75.
491. *Door,* 12/20/72–1/10/73.
492. Ibid., 5/12–26/71; *Union,* 10/8/75.
493. Daniel, 401.
494. *Union,* 10/8/75.
495. Ibid., 9/9/75, 9/10/75, 9/13/75, 9/14/75, 10/1/75, 10/8/75, and 10/10/75.
496. Ibid., 9/17/75.
497. Ibid., 3/11/77 and 6/3/77.
498. Zschiesche interview.
499. Ibid.
500. Livie Ross, "San Diego Firecrackers," *Labor Today,* March–April 1970, 26.
501. *Union,* 1/9/73; *Door,* 12/9–23/71, 1/13–27/72, and 2/10–24/72.
502. *Union,* 1/9/73.
503. Ibid., 4/22/71.
504. *Door,* 6/1–25/73, 8/74.
505. Zschiesche interview.
506. Ibid.
507. *Union,* 11/19/77 and 11/24/77; Harold Keen, "Behind the Steel Curtain at National Steel and Ship," *San Diego Magazine,* 11/80.
508. *Union,* 9/19/78.
509. Ibid., 11/21/79.
510. Ibid., 3/28/80; *Los Angeles Times,* 10/15/90.
511. *Union,* 8/3/80.
512. Ibid., 8/6/80; *San Diego Magazine,* 11/80.
513. *Union,* 8/6/80, 8/7/80, 8/8/80, and 8/13/80.
514. Ibid., 8/8/80.
515. Ibid., 8/29/80.
516. Ibid., 9/3/80.
517. Ibid., 9/4/80 and 9/5/80.
518. Ibid., 9/17/80.
519. Ibid.
520. Ibid., 8/16/81.
521. Ibid., 5/8/81, 5/10/81, and 5/11/81.
522. Ibid., 5/10/81.
523. Ibid., 5/8/81, 5/9/81, 5/15/81, 6/6/81, 6/7/81, and 10/11/81.
524. Ibid., 6/6/81; *Los Angeles Times,* 10/15/90.
525. *Union,* 8/81.
526. Ibid., 9/17/80.
527. Ibid., 9/26/80.

528. Ibid., 10/17/80, 10/23/80, 11/8/80, and 11/10/80.
529. Ibid., 6/6/80.
530. Ibid.
531. Ibid., 9/18/80, 10/11/80, and 1/8/81.
532. Ibid., 1/8/81 and 1/10/81.
533. Ibid., 1/9/81, 1/11/81, and 5/31/81; *Labor Leader,* 11/82; Miguel Salas was expelled and fined $1,000 for "disruptive acts" including the illegal wildcat strike, his link to the bomb plot, and the ship-launching protest.
534. Ibid., 10/1/81.
535. Ibid., 10/13/81 and 10/30/81.
536. Zschiesche interview.
537. Ibid.
538. *Union,* 10/2/84, 10/3/84, and 10/8/84.
539. Ibid., 9/16/86.
540. Zschiesche interview.
541. *Union,* 1/24/87 and 7/11/87.
542. Ibid., 1/7/88.
543. Ibid., 1/9/88 and 3/23/88.
544. Ibid., 10/4/87 and 10/9/87.
545. Zschiesche interview.
546. *Union,* 10/13/87.
547. Ibid., 11/11/87.
548. Zschiesche interview.
549. Ibid.; *Union,* 12/6/87.
550. Zschiesche interview.
551. *Union,* 2/13/88.
552. Ibid., 7/11/88 and 7/13/88.
553. Ibid., 8/10/88 and 9/2/88; Peter Zschiesche comments that "the workers had some gains including a new profit-sharing plan, but also some real losses in the traditional, level wage structures of past agreements." Interview.
554. Fred Lonidier, *Blueprint for a Strike: A Fragmentary Capsule History of the Ironworkers and Other Unions at NASSCO* (San Francisco: San Francisco Art Institute, 1992), 10.
555. As Zschiesche recalls, "They would allow no negotiations of the terms of the ESOP and it remained totally outside of the labor agreement, to be changed or canceled by their will only. This should have been a signal of the new management philosophy that came with the buyout. The previous owners, Morrison-Knudsen, operated with a traditional view of 'industrial relations' that never sought to get rid of the unions. The new management owners began operating as if they were the true voices of the workers, not the unions." Interview.
556. Zschiesche interview.
557. *Union,* 10/7/92.
558. Ibid., 10/26/92.
559. Ibid., 2/21/93 and 9/2/94.
560. Zschiesche interview.
561. *San Diego Business Journal,* 7/22/96; Zschiesche interview.
562. As Zschiesche sums up events in recent years: "In 2000, the Machinists Union negotiated an open-shop, seven-year agreement with NASSCO to preserve their bargaining unit and provide a base to reorganize union membership. A series of representation elections in 2002 left the rest of the yard divided between several international construction trade unions and a new, independent Shipyard Workers Union." Interview.

563. *Union*, 9/11/83.
564. *San Diego Business Journal*, 1/30/95; *San Diego Economic Bulletin*, 11/89.
565. *Union-Tribune*, 8/4/02.
566. Donald Cohen interview, 1/10/03.
567. Ibid., 11/8/02.
568. Ibid., 11/11/02.
569. Center on Policy Initiatives, 2 and 22.
570. Ibid., 2 and 21.
571. Ibid., 2–5.
572. *Los Angeles Times*, 5/31/93.
573. *Union*, 7/4/92, 8/12/92, and 8/23/92.
574. *Los Angeles Times*, 10/12/92 and11/19/92; *Union-Tribune*, 11/13/92 and 11/26/92.
575. *Union-Tribune*, 1/24/93, 2/12/93, 6/24/93, 6/27/93, and 7/2/93.
576. Ibid., 7/2/93.
577. Ibid.; *San Diego Business Journal*, 11/1/93.
578. *Graduate Employee News*, 10/27/95 and 10/31/96.
579. I am a political action vice president on the Executive Board of the American Federation of Teachers, local 1931.
580. *Union-Tribune*, 8/14/97, 8/19/97, and 9/6/01.
581. Ibid., 9/3/00.
582. Ibid., 11/15/00, 12/11/00, and 9/6/01.
583. Ibid., 12/11/99.
584. Ibid., 8/2/02.
585. *San Diego Newsline*, 5/9/79 and 12/80; UDWA, "A Brief History and Background."
586. *San Diego Reader*, 1/31/02.
587. UDWA.
588. *Union-Tribune*, 4/10/00.
589. Ibid., 4/17/00.
590. Ibid., 4/22/00.
591. Ibid., 4/26/00.
592. Ibid., 4/29/00.
593. Ibid., 5/8/00.
594. Ibid., 5/10/00.
595. McGill, 248.
596. *Union-Tribune*, 2/3/90.
597. *San Diego Reader*, 3/4/99.
598. *San Diego Business Journal*, 1/29/96, in vertical files in California room at San Diego Public Library.
599. *Union-Tribune*, 10/5/97, 6/12/98, and 6/13/98.
600. *San Diego Business Journal*, 5/30/97, in vertical files in the California room at the San Diego Public Library.
601. *San Diego Reader*, 3/4/99.
602. Ibid.; *Union-Tribune*, 12/19/98 and 3/9/99.
603. *San Diego Reader*, 3/4/99.
604. *Union-Tribune*, 6/18/99.
605. Ibid., 7/30/02.
606. As Matt Potter of the *San Diego Reader* has pointed out, KPBS, which is owned by the State University system, has received "mega-donations from such powerful and wealthy San Diegans as

the *Union-Tribune*'s Helen and David Copley. The radio station also runs a news operation, along with talk and opinion shows, some of which critics say are sometimes skewed to favor big-money special interests" and maintains a practice of "stonewalling public requests for information about its big private contributions." Potter has also reported that SDSU President Stephen Weber "has joined a group of establishment insiders plotting a battle for control of the San Diego Unified School District board of trustees . . . SDSU memos uncovered earlier this year [2001] revealed that Weber has repeatedly used his authority over the TV and radio stations to impose his will on station management. In light of that, critics worry, KPBS news and opinion operations might discriminate against opponents of Weber's personal political views and favored school-board candidates. The reported presence of *Union-Tribune* editorial writer Bob Kittle at the same meeting is also raising eyebrows; La Jolla resident Kittle, who frequently involves himself in public-education politics, and his wife Luanne own and operate the Rhoades School, an expensive private elementary and middle school . . . located near Rancho Santa Fe." *San Diego Reader,* 2/3/00 and 10/25/01.

607. www.activistsandiego.org.
608. www.surfrider.org.
609. Nancy Cary, "Something Foul in the Air," unpublished manuscript; Environmental Health Coalition, "Info on EHC." The EHC is located at 1717 Kettner Boulevard, Suite 100, San Diego, CA, 92101 (619) 2355–0281.
610. Globalphobics, "Cry of the Excluded Ones," unpublished document.
611. Other information on Globalphobics was gathered from primary documents such as "A Report on the Weekend of Events in Protest of the Free Trade Area of the Americas (FTAA)" and "Globalphobics Network of the Californias." I was present at the April 21, 2001, protest.

Acknowledgments

This book owes a special debt to the staff of the San Diego Historical Society: Greg Williams, Carol Myers, Therese James, and Cindy Krimmel in the Photo Archives; and Dennis Sharp and John Wadas in the Historical Archives. Thanks also to the helpful folks of the California and Periodical Rooms at San Diego's Downtown Public Library. Alessandra Moctezuma, Perry Anderson, Jennifer Cost, Steve Erie, Martin Elder, Matthew Bokavoy, and Jim Mahler—to mention only a few friends—nourished us with invaluable comments and encouragement. In addition to his striking Photo Chronicle, Fred Lonidier advised on overall design. Native San Diegan Abby Aguirre of The New Press was our guardian angel throughout. We thank her and the rest of the New Press gang, including Colin Robinson, Maury Botton, and Steve Hiatt, for making this book so much fun to do.

All royalties from the sales of *Under the Perfect Sun* will go to the Workers' Information Center (CITTAC), a courageous NGO in Baja California that supports the struggles of maquiladora workers and, more generally, advances human rights in La Frontera. We encourage readers to learn more about San Diego's urgent movement for social change and environmental conservation: Activist San Diego (www.activistsand iego.org); the San Diego Coalition for Peace and Justice (www.sdcpj.org); the Environmental Health Coalition (www. environmentalhealth.org); the Surfrider Foundation (www.surfrider.org); the Center on Policy Initiatives (www.onlinecpi.org); and the San Diego–Imperial Counties Labor Council (www.unionyes.org).

Index